The Peasant Betrayed

The Peasant Betrayed

Agriculture and Land Reform in the Third World

John P. Powelson and Richard Stock

CATO INSTITUTE

Washington, D.C.

Library of Congress Cataloging-in-Publication Data

Powelson, John P., 1920—
   The peasant betrayed.

   Includes bibliographical references and index.
   1. Peasantry—Developing countries. 2. Agriculture—Economic
aspects—Developing countries. 3. Land reform—Developing countries.
4. Poor—Developing countries. 5. Developing countries—Economic
conditions. 6. Developing countries—Social conditions. I. Stock,
Richard. II. Title.
HD1542.P68 1990   333.3'1'091724   90-2256
ISBN 0-932790-74-7 (pbk.)

   The first edition of *The Peasant Betrayed* was published in 1987 by Oelgeschlager, Gunn & Hain in association with the Lincoln Institute of Land Policy. The text of the paperback edition has been revised by the authors independently of the Lincoln Institute.

Printed in the United States of America.

CATO INSTITUTE
224 Second Street, S.E.
Washington, D.C. 20003

Contents

Tables

Preface

This revised edition of a work originally published in 1987 confirms the fundamental story. New information reinforces the main conclusion: *Instead of benefiting the peasants—as they promised to do—many states undertaking land reform have enriched themselves.* Thus land reform has become another policy instrument to skim off the "agricultural surplus." It has also enhanced the power of government officials, particularly at high levels, increasing their ability to demand patronage. Reserving for themselves decisions on agricultural inputs, outputs, and timing, they are usually not as good farmers as the farmers. Both because of this and because peasant incentive has been reduced, agriculture itself has suffered. These are the main theses of this book. There are some exceptions, which we try to identify, along with suggested reasons for them.

But our criticisms of implementation do not reflect our attitude toward land reform itself. We favor it. We did not want to reach the conclusions we have reached. One colleague, misunderstanding this, was distraught by an early version of the manuscript. He wrote us as follows:

> Land reforms . . . remain one of the few proven means of promoting equity, standing, and voice for the most exploited people. They are no panacea, but often a pre-condition . . . for equitable economic growth. More importantly, without land reforms, whole generations of the landless poor will live short and nasty lives with little dignity and less security.

We sympathize with the spirit of this critique. More painfully, we agree with all but the first sentence of it. But we disagree that land reform—as it has been implemented—is a "proven means" of promoting equity. It ought to be, but for the most part it is not.

Two propositions underlie this volume. First, the state in most less-developed countries (LDCs) is an interest of its own, or—more accurately—a bundle of interests of all who participate in it. It is *not* the defender of "national" interests or even of a wide spectrum of interests. Political scientists have long known this. But the point has not generally been recognized by economic planners and those who assist planning. Second, despite its rhetoric, the state rarely if ever defends the poor, except where the poor have the political leverage to demand that protection. Above all, many states are biased against small-scale farmers, in both efficiency and distribution of resources. These propositions apply to socialist and non-socialist governments alike. Possibly they would apply to more-developed countries (MDCs) as well, but there they may be offset by counterforces from leverage the poor have gained. LDC governments are far less accountable to their constituencies, especially the poor, than are governments of MDCs. (Beyond this conjecture, however, this book does not cover comparisons with MDCs.)

Thirteen years ago I began a study still in preparation: a history and theory of economic development, largely institution-based. With the aid of a Faculty Fellowship from the University of Colorado, an appointment as Visiting Scholar at Harvard, and a grant from the Lincoln Institute of Land Policy, I began studying the history of land tenure as a prototype institution. In what was originally to be the final chapter of that volume, I began investigating land reforms of the present day to discover whether they followed the pattern I had found in history. But the suspicion that indeed they do required more investigation than could be reported in a single chapter. As a result, the history volume was temporarily set aside, and I turned attention to the present one.

At this point the first of two fortuitous circumstances affecting the present volume occurred. At Harvard, I came into contact with Grace Goodell, an anthropologist with village experience in several Third World countries. Whereas most economists view the poor "from above," and most economic plans are worked out on desks in capital cities, Goodell had lived in villages among those most affected. Her ideas helped confirm the direction of my thought as well as the decision to write this book. Goodell had just done an article on the Philippine land reform, which—in revised form—has become Chapter 2 of this book. This article was published in *Policy Review*, Spring 1983, and we are indebted to the Heritage Foundation for permission to use parts of it. It is the only chapter that had been previously published. Another study of Goodell's is cited in Chapter 5 on Iran.

Other circumstances, more deliberate than fortuitous, were the reading of authors such as Bauer (1972), Bates (1981, 1983), Hopkins (1973), and Lipton (1977), who were thinking along similar lines. Several others—such as Reynolds (1975), Popkin (1979), and Adams, Graham, and Von Pischke (1984)—have been arguing for the astuteness and rationality of the peasant, while at the same time pointing out systematic biases against him. Lele (1972) lists fifteen studies demonstrating the lesser access of small farmers to institutional credit than large farmers.

The second fortuitous circumstance was finding Richard Stock as co-author. Stock was one of the more apt graduate students to come my way. The problem, at first, was that his own thinking had not traveled in the same direction as mine. He was concerned that a book on *The Peasant Betrayed* would be an excuse for the rich and powerful to abdicate their responsibilities toward the poor. ("If everything we try for the poor is negative, then why try?") So we compromised. The investigations lay ahead of us. We were both concerned that the poor in the Third World had been victimized by multiple oppressions, although we each had different ideas of what those oppressions were. But we did agree that our conclusions would depend on evidence we were yet to find.

As our investigations got under way, we found ourselves not alone. Susan Gunn, a graduate student in anthropology who had worked for the American Friends Service Committee in both East and West Africa, told a story about Somalia that was remarkably similar to countries we were studying. We persuaded her to write Chapter 8. Bettina Herr, an economist doing a thesis on Algeria, found aspects of her research that fit in with our directions. We invited her to condense her thesis into Chapter 9. When we told our story to Charles Howe, a colleague in economics just returned from Indonesia, he too found similarities and became enlisted for Chapter 15.

The bulk of the investigation for ten chapters (Bolivia, Egypt, India/ Kerala, Iran, Mexico, Pakistan, Peru, South Korea, Taiwan, and Tanzania) has been done by Stock. He spent three months in the library of the Land Tenure Center at the University of Wisconsin, whose collection of publications on land reform all over the world doubtless surpasses any other. We are grateful to the Land Tenure Center for this resource. Stock returned with numerous notes that required well over a year to assimilate, with the aid of the library at the University of Colorado. My contribution lies in writing four chapters (Introduction, El Salvador, Nicaragua, and Conclusion) and in reworking the materials supplied by Stock, while adding information to them from my own files.

In addition to the resources already mentioned, we are indebted to the Scaife Families Charitable Trusts and the Earhart Foundation for grants that supplied summer salaries, travel costs, and expenses of research assistants.

John P. Powelson

References

Adams, Dale W.; Graham, Douglas H.; and Von Pischke, J. D., 1984. *Undermining Rural Development with Cheap Credit*, Boulder, Colo., Westview Press.

Bates, Robert H., 1981. *Markets and States in Tropical Africa: The Political Basis of Agricultural Policies*, Berkeley, University of California Press.

Bates, Robert H., 1983. *Essays on the Political Economy of Rural Africa*, Cambridge, Cambridge University Press.

Bauer, Peter T., 1972. *Dissent on Development*, Cambridge, Mass., Harvard University Press.

Hopkins, A. G., 1973. *An Economic History of West Africa*, New York, Columbia University Press.

Lele, Uma, 1972. "Role of Credit and Marketing Functions in Agricultural Development," paper presented at International Economic Association conference on

"Agriculture in Development of Low Income Countries," Bad Godesberg, Germany, August 26–September 4.

Lipton, Michael, 1977. *Why Poor People Stay Poor*, Cambridge, Mass., Harvard University Press.

Popkin, Samuel L., 1979. *The Rational Peasant: The Political Economy of Rural Society in Vietnam*, Berkeley, University of California Press.

Reynolds, Lloyd G., 1975. *Agriculture in Development Theroy*, New Haven, Conn., Yale University Press.

1. Introduction: Compassion Is Not Enough

Nineteen eighty-four was not the year of Orwell; it was the year of the drought—a killer whose impact will linger over the rest of the decade. Affecting countries in the north, south, east, and west of Africa, it was most severe in Ethiopia and Mozambique. Pictures of shriveled children held by desperate parents, or of lines of people walking across the desert in hopes of aid in a neighboring country, shocked the readers of Western newspapers. Thousands of people died—we cannot yet know how many. But most shocking of all was the finding that people more than nature were to blame.

> Many disasters attributed to nature, such as floods and droughts, are actually caused by or made worse by human activity, according to a new study of the causes and effects of major calamities (Philip Shabecroft, in *The New York Times*, 11/18/84).

That study—"Natural Disaster: Acts of God or Acts of Man?"—was undertaken by the head of the Swedish Red Cross with an official of Earthscan, an organization monitoring the global environment. Shabecroft continued:

> The famine in Ethiopia, and a developing famine in the Sahel countries south of the Sahara, is caused not by the lack of rain that triggered it, the report said, but by agricultural practices and deforestation that produced soil erosion, by population growth and by political decisions such as an emphasis on cash crops and a failure to develop adequate distribution systems.

In writing of the disaster in Ethiopia, Clifford May of *The New York Times* (NYT, 11/18/84) argued that government policies were among the causes:

> In the decade since this Government [of Ethiopia] came to power in a coup, virtually no land has been irrigated and little has been done to correct environmentally destructive practices. . . . Cutting of forests and overgrazing by livestock has been widespread. *Also, the low prices paid by the state-owned Agricultural Marketing Corporation have discouraged farmers in still-fertile regions from producing a surplus or selling whatever surplus they produce.* (Emphasis added.)

1

In a later article (NYT Magazine, 12/1/85), May quoted a nun, a relief worker in Ethiopia:

> "And then, a few years ago, some people from the Ministry of Agriculture showed up and ordered that all the false banana trees be cut down," she says, referring to a common tropical African plant that resembles a banana tree but gives no fruit. "They said there were other, better crops that could be planted on the land instead.
>
> "Well, what these people didn't realize is that the root of the false banana is what peasants live on in times of famine. It's sort of their own emergency relief food. Without it, thousands just starved to death."

Later in the same article, May wrote:

> As damaging as any of this are the policies of most African governments toward their rural majorities—roughly three-quarters of their populations. This group has been squeezed in the vise of state marketing boards, which purchase farm products at fixed, low prices. The difference between the government's purchase price and its selling price often represents its main source of income, along with foreign aid. In many cases, that money is used to equip armies, construct office buildings, conference centers and all manner of prestigious projects and pay the salaries of civil servants and employees of inefficient government-owned industries.

In May, 1986, the head of Ethiopia's food relief effort defected to the West, declaring that "his government's policies, as much as drought, were responsible for the catastrophic Ethiopian famine of 1984 and 1985. . . . 'The bulk of the government's investment in agriculture continues to be directed to collective and state farms that,' [he] said, 'have proved to be a failure' " (May, NYT, 5/21/86).

Glenn Frankel of the *Washington Post* (in *Boulder Daily Camera*, 11/22/84) added a poignant human dimension by telling the story of an individual farmer in drought-stricken Kenya:

> Muthoka's first problem this year is not drought but seeds. All of his seeds went into last year's planting season, which because of drought produced nothing. That means he must buy seeds from a local cooperative, which in turn gets them from a government board called a parastatal. It has a legal monopoly on the distribution of seeds in Kenya. . . . [But there is] a nationwide seed shortage due in part to extra demand and poor planning by the parastatal.
>
> There is a fertilizer shortage as well. But all of Kenya's chemical fertilizers are imported and high-priced, and Muthoka cannot even consider buying any. . . . Other government-related obstacles lie in the way of his making a living. . . . Kenya gives a legal monopoly on the collection and distribution of corn to a state-controlled parastatal called the National Cereals and Produce Board. Muthoka must sell all his surplus to the board at a price set by the government, not the marketplace. The board's

budget often is stretched thin and its bureaucracy bloated. Payment for a crop can be delayed as much as six months, denying Muthoka the cash he needs to get started on a new harvest and to pay for the few necessities of his life.

Experts say Matheka Muthoka's problems are not atypical. Each obstacle he faces is surmountable, but put together, they are steadily driving down food production in a country of rapidly increasing population.

Following the same line, *The Washington Post* reported (weekly edition, 9/1/86):

The U.N. Food and Agriculture Organization says most African countries adopted policies that gave farmers little incentive to grow more food than their own families could eat. Instead, these policies lured many farmers, the backbone of poor African economies, to cities. There, they stopped farming and started eating imported food, purchased with overvalued currency and foreign aid money. In those years, food imports rose tenfold.

Across the continent, in Mali, the story is similar. Sheila Rule (NYT, 3/8/85) wrote,

While the major cause of the current food emergency is drought, food donors say the fact that this one-party country has become a large food importer and a year-round recipient of international aid is due not only to climatic conditions but also to economic mismanagement. . . .

Until about three years ago this country . . . had cereal marketing and pricing policies that featured state monopolies, low producer prices and subsidized consumer prices. Farmers had little incentive to plant and harvest and, as a result, agricultural production was severely damaged.

The story of Mali is confirmed in Bingen (1985), who studied the state management of land and water in a rice development project (Operation Riz-Segou), and concluded that this project—which did nothing to alleviate suffering from the drought—occurred at the expense of small farmers. Rice, which is actively promoted in several West African countries, serves primarily an urban constituency, and the use of land and water to develop it may not only deprive the poor of resources better used for subsistence crops, but it may reduce employment below the maximum possible for such land, thus impairing the income by which the poor might buy their food.

That Third World governments have been biased against peasant farming is now a commonplace for development economists. Twenty years ago, influenced by the theories of Lewis (1954) and Fei and Ranis (1961, 1964), many economists believed this bias to be a good thing: resources had to be drawn from agriculture to finance industry. Now—with malnutrition, hunger, and agricultural backwardness—economists are taking a second look.

Land reform until now has been one of the sacred cows of economic development. Yet, governments have taken land from aristocrats of the Third World and given it to the state more than to the peasants. *Nominally*, the peasants are owners, but many of the *benefits* are transferred to the state. In principle, these benefits are used for economic development; in reality, many of them are pocketed by state officials.

Furthermore, the overall benefits are reduced by inefficiency when state officials—who know little about agriculture—insist on administering the nation's farms. Often they make the most minute decisions (on what to plant, when to fertilize, how and how much, when to harvest) from the nation's capital, without ever seeing a farm. In many countries, these same officials head up state monopolies that sell the peasant his inputs and buy his output at prices set by the state, for the benefit of the state and its bureaucracy, not the peasant. If sometimes peasants do benefit, often their gains are temporary. What the state gives, the state can take away— and will take away, when it comes under political or economic pressure. There are exceptions to all these statements, but they are few.

How does this condition come about? In many ways, such as through land reform itself. Twentieth-century land reforms in general, have been "by grace" instead of "by leverage." A land reform by grace is bestowed upon peasants—without their having participated in forming it—by a gracious government, which may have conquered the old order—"the landowning aristocracy"—in a revolution, or which may have been elected by an intellectual minority with compassion for the peasantry. But compassion is not enough.

A land reform by leverage, on the other hand, takes time. This is a reform by which peasants, in organizations they have formed and manage, bargain with overlords or government from strength they have already achieved. All the examples we can think of come from Europe and Japan, of the nineteenth century and earlier, and these are not taken up in this book. We will argue that reforms by grace ultimately deprive the peasant of initial gains, in most cases within five years, though it might take fifty. Only through reforms by leverage does the peasant acquire, in the long run, an equitable distribution of welfare and adequate political representation. Therefore, those from the outside who would advocate the peasant would do better to help him acquire economic and political strength than to encourage a land reform of a benefactor's making.

Land is worth the capitalized value of its revenues. If bureaucrats skim these away, leaving the farmer with no more than he could earn as a landless laborer, his newly acquired land is worth zero. If the same happens in a government cooperative, his membership is worth zero. The state can even reduce his value to less than zero, if the peasant has no way to abandon the land. This happened toward the end of the Roman Empire, and it is probably happening in some areas today.

Here and elsewhere, by "peasant" we mean the farmer who himself tills

4

the soil, whether he owns it or not. We may refer to "rich peasants" because it is customary to do so. For the most part, however, our "peasants" are poor.

Worse yet, state officials believe they can manage agriculture. Bureaucrats in Cairo, for example, determine what will be planted on each farm in Egypt, when it will be planted, what fertilizers and seeds will be used, and where and how it will be sold. With little left for them to decide, farmers *on their own land* are but low-level employees of the state. In Egypt, agricultural output per capita has *decreased* at an *average* annual rate of 0.4% per year for nineteen years! (See Chapter 6.) In other countries, where state officials have decided that they are better farmers than the peasants, the story is the same. In Algeria, agricultural output has decreased at an annual rate of 1.85% for the same nineteen years, in Botswana by 2.56%, in Mexico by 0.15%, in Zambia by 1.21%. These are, of course, the worst cases. But agriculture is languishing in many parts of the Third World.

The authors of this book are advocates, ideologically, of land reform, but only in systems that work, that is, those systems or policies that increase the welfare of the rural poor. Unfortunately, our findings lead us to believe that the system that *would* work is the one rarely tried: to expropriate land from oligarchies, give it to peasants in fee-simple ownership, leaving them to sell their land if they wish, produce what they will, borrow and buy where and when they will, and sell their crops wherever they will.

We devote one chapter each to sixteen land reforms: those of Algeria, Bolivia, Egypt, El Salvador, Indonesia, Iran, Kerala (an Indian state), Korea (South), Mexico, Nicaragua, Pakistan, Peru, the Philippines, Somalia, Taiwan, and Tanzania. Two of these (the Philippines and Somalia) are by anthropologists who have done field work in their areas; their perspectives will be somewhat different from those of economists. The rest are written by economists, who have visited most of the countries concerned, but who have relied primarily on library and statistical sources. This is not a random selection of countries. It consists of *all* those that in our judgment meet the following criteria: (1) A significant land reform has occurred. (2) Sufficient information exists, in languages we understand, to write a chapter. (3) Our story must not yet have been widely told.

We exclude India (except Kerala) on the first criterion. Nine areas excluded by the second criterion did offer enough information for vignettes, which appear in Chapter 18: Chile, Honduras, Paraguay, the Philippines under Aquino, Sri Lanka, sub-Saharan Africa, Turkey, Venezuela, and Zambia. Also in that chapter are resumes of two countries excluded by the third criterion: China (whose story is told by Lardy 1983) and Cuba (Mesa Lago 1981). These eleven short stories are intended to show that the findings for earlier chapters extend to a much greater area.

Briefly, our findings are as follows. In most countries studied, the peasant has become worse off over the past two decades. But in a number

5

of countries, he is probably better off, for many different reasons: in Paraguay because the rulers could dole out abundant land at little cost to themselves and, by leaving peasants alone, keep them politically quiet; in Bolivia because the government was too disorganized to control the peasantry; in Kerala (India) because a weak state government in a federated system enabled effective peasant organizations to influence events in their favor; in Taiwan and South Korea because of both peasant political power and strong economic growth; in Indonesia because of "Green Revolution" increases in farm output unusual for the Third World.

Only in Taiwan and South Korea, we will argue, are peasants better off because their political leverage enabled them to demand policies in their favor. Even so, the reforms were authoritarian and did not benefit them as much as they might have, given free institutions and free markets. In Taiwan more than in South Korea, a significant agricultural surplus has been skimmed off by the state.

Some will argue that weather, not land reform, brought about the results we have shown. But the dismal results are far more widespread than drought, for example. Even in the most stricken countries—such as Tanzania—output declines do not correlate with drought, either in time or in place. We assert they must *also* have been caused by government policy.

Most unfortunate of all, anti-peasant policies have been bolstered by well-intentioned elites of the industrialized world, who often believe that peasants are helpless and in need of protection. Illiteracy is confused with ignorance. "Agrarian reform" is defined as "land reform" plus that set of institutions (credit, technology, marketing, and the like) that must be supplied by government. In fact, as we will show, many (probably all) peasant societies have their own well-developed systems of credit, supply, marketing, saving, investment, and communication of technology. The supposition that peasants do not have these capabilities is one of the gross ethnocentricities of the development profession. Gunnar Myrdal's (1968:710) concept of a "Rip Van Winkle world, among people still drowsy with the slumber of centuries" is being displaced by anthropological evidence that peasants are capable and shrewd, and peasant societies are perpetually changing. Often land reform imposes new institutions—such as credit and technical assistance—that supplant rather than improve the old. This abrupt change disrupts village societies completely, emasculating cultures, destroying values and social relationships, reversing directions of change, and throwing peasants into a state of *anomie* out of which they arise with difficulty.

Yet the state could be useful to peasants and to agricultural development. There are reasons for rural backwardness, which the state can help remove or modify. We argue that agricultural development is best promoted by assisting social institutions already in place: by linking informal credit structures with modern ones, as suggested by Solem (1985), rather than supplanting them by a state bank; by improving the knowledge and capabilities of traders already in the market rather than imposing a government trading corporation; by taking cues from peasants rather than giving instructions to them.

In a book whose title, *Undermining Rural Development with Cheap Credit*, tells the theme, Adams et al. (1984) argue convincingly that government intervention in rural credit markets has allowed agriculture to deteriorate by diverting credit into improper channels (mainly political), while depriving those farmers who need it most and can use it best. We ourselves do not condemn a state agrarian bank so long as it neither proclaims its monopoly over peasant credit nor tries to drive out competitors with subsidized interest rates. We do not condemn government buying and selling agencies so long as they do not compete unfairly through subsidized prices, and peasants are free to ignore them if they wish. But if these agencies intrude themselves through sovereign right, even though peasants would be more prosperous taking their business elsewhere, they become a drag on the economy through the resources their officials consume.

The Interests of the State

With the writings of a few pioneers (e.g., Bauer 1972; Reynolds 1975; Lipton 1977; Bates 1981, 1983) the governments of less developed countries (LDCs) are coming to be perceived less as maximizers of social welfare and more as aggregators of private interests, weighted according to their relative contributions toward keeping the government in power. This statement might be made about any government. If it seems especially applicable to LDCs, the reason must be that the socio-economic segments in LDCs vary more widely than in more developed countries (MDCs) in their capacities to defend themselves. Just as income and wealth are more highly skewed in LDCs than in MDCs, so also is political power. Relative to total population, there are more *very strongs* and more *very weaks* in LDCs than in MDCs.

Among the stronger segments are urban industrialists and urban workers. The industrialists gain strength through family connections, education abroad, interrelations with the bureaucracy, and wealth. They wield all the assets to influence government in their favor. The workers gain strength partly by being indispensable to the industrialists and partly through location in the cities, where their concentration makes riots easier and their visibility makes them more dangerous. The peasantry, commanding none of these advantages, is at the low end of power.

Thus it is urban interests and government bureaucrats that benefit from land reform. How? As condition for receiving land, the peasants must agree to restrictions that turn the terms of trade against them, as follows. (These mechanisms vary, of course, from country to country.)

1. The prices of farm products are held low.

7

2. The prices of farm inputs (fertilizer, machinery, seed) are kept high.
3. Peasants are required to sell their outputs to state monopolies. Illegal sales become more visible, so no. 1 is more easily enforced.
4. Peasants are required to buy their inputs from state monopolies. Illegal purchases become more visible, so no. 2 is more easily enforced.
5. Peasants are required to obtain their credits from state agencies.

Often the credits are tied to inputs (e.g., loans made in fertilizer or seed) and repayment is tied to sales (i.e., repayment in crop). Once again, nos. 1 and 2 become more easily enforced. Sometimes a government offers subsidized credit to peasants. Superficially, it would seem that the peasants have gained. But frequently this credit is tied to other requirements on agricultural technology or attachment to government agencies, which reduce farmer efficiency and farm income. The peasant's prior credit sources (which are alleged not to exist, but they do) are driven out of business. When the peasants have nowhere to turn except to government banks, these become perpetually out of funds, or else they direct their funds to richer farmers.

These five mechanisms relate, of course, to private farming. In the state farming of socialist societies, the same effects are achieved by allocating the work load and setting the peasant's wage, while refusing the peasant the right to produce on private land or to sell in a free market. Alternatively, peasants may be *required* to join "cooperatives" (in quotes because the compulsory nature distorts the spirit) whose rules are set by the state. Thus the observations apply to socialist and nonsocialist societies alike.

On the surface, these mechanisms are not always disadvantageous to the peasant. Sometimes subsidized inputs and credits seem to help. Close inspection, however, usually shows that in these cases, only the rich farmer (or the rich state farm) gains. Supply is less than demand, and the favors must be rationed. Someone, of course, must ration them, and this person becomes tempted to receive pay-offs. In principle, the bribe can be anything up to the difference between subsidized price and what the market price would have been. Depending on the degree of control (obverse of the availability of a black market), the public official—by virtue of his monopoly—may even demand a bribe that elevates the cost of the peasant's inputs to higher than he would have paid on the free market.

Typically, a credit bank will be established for the poorest of the peasantry, and just as typically, the poorest will not be able to use it. Bates (1983:127) argues that by returning some of its "take" to a portion of the agricultural community (specially selected "leaders"), the government is better able to keep that whole community under political control. While land reform is not the only mechanism, it is one of those by which state control is established and agricultural saving extracted for the benefit of the state.

Differential access to public goods has been described by Krueger (1974), Buchanan et al. (1980), and others as "rent-seeking." A public good (such as a credit institution) yields a rent (a technical term for an extraordinary profit) when its services are available only to certain individuals who thereby establish a monopoly or quasi monopoly and are able to charge monopoly prices. The rent may accrue to a farmer (of political importance) who receives subsidized credit but whose prices of final output are uncontrolled. Alternatively, a state agency authorized to buy products at monopsony prices, or sell at monopoly prices, may extract the rent itself. In principle, such rents are to be devoted to economic development projects. In practice, they are often paid in rent-like emoluments to state officials.

The Interests of the Rural Elite

In some countries the government is able to implement these policies only with the cooperation of a rural elite (Adams 1986). This elite, to be distinguished from the peasants at large, is able to obtain benefits from the government by cooperating with it to bring ordinary peasants "into line."

We found the following results in the countries indicated. First, government-organized cooperatives tend to be dominated by this elite or their clients (Mexico, Egypt, Iran, Algeria). Second, subsidized inputs will be monopolized by this elite (Egypt, Iran, Pakistan). Third, the nature of government investment in agriculture will be determined by the needs of this group (Mexico, Egypt, Iran, Peru, Bolivia). Fourth, the peasants will become *more* dependent on the state because they exhaust their political capital battling this group. The resources spent in these battles are not available for production (Mexico, Peru). Fifth, peasant agriculture stagnates. Because of greater peasant dependency, the government is able to extract the agricultural surplus more easily (Mexico, Egypt, Peru).

Socialism: The Answer?

Some would argue that the answer to rent-seeking lies in the socialist state. In this state, the government—to which all rents accrue—becomes the protector of the worker and the farmer. Society is described as belonging "to the worker," and all economic decisions are made in the worker's name. In some socialist societies—such as Sandinista Nicaragua and increasingly so in the Soviet Union and China—the worker is allowed considerable decisionmaking at local levels, but he is not be permitted to decide the basic structure (private property, cooperative, state farm, degree of mixture of the above).

Each real situation, however, is more complex than the generalization of the preceding paragraph. Which worker's interest does the state defend? In classical Marxism, it is the urban worker. The Soviet Union has defended the urban worker at the expense of the rural, and on this point Soviet and Chinese ideologies diverge. A further complication is the

9

divergence of long run from short run: whether the socialist society is capable of economic advance which over the long run will raise the standard of living of workers and farmers above what it would have been in a more decentralized society.

Our own reading of history leads us—in the long-run interests of workers and farmers—to prefer a dispersion of power rather than its concentration. The benevolent centralized power, like the governments of the Soviet Union, China, Cuba, Tanzania, and Nicaragua, is subject to three hazards.

First, the benevolent originating unit (Lenin, Mao, Fidel Castro, Julius Nyerere, and the Sandinista junta, respectively) creates or preserves a power *position*, which becomes attractive or threatening to others. Without checks and balances, there is no stable equilibrium over the long run. So long as the power position exists, it can be seized.

Second, the benevolent originating unit is mortal; its replacement over time is apt not to be so benevolent to workers. We saw this as early as the French Revolution and more recently in Soviet and Polish attitudes toward the Solidarity union.

Third, and perhaps the most important, the economy is complicated far beyond the imagination of the benevolent originating unit or its supporters. Economic policy has impacts they do not dream of. For example, controls to keep food prices low for urban workers result in discouraging farm output, even in command societies; failure to factor interest rates into investment decisions leads to shortages in specific lines, and the like.

These three hazards combine into one effect. The benevolent government-patron in a socialist state believes that it knows the best interests of the peasant even more than the peasant does. ("It" refers to the collective group which manages the government: a politburo or junta, for example.) In fact, however, as our anthropologists (Goodell in Chapter 2 and Gunn in Chapter 8) bring out, peasants have methods of coping with their problems, about which the benevolent patron knows nothing. If these coping methods are destroyed through the imposition of a state structure (for credit, marketing, or whatever), and if the state structure does not work or works imperfectly (as is almost always the case), the question is whether the peasant has lost more in the demise of his coping methods than he has gained through whatever the government has done for him. We will argue that in most cases, he has lost more. Furthermore, peasant problems are usually local-specific, requiring local-specific treatment; the government, however, is usually capable only of uniform, nationwide treatments.

New Agencies, or Improve the Old?

In addition to equity in land distribution, land reform by grace is "justified" by two propositions: first, that peasants—being weak, uneducated, and ruled for so long by feudalistic landlords—are incapable of

10

organizing their own institutions of marketing and credit; and second, that "monopolistic" moneylenders have long dominated rural credit, charging usurious rates. Therefore, it is often argued, the state must provide them with technical assistance, marketing structures, and credit. But marketing and credit institutions always exist. Often, as we will show in the chapters that follow, the state presumes a tabula rasa: no economic culture. Therefore, it starts from scratch. In so doing, it destroys the existing institutions.

The close integration of credit with marketing in village societies requires that we address the two propositions together. First, moneylenders are rarely monopolistic and only sometimes are they rich. (If they were monopolistic, the solution would lie in more moneylenders, not fewer.) Often they are respected members of the community who provide credit in tiny amounts for a few days only; generally, the banking system cannot do this. Tun Wai (1976:58) has found that in many countries professional moneylenders and landlords provide only a small portion of informal rural credit (India, Bangladesh, and Nepal are exceptions), while relatives and friends supply substantial amounts. The "usurious" rates (say, 150%) that we frequently hear about are exceptional; Tun Wai (1977:304) finds a large number of "usual" rates in the range from 20% to 40%. Perhaps even these rates are high; if so, the cause doubtless lies in scarcity of credit and risk of default. These, then, are the problems to be addressed. Why is credit scarce? Why is the default rate high?

Second, one reason why the marketing system appears deficient is that observers of it do not reckon in peasant terms. As Goodell points out in Chapter 2, peasants in Santa Rina (real village, fictional name), Philippines, were accustomed to buying fertilizer by the teaspoon, but they required flexibility and immediate availability; neither of these the government agency could supply. Where peasants have wished to enter the money economy with their sales, it has not been their own deficiencies that have prevented them but restrictions imposed by either landlords or government. The aftermath of the Bolivian agrarian reform—see Chapter 7—makes this point clear. The Bolivian government was unable to dominate the peasants, not because it did not want to do so but because it was too weak to do so.

Third, and possibly the most important of all, traditional peasants have always had their own political structures, capable of negotiating on their behalf. This is so even when they have lived on feudal haciendas or their equivalent. On the mere assumption that the government is representative of the people, the true representatives of villages may be either co-opted forcibly into the higher bureaucracy or destroyed politically.

Thus, most of the twentieth-century land reforms have destroyed the political and economic institutions that peasants have developed over centuries, substituting nationally uniform organizations that either are inefficient, do not work, or deteriorate the welfare of the peasants.

11

Conclusion

Land reform—much needed in the Third World for both equity and efficiency—has become one of the instruments by which the "agricultural surplus" (amounts produced by farmers above subsistence) has been skimmed off by the state, ostensibly to promote economic development. The resources are often misused, however, through either direct corruption or extravagant, wasteful projects to promote the political or territorial interests of powerful people. Usually land reform agencies are manipulated to serve the urban bias in government policy. Furthermore, the imposition of state-sponsored programs upon village people destroys village cultures and institutions, preventing them from developing rationally as local circumstances require. Worse yet, these policies combine with population growth, overgrazing and other agricultural practices, to depress agriculture so much that Third World nations cannot cope with natural disasters—such as drought and flooding—when they occur, as they did in Africa in the mid-eighties. These misfortunes occur whether the government is socialist or nonsocialist.

Land reform *is* needed in LDCs. Land has been inequitably divided, monopolized by powerful individuals, and old agricultural systems have been inefficient. But for reform to be effective, the philosophy of paternalism must end. Until the government becomes representative, peasants must view it as adversary, not as protector. Peasant defenses and political power from below must be developed, so that reforms will occur by leverage, not by grace. Many peasants, of course, are already aware of the dangers of powerful politicians, both local and national, and of urban-biased governments. But the rhetoric of governments, as well as of most foreign supporters of land reform, has yet to reflect this political reality.

References

Adams, Dale; Graham, Douglas H.; and Von Pischke, J. D., 1984. *Undermining Rural Development with Cheap Credit*, Boulder, Colo., Westview Press.

Adams, Richard H., 1986. "Bureaucrats, Peasants, and the Dominant Coalition: An Egyptian Case Study," *Journal of Development Studies*, vol. 22, no. 2: 336–354.

Bates, Robert H., 1981. *Markets and States in Tropical Africa*, Berkeley, University of California Press.

Bates, Robert H., 1983. *Essays on the Political Economy of Rural Africa*, Cambridge, Cambridge University Press.

Bauer, Peter T., 1972. *Dissent on Development*, Cambridge, Mass., Harvard University Press.

Bingen, James R., 1985. *Food Production and Rural Development in the Sahel: Lessons from Mali's Operation Riz-Segou*, Boulder, Colo., Westview Press.

Buchanan, James M.; Tollison, Robert D.; and Tullock, Gordon, 1980. *Toward a Theory of the Rent-Seeking Society*, College Station, Texas A&M University Press.

Fei, J., and Ranis, G., 1961. "A Theory of Economic Development," *American Economic Review*, June.

Fei, J., and Ranis, G., 1964. *Development of the Labor Surplus Economy*, Homewood, Ill., Irwin.

Krueger, Ann O., 1974. "The Political Economy of the Rent-Seeking Society," *American Economic Review*, June.

Lardy, Nicholas, 1983. *Agriculture in China's Modern Economic Development*, New York, Cambridge University Press.

Lewis, W. Arthur, 1954. "Economic Development with Unlimited Supplies of Labour," *The Manchester School of Economic and Social Studies*, May.

Lipton, Michael, 1977. *Why Poor People Stay Poor: A Study of Urban Bias in Economic Development*, Cambridge, Mass., Harvard University Press.

Mesa Lago, Carmelo, 1981. *The Economy of Socialist Cuba: A Two-Decade Appraisal*, Albuquerque, University of New Mexico Press.

Myrdal, Gunnar, 1968. *Asian Drama: An Inquiry into the Poverty of Nations*, New York, Twentieth Century Fund.

Reynolds, Lloyd G., 1975. "Agriculture in Development Theory: An Overview," in Lloyd Reynolds, ed., *Agriculture in Development Theory*, New Haven, Conn., Yale University Press.

Solem, Richard Ray, 1985. Project Identification Document, *Small Farmer Credit*, Washington, D.C., Agency for International Development.

Tun Wai, U, 1976. "A Revisit to Interest Rates Outside the Organized Money Markets of Underdeveloped Countries," International Monetary Fund Institute, document DM/76/54, xerox.

Tun Wai, U, 1977. "A Revisit to Interest Rates Outside the Organized Money Markets of Underdeveloped Countries," Rome, *Banco Nazionale del Lavoro Quarterly Review*.

2. The Philippines

*Grace Goodell**

Background

Land reform in the Philippines has roots extending for almost eighty years, but they have been shallow. The first efforts were made shortly after the United States won the islands from Spain in 1898. The American government purchased the friar estates** from the pope in order to parcel them out to the tillers upon them. But the estates were redistributed slowly and very selectively.

After World War II, with the Huk peasant rebellion raging in rural Central Luzon, the young independent nation's Rural Progress Administration resumed redistribution. Although aided by an American advisor who drafted a detailed program, the poorly funded "landed estates policy" received no support from Philippine political elites. Even a public commitment by Magsaysay—a most popular president—lacked credibility. Similarly, President Macapagal never seriously tried to implement the comprehensive Land Reform Code of 1963 he had sponsored. Nor did President Marcos, throughout his first term of office (1965–69). Philippine

NOTE: This chapter, the only one in the book that had been published before, appeared in *Policy Review*, vol. 24 (Spring 1983). It inspired the authors to research the remaining case studies of this book. Both for this reason and because the policies and relations expressed here are prototypes for other land reforms studied, the chapter is included with minimal modifications. It speaks in present tense of events now past. For the Philippine land reform experience under President Aquino, see p. 375–379.

*The data informing this study were collected during three and a half years of anthropological field work in Santa Rina and nearby villages, as well as eighteen months of participant observation in several of the key government agencies and private rural banks and on the basis of familiarity with the government's programs nationwide. In accordance with standard case-reporting procedures in anthropology, the names of Santa Rina and all persons (except well-known public figures) have been changed. Names of the state of Nueva Ecija and Planters' Products have not been changed.

**For a description of the friar estates, see Roth (1977).

villagers continued to pay exorbitant rents to their landlords, which seriously inhibited their farming initiatives (Takahashi 1969).

Thus it is no surprise that intense public demonstrations demanding legislative revisions in the law and then their implementation marked Marcos' second inauguration. These demonstrations continued for months. Thousands from the countryside around Manila were joined by students, clergy, urban trade unions, and representatives of the Philippines Public School Teachers Federation. Finally, along with the proclamation of Martial Law in 1971, Presidential Decree 27 became the cornerstone of Marcos' New Society, "for the emancipation of the tiller from the bondage of the soil." On the law's first anniversary, Marcos asserted that "land reform is the only gauge for the success or failure of the New Society. If land reform fails, there is no New Society."

With these many decades of discussion and preparation, Philippine elites were hardly caught off guard. Those who most clearly saw possibilities for using it to their own interests were, naturally, government officials and their circles. Many of these had already begun to transfer their agricultural interests from landholding and farm management to the New Society's multifarious bureaucratic forms of managing the entire agricultural sector.

The State Replaces the Middlemen

The conventional wisdom of development economics maintains that the danger inherent in land reform is that the peasant may be delivered into the hands of middlemen, who are considered more evil than landlords. For decades Third World planners and their Western mentors have waged war against "middlemen," a pejorative term for the entire private sector serving rural areas. But given land reform, who will replace the landlord's credit and other services to the peasant? Will middlemen be any improvement?

Conventional theory further assumes that an integrated government program is needed to replace the services that landlords, dozens of middlemen, and the farmers themselves used to provide for the village. To many economists—particularly those in central planning offices—an integrated package seems sensible. By reducing collection risks on small loans, the package would be fiscally sound. It would compel modern practices. For the planner, it would tighten central control over the masses of farmers and the untidy capitalist sector serving them. And the bureaucrats argue that a package enables the state's machinery to replace the avaricious middlemen in all three of their major areas of former oppression: credit, input supply (along with guidance into the new technology), and harvest procurement. But the small farmers with whom I lived in a Philippine village found otherwise. Instead, the integrated package robbed them of all managerial or entrepreneurial options, while reducing their output and their earnings.

16

Despite its economic jargon, the intention behind integrated and packaged Third World agricultural programs is clear. In Paul's (1966:413) words:

Making loans against delivery contracts the proceeds of which are used for repayment of the loans before the balances are remitted to the producers . . . means that credit and marketing must be closely allied. A further step in the same direction would be to tie in more closely the introduction of new agricultural techniques with the administrative systems used for the extension of credit and marketing. . . . The need for credit can be used as leverage to speed up the adoption of new methods. . . . [Supplies] should be furnished in kind through the same channels as credit and thus paid for by the proceeds arising from the delivery contracts. . . . Millions of farmers throughout Asia must have seasonal credit in order to subsist throughout the year. Various ways must be devised whereby this need is used as leverage for generating more rapid progress in the introduction of new methods.

Such a plan need not be restricted to land reform beneficiaries; but land reform does make it easier to require farmers to join "their" cooperatives, which then act as the government's integrating apparatus.

Over and over in its definitive Sector Policy Paper on agricultural credit, the World Bank (1975) insists upon government-controlled, packaged loans to the small farmer, ignoring alternatives and not recognizing inherent dangers. For nearly a decade, the bank tells us, "integrated agricultural development" has comprised an "important credit activity"

necessitating the packaging of credit together with extension and infrastructure. . . . All components of a [World Bank] production package should be, and usually are, financed under such schemes. . . . Clearly there is a need to think of production packages for the farm as an entity and to finance all complementary components. . . . To make the credit program a success, the government must provide the complementary inputs. . . . The package approach is to be preferred since it provides the farmer with credit plus all the ancillary services he requires.

Indeed, credit and inputs distributed in kind in such a comprehensive government package constitute two of the bank's ten unequivocal "principles" of agricultural credit for the Third World (World Bank 1975).*

Packaged Agricultural Services in the Philippines

But how does such a program of government-packaged agricultural services for small farmers actually work in the nitty-gritty at the local level? The present case study examines the network of complementary programs

*See also World Bank (1976) for the full country report on the Philippines. For further perspectives on an integrated development program, see ILO (1974).

for establishing state control over the small rice farmers of the Philippines' rich irrigated lowlands. The government of the Philippines, with the help of aid agencies, evolved this scheme over many years. But it crystallized in its most comprehensive form in 1972 at the time of land reform. Except where noted, this case is typical of schemes in many developing countries.

The village of "Santa Rina," Nueva Ecija, is in the center of Manila's fertile rice bowl. The average small-farmer holding in Santa Rina, and in the Philippines as whole, is 5 acres. In Santa Rina this yields two crops of rice a year. Like most villagers in Central Luzon, Santa Rina farmers can reach the moneylenders and other private middlemen of a nearby provincial town within a few hours' travel by jeep.

Centered on the "supervised credit" program called Masagana 99 (which refers to an abundant harvest), the state's campaign fundamentally arrogated to itself responsibility for all financial, supervisory, and marketing services for rice (which had traditionally been offered by landlords and the middlemen). Some of the government's agencies attracted top Philippine expertise. One, included in this study, was managed by graduates of the Asian Institute of Management, founded by faculty members and Philippine alumni of the Harvard Business School.

At the time of land reform in 1972, scientists had just released the new varieties of high-yielding rice that promised extraordinary yields. While the small rice farmer (generally literate) had used almost no fertilizers and pesticides previously and hardly knew how to select or apply them, state planners and scientists calculated that he would need hundreds of dollars' worth of chemicals each season to realize the potential of the Green Revolution. After teaching him his need for these, the government then offered him a loan to pay for them. Finally, by combining land reform with the Green Revolution's drive for national self-sufficiency in rice, and with a concerted effort to "integrate" all agricultural services, Manila was able to secure international backing and expert guidance.

Various middlemen serve the rural areas, but here we must draw particular attention to those who carry new agricultural information out to the small farmers. Their contribution is crucial at the time of land reform when the landlord ceases to provide managerial direction, and also in periods of sudden technological improvement. Besides the farmers' own rapid telegraph from field to field across the landscape, the input suppliers of the private sector more effectively diffuse innovations in farming practices than does an agency like the Philippines Bureau of Agricultural Extension—and at no cost to the state.

Rather than complement the teaching networks of these private sector information middlemen—progressive farmers in each village, merchants, seed growers, agricultural supplies salesmen, and even rice traders—the Philippine government's integrated agricultural program set out to displace them. Until then, the Bureau of Agricultural Extension had served the small farmer for more than fifty years as an independent agency.

18

Integration of government services now meant combining two monopolies: one over the dissemination of information about the new rice technology and another over input supplies.

Three cornerstones supported the government's integrated credit and agricultural program. First, Masagana 99 offered low-interest loans—12% per season—that undercut the private market's 50% or higher. To qualify for land reform and this supervised credit, a farmer had to join his village cooperative. His loan might be administered through a rural bank, but increasingly it was handled through a government bank, a Manila-based development firm, or another state or parastatal agency. Only one program was authorized to serve each village. In line with the planners' advice cited above, the loan comprised a fixed package of inputs issued in kind, plus just enough cash to cover labor costs. This credit package for any given cropping season was approximately the same throughout the nation, between $100 and $150 per hectare in 1982.*

To make sure they have the chemicals on hand when they need them, the program technician supervising Santa Rina farmers (an agricultural college graduate) prescribes all inputs at the time that he approves their loans—before planting. Each farmer then takes his purchase order to the supply store specified by the technician, which gives him his fertilizers and insecticides, and sometimes new seeds, and charges them to his Masagana 99 account. Because of the shortage of trained personnel, and in order to reduce administrative costs while assuring a more integrated supervision, the crop technician serves also as the farmer's loan officer. In particularly intensified programs not far from Santa Rina, the technician lives in the village and even supervises the farmers' timing of critical field operations and the distribution of irrigation water.

In many parts of the Philippines the program is administered by the private rural banks; indeed, they must agree to do so when receiving their license. Since a farmer can draw his Masagana loan from only the one bank or credit program appointed to his village (to simplify the task of credit ratings), he has no choice on which one to patronize and no opportunity to play off agencies against each other for better services. Thus, Masagana 99 insulates its borrowers from the dangers of greedy private moneylenders, but not from the state itself. Loans may be issued only through the state-controlled "farmers' cooperatives" (in quotations because they were not formed at farmer initiative); official lending agencies are strictly assigned to prevent farmers from shopping around; loans are subject to fixed government rates and regulations (as well as to periodic government amnesty on all outstanding Masagana debts); and the state's technical recommendations, state-controlled inputs, and often state procurement policies attempt to determine all farming operations so far as is possible.

*Ministry of Agriculture (1974:2) (also later editions).

The State Monopoly on Distribution

The second cornerstone of the Masagana 99 integrated credit scheme is the government's distribution system for the indispensable chemical inputs. Since farmers had previously used few chemicals in traditional agriculture, the government feared that in promoting the Green Revolution it would drive them into the jaws of capitalist middlemen who might sell them unnecessary, overpriced, or adulterated inputs. To guard against this and to facilitate the nationwide distribution of chemicals in response to the anticipated demand, the government financed the establishment of Planters' Products as, in effect, the sole retail chain for agricultural chemicals throughout the country, and the sole fertilizer manufacturer and distributor in the nation's more prosperous agricultural regions. The first prerogative is closely connected to the second. No retail chain could sustain itself only on the sale of pesticides. Thus, all Planters' requires is a monopoly over the lucrative fertilizer distribution in order automatically to restrict competition on the sale of complementary inputs like pesticides.

Planters' Products was founded in the early 1970s by Philippine sugar barons who foresaw the enormous commercial opportunities of the new rice technology, especially if it became linked to government credit and compulsory government supervision. Financed and generously protected by the government, Planters' Products is formally held by all farmer-patrons as stockholders. Yet, although among the top ten firms in the nation in volume of sales, the company has never issued a dividend to these "stockholders." The president of Planters' Products also controls the nation's sugar interests; top government officials sit on its board.

Planters' Products has therefore enjoyed a number of advantages: government patronage and the fear instilled by martial law; foreign funds for agricultural credit flowing through tightly guarded channels; a presidential commitment to the new rice technology; and participation in the integrated model for agricultural success. These have helped it move quickly along from blocking the Chinese middlemen to securing a monopoly over fertilizer production and distribution; then to monopolizing retail sales of pesticides and herbicides, supplanting not just the Chinese but foreign suppliers as well (Bayer, Ciba-Geigy, Shell, among others); then to acquiring an exclusive franchise for repackaging selected imported chemicals under its own label; and finally, to becoming the supplier for all government agricultural loans. The company is the middleman for loans under Masagana 99; for all loans extended through the Agricultural Credit Administration and its multifarious programs; for all loans offered by the state's extensive Area Marketing Cooperatives and village-level farmers' cooperatives; and for all loans processed through the state Land Bank, the Ministry of Agrarian Reform, and most compact farm and corporate farm programs. Finally, in 1978, after seeing impending weakness in the Masagana 99 program, Planters' Products established its own government-funded P200 million credit line directly to the farmers, in the process tapping the state cooperatives and their personnel to advertise, distribute, and monitor the company's loans and to collect from borrowers at harvest as part of their official duties to the village cooperative.

The third cornerstone of the government's integrated agricultural program is the National Grains Authority (NGA), also established by sugar baron elites with antimiddleman bias. The NGA purchases rice from small farmers either directly or through special credit programs and village cooperatives. Only small farmers are entitled to benefit from its higher purchase price. In many of the government's credit programs, farmers are required to sell their produce to NGA. When farmers do so, their loan remittances and other expenses (irrigation fees, land amortization payments, etc.) are deducted before they are paid for their harvest. A World Bank study refers to "the improved market opportunities" this NGA connection offers.*

These three cornerstones appear to support a rational economic plan. By offering a cheaper interest rate than the private sector, this plan brings farmers into the Masagana 99 program and hence into government cooperatives. By tying their lump-sum loans to the new technology through the technician's purchase order, the plan forces them to modernize their farming according to the scientists' and policy-makers' "superior" knowledge. Combining the chemical inputs and seeds into a single compulsory technology package offered through Planters' Products guarantees farmers reliable inputs and protects them against fraud, while at the same time improving the likelihood of a good harvest and hence of the government's recovering its investment. Undercutting the private traders' price at harvest encourages or even requires the farmers to sell to the state grain authority, through which the government repays itself (since Masagana credit is extended without collateral). The Land Bank and other agencies receive their payments and fees at the same time. Its pricing policy raises the price of rice on the private market as well, replenishes the government's grain holdings for national distribution and emergency, and thereby is held to minimize the country's net losses through storage damage. Finally, the plan consistently protects the farmer from extortionary middlemen.

All the above sounds ideal, but it has not turned out that way. In the first five years of Masagana 99, the Philippines enjoyed a 30% rise in national rice production. At first glance, this seems impressive. But it was principally due to the new high-yielding seeds themselves, which would have produced an increase in production whatever the complementary services.

But there is evidence that they might have performed better without the government package. In provinces where participation in Masagana 99

*For this and other references to a recent confidential World Bank study, "Philippines Sector Survey: Agricultural Support Services," see Bello et al. (1982).

21

dropped drastically as early as 1977, farmers steadily increased their purchase of new seeds and inputs and have produced a continuous rise in crop yields. With even 85% to 90% of the farmers out of the program, these areas boasted as much as a 15% yield gain in some years, at least as high a rate as during the years of full participation.

When the effective use of capital is fed into the equation, moreover, the comparison between Masagana 99 and the private sector is seen to be even more favorable to the middlemen and the farmer on his own. Even before the decade was out, Philippine farmers had accrued a one-billion-peso debt to Masagana 99 ($143 million). Because the government fears that farmers would riot and production would drop if it took strong measures to ensure loan repayment, it continually reschedules delinquent farmers' loans. Thus it is impossible to know what the Masagana collection rate actually is. But some idea of the proportions is shown by figures for the wet season of 1977, when 366,000 outstanding unpaid loans contrasted with 131,000 current loans (Bello et al. 1982:79). By contrast, the private sector of Santa Rina averages a 90% collection rate (Goodell field work).

Nevertheless, because of its ability to draw upon foreign aid and the taxpayer's purse, the state's integrated policy is winning the battle against private middlemen. In the first four years of the program, the private sector's share in institutional finance for agriculture dropped from 81% to 50% (Central Bank 1980), and the informal sector suffered more severely. After only seven years of Manila's consolidated thrust into the countryside, almost all farm credit programs of private banks were bankrupt. Many of the banks themselves collapsed under the weight of parasitic dependence, waste, and corruption of the Masagana program's paternalism. By 1976, 500 banks, which had by then become dependent on the program, had been disqualified (Bello et al. 1982:79). Rural banks, in general, had become over-dependent on the program, losing their portfolio diversification and thus an ability to stand on their own. And, finally, the country's lively network of rural banks had lost its ability to mobilize local savings. Out of thirty-two rural banks in the prosperous province of Nueva Ecija, several of which had flourished for nearly twenty-five years, only three remained in good health by 1981. In virtually every case, the decline of private banking services could be attributed to the government program.

Parallel to this massive erosion of the private financial sector in the provinces is the government's systematic undermining of private retail initiative serving the farmers. Planters' Products, financed and granted monopoly operations by the state and owned by government elites, has taken over almost all agricultural supply stores in the country. The only potential competition to Planters' on its scale, Atlas, no longer has its own warehouses, distributors, or even retail outlets. All private retailing chains for farm supplies have been extinguished. No longer do independent salesmen bring to the farmers the challenges of alternative inputs. The Chinese middlemen have been driven underground; private seed growers have been forced into the state's association for them; all rice millers and traders are circumscribed within the state's procurement and pricing policies; and the state reserves a monopoly on exporting rice. Despite nearly universal adoption of the new rice technology in the irrigated lowlands, not one of the hundreds of thousands of village entrepreneurs sells the supplies that farmers need.

While rice production continues to expand, the private sector's participation in processing, storing, marketing, and investing new capital has remained at a standstill for several years and now is actually being displaced by NGA expansion, which includes new warehouses and sizable port facilities. The sharp reduction in seasonal price variation, due to government intervention, has eroded the private sector's profit margins so that it is less able to finance post-harvest facilities, such as processing, storing, etc. And so the state intervenes further. Finally, the agricultural extension service, one of the oldest in the Third World and potentially a major stimulant for rural experimentation and enterprise, has been reduced to a mere puppet of the state's and the elite's commercial monopolies.

Farmers are now worse off than they were under the landlords. To settle a disagreement over a loan, a peasant must penetrate the Central Bank of the Philippines, a maze of corridors and guards in downtown Manila. To argue over the price of Carbofuran, he must seek out the National Food and Agriculture Council, somewhere within the Ministry of Agriculture, itself somewhere within the government complex, somewhere in distant Quezon City. Farmers are well aware of their dependence. But, in exchange for these critical losses, have they not at least gained land reform? Hardly. Once the state had monopolized ancillary services, it ceased implementing the land reform (no longer needing it for its own purposes), with only a fraction of the eligible lands actually transferred.

In the confidential study previously cited, the World Bank has found Masagana 99's integrated agricultural program to be a national disaster: a correct judgment, but even in a confidential appraisal the bank misses the crucial issues. For example, it points out the grave ecological effects of the farmers' present widespread use of the wrong types of fertilizer, and the much higher cost of these over the ones they ought to use. But the bank treats this as merely a technical matter or, worse yet, as the fault of the extension service or of farmers' ignorance. It does not recognize that these deleterious compounds are precisely the ones manufactured by the Planters' factory in Bataan, while the farmers' access to the more beneficial and economic fertilizers they prefer is precluded by the state's import protection. Thus there is no mere "technical error," but a determined policy for Planters' Products to make money. In another passage, the bank team is mystified that a capitalist enterprise like Atlas (owned by a political rival of former President Marcos) spends nothing on trying to market its products in competition against Planters'.

The Worm's Eye View from Santa Rina

Let us now see the state as middleman in real life in Santa Rina. Some 150 families live in Santa Rina village; all are farmers or landless laborers. A jeep passes through Santa Rina daily going to and from the main highway, from which one can continue on to the provincial capital an hour away. But all government business, including Masagana 99 loans, must be transacted in the municipality to which Santa Rina "belongs," located in the opposite direction, difficult to reach by an infrequently traveled road, and offering far less choice than the provincial capital. Eight moneylenders and six rice buyers (all petty middlemen, small farmers themselves) live in Santa Rina and till their lands there. The village boasts seventeen small stores. Santa Rina has a school with three grades, no electricity, a half-built chapel, and a farmers' cooperative so ineffectual that it has ceased to meet. It is not a village dominated by a few rich families, nor was it ever controlled by a single landlord.

The large estates, to which some of Santa Rina's lands originally belonged, were broken up by land reform, though at least half of the village's fields have not yet been surveyed for reform. Still, any farmer in the community can apply for Masagana 99's supervised credit. The bank authorized to administer Santa Rina's loans is owned by a provincial family, Judge Luz and his wife. Since the government program began, this bank has held a monopoly on all Masagana 99 loans throughout the municipality's thirty-odd villages. It used to have its own agricultural credit program, but as that cannot compete with the government's program, it has been closed.

The first problem for Santa Rina farmers in the integrated agricultural program is that, like most rural bankers in the Philippines, the Luz family also owns an agricultural supply store. When the Masagana 99 technician issues a farmer a purchase order for chemicals, he restricts it to the bank's outlet store, where Masagana borrowers are charged prices up to 15% higher than customers paying cash, even for the same chemicals. The bank technician's task of designating which chemicals a farmer must purchase encourages him or the bank to require inputs that may be unnecessary or adulterated, whose period of viability may have expired, or chemicals dumped on the Masagana market under a Planters' Products label when in fact they have been banned throughout the country. The program's Santa Rina borrowers suffer all these eventualities. Unlike earlier years, they have no alternative source of supply. In a pilot study of randomly selected pesticides purchased at Planter's retail stores that Santa

24

Rina farmers patronize, 75% contained chemicals adulterated to more than twice the acceptable standard deviation.

In addition, through the government's agriculture controls and Planters' fertilizer monopoly, rice farmers pay 50% above the world market price for urea, the fertilizer most valuable for their crop and soil conditions (*Philippine Times*, 2/18/82). Thus, the government's "socialized" agricultural program, with its elaborate designs to shield naive farmers from "rapacious" capitalists, places them instead at the mercy of a money-lending monopoly. It also puts them in the hands of a monopoly retailer as well as a monopoly wholesaler for their inputs, forcing them to pay higher prices than offered by those against whom they are being protected. Even those farmers preferring to borrow from the private sector are left defenseless against manipulation and fraud in acquiring inputs. The chemicals which could have been inspected by the government are not.

A second problem in the state's program is that the chemicals farmers must purchase with the loan often have little or no relevance to the actual needs of their crop. Indeed, they are issued at the time the loan is approved, before the crop has even been planted. Thus the farmers are not only forced to buy the wrong kind of fertilizer, they must tie up their capital before *any* fertilizer is needed at all.

There are other examples of waste caused by this contradiction. In 1979 the standard government recommendation for Masagana loans required all Santa Rina borrowers to purchase specific insecticides against brown plant hoppers, although 92% of the farmers in the province were planting a rice variety highly resistant to that pest (Goodell 1979:5–6). In six villages near Santa Rina, an intensified Masagana 99 program issued its members over $300,000 worth of redundant pesticides in a single year, while the farmers complained that they had no need for these chemicals.

Integrating all aspects of an agricultural program under state control also jeopardizes timing, which is decisive in modern farming. Monopoly distribution systems provide little incentive to maintain inventories responsive to their clients' needs. Frequently Santa Rina farmers find that Judge Luz's supply store has none of the necessary chemicals when an infestation breaks out or when the crop needs additional fertilizers. Turning to other merchants would double their expenses since they have already assumed a packaged debt at Judge Luz's store.

The already serious conflict of interest—between Judge Luz's bank serving as advisor and financier to the Santa Rina farmers while he is their only source of input supplies—is sharpened by the farmers having no choice on the source or size of their Masagana loan. But the rural bank is not accountable for these distortions, which affect public funds, not those of Judge Luz himself. For example, though collections are notoriously poor, Judge Luz has only to achieve 60% repayment to qualify for 100% coverage by the Central Bank (Memo 1981). As a result, he has loaned funds earmarked for small-farmer rice production to his cousin for an orchid business, to his brother for an electrical appliance store, and to his mother-in-law for a trip to Los Angeles: all in the names of farmers in the local cemetery.

But even when Judge Luz does not collect 60% of the outstanding loans, the government periodically revs up Masagana with a new program, available to all farmers regardless of their previous repayment record. Its funds run after farmers, not the other way around. With rice production now contingent on monopolies and handouts, the very stability of the state depends upon perpetuating corruption and exploitation.

The conflict of interest of the bank technician both administering loans and dispensing farming information leads to more contradictions. Those very farmers who most need to improve their agricultural practices usually hide from the technician, because they are his worst defaulters. Similarly, during a pest or disease outbreak when farmers most need his advice, the technician is loath to enter the village because his supply store invariably runs out of stock.

Curiously, Judge Luz is in the same double bind at his level as are the Santa Rina farmers at theirs; he cannot compete for the farmers' business on his own terms because of Masagana 99's much lower interest rate, so he has had to accept the government's offer to become its outlet for Masagana credit. Even if his technician is honest and professionally competent, he is limited to government-approved recommendations (predominantly for Planters' inputs) when he issues the government loan, just as his supply store is constrained by Planters' licensing powers. In short, though Judge Luz has his monopoly over loans and inputs in the municipality, the monopolies of the state and Planters' Products rule him at the national level.

All the above applies to the farmer as he plants and cultivates. At harvest, a new set of problems arises. Many Masagana programs require that the farmer sell rice to the NGA. Furthermore, he must sell the entire harvest at once, instead of incrementally. Harvest, of course, is the time when prices are lowest. The farmer is not allowed to store part of his crop until he can charge higher, off-season prices. He suddenly becomes a "millionaire for a day," and the temptation to spend indiscriminately is great.

Santa Rina farmers trying to sell their rice to the NGA usually wait from three to seven days in line outside the warehouse with their grain, sleeping there at night to hold their places in the queue—whereas they might have sold to any private dealer of their choice in fifteen minutes, had they been allowed to do so. The question is not simply one of inconvenience: if it rains during this time, their rice becomes wet and commands a lower price.

What does a farmer find when he does reach the head of the line? The government has advertised that it is prepared to pay a higher price than the private retailers yet says nothing about "quality control." Claiming that their scientific instruments are more accurate than the farmers' own judgment, the NGA tester brings down the price—on "quality" grounds—to that of the retailers outside or lower. Since farmers cannot ascertain the state's actual average buying price, even week-to-week, they have no leverage against this false inducement. The private middlemen, on the other hand, would supply Santa Rina's house-to-house "wireservice" with copious daily information about the markets, gratis. Furthermore, when farmers can sell to the middlemen locally, quickly, and in small quantities, if they do not like the price offered by one, it is easy to go down the road to another.

Who, then, would ever voluntarily sell to NGA? Many farmers must sell to NGA as part of the Masagana package. In conversing with those in the line outside NGA, one discovers among them the many bankers and others who administer Masagana programs. They identify themselves as small farmers—thus qualifying for the NGA procurement program—by presenting their client's co-op cards (and other necessary documents), which they require the farmers to turn over to them as a condition for the loans. Still others are prosperous rice traders in the private sector, who, with their natural links to NGA officers, persuade them to drive the farmers back into the private sector through low "quality control" prices in order to purchase the traders' rice instead—at the subsidized price. Thus the purpose of government rice procurement—to offer higher prices as an incentive to small farmers—benefits the provincial elites instead.

A second justification for NGA, safer national rice storage, is nullified by government mismanagement and private sector efficiency: the NGA suffers "appreciably higher" loss due to storage damage than the private sector. A third justification, distribution to rice-short regions, is fulfilled more effectively by the middlemen, who vigorously seek out areas of grain shortage, whereas NGA is centralized in Manila.

Farmers selling to the NGA, moreover, are not paid on the spot, as they would be if dealing with private middlemen. Instead, the NGA deducts from the value of each farmer's delivery not only his Masagana 99 loan and its charges, but also sundry debts and fees over which the farmer has no choice and which he certainly would not pay if given the choice. Calculating all these deductions delays his remuneration at least six weeks.

Furthermore, irrigation charges are deducted even when water delivery had been unsatisfactory or damaging; land reform amortization is deducted before the farmer agrees to the terms of the settlement; co-op membership fees and mutual liability against other farmers' delinquency are deducted even when the co-op has been disbanded; rescheduled dues on past debts are deducted, at compound interest that no farmer is able to monitor; and various other arbitrary claims by the state are deducted as well. An example: compulsory life insurance for all co-op members. Yet, with their close family ties, villagers would hardly choose to invest in life insurance, especially since they have never yet seen any benefits paid to families of the deceased.

All of these charges are packaged into the small farmer's loan, so he must pay them if he is to receive any agricultural advice at all. Since farmers financing their crop on their own withhold payment from any government agency until they are satisfied with the services they receive, these automatic deductions through both "their" cooperative and the NGA deprive those within the scheme of the only leverage they have over the government's performance.

Finally, the very comprehensiveness of the state's integrated scheme appears to the Santa Rina farmers as a trap. It pits the obligations that land reform and modern agriculture force them to assume against their future standing as borrowers. Farmers the world over must borrow to finance their crops. In the Third World the private sector is far too disorganized to maintain a watertight credit rating system, so villagers can always play middlemen off against each other. While they cannot endlessly avoid their responsibilities, the freedom and informality of the private sector ensure the flexibility that efficient agriculture demands. In contrast, the state's complex net of institutional approvals and verifications, identification cards, and restricted access to services through appointed agencies seems expressly designed to deprive them of bargaining power for capital.

When the state does offer land reform beneficiaries a choice between itself or the private-sector middleman, they vote with their feet for the latter. A decade after the land reform, voluntary subscription to Masagana 99 has fallen from 98% of all eligible farmers (Central Bank 1977) to 21% in Santa Rina (Goodell field research). Certain high officials (not wishing to be quoted by name) estimate that nationwide it has fallen to 1%. In order to retain the freedom to make their own decisions, most farmers prefer to pay 50% interest rates or more to "rapacious" capitalists rather than a mere 12% for Masagana's benefits. Of course, farmers eagerly sign up for a new government program if it grants them amnesty on their outstanding Masagana debts. But in a few seasons they fall into arrears once again. The astounding rate of default among farmers who still have the funds for luxury items—the prosperity found in villages that disqualify themselves from the state's integrated program—speaks for itself. In Santa Rina, 86% of all farmers disqualifying themselves from the government's cheaper credit program through persistent default admit that they could afford to resume repayment if they wanted to do so (Goodell field research).

The farmers' preference for the private sector has undermined other pillars of the state's well-knit program as well. In land reform areas, under-the-counter sales of non-Planters' chemicals in Planters' stores are rampant. Masagana technicians thrive on bribes paid them for recommending these chemicals instead of Planters'. The black market for seeds not licensed by the state flourishes. As the government allows new Masagana programs with stricter surveillance to proliferate, as the Land Bank itself moves into the fray to recover its claims directly through supervised loans, and as recalcitrant beneficiaries are threatened with well-publicized management takeovers by the state-controlled cooperatives, membership in the state's integrated program dwindles.

In Manila's rice bowl, no new scheme for reversing the erosion of Masagana's control lasts more than several years. Indeed, during a run of bad seasons it is not uncommon for some Santa Rina farmers to hand their recently won land deeds back to their old landlords, seeking refuge there rather than in the state's integrated package. According to a 1983 agricultural economics survey of lowland rice farmers, conducted by the International Rice Research Institute, the average *income* per hectare is no higher now in Central Luzon despite higher yields, these many government programs, and land reform than it was in 1972–78.

The Middleman Unvanquished

What does the private middleman offer that the farmers prefer to the state's more favorable interest rates and its paternalistic protection? These middlemen do not attach strings to their services. Even individual firms make little effort to coordinate their own responses to farmers' needs. Private middlemen who lend money, sell inputs, and buy rice at harvest have no expectation that a Santa Rina farmer will return to them for any other service in the future. Farmers skillfully keep their options open, especially as higher rice yields increase their mobility.

Second, the private sector is very flexible. In contrast to the government's packaged credit and technology, it is willing to deal in any unit of capital, input, produce, or even any unit of time. A farmer can borrow whatever amount he needs, however small, requesting a loan for twenty-four hours or for several years; interest rates vary accordingly. The village moneylender will never ask how the farmer plans to use the loan—much less will she volunteer advice—because that is none of her business. Village and urban retailers are prepared to sell a farmer half a cup of ammonium sulfate or four tablespoons of Brodan. In any village store in the Philippines you can purchase a single Marlboro cigarette. "If this were Masagana 99," one farmer observed as he stopped by the village store for a smoke, "everyone within five miles would have to buy six cartons of the same brand and guarantee each other's repayment before I could pause for a light."

Most of the loans made by private middlemen last for one or several months rather than an entire season. Days make a difference when capital is scarce. Farmers will delay applying fertilizer until as close to harvest time as possible, in order to make sure the crop and the weather justify the investment, and to keep the number of days they actually hold a loan to a minimum. This rapid recycling of the village's own resources is a far more efficient use of capital than the government's cumbersome season-long packages.

Such plasticity also lends itself to conditions of rapid economic development even where land reform has created a tabula rasa, as it were, for a large and diversely endowed population. It assures farmers of a wide range of choice, the opportunity to make last-minute decisions, and the option to purchase not a whit more than they actually need. This flexibility enables them to adjust their strategies to their differing circumstances, managerial skills, and family assets. All of these vary considerably even in a peasant village, and more so as the years progress after land reform. Poorer farmers, those with greater family demands, or those slower to master the new technology need not assume a heavier debt than they can meet. More prosperous farmers are not held back by the rigidities of nationally packaged prescriptions. Each can tailor his crop management according to his particular requirements and capacities.

Nor can the state's prescribed and packaged technology encourage farmer experimentation, since borrowers under such supervision are left few, if any, choices. Packaged technology offers no opportunity to purchase inputs in small enough quantities for inexpensive field tests. With virtually no government experimentation conducted locally, the combination of Masagana 99 and Planters' Products stifles leadership in serious innovation while fostering risky fads on a national scale. Like all monopolies, when it does err, the state's integrated agricultural program threatens to institutionalize mistakes on a large scale. This can pose a grave threat to the nation, as was seen in 1973–74 when Masagana 99 borrowers, using technology standardized throughout the Philippines, fell prey to the same tungro epidemic from one end of the country to the other.

But does not the private sector charge high interest rates for agricultural loans? It does so, but it rarely requires a written agreement, which might intimidate the borrower. It transacts business in the farmer's own language, while government forms are in English, which he cannot understand. A farmer, moreover, can do business with village middlemen on the spur of the moment without transportation costs, without waiting for approval, without subjecting himself to the incomprehensible and humiliating demands of state officials. Village and provincial-level middlemen remain at the beck and call of clients night and day (farmers even know where their landlords reside in the municipality or in Manila), because clients call on middlemen for many personal services, for connections with powerful people, for advice and emergency assistance. A high interest rate may very well reflect the value of services, while also providing the private lender the leeway to extend loans according to circumstances or to absorb those that cannot be paid. Given the competition among middlemen, there is no evidence that any of them are becoming rich.

Furthermore, the private sector cannot, like the state, use force to collect payment. It cannot threaten the farmer with jail, with repossession of his land title if he is a beneficiary of land reform, or with management take-over through the cooperative. Finally, private individuals and institutions providing agricultural services in the province have no links with national agencies, through which they might otherwise distort the market. Compared with the size of Planters' Products or the government's banking programs, they are small. Provincial middlemen are too numerous, too fragmented, and engaged in too much competition against one another to match the state's monopoly.

Admittedly, provincial-level middlemen do attempt to dominate certain spheres within the municipality. No doubt the prejudice against middlemen in general was originally rooted in empirical evidence, particularly during the economically static conditions of earlier years. But when they dominate successfully today, it is always with the assistance of the state, which grants exclusive licenses and monopolies.

Because they are part of the villagers' social fabric and because they are so free to fill any gaps that appear, the private middlemen offer countless important supplementary services in the countryside, often without charge. During the lean months before harvest, farmers accumulate debts at the village stores owned by some middlemen. Because villagers are bound by personal relations impossible to develop with a state official, borrowers use these stores to their advantage rather than—as in Planters' case—the other way around. While the village storekeeper's prices exceed those in town by some 5% to 10%, she (and many middlemen are, in fact, women) does not charge her clients interest, and she will buy almost any item on request during her frequent shopping trips to town. If her customers or farmers holding crop loans harvest low-quality or moldy rice, which the government would not accept, the village middlemen can be pressured to buy it as payment for a farmer's debts. Should she reject such a farmer's bad rice, her fellow villagers would make her uncomfortable. And by not charging compound interest on outstanding debts, the middleman provides an invaluable form of crop insurance. It is in these ways that the middleman absorbs costs that may be compensated by the high interest rates.

In Santa Rina, the village middlemen perform other services as well. When a borrower mortgages his land to her for a given period of time (she can never in fact lay claim to the title), she usually hires him to continue working it; she often invests in it, and her more efficient management serves as a good example to him. The state's management take-over (or token sentence to a few days in jail) contributes nothing in this way to improve his land and working practices.

Furthermore, many village middlemen are the most progressive farmers in their communities. Simply by farming in Santa Rina, they provide more effective demonstrations of new agricultural practices than any of the

31

state's extension classes. This behavior contrasts with that of the government credit and extension agents, who—the farmers know—being tied to monopoly profits, are more concerned to further Planters' sales than to promote the farmers' savings.

Finally, as a citizen of the village, the upwardly mobile middleman presents a dynamic example to other villagers. In her venturesome spirit, she proves that the world beyond Santa Rina is accessible to ordinary farmers, that they can enter into partnership with provincial townsmen as equals, seek bargains as far away as Manila, and try new enterprises. It is the middlemen who first send their children to high school beyond Santa Rina. It is they, not the officials administering Masagana programs, who advance the community's civic interests and spearhead demands that the government perform more effectively. Farmers can identify with these fellow villagers. The state has attempted to fill their roles itself through the farmers' cooperative. But how can a government official from town, who himself has power over the farmers, address their needs, especially when these needs are to check government corruption and to remedy empty promises?

After the Middleman—What?

What have been the consequences when the state and its funders and planners set out to displace hundreds of thousands of village- and provincial-level middlemen and to substitute for them their own agencies? In one village near Santa Rina, the government's integrated agricultural program succeeded in eliminating two middlemen and a rice buyer who had moved to town in search of better economic opportunities. They could no longer compete with the intensified Masagana program. They took with them their economic resources, their management skills, their network of urban contacts, and their familiarity with the ins and outs of life beyond the village. They took also their leadership, their experiments, their families active in civic affairs, their celebrations open to all, their stories about travel elsewhere in the country, not to mention their stores, moneylending, jeeps, television sets (available to everyone each evening), and their congenial characters. One old man, no longer able to walk to the fields, must now assume leadership there.

The private sector serving the countryside is part of a complex social ecology comprising numerous organisms well integrated into the environment. Over time these very flexible "middle" men and women are subject to local pressures for change; the living system of which they are a part is patchable. There are in fact numerous ways for a small-scale Asian farmer to borrow money, numerous ways to cultivate rice, numerous ways to profit from 5 acres of land—not just one way as the planners and their funders insist. Many of these ways are described by Wheelock and Young (1973). The multiplicity of options in the private sector allows a family to

32

slip over easily from one way of doing something to another. Surely the problem of how to keep Santa Rina's middlemen from leaving the village should pose a far greater worry to the state than how to eliminate them. That is, unless the state *wants* to eliminate those structures in local and provincial society that stand in the way of its domination of rural economic life. The case of what lies behind the Philippine land reform, so sparsely won, by so few, after so many decades of promulgations—this case makes us realize how determined the state can be to relinquish hold only when in fact is has first established even tighter control.*

Authors' Note

This chapter was written before the election and coup of 1986. In January, 1986, just before the election, one of the authors (Powelson) visited the Philippines and talked with farmers and agricultural technicians in Silang County. Although the conversations were impressionistic and do not constitute a formal study, nevertheless the consensus is worth mentioning.

First, the Masagana 99 Program, to which Goodell refers, is now ended. All agree it was a failure. Even before the end of the Marcos regime, farmers had become free to borrow where they like, and informal mechanisms were being reconstituted in the countryside. Still, farmers complained about lack of credit, in that large banks—both private and government—tended to absorb the national credit supply, and only local resources were available for local needs.

Second, the farmers consulted were virtually unanimous that the land reform had been a failure, primarily because sugar plantations had been exempt. Much farmland was reported to have been planted in sugar in order to escape the reform. The main sugar mills and sales outlets were reported to be in the hands of Marcos "cronies," a point that was confirmed immediately after the coup. These establishments are said to have been operated inefficiently, with inflated costs enriching their owners. As a result, Philippine sugar became overpriced on the world market. Recovery from this abnormality is doubtless one of the main challenges to the Aquino government.

The main obstacle to effective land reform is probably summed up in the following paragraph, which an agricultural technician from a private agency in the Phillipines wrote to Powelson in April 1986:

> This is a small community where I have been working for two years now. The land is going to be sold to a developer in violation of tenants' rights under the land reform law. It is a shame to think that a whole community

---

*The *anthropological* case study of Santa Rina presents many characteristics of state intervention very similar to those we will document with *economic* studies from other countries in subsequent chapters.

of people I know will be forced off the land and committed to a life in the streets or as landless agricultural workers. We have at last concluded that it is unrealistic to suppose they will ever own the land according to the provisions of the law. First, officials of the Ministry of Agrarian Reform are unresponsive. Second, the landlord is protesting tenant rights. Although he has no basis to do so, the court case may drag on for years while the political situation changes. Finally, the tenants don't have enough money to fight it. At best, we hope, the courts will recognize the rights of tenants to remain on the land for the time being, under current arrangements.

References

Barker, R., 1981. "Rice Marketing in Asia," *Rice Research Strategies for the Future*, Quezon City, Philippines, International Rice Research Institute.

Bello, Walden; Kinley, David; and Elinson, Elaine, 1982. *Development Debacle*, San Francisco, Institute of Food and Development Policy.

Borton, Raymonde E., ed., 1966. *Getting Agriculture Moving*, vol. 2, New York, Agricultural Development Council.

Central Bank of the Philippines, 1977. "Rural Banking System in the Philippines," *Annual Report*, Manila.

Central Bank of the Philippines, 1980. "Private Sector Participation in Masagana 99," Department of Agricultural Credit, internal paper, Manila.

Goodell, Grace, 1979. "Technology's Road from IRRI to the Farmers," in "Memos from the Barrio" (series distributed to senior staff of International Rice Research Institute), Economics Department, IRRI, Los Baños, Laguna, Philippines, October 30.

Hanisch, Rolf, 1977–78. "Decision-Making Processes and Problems of Implementation of the Land Reform in the Philippines," *Asia Quarterly*, Part I in 1977, vol. 4; Part II in 1978, vol. 1.

ILO (International Labor Organization), 1974. *Sharing in Development: A Programme of Employment, Equity, and Growth in the Philippines*, Geneva.

Memo, 1981. Memorandum from Executive Officer, Credit Committee, National Food and Agriculture Council, Ministry of Agriculture, Manila, May 24.

Ministry of Agriculture of the Philippines, 1974 (and later editions). *Masagana 99*, Manila.

Paul, A., 1966. "Credit's Role in Improving Agriculture," in Borton (1966).

Roth, Dennis Morrow, 1977. *The Friar Estates of the Philippines*, Albuquerque, University of New Mexico Press.

Spinks, G. R., 1970. "Attitudes Toward Agricultural Marketing in Asia and the Far East," *Monthly Bulletin*, Rome, Food and Agriculture Organization, January.

Takahashi, Akira, 1969. *Land and Peasants in Central Luzon: Socio-Economic Structure of a Philippine Village*, Honolulu, East-West Center Press.

Wheelock, Gerald C., and Young, Frank W., 1973. *Macrosocial Accounting for Municipalities in the Philippines: Rural Banks and Credit Cooperatives*, Ithaca, New York State College of Agriculture and Life Sciences, Cornell University.

World Bank, 1975. *Agricultural Sector Policy Paper*, Washington, D.C.

World Bank, 1976. *The Philippines: Priorities and Prospects for Development*, A World Bank Country Report, Washington, D.C.

3. Mexico

"They have to come to us first if they want land," says an official with the peasant confederation. "Even if they get land, they have to come to us to get water. If they get water, they still need credits and fertilizer. The party will never lose control of the countryside" (Frazier, in *The Wall Street Journal*, 2/14/84).

Mexico's revolution of 1910–17 was fought in the name of Land and Liberty. Article 27 of the Constitution of 1917 vested ownership of all lands initially in the nation, but the government had the right to transfer land to private citizens subject to whatever restrictions it might determine in the public interest. In a compromise between the "revolution of the south," which fought for communal farming (*ejidos*), and the "revolution of the north," where small private properties were in favor, the revolutionary government decided on both forms, to be determined according to local needs.

Land redistribution, however, has been gradual, occurring over decades although bunched up in certain presidencies, such as that of Lázaro Cárdenas (1934–40). Presidents have vied with each other for expropriating large farms, dividing them into *ejidos* and small private properties. The last major expropriations took place in 1975. Since then acreage redistributed has been small, presumably because there is no more land to give.

In principle, the *ejido* contains a communal plot for the village, with individual plots assigned to *ejidatarios*. Some (collective *ejidos*) farm as corporations; others (individual *ejidos*) farm individual plots; some are mixed. The "problem of the commons" (who will take care of it? who will improve it?) – solved in other countries by its division into private properties – has been perpetuated by law in Mexico. Furthermore, the private assignments cannot be sold, mortgaged, or given away, but they can be inherited. An *ejidatario* who abandons his land loses it.

All these problems have been "solved" by subterfuge. An *ejidatario* who would seek employment in the city may – with an appropriate bribe to local officials – arrange that his abandoned land shall be assigned to another *ejidatario* or even to a private outsider who then makes him a monetary "gift." In ways such as these, both the communal land and individual plots have been partly conveyed into de facto private property, some of it attached to lands officially outside the *ejido*.

35

Land expropriations over fifty years have contributed much to the instability of Mexican agriculture. Had they been done once for all after 1917, the uncertainty might have vanished. A "large" farm in Mexico, most of them in the irrigated Northwest, now typically contains about 100 hectares. With rapid population growth, the increased numbers of landless peasants continue to demand the land the revolution has promised them. The government, concerned that further distributions not only are politically impossible but would diminish agricultural output, has vacillated. Cruelly enough, parched scrubland in the south has been doled out in small quantities to farmers who quickly discover that no living can be earned on it.

Despite the revolution, the Mexican land reform has always been one of grace rather than leverage, as is illustrated in Morelos. Here the distribution carried out on the spot in 1917 was ignored by the central government. Villages were required to petition for the land for which they had fought. Many asked for restitution of plots taken from them by haciendas in the nineteenth century. But the government preferred to grant land (*dotación*) rather than restore it (*restitución*).

> Agrarian reform was not going to legitimize the historic rights of the village to the land nor strengthen their autonomy . . . On the contrary, it was going to distribute the land as a unilateral concession from the State, like a favor from a powerful figure who retains for himself the right to watch over the fulfillment of his supreme edict and to intervene overtly in its administration to create a political clientele (Warman 1980:136).

Peasant Organizations

To champion the peasant vis-à-vis the landed aristocracy, Cárdenas enhanced the power of the state, making the peasants increasingly dependent upon it. Although the landed aristocracy lost much during Cárdenas's presidency, it maintained a continuing presence, and the government's influence in the countryside extended only as far as the state's military power. There was no sense that a particular piece of land would automatically become the peasants' through the law of the land. Only through political dependency on the official party could that occur. Furthermore, when the field of battle had been lost, the old aristocracy tried to infiltrate the party. Some argue that a counterreform occurred from the last year of Cárdenas's presidency, gaining headway during the forties.

Thus the state and the peasants needed each other and land reform was the economic issue of their joint political survival. Only through this observation do we understand both why hacienda land was not expropriated once for all in 1917—the state was not powerful enough, nor did the revolutionary generals necessarily want to—and why land reform and indeed the revolution continued for at least fifty years.

This bizarre relationship was different from all other countries whose land reforms we have studied. Elsewhere, the state generally wrote the rules for land tenure; it expropriated properties that were violating them; and it either gave legal title to existing tenants or formed cooperatives or state farms. The entire process was accomplished in a few months in Peru, two years in Egypt, Taiwan, and Japan, four years in the People's Republic of China and South Korea, and similar periods elsewhere. In Mexico — quite apart from the half century over which the total process occurred — the average length of time between an initial petition for land by a group of peasants and the provisional grant — when they might start farming — was five years. On average, another seven years was required for the *ejido* to gain definitive title. During this period, peasants had to be on guard against landowner violence. They also needed enough funds to bribe middle- and low-level officials who might influence the decision. *This entire process fostered dependency on the apparatus of the state.* Indeed, leaving *ejidos* in a "partially legitimated" state helped to secure their political loyalty (Hewitt 1980:30). On the other hand, landowner access to government policymakers also prolonged the proceedings.

Peasant Leagues and the Revolutionary Party

Peasant leagues were formed in several states during the twenties (Salamini 1971:114). The most powerful of these grew up in states with strong governors or military leaders who loaned official support: Tejada in Veracruz; Portes-Gil in Tamaulipas; Cárdenas in Michoacan. In 1926, the leagues of sixteen states combined into the Liga Nacional Campesina (LNC). The LNC advocated carrying out Article 27 of the 1917 Constitution, which provided for land reform.

In 1929 President Calles organized the National Revolutionary Party (PNR) in order to gain control of the innumerable political factions, but when the PNR tried to absorb LNC at the 1930 Congress of the latter, LNC split into three parts. When Lazaro Cárdenas became president of the PNR in 1930, he tried to consolidate all peasant organizations into a national unit. By 1933 the Confederación Campesina Mexicana (CCM) was formed to back Cárdenas's bid for the presidency, and within a short time, it had become the dominant organization.

The CCM then set up peasant leagues in every state while campaigning for Cárdenas. In the 1933 convention of the PNR, the CCM's agrarian delegates won endorsements in the party platform for speeding up the land reform; for creation of an independent Agrarian Department; for peasant participation on the State Agrarian Commission; and for peasants resident on the hacienda to be allowed to benefit from land reform (Huizer 1970:465–66). After Cárdenas had won the presidency in 1934, CCM used central government personnel to recruit and organize local peasant leagues; it also received federal subsidies. The independent peasant leagues (of the various states) had all been effectively destroyed (Salamini 1971:114ff.).

37

The official incorporation of the peasantry into the party was accomplished during the Cárdenas presidency. In 1935, Cárdenas asked Portes-Gil and the PNR National Executive Committee to re-organize state agrarian leagues in every state, in order to bring them together into a national organization. Communities were legally required to establish such leagues in order to petition for land (Huizer 1970:468). The leagues sent delegations (expenses paid by the government) to a congress in 1938 that established the Confederación Nacional Campesina (CNC). The PNR, now converted into the Partido de la Revolución Mexicana (PRM), became organized into four sectors, of which the CNC was one, the others being labor, the army, and the "popular sector" (a loose amalgamation of middle classes).

Although the CNC had been intended as advocate for peasants before the state, it turned out instead to be the state's avenue to control the peasantry. First, it depended on government subsidies. Second, while each *ejido* belonged to the CNC as a collective, during the forties, state and regional officials tended to be non-peasants. They depended on their superiors for their promotions, not on the peasants for their jobs, and their careers lay in the politics of the nation. Their roles ceased to be those of advocates. The monopoly of the state over "legitimization of agrarian change" was responsible for the dominance of the state (Hewitt 1980:21).

Thus the ambiguity of the revolution when the fighting ended (1917–20), the continued power presence of hacienda owners, and the precariousness of the revolutionary government during the twenties threw peasants and government into mutual dependence. But why did the government win? Why did the peasantry end up depending on it, and not vice versa?

The answer to that intriguing question encompasses a broader set of questions than land reform; we therefore allude to it but do not address it. For example, labor's relationship with the government was similar to that of peasants. The unions too were brought within the orbit of the party (although minor unions, such as the communist, remained alive outside). The "civilianization" of the army has been much-touted as a move away from military politics and toward civilian democracy, yet in Mexico it was part of a wider process. As other organizations were absorbed into the government, why not the army? Business also developed an ambiguous dependency on government, one that is still in flux. Thus government was the focal point for all these organizations. Since it both commanded resources and could play one group against another, it turned out that all groups depended on government, not vice versa.

The dependency proposition is tested negatively in research by Salamini (1971:153–71) on three municipalities in Veracruz—La Antigua, San Andrés Tuxtla, and Alamo-Temapache—seeking a "correlation between strong local peasant movements and sweeping agrarian reform." He concluded that "peasant leadership was unable to bring about lasting changes in the agrarian structure of the state."

In La Antigua, which contained 10,000 hectares, half in crops such as sugar, corn, beans and tomatoes, half in cattle, the sugar mill and the best acreage around it were excluded from expropriation in the twenties. Local supporters of reform were continually harassed by landowners and their leaders were murdered. Petitions were decided and the post-reform "socio-political structure [was] not strikingly different from pre-revolution" (Salamini 1971:102). In San Andrés Tuxtla a number of commercial crops (tobacco, bananas, sugar cane, coffee, and cotton) were grown, but cattle took half the acreage. Large tobacco haciendas for export dominated in the late Porfiriato. Despite intense activity of peasant leagues and some land redistribution in the late twenties and early thirties, cattlemen and large owners continued to dominate, partly through violence. In Alamo-Temapache, agriculture followed oil discovery. Because of the power of landlords and lack of population pressure, land reform was not pressed very hard.

Thus land reform was ineffective when left to peasant leagues. It required the support of the state. But when it received this support, it was modeled after the needs of the state, not those of the peasants.

Credit

The Agricultural Credit Law of 1926 established the National Agricultural Credit Bank (NACB), which loaned mainly to medium- and large-scale farmers. It also authorized regional banks to serve *ejidos*. These banks in turn helped organize several hundred unlimited-liability credit cooperatives within *ejidos*. Under the 1926 law, 39.5 million pesos were loaned in 1926-35. Of this amount, 32.9 million pesos went to 1,441 individual farmers and 6.6 million pesos to 338 credit cooperatives composed of 18,520 small farmers (Sanderson 1981:84). Yet credit dispensed at the regional level—instead of through local banks or cooperatives seeking credit from multiple sources—enabled the state to reward or punish *ejidos* and to promote its favored crops, its favored areas, and its favored people.

In 1935 (under Cárdenas), these regional banks were reorganized into the National Ejido Credit Bank (hereafter, Ejidal Bank). But the distribution of this credit was lopsided. In 1936, the Laguna Cotton Region (expropriated by Cárdenas, see below) received almost all of it (Sanderson 1981:120), and consistently during the forties and fifties it received one-third (Senior 1958:102). To be eligible for credit in La Laguna, the *ejidos* were required to buy shares in the bank. But the government was always the majority holder, therefore the principle decisionmaker. The rest of the credit went mainly to a few regions specializing in export crops (Yucatan for henequen; Mexicali for cotton, fruits, and vegetables; Michoacan for sugar; and Yaqui Valley for wheat and cotton). Even today, roughly half of state credit for agriculture goes to Laguna, Yaqui, and Yucatan (Sanderson 1981:120).

The distribution of Ejidal Bank credit by crop between 1938 and 1951 is shown in Table 1. Cotton and wheat (grown almost exclusively in irrigation districts) take up over 50% in most years. Corn, the major consumption crop of Mexican peasants, received only 20% on average.

Uncontrolled by any effective regulatory agency, the Ejidal Bank became semi-autonomous. Its inefficiency and corruption—frequently brought to light in the forties and fifties—caused continual peasant discontent. For example, in the early years of the bank, each *ejido* was required to place 5% of its community earnings into a "social fund." Little accounting was made, and in 1942 the bank allowed the social funds to be abolished. Rumor held that key bank officers had sold farm machinery at inflated prices to the funds. In 1942, peasant organizations complained that zone chiefs had "persuaded" peasants to cultivate private plots for them. This time an investigation was made, and seven chiefs were discharged. But in 1953, when the new head of the Torreón agency uncovered widespread fraud by bank employees, his finding created a furor and he himself was dismissed (Senior 1958:138–39).

In 1947, local credit societies were placed under direct control of the Ejidal Bank. Thus the bank made all decisions on capitalization, marketing and credit in the *ejidos*. In the forties and fifties, it had thirty-five regional agencies, of which La Laguna was the largest. This region was divided into thirteen zones, each headed by a zone-chief with an assistant chief for each *ejido* cooperative. The bank continued to be responsible for the marketing of the region's cotton crop.

Senior (1958:105) attributes the success of the Ejidal Bank to its "casting loose those *ejidos* which were no longer good credit risks." During most years from 1940 to 1970, only 13% of *ejidatarios* in all of Mexico received credit, and they tended to be the same ones year after year (Sanderson 1981:142). Hewitt (1980:29) reports that from 1950 to 1970, the Ejidal Bank in an average year loaned to 32,000 *ejidatarios*, or only 2% of *ejidatarios*. (We cannot reconcile Sanderson's and Hewitt's figures, but both percentages are so low as to make the point.) At the same time, private banking credit for large commercial farmers was growing rapidly (Table 2). *Ejidatarios*, of course, could not receive private credit because of their lack of ownership.

Besides providing credits and selling output, the Ejidal Bank owned processing plants (ginning mills, decorticating plants), ran a central repair shops for farm machinery, and set up consumer cooperative stores. Thus it was omnipresent, dabbling in a wide range of activities besides credit.

In his attempt to rival Cárdenas as Mexico's chief agrarian reformer, President Echevarría Alvarez (1970–76) not only distributed land, but combined the Ejidal Bank with NACB and the Banco Agropecuario (established in 1965), to eliminate duplication. The new agency became the National Rural Credit Bank. Although two-thirds of this bank's loans went

Table 3.1

NATIONAL EJIDAL CREDIT BANK: SHORT-TERM LOANS GRANTED, 1938–51, BY CROP (PERCENTAGES)

	1938	1939	1940	1941	1942	1943	1944	1945–46	1946–47	1947–48	1948–49	1949–50	1950–51
Sesame	1.9	0.8	0.7	1.4	2.4	3.5	1.1	1.9	3.5	3.7	5.4	4.6	2.5
Cotton	30.4	27.0	23.2	23.7	28.2	36.0	38.2	30.6	24.6	31.2	24.8	26.5	30.4
Rice	3.3	4.3	6.2	5.7	8.0	5.7	8.9	11.6	15.0	7.1	8.6	9.8	8.8
Peanuts	0.4	0.3	0.4	1.1	1.4	1.8	1.2	0.4	0.9	0.6	0.8	1.0	1.0
Coffee	0.9	1.8	3.0	3.4	3.1	2.7	2.7	3.4	3.1	2.5	4.3	3.1	2.2
Sugar cane	4.6	4.1	11.7	12.8	12.5	10.3	9.4	9.7	10.5	10.5	5.3	3.3	2.5
Chilis	0.5	0.5	0.5	–	0.7	0.6	0.9	3.4	2.4	1.7	0.5	0.5	0.9
Beans	2.6	2.6	1.4	1.6	1.4	1.0	1.3	0.8	2.6	2.2	2.9	2.8	2.3
Chickpeas	3.0	1.6	1.6	1.6	2.8	1.3	1.0	1.5	1.8	1.5	2.5	1.4	0.5
Corn	18.6	23.4	20.9	21.9	17.6	16.1	17.5	14.6	12.2	14.0	21.1	21.4	21.8
Bananas	0.7	2.6	2.1	2.3	1.0	1.9	0.8	0.5	0.5	0.6	0.1	0.7	0.5
Wheat	26.5	27.0	25.4	22.6	17.4	14.2	13.2	13.6	17.2	20.3	21.1	21.8	24.4
Misc. products	6.5	3.9	2.8	1.8	3.7	4.9	3.9	7.6	5.7	3.6	2.9	3.2	2.2
Total	100.0	100.0	100.0	100.0	100.0	100.0	100.0	100.0	100.0	100.0	100.0	100.0	100.0

SOURCE: Calculated from IBRD (1953:210, Table 31).

41

Table 3.2

PUBLIC AND PRIVATE CREDIT AVAILABLE TO AGRICULTURE, 1940–1970

Period	Ejidal Bank		Agricultural Bank		Private Formal Credit	
	Average Annual % Growth	% of Total	Average Annual % Growth	% of Total	Average Annual % Growth	% of Total
1940–50	2.6	38	68.0	28	8.8	36
1951–60	12.9	40	4.4	14	13.7	46
1961–70	0.9	16	3.4	13	11.8	71
1940–70	5.4	26	25.2	15	11.7	59

SOURCE: Sanderson (1981:142).

to *ejidatarios* in 1976, most were still directed to the North and Northwest and to commercial crops (Yates 1981:207–8). Two-thirds of the cotton acreage, 60% of the wheat acreage, but only one-third of the corn acreage benefited from public credit. The bank often purchased both the inputs provided to farmers and their output (at prices set by the state).

Yates's explanation of this poor performance—a lack of farmer creditworthiness—is a non-explanation. It merely raises the next question: why are farmers not creditworthy? We suggest that systematic deprivation, by the state, of most farmers of the inputs necessary for successful agriculture constitutes a vicious cycle: it is both caused by and cause of a gross maldistribution and economic distortion of credit, which lies at the root of Mexico's farm problem.

Irrigation

The state has wielded its great power over agriculture by concentrating resources in the irrigated zones of the Pacific Northwest, to the deprivation of the rest of the country. Has this policy been successful?

Reynolds (1970) argues emphatically no. Applying multiple regressions, he attempted to explain output by inputs of land, labor, and capital. Any residual (i.e., not explained by these inputs) is attributed to productivity. In Table 3, the growth of combined inputs (column 2) is subtracted from the growth of output (column 1), and the difference is called productivity increase (column 3). Productivity growth has been greatest in the South Pacific zone and moderate in the Gulf and Center. These are the very areas in which the least inputs have been applied. The North Pacific and North, with greater application of inputs, have shown the lowest rates of productivity growth. The implication is that if the deprived areas had been the

Table 3.3

THE GROWTH OF MEXICAN CROP PRODUCTION, INPUTS, AND
PRODUCTIVITY, 1929–59 (COMPOUND ANNUAL GROWTH RATES)

	Growth of Outputs	Growth of Inputs	Growth of Productivity
North	5.0%	4.2%	0.8%
Gulf	4.5	2.7	1.8
North Pacific	5.8	5.6	0.2
South Pacific	5.7	2.9	2.8
Center	3.5	1.8	1.7
Mexico	4.5	3.2	1.3

SOURCE: Reynolds (1970:124).

privileged ones (i.e., resources directed to them) and vice versa, Mexican agricultural output would have increased dramatically—or at least far more than it actually did.

The principal input into the North and Northwest was irrigation. From 1936 to 1973, irrigated acreage in the whole country increased from 1.0 million to 4.7 million hectares (Lehman 1981:261), with most going to areas of private ownership in the North and Northwest. Forty percent of the irrigated acreage was in Sonora, Sinaloa and the Rio Colorado District of Baja California (Yates 1981:70). From 1940 to 1970, 86% of public investment in agriculture, or 12.7% of the federal budget, went to irrigation (Lehman 1981:261). After a dramatic drop during the Cárdenas years, private irrigated land increased from 45.6% of the total in 1940 to 59.4% in 1960 (Table 4). The irrigation law of 1947 held that irrigated acreage of up to 800 hectares could be held privately in areas declared "mountainous" or "dry." Application of this law depended on bribery or personal prestige, however (Greenberg 1970:23).

Why did the government invest heavily in irrigation in the North and Northwest if a greater economic payoff was possible in the South Pacific, Center, and Gulf? The obvious answer—that it did not know this in advance—is inadequate. (Projections might have been made.) More likely, irrigation presented greater possibilities for a power base. Water was a plum which could be dangled in front of farmers in exchange for political support.

The Constitution of 1917 made surface water the property of the nation. Although the Irrigation Directorate was formed in 1921, little was done during the twenties. Later in the decade the National Irrigation Commission (CNI) was established to manage all irrigation works as a public utility and to develop new ones. In the initial districts of the far north, estab-

Table 3.4
LAND ON FARMS BY TYPE OF TENURE, 1930-1970

	Acres (000's)		Percentage Distribution	
		Private Farms and Communities		Private Farms and Communities
	Ejidos	Communities	Ejidos	Communities
		Total Arable		
1930	4,337	28,078	13.4	86.6
1940	16,202	19,061	45.9	54.1
1950	19,303	24,132	44.4	55.6
1960	21,685	28,024	43.6	56.4
1970	26,257	21,033	55.5	44.5
		Irrigated Arable		
1930	541	3,603	13.0	87.0
1940	2,457	2,059	54.4	45.6
1950	3,014	3,172	48.7	51.3
1960	3,529	5,158	40.6	59.4
1970	4,349	4,504	49.1	50.9
		Grassland		
1930	8,789	155,515	5.3	94.7
1940	26,338	112,463	19.0	81.0
1950	40,846	125,648	24.5	75.5
1960	48,466	146,970	24.2	75.8
1970	63,937	130,034	33.0	67.0

SOURCE: Yates (1981:154).

lished during the thirties, water was to be assigned preferentially to illegal migrants returned from the United States, other residents of the area, and alumni of agricultural schools. However, these districts—centered on a dam or other irrigation work—became one of the main vehicles by which government gained control over agricultural production. In 1964, they constituted 27.8% of arable land (Greenberg 1970:27).

In 1935, when there were twenty-eight of these districts, ministries vied for them; the National Agricultural Credit Bank won ten. In 1944, however, these ten were returned to the CNI. In 1947, when the CNI and related agencies were combined into the Ministry of Water Resources (SRH), the operation of irrigation districts was divided functionally between SRH and the Ministry of Agriculture, the latter performing administrative duties (operation, maintenance, and colonization) and SRH planning and constructing new works. In 1951, however, all functions except colonizing were returned to SRH. Since none of these moves appears to be explained by administrative logic, we can only assume that they depended on which politician, located in which agency, was ripe for political reward.

Initially, the district manager (employee of SRH) would ally himself with local policiticans to run the districts as personal fiefs. Land contracts and water rights were the treasures they might award. At first only rich farmers could afford these. To aid the small farmer, a schedule of payments was arranged (10% down, advanced by CNI; the balance over twenty years at 4% interest). In practice, a farmer paid 20% of his total harvest to CNI for land and water, or 30% if tools and seed were provided as well (Greenberg 1970:28). An opportunity for corruption came at the end of three years if the down payment had not been repaid. CNI could expel the small owner without returning payments already made. Instead, these would reduce the down payment of the next applicant.

Abuses such as these led to pressure for farmers to participate in district governance. In response, President Ruíz Cortines (1952–58) established Directive Committees, whose members were the district manager, representatives of the Ministry of Agriculture, the National Agricultural Credit Bank, and the Ejidal Bank, plus representatives of smallholders and *ejidatarios*. Because the SRH and Ministry of Agriculture could veto their actions, however, these committees had no power. "The Ministry of Agriculture did all the planning and made all decisions about what was grown in the districts, as well as [retained] a voice in who got what machinery, what seeds and what fertilizers. . . . The SRH . . . retained full control of all multi-use works. Local politicos were often rewarded for their loyalty to the PRI by being given positions on the Directive Committees" (Greenberg 1970:29).

Using a sample of sixteen irrigation districts covering 60% of publicly irrigated land in 1971, Schramm and Gonzales (1977: 19) calculated that average user charges constituted between 38% and 45% of expenditures for operations, repair, and maintenance, and only 10% of total irrigation costs. The rest was therefore a subsidy to landowners. Because of interlocking relationships between powerful landowners and local governments, Schramm and Gonzales (1977) were pessimistic about near-term change.

While irrigated acreage contributes between 45% and 50% of total Mexican crop output, the proportion of marketed output is about 66% (Yates 1981:77). While the crop mix of irrigation districts has been diversified dramatically over the last twenty years, cotton dominated as early as the mid-forties, and accounted for 53% of irrigated acreage in the mid-fifties. Thus we see the government's early emphasis on the principal export crops, of which two, cotton and sugar, required extensive irrigation.

While the *ejidos* in the irrigated districts are privileged compared to *ejidos* everywhere, they still are subordinate in their own districts. But their experiences have varied. To present this diversified picture, we have selected four case studies, below.

La Laguna*

Despite peasant agitation during the 1920s, the principal landowners of La Laguna, a traditional cotton-growing region in an irrigated oasis on an arid plateau bordering Coahuila and Durango states, had avoided land reform by contributing regularly to national political leaders (Senior 1958:50). Finally, in 1936, bowing to continued agitation, President Cárdenas expropriated over 400,000 hectarés in the area: 75% of the irrigated land, 25% of the nonirrigated land. Thirty thousand peasants were settled in 300 *ejidos*. Owners retained 150 irrigated hectares of their choice.

Cárdenas' reform was accomplished in forty days, which resulted, in part, in an uneven quality distribution: "The redistribution was far too hasty to permit optimal results. So many petitioners qualified for land that the original holdings were fragmented, with subsequent loss of scale economies" (Reynolds 1970:150). The point of such distributions was to encourage efficient use of irrigation ditches and to receive federal loans, but Reynolds reports that even after receiving the bulk of ejidal credit, La Laguna was less than an exciting success (see Table 5).

Unevenness in land distribution among *ejidos* showed up on the proportion of wells to acreage. Two such wells would normally increase cotton yields by 40% and wheat yields by 33% (Senior 1958:107). Choosing their own lands, the former owners naturally retained what wells they could. After expropriation, private farmers—with their better access to capital—drilled more wells (Wilkie 1971:55). By 1948, 62% of the wells were in private hands, helping to water 30% of the total cultivated acreage, while 38% were owned by the *ejidos* with 70% of the land. Since only surface water was controlled by the Irrigation District, subsurface water went to whoever tapped it first.

Crop Structure and the Ejidal Bank

Because economies of scale were expected, most *ejidos* were initially collective, in both land and work. But it was early discovered that private farming was more efficient: *ejidatarios* who irrigated their own crops at their assigned times wasted less water (Wilkie 1971:55). Thus many *ejidos* were parcelized. By the mid-forties, most had become mixed. Soil preparation and planting were done as a group but cultivating and harvesting by individuals. Crops had to be marketed through the Ejidal Bank, which reimbursed itself for loans and distributed remaining proceeds to the

*Senior (1958) has written a general study of the land reform in La Laguna, and Wilkie (1971) has made a case study of one *ejido* (San Miguel) in the region. We draw on both for this summary.

Table 3.5
Mexican Cotton Production, 1944-45 to 1953-54

	Area						Production					
	1944-45		1949-50		1953-54		1944-45		1949-50		1953-54	
	ha	%	ha	%	ha	%	ha	%	ha	%	ha	%
Laguna	134,103	36.7	121,930	15.8	140,170	16.2	43,104	44.1	56,401	21.7	53,545	15.3
Mexicali Valley, B.C.	61,884	16.9	125,154	16.2	197,214	22.9	14,625	15.0	51,313	19.7	91,310	26.1
Matamoros, Tamps	91,845	25.1	305,000	39.6	223,658	25.9	22,310	22.9	80,215	30.8	76,689	21.9
Juarez Valley, Chih.	13,301	3.6	36,200	4.7	34,557	4.0	3,239	3.3	10,580	4.1	13,843	4.0
Delicias, Chih.	29,023	7.9	36,650	4.8	54,791	6.4	5,744	5.9	13,806	5.3	21,807	6.2
Don Martin, N.L.	15,701	4.3	29,300	3.8	18,850	2.2	4,399	4.5	9,493	3.7	6,842	2.0
Sonora-Sinaloa	15,100	4.1	96,540	12.5	184,794	21.4	3,208	3.3	31,101	12.0	76,360	21.8
All others	4,859	1.3	19,760	2.6	27,564	3.2	957	1.0	7,110	2.7	9,579	2.7
Total	365,816	100.0	770,534	100.0	862,748	100.0	97,586	100.0	260,019	100.0	349,975	100.0

SOURCE: Senior (1958:242, Table 27).

ejidos. Under the early collectivization, profits had been divided according to days worked; under the later mixed system, according to the harvest from each plot.

In addition to marketing, the Ejidal Bank could influence the structure of *ejidos* through its credit operations. In order to supply credit only to those considered good risks, it encouraged the formation of more than one cooperative credit society within each *ejido*. In this way, the poorer *ejidatarios* could be left out of the societies to which the bank was offering its resources.

During the late fifties and early sixties, when cotton prices fell and costs of production were increasing, the per capita income of San Miguel *ejido* stagnated. Feeling that the *ejido* was not being properly managed and that they could function better on their own, some members decided to separate, taking their land with them. The majority opposed this move, fearing the Ejidal Bank would no longer provide credit to the remaining members. Violence erupted after five years of argument. Irrigation water was cut off to the separatists, who then occupied "their" fields claiming they would not leave. Some members of the main group came with guns, and the leader of the separatists was killed.

Curiously, these two stories demonstrate no clear "party line" on dividing up *ejidos*. In the first case, the bank was in favor. In the second case, the bank took no position, but peasants' attitudes opposed to division were shaped by what they thought the bank would do. The only consistency is the paternalism and overbearing influence of the bank, which extended far beyond its initial purpose of providing credit.

In other ways also, the bank interjected itself into farming decisions; for example, it would offer credit only for cotton and wheat. Since no credit could be obtained elsewhere, this decision meant that only cotton and wheat could be grown, even if enterprising farmers wished to grow something else. Not only that, but cotton could be sold only to the bank. During the late forties an active black market in cotton grew up, which countered the bank's stranglehold. In fact, so much cotton was sold in the black market that official production figures for the *ejido* are probably not accurate (Senior 1958:138–9, 190).

Peasant Representation in the Ejidal Bank

During the late thirties and on into the forties, a number of organizations vied for the opportunity to represent the peasants before the Ejidal Bank. Rather than allow peasants to settle the matter for themselves, the Ejidal Bank stepped in to end the "disorder." It set up an umbrella committee of members of the contending peasant groups. This committee in turn organized fifteen advisory committees of "responsible" peasant leaders (Senior 1958:120). These committees obtained wide-ranging authority over education, grievances, agricultural production, health, administration and credit. They worked closely with the zone chief of the bank. Elections to advisory committees were held in 1938, after which a Central Committee of Ejidatarios was formed in Torreón. Thus the Ejidal Bank took advantage of the competition among peasant groups to establish its own, paternalistic organization. Satisfied with this framework, Cárdenas' government recommended its extension to other parts of the country.

Beginning in 1940, two leagues competed for peasant support: the State League of Agrarian Communities, affiliated with the government-sponsored National Peasant Confederation (CNC), and the newly organized, independent Central Union of La Laguna, formed by zonal representatives under a law of 1939, which authorized such unions nationwide. (We consider it pertinent that a law was required.)

Battle lines were drawn on the basis of how much each organization could do for the *ejidos*. The Central Union had defended a number of *ejidos* whose enterprises (cotton gins and equipment pools) had been taken over by the Ejidal Bank on the finding that their debts were excessive. In addition, equipment centers belonging to the Central Union had been taken over. As a result of these take-overs, the bank increased its cotton ginning from 35% of ejidal totals in 1936 to 99% in the 1950s. These actions elicited strong protest from the Central Union, but to no avail.

The Central Union also defended the priority of *ejidos* (over private owners) to irrigation water, which had been assigned by law, but the union was continually put off and the law continually not observed.

The State League of Agrarian Communities, on the other hand, called for support of peasants because of what it could do for them through its influence with the National Peasant Confederation and the Ejidal Bank. The league supported the Ejidal Bank even in cases where peasant interests appeared to be in jeopardy. In the corruption case of the fifties (see section on credit, above), the league endorsed removal of the manager as a "disturbing influence" (Senior 1958:188). When the Central Union requested a loan to initiate grape cultivation in certain *ejidos* where the soil was appropriate, the State League lobbied against it, on the ground that some *ejidos* would be favored over others. It was, however, a case of one peasant union arguing, on political grounds, against loans to *ejidos* associated with its rival.

By the fifties, most *ejidos* had affiliated with the State League rather than the Central Union. Was that because they honestly preferred the paternalizing state, or because the system was so rigged that the Central Union, or any agency independent of the state, could not succeed? We are led to believe the latter: the State League must have expected "goodies" from the Ejidal Bank in exchange for supporting the bank on issues that would build up its power. By exception, the San Miguel *ejido* remained with the Central Union, which had supported it in a law suit against the Ejidal Bank (Wilkie 1971:51-2).

Even so, the Central Union was not entirely "clean." After its organiza-

49

tion, no further elections were held. Despite regulations to the contrary, its initial officers remained until 1953 (Wilkie 1971:52).

Impact of the Ejidal Bank

Cotton production in La Laguna dropped precipitously after the fifties (Reynolds 1970:112). Drought and the lowering of the water table (through too many wells) are the conventional reasons. Production shifted away to newly irrigated plains on both the east and west coasts. But even after the drought had ended, La Laguna's position could not be regained. No one, of course, can answer whether drought or mismanagement was the prime cause. Surely, however, the rigidity of the Ejidal Bank, with its pervasive power into so many lines of activity, hindered the peasants from developing cotton as they might have and from flexing into other types of production if cotton should fail.

Atencingo

Atencingo (in Matamoros, state of Puebla) was a sugar hacienda and mill (123,000 hectares, of which 12,000 to 15,000 were irrigated) begun through an initial acquisition by William Jenkins, an American, when he foreclosed a mortgage in the early twenties. Piece by piece, he purchased other large properties in the area. Since much of the land had not been planted during the Revolution, Jenkins had it cleared, imported new varieties of sugar cane, and built a railroad to connect the mill with the fields and with the main line to Mexico City. By 1934, his was the most productive sugar mill in Mexico.

In 1923 villagers began petitioning for land from this complex. Jenkins fought the petition, using his extensive political contacts and allegedly by assassination of peasant leaders (Ronfeldt 1973:15). Nevertheless, by 1935 peasants had been granted 155,600 hectares from the Jenkins enterprises, which included none of the irrigated sugar cane land that served Jenkins's mill. Before Cárdenas, it was common practice to grant peasants some access to land but not to the most productive land (Eckstein 1970:297).

In an audience with President Cárdenas in 1937, villagers obtained an order that the sugar heartland should be turned over to them. But Jenkins organized the resident peasants and mill workers to petition that the area be turned over instead to them. At the same time, he backed elements in the government who contended that the area was fit only for sugar cane growing, which was not true; therefore, any resulting ejido should be a collective required to grow cane for the private mill.

Despite a last-minute invasion by the villagers, this maneuver worked: Jenkins retained 150 irrigated hectares and the mill. The ejido, a 9,000 acre collective, existed on paper, but the lands were operated just as before. Ejidatarios were paid the same daily wage and they could not farm on their own or switch to a different crop. Instead of distributing profits equally, the mill administration paid a certain portion as bonuses to loyal employees. Any workers who protested were run off or killed, with bodies eventually appearing in the cane brake (Ronfeldt 1973:44). Opposition developed despite the terror, but the Alemán presidency was not an encouraging environment and the governor of the state at that time was a close political ally of Jenkins.

Although the 1946 elections brought an even more conservative president (Ruíz Cortines), at the state and local levels the new officials were not closely associated with Jenkins. Under a charismatic leader, those unfriendly to Jenkins took control of the *ejido*. They wanted to diversify into higher-yielding crops, but the original *ejido* grant forbade this. So they took advantage of a 1943 decree from Alemán permitting every *ejido* to cultivate 10% of its acreage in corn. From this, they slowly diversified a small acreage into more highly valued crops. Apparently, they had no difficulty finding private sources of credit or marketing channels, another indication that perhaps peasants are sufficiently astute not to need government paternalism in these areas.

Even with small crops occupying part of the land, sugar increased in the first two years of ejidal control. But the mill administration set out to bankrupt the collective *ejido*. Legally, the mill was the sole source of crop credit, collected annually after harvest. So the mill left some cane uncut, charging the cooperative (*ejido*) for the loss. In the first year, the cooperative arranged an alternative buyer. Still, the mill could not process all the cane because of breakdowns. It refused to allow the independent transaction anyway, claiming the uncut cane as collateral for the credit. After the same had occurred a second year, the *ejidatarios* cut back on sugar cane production in protest.

After two years of this dispute, the state government set up a commission, headed by the governor, to supervise the *ejido*. The new manager, a personal aide of the governor, worked closely with the mill administration and "bribed" some of the former ejidal leaders with lucrative jobs. In the late fifties, a new opposition emerged, with personal ties to the federal rather than the state bureaucracies. This opposition called a strike for diversification and parcelization right before the crucial harvest of 1959.

The strike caused federal authorities to intervene in 1961. They restored ejidal control but ordered the continued production of sugar for the mill. The new cooperative leaders complied; in return, their friends in the government helped them stay in power. All talk of parcelization and crop diversification ended.

"Trouble" was therefore postponed for another ten years. But leaders of the nine villages of which the *ejido* was composed began to demand more powers at the village level. In 1971, the *ejido* was divided into nine credit societies.

Ronfeldt (1973:223) sums up the government involvement as follows: "The ejidatarios offered the government their loyalty in exchange for local institutional power, which at times enabled their leaders to wrest a slightly greater share in the region's agricultural wealth from the mill administration." But only a small portion of the *ejidatarios* benefited; it is not clear that they represented the rest. Ronfeldt (1973:218) adds that the ordinary members "had little political or economic power. . . . They were highly dependent and subordinate partners in the larger political and economic system. Their political and economic conditions were basically imposed from without. . . . What happened in Atencingo depended decisively on what happened in Mexico City and Puebla."

The Morelos Sugar Zones

The sugar zones in Morelos illustrate how the government—eager for foreign exchange—can force farmers to produce export crops even though crops for domestic consumption might alternatively be up to four times as profitable for them. In 1970, Stringer studied District Sixteen, which includes three-fourths of the 44,000 irrigated hectares in Morelos. In the present section, we abstract from his study.

By a decree in 1943, the Ministry of Water Resources (SRH) was put in charge of all sugar-cane refinery and supply zones (Stringer 1972:301). Each zone became an irrigation district; sugar was required to be grown on one-half the land. "In reality mill owners chose the best land of the surrounding area" (Purcell 1981:215) as their sources of cane supply.

These owners were organized into an association (formed in 1932 to set production quotas during the depression). This organization—UNPASA (Unión Nacional de Productores de Azucar, S.A.)—was designated by the government as the sole supplier of sugar to both export and domestic markets (Purcell 1981:215). By decree in 1944, the cane price was tied to the industry's refinery price. The farmers received a price based on the refinery's weights and the percentage of sugar that it extracted. Since the farmers had no method of controlling either the weighing or the extraction, they had to take the refinery's word for both, and they suspected they were being cheated. They were also dependent on the refinery for fertilizer and insecticides (not being allowed to buy them elsewhere). The refinery deducted the cost of these upon paying the proceeds to the farmers; furthermore, payments for cane were made in three installments, spread out for nine months after the cane had been harvested.

The state required that sugar and rice be rotated, each for three years. Half of the rice crop was financed by the Ejidal Bank, which owned three of the seven rice mills in the state. During a period of five years (probably 1964–69; Stringer is unclear), 90% of its loans in the state were for rice.

Stringer argues that the farmers felt detached from their land because they had virtually no control over what they planted on it; where they would secure their credits or buy their inputs; where they would sell their outputs, or for how much. Even the harvesting was done by day laborers, of whom 60% were from other states at a time (the dry season) when there was little work to be done on the nonirrigated plots in the state.

52

Finally, although farmers were forced to grow sugar and rice, Stringer (1972:303) calculates that revenues might have been multiplied several times if fruits, flowers, and vegetables had been grown on the same acreage. For the more common crops of the region, he estimated the following net monthly incomes, in dollars per hectare:

Crop	$ per hectare net/month
Sugar, first year	9
Sugar, second year	11
Sugar, third year	7
Rice	26
Alfalfa	28
Tomatoes	40
Hay	40
Feed corn	39
Maize corn	30
Beans	23.

Stringer (1972:303) concludes that

> Since both irrigated landowners and use right holders (*ejidatarios*) are obliged to cultivate sugar cane, the former peons have neither the land nor the water rights they fought for. . . . Were farmers within irrigation districts free to cultivate more remunerative crops, . . . were NECB (the Ejidal Bank) to provide credit for crops other than rice, the state's agricultural resources would be more rationally allocated, consumers in Morelos and Mexico City would be supplied with less expensive fresh produce, increased earnings would be invested in irrigation of arable land, and increased rural employment would result.

The Yaqui Valley of Sonora*

The irrigated Yaqui Valley, source of 25% of Mexico's wheat and 10% of its cotton in 1970 (Freebairn 1970:213), was home to a land concession sold by the Díaz government in the nineteenth century and purchased by the Richardson Land Company of California in 1904. By 1926, the company had irrigated and cultivated 44,000 hectares. Claiming that the ownership limitations of the original concession had been violated, the government expropriated the property by buying all company shares. Governance of the valley's water resources was entrusted to the National Irrigation Commission (CNI).

A political confrontation between President Cárdenas and the state governor Yocupicio of Sonora precipitated land reform. Strongly backed by the hacienda owners as well as a personal following of Yaqui Indians,

*This case study is drawn primarily from Freebairn (1970).

Yocupicio won the state elections of 1936 even against the official Party candidate (Sanderson 1981:114). To garner political support against Yocupicio, the government announced land reform in the Yaqui Valley in 1937. The owners argued that the Valley was exempt from reform under the terms of the Richardson concession, but a government commission ruled against them.

Some 17,400 irrigated hectares and 36,000 nonirrigated hectares were expropriated and handed over to thirteen newly formed *ejidos,* provided they would allow the Ejidal Bank to organize them as "productive cooperatives" (Freebairn 1970:220). But they had no membership capital; right from the start, they were in debt to the bank for farm machinery and working capital. Furthermore, all money transactions of the *ejidos* were supervised by field officials of the bank. Wages and profits were paid according to time worked. In short, although nominal management was retained by the *ejido,* effective authority had been removed from the peasants and taken over by the bank.

From 1938 to 1943—mostly years of World War II when the price of grain was high—the *ejidos* were successful. Irrigated acreage expanded, and most *ejidatarios* in the Yaqui Valley had 20 to 30 hectares of irrigated land each. This quantity shows that they were favored compared with *ejidatarios* elsewhere. By the sixties, however, only one small group (forty *ejidatarios*) worked only one *ejido* as a collective. All other land was parcelized, in a trend begun as early as the forties. We deduce that the peasants wanted their properties to be private from the fact that 25% of the plots were illegally rented. Contrary to the spirit of the land reform, many *ejidatarios* were doing little of the physical labor themselves (Freebairn 1970:229), the rest being done by tenants and hired workers. Furthermore, the bank itself promoted parcelization, possibly so that it could discriminate among its borrowers.

Discrimination against *ejidos* is found in the allocation of land. In the irrigation districts of Sonora, *ejidos* held 29.3% of the land and private owners the rest. In the mountains, where land was poorer, the *ejidos* held 62.3% (Sanderson 1981:249).

The Problems of the Seventies and Eighties

After decades of undermining agriculture, the government discovered, beginning in 1971, that Mexico was forced to import its basic food needs. At first, the problem seemed not so serious, since exports of oil and commercial crops (sugar, strawberries, and tomatoes) more than sufficed to pay for the imports. But these sources of revenue did nothing for the rural poor, whose incomes depended on smallholder productivity. Finally, as the oil glut came upon the country in the early eighties, an increase in agricultural overall agricultural productivity became imperative.

But the switchover was not sudden. Indeed, the main conflict of the

54

mid-seventies lay between further land distributions and increased productivity. Eleven days before his term ended in 1976, President Luís Echevarría, a spokesman for the former, confiscated 89,000 hectares in the Northwest, leaving to his successor, José López-Portillo, the task of distributing them. Encouraged by Echevarría's act, peasants occupied other lands in the neighborhood. Declaring that the land problem would not be solved by distribution into ever-smaller parcels, López-Portillo worked out a compromise by which some of the expropriated land was distributed and some returned. With a show of force, he cut off the impending crisis, announcing at the same time that there was no more land to be distributed.

Abetted by oil revenues, the government's main response to agricultural deficiencies has been to intrude itself further. To improve productivity on the *ejido*, the López-Portillo administration tried to promote collectivization: turning private into collective *ejido* land (NYT, 1/9/79). The experiment was only a regurgitation of the initial model for collective *ejidos* and it failed for the same reason as that model: the farmers' attachment to private plots.

In 1980, López-Portillo announced a more ambitious plan, called the Mexican Food System (SAM, for Sistema Alimentario Mexicano):

> The key to the Mexican Food System appears to be coordination of all aspects of the cycle, from credit for seeds, fertilizer and machinery, through technical assistance for planting and harvesting, to improved transportation and storage facilities, nationwide marketing and occasional price subsidies. The Government, according to the President, will "share the risks" of the peasantry (Riding, in NYT, 4/9/80).

Additionally, the López-Portillo administration attempted to fortify Copalmar, an umbrella organization coordinating all government agencies dealing with Indians, rural health, and rural poverty. Copalmar had already showed some promise by building and staffing 2,105 rural medical units. But in 1980, it planned to expand its orbit into food, by "building 200 large storage areas to supply more than 6,000 village distribution points" (NYT, 9/21/80). "We are going to break the power of the transportation middlemen because we have our own trucks, boats, and even planes," explained Mr. Ovalle, who was the coordinator of Coplamar (Riding, in NYT, 9/21/80).

In all of its endeavors, SAM failed. It was intended to raise guaranteed prices for basic food crops, subsidize increased use of credit, high-yielding seeds, and fertilizer, and extend crop insurance. All these objectives fell before the budget crunch of 1982.

Gonzales (1987:137) discusses the impact in the state of Morelos:

> Several direct observations of this crop showed a marked difference between the yields obtained from the so-called improved variety . . . and

55

those of the local criolla variety. Usually the improved was smaller and infested with mold while the criolla was less moldy and had a larger size and yield. Interviews with peasants suggested that most of them mistrusted the improved variety and were unwilling to plant it. But they were forced to take the technological package as a whole; otherwise they would have no access to agricultural insurance nor to an advance in wages.

Banco Rural (BANRURAL) did increase its credit in 1981, only to fall back to pre-SAM levels in 1982 (Pessah 1987). It did so at negative real rates of interest (12% nominal rate in the face of inflation over 20%), and its distribution was uneven over regions. Credit was conditioned on the acceptance of the whole technological package.

Sanderson (1986:265) summed up SAM as follows:

> The SAM's optimistic feeling that such agencies could somehow be transformed from the co-optative mechanisms of social control to the progressive vanguard of rural change after four decades of evidence to the contrary staggers the imagination and gives credence to a cynical interpretation of the SAM as a sop to elite campesinistas and their partisans.

Under the presidency of de la Madrid (1982-1988), two other initiatives have been taken, PRONAL and PRONADRI (Programa Nacional de Desarrollo Rural Integral). We know of no studies to date on the performance of these agencies.

When peasant interests conflict with those of the government itself, the government's attitude is exemplified by an amendment to the constitution in 1978, which permitted expropriation of lands (peasant or other) needed for drilling. This amendment set the stage for confrontation:

> Mexico has sent troops to the country's rich southeast oilfields to remove roadblocks set up by angry peasants who are demanding compensation for land expropriated by the national oil company (Pemex). . . . Frustrated by the slowness of the bureaucracy and Pemex's limited interest in their problems, peasant groups have taken to blocking the paths through their fields to the oil wells. . . . Pemex has used helicopters to carry technicians to the blockaded wells (Riding, in NYT, 2/22/79).

By the mid-eighties, not only had the oil glut arrived, it became increasingly apparent that much of the revenue from oil had been pocketed by politicians for investment in the United States. Mexico's resulting balance of payments deficits made it extremely improbable that the government would pursue any of its programs to benefit the peasants.

In fact, Mexico's agricultural output per capita was less in the middle eighties than it was in the early sixties (Table 6). One reason, of course, was the strong population growth. But surely another was the set of policies associated with the land reform, in which the government had

Table 3.6

ANNUAL PERCENTAGE INCREASES IN AGRICULTURAL VALUE
ADDED, TOTAL AND PER CAPITA, FOR MEXICO, 1960–70,
1970–80, AND 1980–87

Year	Value Added	Per Capita
1960–70	4.68	0.80
1970–80	3.99	0.64
1980–83	2.04	−0.72
1983–84	2.69	0.48
1984–85	3.75	1.66
1985–86	−2.72	−4.77
1986–87	1.62	−0.64

SOURCE: Calculated from Inter-American Development Bank, *Economic and Social Progress in Latin America: 1988 Report*, Tables A-1 and B-7, pp. 534, 544.

attempted to oversee the operations of the peasantry, requiring them to buy their inputs from and sell their outputs to official agencies (including the Ejidal Bank) at prices set by the government. In so doing, the government made agriculture less profitable than it might have been.

Are *ejidos* more efficient than private farms? A number of researchers have raised this question, with no conclusive answer. Reynolds (1970:145) found that "between 1930 and 1960 there was an almost perfect negative correlation between the regional growth of per capita agricultural production and the share of ejidal land under cultivation (Table 7). This suggests that the *ejido* system which emerged from the Revolution may have retarded agricultural development over the long run."

Reynolds points out, however, that before 1930 the correlation is not so clear. He adds that many other factors are pertinent than whether land is ejidal or private: "While suggestive, [the evidence cited] is far from sufficient . . . that *ejidos* were less productive than private farms, since allowance must be made for differences in the quality of the soil, climate, degree of public and private investment, rural education, and proximity to markets of each tenure class as well as the contribution of each class to the overall productivity" (p. 147).

In another study—also inconclusive to our mind—Eckstein (1966) collected data from 667 *ejidos* from 1940 and 815 *ejidos* and 651 private farms in 1950. Dividing them into sixteen regions, designated as high-income (ten) and low-income (six), he compared the operating results of *ejidos* with those of private farms within each region. He found that in high-income regions, where adequate inputs were available, collective *ejidos* outper-

Table 3.7

RANK ORDERING OF THE GROWTH OF PER CAPITA
AGRICULTURAL PRODUCTION (1930–60) AND THE PERCENTAGE
OF EJIDAL LAND UNDER CULTIVATION (1950)
(RANKED IN DESCENDING ORDER)

Rate of Growth of Agricultural Production per Rural Dweller (1930–1960)	Share of Ejidal Land to Total Land under Cultivation (1950 or 1960)
1. South Pacific	1. Gulf
2. North	2. Center
3. North Pacific	3. North
4. Center	4. North Pacific
5. Gulf	5. South Pacific

SOURCE: Reynolds (1970:145).

formed individual *ejidos* and did as well as private farms. In low-income areas, the individual *ejidos* did better.

But he concludes that collective *ejidos* did not reach their full potential for three reasons. First, from 1940 on, the political climate turned against collectivization as a form of communism. The government, through the Ejidal Bank or otherwise, actively encouraged parcelization as well as individualization of credit. The rural élite of course favored this policy. Second, internal conflicts within the collective—over profit and parcel distribution—fragmented the polity, causing collectives to split into two or more, as well as into de facto private property. Third, "mismanagement of assets" (a euphemism for corruption) at both *ejido* and state levels drove many *ejidos* into or close to bankruptcy.

More recent studies (Mueller 1970; Dovring 1970; Nguyen and Saldivar 1979) have found *ejidos* to be just as efficient as private farms. However, because half or more *ejido* land in several irrigation districts had been rented to private farmers (Yates 1981:181), this comparison loses its value.

Whether *ejido* or private property is more efficient is therefore a loaded and complex question. It really divides into two: which of the two is more efficient given all the political interference, economic intervention, inequalities in distribution, and corruption, and which would be more efficient if these could be corrected? But the second is a non-question, for we know of no area in the world where state-enforced collectivization has not been plagued by many, if not all, of these "inconveniences."

With greater government attention to agriculture from the mid-seventies into the eighties, per capita output ceased to fall. Instead, the growths of population and farm output have just kept pace. It would therefore *seem* that even if Mexicans are not eating better in the eighties than in the seventies, at least they fare as well as they did before. Alas, this is not so! As their incomes rise, the middle groups eat more. As *their* per capita food consumption increases, all the less is left over for the poor. Unless overall output *increases* relative to population, the poor will become hungrier.

References

Austin, James E., and Esteva, Gustavo, eds., 1987. *Food Policy in Mexico: The Search for Self-Sufficiency*, Ithaca, N.Y., Cornell University Press.

Ballance, R. A., 1972. "Mexican Agricultural Prices and Subsistence Farming," *American Journal of Economics and Sociology*, vol. 13, no. 3: 295-306.

Barkin, David, and King, Timothy, 1970. *Regional Economic Output*, Cambridge, Cambridge University Press.

Chevalier, Francois, 1963. "The Ejido and Political Stability in Mexico," in Veliz (1967).

Dovring, Folke, 1970. "Land Reform and Productivity in Mexico," *Land Economics*, vol. 46, no. 3:765-76.

Eckstein, Solomon, 1966. *El Ejido Colectivo en Mexico*, Mexico City, Fondo de Cultura Económica.

Eckstein, Solomon, 1970. "Land Reform and Cooperative Farming: An Evaluation of the Mexican Experience," in Raanan Weitz, *Rural Development in a Changing World*, Cambridge, Mass., MIT Press.

Freebairn, Donald K., 1969. "The Dichotomy of Prosperity and Poverty in Mexican Agriculture," *Land Economics*, February.

Freebairn, Donald K., 1970. "Changes in Ejidal Farming in Northwest Mexico's Modernized Agriculture: The Quechehueca Collective, 1938-1968," in Robert Stevens, *Tradition and Dynamics in Small Farm Agriculture*, Ames, Iowa State University Press.

Gonzales, Gustavo Viniegra, 1987. "Generating and Disseminating Technology," in Austin and Esteva (1987).

Greenberg, M., 1970. *Bureaucracy and Development: A Mexico Case Study*, Lexington, Mass., D. C. Heath.

Hewitt de Alcantara, Cynthia, 1980. "Land Reform, Livelihood, and Power in Rural Mexico," in Preston (1980).

Hicks, Whitney W., 1967. "Agricultural Development in Northern Mexico," *Land Economics*, November:343-402.

Horowitz, Irving, 1970. *Masses in Latin America*, New York, Oxford University Press.

Huizer, Gerrit, 1970. "Peasant Organization in Agrarian Reform in Mexico," in Horowitz (1970).

International Bank for Reconstruction and Development, 1953. *The Economic Development of Mexico*, Baltimore, Johns Hopkins University Press.

King, Russell, 1977. *Land Reform: A World Survey*, Boulder, Colo., Westview Press.

Kirk, Rodney Carlos, 1980. "Agrarian Reform and Disguised Unemployment," *Papers in Anthropology*, vol. 21, no. 1:11-21.

Landsberger, Henry, ed., 1974. *Rural Protest: Peasant Movements in Social Change*, New York, Macmillan.

Lehman, David, 1981. "Peasantization and Proletarianization in Recent Agrarian

Changes in Brazil and Mexico," in Steve Jones, P. C. Joshi, and Miguel Murmis, eds., *Rural Poverty and Agrarian Reform*, New Delhi, Allied Publishers.

Michaels, Albert L., 1970. "The Crisis of Cardenismo," *Journal of Latin American Studies*, vol. 2, no. 1:51–79.

Mueller, M. W., 1970. "Changing Patterns of Agricultural Output and Productivity in the Private and Land Reform Sectors in Mexico, 1940–60," *Economic Development and Cultural Change*, vol. 18, no. 2:252–66.

Nguyen, D. T., and Saldivar, M. L. Martinez, 1979. "The Effects of Land Reform on Agricultural Production, Employment, and Income Distribution: A Statistical Study of Mexican States," *Economic Journal*, vol. 89, September:624–35.

Pessah, Raúl, 1987. "Channeling Credit to the Countryside," in Austin and Esteva (1987).

Preston, David, ed., 1980. *Environment, Society, and Rural Change in Latin America*, New York, John Wiley & Sons.

Purcell, Susan Kaufman, 1981. "Business-Government Relations in Mexico: The Case of the Sugar Industry," *Comparative Politics*, vol. 13, January:211–33.

Reynolds, Clark, 1970. *The Mexican Economy: Twentieth Century Structure and Growth*, New Haven, Conn., Yale University Press.

Ronfeldt, David, 1973. *Atencingo: The Politics of Agrarian Struggle in a Mexican Ejido*, Stanford, Calif., Stanford University Press.

Salamini, Heather Fowker, 1971. *Agrarian Radicalism in Veracruz, 1920–1938*, Lincoln, University of Nebraska Press.

Sanderson, Steven, 1981. *Agrarian Populism and the Mexican State: The Struggle for Land in Sonora*, Berkeley, University of California Press.

Sanderson, Steven, 1986. *The Transformation of Mexican Agriculture*, Princeton, N.J., Princeton University Press.

Schramm, Gunter, and Gonzalez, V. Fernando, 1977. "Pricing Irrigation Water in Mexico: Efficiency, Equity, and Revenue Considerations," *Annals of Regional Science*, vol. 11, no. 1:15–35.

Senior, Clarence, 1958. *Land Reform and Democracy*, Gainesville, University of Florida Press.

Stringer, Hugh, 1972. "Land, Farmer, and Sugar Cane in Morelos, Mexico," *Land Economics*, vol. 48, no. 3:301–3.

Véliz, Claudio, ed., 1967. *The Politics of Conformity in Latin America*, London, Oxford University Press.

Warman, Arturo, 1980. *We Come to Object: The Peasants of Morelos and the National State*, translated by Stephen K. Ault, Baltimore, Johns Hopkins University Press.

Wilkie, Raymond, 1971. *San Miguel: A Mexican Collective Ejido*, Stanford, Calif., Stanford University Press.

Winder, David, 1977. "Land Development in Mexico: A Case Study," *Institute of Development Studies Bulletin*, vol. 8, no. 4.

Yates, Lamartine, 1981. *Mexico's Agricultural Dilemma*, Tucson, University of Arizona Press.

4. Tanzania

To people everywhere—social scientists and others alike—Tanzania in the sixties was a shining hope for Third World development. President Julius Nyerere was a forceful leader and teacher (*Mwalimu*), dedicated and uncorrupt, who would bring his country into a new socialism, built upon traditions of villages and cooperation among humble Africans.

By the mid-1980s, the dream was shattered. Instead of becoming foundation blocks, African traditions had been destroyed. Instead of by cooperation among villagers, economic and political modes were ordered by strangers from a faraway central government. Vast numbers of people had been moved, some at gunpoint, from where they wanted to live to where they did not want to live. Some of their homes were burned so they would not return. Instead of cooperation, there was bitterness. Instead of producing, people were idle. Instead of abundance, there was hunger. In 1980, Nyerere admitted that his people were worse off than in 1970; and in 1970, they had been hardly better off than at independence, in 1961.

What happened? Instead of true traditions, which were widely diverse from tribe to tribe, Nyerere's vision was grounded on an Africa that never was. Institutions conceived in theory and designed in standard forms and shapes abruptly displaced diverse ones forged over centuries by local need. But they could not work. When he and his government tried to graft that vision upon the country, each tribal people, for its own reasons, refused to let it take hold. As a result, agriculture, trade, and other production declined. The drought in the early seventies was a convenient scapegoat, but as Coulson (1982:260) points out, plantings failed widely even in areas where rainfall was sufficient.

Background

Before the colonial era, the territory that is now Tanzania was ruled, like most of Africa, by tribes and native kingdoms. Tanganyika was itself a foreign body, implanted by Germans in 1884 and assumed by the British after World War I. Still, the British policy was one of indirect rule. So long as taxes were paid, the peace kept, the land secured against rival powers,

NOTE: Kenneth B. Powelson researched and wrote parts of this chapter as part of an honors thesis in Harvard College. We are also indebted to Michael Kirby for help in assembling materials.

and trade promoted, the British paid little attention to tribal ways of life, including how land was farmed.

In the middle of our present century, the nationalist leaders of Tanganyika Africa National Union (TANU) assumed two roles. The first, to negotiate independence, seemed to the world to be their only purpose. But the other—to forge a nation—has dominated their minds and frustrated their effectiveness ever since. Tanzania was not a nation; it was a conglomerate of Sukumu, Nyamwezi, Hehet Nyakyusa, Chagga, Gogo, Luo, Tatogo, Masai, smaller tribes, and Swahili-speaking Arabs. The African tribes, furthermore, were divided into groups, such as Ngoni, Yao, Bantu, and Nilotics that had fought each other for generations. It was as if TANU had crafted an empty nation, composed of drawing-board organizations and institutions never tried out on real people, and then poured its diverse peoples into that nation.

One of the first acts of the new nation was formally to strip tribal chieftains of all political, administrative, and judicial authority in local government. Ethnic groupings were amalgamated where possible, to prevent tribal issues from crystalizing into local political movements (Hill 1974:208). TANU simultaneously stipulated that its own district chairmen should become ex officio chairmen of the newly formed District Councils, and only TANU members would be allowed to run for membership in those Councils. Tribal groups opposed this intrusion to no avail (Hyden 1980:84).

The land reform—or Ujamaa villages—did not fail solely for the classic reasons: that cooperatives work when designed by co-operants and not when forced upon them; that bureaucrats do not know how to farm; and that state servants milk those over whom they gain power. It failed in part for those reasons but also because the whole experiment failed. Ujamaa was part of the empty nation.

Every society has its ways of holding farmland and doing business. While Nyerere believed that in African tradition land had been held in common, it was never held in common by all Africans, even within a tribe. Different layers of rights (to cultivate, to live on, to pass over, to hunt on) belonged to different people; they were inherited by kinship, in some tribes through the mother's side, in others through the father's, and in still others through the mother's side but controlled by the daughter's husband. Lands were redistributed periodically, usually by tribal elders, but always according to tribal rules.

Members of tribes and lineage groups thus had far more right to land than is implied in Nyerere's (1967:166) statement, in which he tried to elevate a tribal tradition to a national level:

> . . . To us in Africa land was always recognized as belonging to the community. Each individual within our society had a right to the use of land. . . . But the African's right to land was simply the right to use it; he had no other right to it, nor did it occur to him to try and claim one.

Tribes would also migrate to new land, never capriciously, but always in response to military or economic pressures. Furthermore, in ordinary migration

> the old traditional settlers went to places normally where their relatives, though not necessarily closely related, clan and lineages live. The duty of these groups to their kinsmen was to provide them initially with provisions while the newcomers were preparing their new fields for self sufficiency first in food products. They also helped the settlers initially to make temporary houses. These services were voluntary. By custom they were expected (Bakula 1969:12).

When the TANU government decided upon forced migration, into areas where the settlers did not have the security of a family to greet them, where they faced a new set of rules not only for land tenure but also for government and the administration of justice, rules not of their own making and that ignored tribal traditions, it was small wonder that the intended beneficiaries were not as appreciative or cooperative as the government had expected.

Voluntary Cooperatives

Yet cooperation and change were also part of tribal cultures, and out of this voluntary cooperation a nation might alternatively have created itself. Cooperation within a tribe derives from the benefits of help at critical junctures, but each farmer must know that the work he does for others will be returned at the appropriate time, though maybe not in exact quantity. Around this philosophy, traditional work groups have evolved (Gulliver 1971:chs. 6–7). Nyerere, on the other hand, perceived give-and-take to depend on what was morally right. While Western social philosophers laud his idealism, for Africans in Tanganyika in the twentieth century, cooperation was founded on well-recognized mutual obligations. To be thrust into a situation where these obligations were no longer assured—and social conscience was to be relied on instead—was not acceptable to them, especially when they, not those who had thrust them, would take the risks.

In the 1950s a voluntary cooperative movement grew beyond traditional functions and spread rapidly in the coffee and cotton regions. It did not come because of a swelling of mass participation, as Nyerere had envisioned, but in response to perceived opportunity. Paul Bomani, a cotton trader and head of The Mwanza African Traders' Cooperative Society, organized a producer's cooperative because of difficulties of African traders in competing with Asians (persons of Indian origin now living in Africa), who had dominated cotton marketing. Bomani created a movement for independent scales, since producers feared the Asians were giving short weight. Working through traditional native authorities as well as cotton traders and large cotton farmers, Bomani organized The Victoria

Federation of Cooperative Unions (later Nyanza Cooperative Union). Unlike the cooperatives later imposed by the government, this union, and others throughout the coffee and cotton regions, were initiated, organized, and controlled by African traders and farmers.

A TANU case worker (1975:115) reported another case of voluntary cooperation in Sukumuland. Four farmers combined their separate herds; they invested in a shelter, veterinary medicine, and quality feed. Deciding they needed ten more farmers for an optimal-size unit, they selected their partners for trustworthiness. To protect against initial losses, each verified the health of the cattle of the others. After a few years they increased their milk production enough to afford rights to high-quality bull insemination.

Still another example of voluntary cooperation—this one later destroyed by the central government—was the Ruvuma Development Association (RDA), described by Coulson (1982:263–71). Nyerere had taken a personal interest in this association. Consisting at its largest point of seventeen villages and 400 families, it had started in 1962–63 as just one village, organized by the TANU Youth League, to increase farm output, ensuring self-sufficiency and later commercial cropping. At first, both common plot and private plots were used, but over time the common plot increased its size relative to the others. The villagers started a primary school that stressed training for local occupations, including farming, and a small dispensary credited with lowering infant mortality rates. With the help of a personal loan from Nyerere they bought a grain mill that competed for business with the local cooperative union. Experimenting with tobacco cultivation, they found the returns too small and abandoned it. (Their refusal to grow tobacco despite the government's minimum acreage regulations later on earned them the enmity of the regional authorities.) The association gradually increased its membership.

What are the requisites of voluntary cooperation? First, corruption must be eliminated by careful controls; each member must be accountable to the others through discussion and inspection. Next, each must perform a function that others recognize as valuable; the benefits must be perceived as mutual. Third, there must be no "free riders." The idea of mutual benefits is obvious, quickly perceived by Nyerere. The problem of free riders is more complex; it can be handled only by their exclusion. But mutual accountability is the most elusive of all; it cannot be forced.

Unfortunately, self-help projects under community control did not relate well to the government's ideas of planning. Kleemeier (1984:185) cites four reasons. First, communities learned to play the development game. They would initiate a project they knew they could not finish to force the government to do it for them. Second, peasants preferred public infrastructure (roads, schools, health services), while government wanted projects that directly increased production. Third, "self-help strengthened the formation of local elites," whereas the government wanted no intermediaries between it and the peasants. Fourth, because government spending followed self-help agriculture, which was generated unevenly throughout the country, government favors were also unevenly distributed, with consequent political complaints.

Compulsory Cooperatives

The concept of compulsory cooperatives arrived with independence, when there were few cooperatives in food-growing areas. The government decided to expand them rapidly, from 857 in 1961 to 1533 in April 1966. With a big push by government and TANU, cooperative membership grew from 361,000 at the beginning of 1963 to 453,000 at the end (Pratt 1976:178); output marketed by cooperatives increased from 145,000 tons in 1960 to 496,000 tons in 1965.

To force the expansion in cooperatives, the government drew on its marketing boards. These had been started during the forties, when the British felt a wartime need for more rapid collection of grains. The Colonial Grain Storage Department became the dominant buyer and seller of maize and other food crops. This department was abolished in 1956, after market miscalculations had led to substantial losses. Since that time, the grain trade had been in private, albeit largely Asian, hands. After independence (1961), the new government issued a compulsory market order, designating the local cooperative as sole buyer of marketed output. To enforce the order, it forbade the transport of grain across district lines without government permission.

The new cooperatives were creatures of the state, organized from the top down. Despite local elections, peasants did not perceive them as under their control, an attitude reinforced by their suspicion of being cheated. Kriesel et al. (1970, quoted in Coulson 1982:149) estimated that the "single channel marketing" of maize caused consumer prices to rise by 50% from 1964 to 1969, while prices paid to producers did not rise at all. Since cooperatives sold as well as bought in the food-growing regions, the peasants were well aware of this margin.

The growth of cooperatives had been, in part, Nyerere's response to large farms and plantations, which he perceived as inimical to socialist equality. TANU's initial thrust against foreign-owned farms succeeded, in that it caused most expatriate farmers to leave in the mid-sixties. But the thrust continued, being directed against Africans who accumulated land (Coulson 1982:146). The answer was not to break up their farms, however, but to force them to sell only to government-sponsored cooperatives.

Yet the "top down" development of the cooperatives led to inefficiencies and corruption. Although the structures created by government opened the probability of corruption, Nyerere insisted on investigating and punishing it when it occurred. In the middle sixties, a number of Special Commissions of Enquiry examined the cooperatives, including those of the main cotton growers and the main coffee growers, and discussed numerous dodges on the part of elected and salaried officials. For example, credit channeled through cooperatives had been assigned by bribery. Small tractors provided by government to cooperatives had been rented by co-op officials who pocketed the proceeds. Bookkeeping deficiencies hid the defalcations. Local cooperative officials made sure they had access to government credit. Being officials, they felt little pressure to repay these loans. They also reimbursed themselves "generously" for expenses incurred in cooperative work.

The 1966 President's Special Commission of Inquiry into Cooperatives blamed lack of training and rapid expansion, which had outstripped the capacity of the Cooperative Development Division (CDD) to supervise local cooperatives. While this may be true, corruption and inefficiency also plagued the older cooperatives in coffee and cotton areas, for which CDD supervision was not necessary. Rather, the two types had in common that—although members elected their officials—appointed officials of the regional cooperative union made the major decisions. These officials also appointed secretaries to the local cooperatives, who might connive with local committeemen to form a power base.

The government's solution to this self-induced problem was to take direct control of sixteen regional cooperative unions; to intervene in the election of committeemen in others; and to supervise more tightly the recruitment of union staff (McHenry 1979:80). The Arusha Declaration of 1967 then called for greater government intervention into all aspects of the economy, including rural development. By 1974, 2,500 primary cooperatives (Table 1) had been grouped into Regional Cooperative Unions (Bernstein 1981:294).

Socialist Villages

> Jamaa, n, a number of persons gathered or collected together, family, society, company, assembly, gathering, meeting. (Oxford University Press, *Standard Swahili-English Dictionary*)

"U" is a prefix indicating general quality (e.g., *moja* means "one"; *umoja* means "unity"). Thus *Ujamaa* means familyhood, the quality of being a society, etc. Where Nyerere's writings have been translated into English as "socialism," generally the Swahili term that he used is *Ujamaa*.

As early as 1960, a World Bank mission to Tanganyika had recommended the establishment of "supervised settlements in thinly inhabited areas." This followed a long history of similar recommendations by various colonial commissions. The Village Settlement Agency, set up in 1962, had facilitated the settlement of thirty villages. These did not become self-reliant, however. Some of the later plans for cooperative villages were extensions of rural resettlement undertaken early in independence

Table 4.1
GROWTH OF COOPERATIVE MOVEMENT, SELECTED YEARS,
1934–73

Year	Number of Societies	Number of Members
1934	23	16,800
1935	37	33,474
1943	45	44,717
1948	77	58,012
1953	198	156,276
1958	546	318,900
1963	1,201	458,953
1968	1,694	643,720
1973	2,299	873,260

SOURCE: McHenry (1979:29).

(Boesen et al. 1977:37–38). Nyerere himself said that "we had talked villagization since 1962 and it was time to act" (Bernstein 1981:305).

In *Socialism and Rural Development*, Nyerere cited the increase in agricultural output as a reason for villagization, although he did not explain precisely how it would come about. He attacked the peasant who expands his farm to 10 or 20 acres as an enemy of economic quality. Although he admitted that these farmers had shown how to increase food production substantially, he felt that their continued growth would kill the spirit of *Ujamaa*. He called for "rural communities where people live together and work together for the good of all." These he envisaged as cooperative villages based on communal production and division of labor—people should be persuaded to set up *Ujamaa* villages, not be forced by government or TANU. Although some crops had to be grown on plantations, which the government would run, workers would know that profit would not be paid to company shareholders but would stay within the community for further investment.

But voluntary cooperation comes slowly, and the government was impatient. Supporting *Ujamaa*, Mwapachu (1976:13), the District Development director for Shinyanga, wrote that "undoubtedly planned villages will contribute to the birth of a development conscience so crucial in the development planning system." But he also argued that coercion was necessary:

> . . . The 1974 Operation Villages was not to be a matter of persuasion but of coercion. As Nyerere argued, the move had to be compulsory because

Tanzania could not sit back and watch the majority of its peoples leading a "life of death." The State had, therefore, to take the role of the "father" in ensuring that its peoples chose a better and more prosperous life for themselves (p. 3).

Four policy decisions in 1969 reflected both this impatience and an increasing willingness to use force.

First, a Presidential Circular ordered that priority for government funding should go to *Ujamaa* villages. Given their scarcity, funds for rural development would in fact go only to *Ujamaa* villages. Since officials sent by government to regions were under high pressure to establish *Ujamaa* villages, local people began "trading." They would agree to establish a communal plot in exchange for some "goodie": a well or primary school. But once villagers discovered that the "goodie" would be approved, their commitment to *farming* the community plot vanished.

Second, the first forced relocation occurred in Operation Rufiji. Farmers on the Rufiji Riss Hood plain were moved to the surrounding ridges, ostensibly because of severe flooding. Although the colonial government had periodically provided food relief in these areas during heavy floods, the agricultural region was so rich that good years more than made up for periodic flooding. Instead of storing food, which would probably have been the most efficient means to attack the problem, the government decided to move the people. But the new areas were less fertile, and the residents found it impractical to commute back to their river valley fields. Despite indications that over time the operation would fail, the government in 1969 pronounced it a great success, making it the model for regionwide movement of people in 1970–72.

Third, fifteen state farms were established. The Second Five Year Plan (1969–79) called for considerable investment in these farms, to make Tanzania self-sufficient in grain. Sixty percent of sisal production, all on large plantations, was nationalized right after the Arusha declaration (1967). In the early seventies, expatriate wheat farms in the Northern Highlands were also nationalized, put under the direction of NAFCO (National Agriculture and Food Corporation), to which the task of achieving self-sufficiency in food was assigned. Thus the difficulties of obtaining peasants' cooperation would be resolved by making them state employees rather than independent farmers.

Fourth, The Ruvuma Development Association (RDA) was disbanded. In a meeting that lasted all of July (1969), the TANU central committee discussed the meaning of *Ujamaa*, reviewing both Operation Rufiji and the RDA. Because the committee disliked intensely both the independence and the politicizations of RDA, it voted for RDA disbandment in September. Soon thereafter, the minister of Rural Development and certain members of the committee flew to Ruvuma to announce the decision (Coulson 1982:271). The assets of RDA were confiscated by the state.

Regionwide villagization was undertaken in 1970–72 in four different regions. Presidential Planning Teams were also sent to a number of the poorer regions, to plan new villages (Bernstein 1982:299). The official in charge of villagization in Mtwara was considered so successful that he was sent to Iringa to conduct the same operation there. "Operation Dodoma" moved 30,000 pastoral families into large villages. More villagization occurred in Kigoma and Chunya districts, but no further operations were conducted in 1973 (see Table 2).

Growth of Villages and Village Population

Village formation in the years 1970–72 took place so rapidly that it skirted the cooperative principles expounded by Nyerere (Bernstein 1982:299). Rural population was concentrated in large villages, with little thought to location choice other than access by road. Farming was done on an individual basis even where initial ploughing had been done by the government.

Raikes (1975) divided *Ujamaa* villages into five types, as of the end of 1973:

1. Self-initiated, a small proportion of the total.
2. Existing villages that were designated *Ujamaa*, with no real change.
3. "Bribed" villages, with some communal production started in exchange for government funds.
4. Villages formed by coercion during 1971–72. These were the most common type.
5. "Kulak" villages, formed when wealthier peasants would join to take over an expatriate farm. There were only a few of these.

In their detailed study of *Ujamaa* villages in Westlake Region from 1968 to 1973, however, Boesen et al. (1977) characterized the government approach as combining a "bureaucratic insensitivity to village needs" with a "movement toward large scale control techniques." Raikes (1975) (quoted in McHenry 1979:151) asked why persuasion was not sufficient. He answered his own question: "There were not enough trained political cadres at any level." Locally assigned government officials carried out the operations; they were sufficiently numerous, and they had access to funds. Boesen et al. (1977:16) doubt that the government really intended to implement *Ujamaa* through bureaucratic control. Rather, local administrative officials, left to interpret *Ujamaa* as they wished, implemented it without regard for local opinion. The cooperatives had come under increasing government control and had never been an avenue by which peasant interests could be expressed. One District Development officer described the situation, paternalistically: "Many committees [of local citizens] do not understand what is required to be done to bring a revolution of rural development to their areas" (Finucane 1974:88–9).

Table 4.2
Growth of Villages and Village Population, 1969–76 and 1980

	1969	1970	1971	1972	1973	1974	1975	1976	1980
Total no. of villages	809	1,956	4,464	5,556	5,628	5,008	6,944	7,684	8,124
Village population (millions)		0.53	1.55	1.98	2.02	2.56	9.14	13.00	
Average size		272	345	357	360	511	1,260	1,692	1,970

SOURCE: Bernstein (1982:232), except 1980: COPAC Information Note (1980:46).

Resistance and lack of "effective" control at the local level precipitated a profound governmental reorganization in 1972. Local, elected governments were abolished, being replaced by senior civil servants from the technical ministries in Dar es Salaam. Local political decisionmaking was thus destroyed (Coulson 1982:254). In a curious "newspeak," this move was entitled "decentralization," possibly because the central government became proliferated over the countryside. TANU was reorganized so that salaried officials, often from a different region, replaced local volunteers. Locally assigned party officers, who did not look upon the villages as their constituencies, were more concerned with pleasing their higher-ups than the local people. Samoff (1983:92) explains "decentralization" as an attempt by government to legitimize its power through emphasizing its "expertise." In this way, local authority and local expertise were undermined.

Kleemeier (1984:189) finds evidence that the government had never intended truly to entrust major decisions to local people. A committee headed by Cranford Pratt (in the late sixties) was commissioned to study the feasibility of decentralization. Its report was never released, apparently because it recommended regional elected governments with substantial power. Instead, the government's decentralization plan was based on a study by McKinsey & Company (corporate management consultants). Each region would become a separate department, with an annual budget through which the government might control its planning. The McKinsey report presumed that 40% of the budget would be controlled locally; in fact, this amount averaged 14% (Kleemeier 1984:190). Since communities had little say in their own budgets, they proposed projects with no sense of appropriate quantity or timing: "The situation encouraged exaggerated budget estimates from the regions, wasted effort in documenting unfunded projects and inhibited long range planning, since regions got such a small percentage of their requests" (Kleemeier 1984:12).

Villagization: 1973-75

Official government pronouncements explained *Ujamaa* villagization as a means of providing common facilities (water, schools, clinics, electricity) more economically to the population (McHenry 1979:151). In addressing the First National Assembly in 1962, Nyerere promised:

> The government will do everything possible to enable the peasants of Tanganyika to live together in village settlements. If you ask me why the government wants the peasants to live in village settlements, my answer is equally simple: without living in village settlements, they cannot get the essential modern facilities.

These facilities were to include

> universal primary education by 1989 (revised to 1977), various per capita targets for rural health centres, dispensaries, hospitals and doctors by

71

1980, and a piped water supply within 400 metres of all Tanzanians by 1991 (revised to . . . "a source of clean, potable, and dependable water to every village as a free basic service") (Kleemeier 1984:193).

On other occasions, Nyerere suggested that increased agricultural production was also an important reason for villagization.

Coulson (1982:256) questions whether these were the ultimate motives:

> . . . There were some areas, such as the Sukumu heartland, where people were moved even though the population density was so high that most of the services could have been built within two or three miles of the majority of holdings. Furthermore, the government never did explain precisely the mechanism by which production would be increased through villagization.

Citing Masefield (1955:66), Coulson (1982:258) argues that the type of farming of many Tanzanians requires dispersed rather than concentrated settlement. Especially is this so with cattle, which need both a wide range area and the proximity of the owner to put them in the kraal (thorned enclosure to protect them from lions) at night, take them out in the morning, and tend them in emergencies. To concentrate their owners in villages would curtail grazing.

If services could be provided in many areas without forced villagization, and if agriculture were better served in some areas by dispersion, then why was villagization enforced *uniformly* throughout the country? There may have been political motives as well, for on numerous occasions government officials condemned tribalism, which implied separatism: the central government might fall apart. To concentrate citizens in villages, with mixed tribal identities, would diminish the authority of tribal chiefs and facilitate political control. Also, to demonstrate its "expertise" in agriculture and rural development, the government needed to deploy people into situations conducive to exhibiting that expertise.

Up to May 1973, 15% of the rural population had moved into 5,600 villages—in poorer regions more than in richer. Only one of the nine better-off regions (the coast) had more than 10% of its population in villages, whereas seven of the least well-off regions had more than 20% (COPAC 1980:3). It is not clear whether the government used the poorer regions for pilot projects—possibly believing them to be in greater need—or whether the poor were more malleable politically.

In 1973, the government decided that the slow pace of villagization was no longer tolerable. In September, the Biennial Conference of TANU approved a resolution that the entire population should be in villages by 1976. In a speech in Kigoma in November, Nyerere said that force might be necessary both to villagize people and to speed production. He endorsed the goal of 1976 in a Presidential Order.

In 1974, 4 million people were forced into villages. Throughout the rural areas, the operation was organized by Regional Commissioners with the aid of the newly "decentralized" civil servants. New village sites were chosen by ward development committees, salaried government, and party officials who in no way represented the local people. The sites were approved by Regional or District Development Committees, whose role had expanded with "decentralization." Local militia (from the towns) both intimidated the subjects and transported them. Houses were sometimes torn down and sometimes burned; stored crops were often lost. As word of these methods spread, peasant compliance became easier (Coulson 1982:252-3). The government has officially acknowledged the use of force (Bernstein 1981:45), and officials directly involved have agreed that the decision was deliberate.

The campaign continued in 1975 with an additional 2 million people. Bernstein (1981:44) estimates that while 1.5 million people had been villagized between 1967 and 1973, the number jumped to 11 million from late 1973 to 1977. Some of those 11 million may have been designated as living within a new village without being actually moved. Nevertheless there seems little question that at least 6 million people were moved against their will during those two years. The population of Tanzania at the middle of 1978 was 17.44 million (IMF:IFS).

The threat of force was probably the most effective means of ensuring compliance. At the same time, the principal vehicles through which peasants might express themselves, "the cooperative movement, the labor movement and all other significant organized groups had been incorporated into the party or government" (McHenry 1979:151) and therefore could offer no opposition.

With mass villagization, the ideals of *Ujamaa* became lost. Cooperative farming and community services fell by the wayside because of lack of interest on the part of the peasantry and lack of budget on the part of the government. Bernstein (1982: 305) describes *Ujamaa* as merely "an interlude in a well established tendency to villagization and rural development through direct state intervention."

After Villagization

Some observers believe that, whatever the error, forced villagization was part of a national strategy to increase agricultural output. With their uniform system of governance and control by full-time government officials, the villages could be the vehicle for agricultural extension and introduction of modern farming methods.

The political structure of the villages lends some credence to that proposition. The legal framework for village government was laid down in the 1975 *Ujamaa* Villages Act, Registration, Designation and Administration. In this, the village was set up as a cooperative society. An assembly of all adult residents would elect a Village Council and would approve the budget and accounts annually. Each Village Council would elect a chairman, secretary, and treasurer, except where the TANU party (now CCM—Party of the Revolution) had a local branch, in which case its chairman and secretary would automatically be chairman and secretary respectively of the village. The Council would carry out village business with state agencies and parastatal companies.

In 1978, however, the government announced that full-time village managers, whom it would pay, would be appointed to every village. In 1979, 52% of the surveyed villages had managers. They were mostly junior staff from the agriculture extension service; some had been primary school teachers. Although paid by the Ministry of Manpower Development and supervised by government-appointed regional authorities, they were presumably responsible to the Village Councils. Clearly, they were an attempt for closer government control at the village level.

Each village was to be a primary level cooperative, serving as intermediary for villagers both in the agricultural input markets (for fertilizer and credit) and in the output markets (by gathering the village surplus for sale to crop authorities). Each village was encouraged to set up a village store to compete with private retailers.

A study in 1979 revealed that 72% of villages surveyed had communal plots, although the percentage varied greatly among regions (COPAC 1980:11–12, 19). But these farms covered only 2–3% of cultivable village land, even though they averaged 45 hectares. Many of these communal farms were not farmed communally but were split into individual or small group plots. In some villages, the incentive to work communal plots was reduced because the income (from cash crops) was spent on village overhead rather than distributed to workers. Cash crops were grown on many communal farms. According to the COPAC survey, production on communal farms was declining, although the evidence for this estimate was not given.

In 1980 the government ordered all villages to start communal plots of at least 100 hectares, but we do not yet have information on how this order had been implemented. The very fact that the order had to be issued would indicate that the government felt that compliance with the idea of communal plots had been less than satisfactory, and that a governmental order was necessary.

How did the government fare in providing the common facilities that presumably justified villagization? Budgeted expenditures on rural social services declined as a percentage of the national budget from 1973 to 1979 (Table 3). Furthermore, maintenance expenditures lagged. In only one out of nine regions in which water expenditures were studied were recurrent expenditures above 20% of capital (the percentage that the World Bank sees as necessary). In seven of the other regions, recurrent expenditures averaged only 5.1% of capital (Kleemeier 1984:193–94). The percentage of villagers with access to clean water actually declined in the lake region, because maintenance was neglected. Kleemeier further suggests an expla-

Table 4.3

BUDGETED EXPENDITURES FOR RURAL EDUCATION, HEALTH, AND WATER SERVICES, 1973–79 (IN THOUSANDS OF 1970 CONSTANT TANZANIAN SHILLINGS)

	Domestic Funds	Foreign Funds	Total Funds	Percentage of Development Budget
1973	42,453	115,195	157,648	–
1974	53,313	70,538	123,851	–
1975	65,753	117,623	183,376	13.3
1976	44,293	159,417	203,710	13.4
1977	47,803	108,882	156,685	9.1
1978	75,940	95,270	171,210	7.7
1979	68,640	74,031	142,671	5.6

SOURCE: Kleemeier (1984:194).

nation not only in lack of funds, but in the failure to involve local people in the projects:

> . . . Villagers had participated very little in the projects except through "self-help contributions" which were more a form of labor tax. Furthermore villages tended to look upon social services as something promised and owed them by the government, and therefore the latter's responsibility to maintain. The result was that the villagers themselves did little to maintain the projects nor were they given the skills to do so (p. 194).

Output, Markets, and Prices

> [There was] a substantial deterioration of real prices and incomes from crop sales during the 1970s. When taken in conjunction with a concomitant deterioration in the efficiency of agricultural marketing the analysis suggests that price policy had a major adverse impact both on peasant living standards and on the economic performance of Tanzania since the mid-1960s (Ellis 1982:263).

Ever since independence, the Tanzanian government has increasingly and persistently co-opted production decisions, pricing, and marketing of agricultural crops, and activity in these fields has become more and more coercive. By the end of the seventies, the standard of living of Tanzanian peasants had deteriorated so much that some observers believed no net progress had been made since colonial times.

We have seen how compulsory cooperatives had been woven into the structure of marketing boards inherited from the British. During the sixties, the "three-tiered system" emerged, in which some 2,300 local cooperatives collected crops in villages, passed them on to twenty regional cooperative unions, which in turn delivered them to marketing boards. Among these, the National Agricultural Products Board acquired maize, rice, wheat, oilseed crops, and cashew nuts. Others were sold to crop-specific marketing boards. Wholesale prices (into-store) were set by the Economic Committee of the Cabinet with the advice of the appropriate technicians from the Department of Agriculture.

Agricultural crises occurred during 1973 and 1974. These were years of drought, but output declined even in areas of adequate rainfall. Furthermore, over two decades the yearly changes in agricultural output have not correlated with rainfall. Therefore, we must assume that other factors than weather bore the main responsibility. Among these, government policy—on both villagization and prices—appears the most likely.

In response to the shortages of 1973-74, the government converted the marketing boards into crop authorities, with more direct responsibilities toward collecting and marketing the output. The three tiers were now collapsed, and crop authorities bought directly from village producers. Instead of into-store prices, the government—still at Cabinet level in Dar es Salaam—fixed prices paid to growers. These prices were determined eighteen months before the crop year. The belief that prices could be fixed that far in advance may well have indicated the naivete of the bureaucrats on agricultural matters, or else their greater attention to political and administrative than to economic reasons. Minimum acreage requirements were set for each village's plantings of specific crops. All collection, transporting, processing, storing, and selling of crops (in both domestic and foreign markets) were the monopolies of the crop authorities. By the end of the decade, only fresh fruits and vegetables, commonly sold in village markets, were exempt. It was illegal to sell wheat to one's next-door neighbor.

Furthermore, the producer price was set as residual, after the wholesale price had been estimated and crop authority marketing costs deducted. The latter were based on past performance, with prior inefficiencies therefore built into subsequent budgets (Ellis 1982:266).

Not only were producer prices low, they were established uniformly at the village level, with no adjustment for transportation. With payment at official prices, therefore, there was no economy in selling locally (more efficient) rather than transporting products across the country. But farmers in border areas, for whom smuggling was an option (mainly from the Kilamanjaro region into Kenya), would either do so or sell in the local black market. Against the advice of the Ministry of Agriculture, the government was forced, finally in 1980, to pay premium prices to border areas, in order to capture what would otherwise be smuggled.

Ellis' (1982) calculations (Tables 4 and 5) show that the net barter terms of trade (prices of foodstuffs sold compared with the consumer price index, representing goods that farmers buy) were moving against the farmers from 1970 to 1980, with a short reverse movement for some crops in the latter years. Table 4 shows the percentage changes in producers' prices deflated by the consumer price index. Table 5 shows the percentage change in the net barter terms of trade (ratio of prices of foodstuffs sold to the consumer price index). Thus the two tables present similar information in different ways. Table 6 depicts Ellis' (1982) estimates that farmers' net real income terms of trade (farmers' incomes – i.e., prices times volume sold – deflated by consumer price index) were also declining for the decade. For export crops, this trend was continuous, while for domestic crops the decline was reversed in the late 1970s but not sufficiently to offset the earlier losses. Finally, Table 7 shows that the index of agricultural output, both overall and per capita, rose from 1961 to the early 1970s and then fell during the period of massive state intervention (in the late seventies).

Only in 1987, when pushed to do so by the International Monetary Fund, did the government allow farmers to sell products more freely and charge market prices (Davidson in WSJ, 1/27/88). Thereafter, Tanzanian per capita income increased for the first time in several years.

Table 4.4

PERCENT CHANGE IN FARMERS' PRICES DEFLATED BY CONSUMER PRICE INDEX (COMPARISON OF CROP YEARS 1973–74 WITH 1969–70 AND 1979–80 WITH 1973–74)

	1969–70 to 1973–74	1973–74 to 1979–80
Export crops		
Cashews	−38.4	−24.0
Coffee	−33.9	−18.6
Cotton	−36.0	+2.3
Pyrethrum	−43.5	−20.3
Tobacco	−20.5	−37.1
Domestic crops		
Maize	−27.4	+20.4
Paddy	−32.5	+4.6
Wheat	−38.4	−5.8
Groundnuts	−23.0	+38.3
Sunflowers	−19.3	+1.2

SOURCE: Ellis (1982:268).

Table 4.5

NET BARTER TERMS OF TRADE OF SMALLHOLDER CROP PRODUCERS, 1970–80 (PERCENT INCREASE OR DECREASE)

	1970–1975	1975–1980	1970–1980
6 export crops	−41.4	−2.0	−42.6
13 domestic crops	−27.1	+15.8	−15.6
3 staple grains	−30.1	+13.2	−20.9
4 drought crops	+14.0	−8.4	+4.4
6 oilseeds	−34.3	+24.5	−18.2
All 19 crops	−40.2	+7.2	−35.9

SOURCE: Ellis (1982:273).

Table 4.6

INCOME TERMS OF TRADE OF SMALLHOLDER CROP PRODUCERS, 1970–80 (PERCENT INCREASE OR DECREASE)

	1970–75	1975–80	1970–80
6 export crops	−32.7	−14.6	−42.5
13 domestic crops	−66.5	+237.9	−10.2
All 19 crops	−38.3	+7.9	−33.4

SOURCE: Ellis (1982:273).

Parastatal Companies

. . . The crop parastatals constitute the core institutional apparatus which regulates the exchange relationships between the productive basis of the economy in agriculture and the state. *Their deteriorating efficiency and spiraling deficits imply both the progressive intensification of real resource transfers out of the rural economy and the dissipation of those resources in unproductive current expenditures.* In addition, the inflationary effect of their deficit financing by bank overdraft further exacerbates the decline in real returns to peasant crop producers (Ellis 1982:277; emphasis added).

Parastatal companies – government corporations that in principle respond to specific ministries but that in practice operate autonomously – are one way Tanzania has transferred resources out of small-farm agriculture and into an ever-growing bureaucracy. The marketing margin

Table 4.7
INDEX OF AGRICULTURAL OUTPUT, OVERALL AND PER CAPITA, 1961–86 (1974–76 = 100)

	Overall	Per Capita
1961	54	77
1962	56	78
1963	61	83
1964	60	79
1965	60	77
1966	69	87
1967	67	82
1968	69	83
1969	77	90
1970	92	105
1971	91	101
1972	94	102
1973	93	99
1974	95	98
1975	99	99
1976	107	104
1977	106	100
1978	106	97
1979	108	96
1980	111	96
1981	114	95
1982	112	90
1983	118	92
1984	124	93
1985	125	90
1986	128	89

SOURCE: Overall index from United Nations Food and Agricultural Organization, *Production Yearbook*, 1973, 1983, and 1986. Data for 1961–71 are based on 1961–65 = 100 and were spliced at year 1972. Data for 1984–86 are based on 1979–81 = 100 and were spliced at 1983. All data were converted into base 1974–76 = 100.

(percent of final sales value appropriated by government) increased from 33.6% in 1970 to 58.4% in 1980 (Ellis 1983:227). The difference between these two percentages is an implicit transfer from peasants to the state.

Had these resources been spent on agricultural research, extension, and input distribution, or even on development projects outside of agriculture, they might in some way be justified. But none of these was forthcoming in the quantities paid for. Ellis (1983:232) explains the waste through the expansion of permanent personnel for seasonal activity and the duplication of overhead capital and trained personnel across crop parastatals.

When cooperative unions were abolished in May 1976, each of the main agricultural parastatals was assigned a district (or districts) from which it would collect all crops at the village level and process or market them thereafter. But most parastatals were not prepared for this diversification; the experience of each lay in an individual crop. Besides the government policy of low prices, peasants had three principal sets of problems with the new parastatals.

First, most crop parastatals did not have the necessary transportation equipment. Some would have surplus and others not enough; interorganizational jealousies prevented them from coordinating pools. Most of their equipment came from the now abolished cooperatives, which, according to a report of the Prime Minister's Commission on Re-establishing Cooperative Unions (PMCCU 1980:75), had used their fleets effectively for all aspects of input and crop distribution. These fleets were now split up among parastatals: the regional transport companies and the crop authorities, with no heed to efficient allocation or complementarity. Soldiers were sent to the offices of cooperative unions to ensure that no equipment was carted off when the cooperatives were abolished.

Second, with no control over their own marketing, peasants did not know whether their crops would be collected before they rotted (PMCCU 1980:53). Crops were often collected long after they had been purchased, and the peasants were held liable for spoilage in the meantime.

Third, the crop parastatals usually delayed payment, from three months to two years. The Prime Minister's Commission (PMCCU 1980:52) correctly stated that these delays represented the rich borrowing from the poor, and the peasants were keenly aware of this fact.

In all of these respects, the peasants were powerless. Under the cooperatives, they had had some control over the leadership. But there was no way to force action by the parastatals.

The 1982 Task Force on Agricultural Development

Recognizing that the agricultural sector was in serious decay, in 1982 the government established a Task Force to make recommendations. In its final report of April 1983, the Task Force presented tables showing substantially the same results—declining agricultural output—reflected in Table 7. (Therefore, reproduction of the Task Force tables here would be redundant.)

> According to the Task Force Report there were four legally recognized tenures in existence: government leaseholds; rights of occupancies [sic];

customary land tenure laws; and the collective tenure system. However, it is not known where the Task Force observed the four tenure systems—since 1969, there has been only one tenure in Tanzania—the right of occupancy. The occupation and use of land according to native law and the custom constitute what is generally termed "deemed right of occupancy" (Gondwe 1986:32).

Gondwe, a member of the Law Faculty at the University of Dar es Salaam, goes on to report that in a private conversation with a senior official in the prime minister's office, he was told that "Tanzania has yet to boast a single *Ujamaa* village."

While other socialist countries (such as the Soviet Union and China) are reverting toward private farming as a way out of their agricultural slowness, Tanzania is equivocating. The new agricultural policy (AGRIPOL) outlined by the Task Force recommends that land allocations to Village Councils, under the Villages Act of 1975, shall be made for at least 999 years, with heritable leases, not alienable, to be awarded to village members. However, lands subject to these leases may be reclaimed at any time by the Village Councils, with compensation to the leaseholder for improvements. Block farms (presumably cooperatives) are also recommended—to continue for a "sufficiently long period," with lots thereafter surrendered to the Village Council for re-allocation. The Ministry of Lands would be responsible for implementing this scheme.

Some have argued that the heritable leases constitute a "new deal" for farmers, who may henceforth farm privately. Perhaps. With alienation ruled out except by permission of Village Councils, and with those councils holding the right to redeem the farms at any time, the ultimate power, it would seem, still lies with them.

Conclusion

Tanzania's social experiment has failed. The welfare of farmers and consumers has seriously deteriorated over the past quarter century in the following ways.

First, the terms of trade moved strongly against all farmers from 1969 to 1974, for producers of both export and domestic-consumption crops. The decline was greater for export crops than for domestic.

Second, from 1970 to 1975, government increased the prices of drought-resistant crops, believing an expansion in the output of these was necessary. In fact, however, they expanded excessively; in non-drought years they were not the crops required for the general market, since, for example, consumers would eat cassava in limited quantities, fresh, and not in chips or other manner in which it could be stored. Therefore, after 1975, the price increase for drought crops was reversed.

Third, in response to the crisis years of 1973-74, government moderated the drop in prices of export crops and reversed the decline for crops of domestic consumption. Whereas in 1973-74 the export crop price index was 92.2% of the price index for domestic crops (1969-70 = 100), by 1979-80 it had declined to 68.0% (Ellis 1982:269). However, the price increases were not sufficient to overcome losses to farmers from previous real price declines. World prices of export crops were increasing in the mid-seventies and did not begin to decline until approximately 1979. Therefore, the government's price policy discriminated strongly against exporters in the latter part of the decade.

Fourth, the spread between prices paid and received by the crop authorities has been increasing.

Fifth, Tanzania is not much better able to feed its people in the mid-eighties than it was in the mid-sixties. From 1961 to 1982, food production increased at an average rate of 3.0% per year, while population increased at a rate of 2.8%. The difference—that per capita output increased by 0.2% per year on average—is minor, probably within the margin expected for error in such data.

Sixth, incomes of farmers producing for export declined steadily during the decade of the seventies. Incomes of those producing for domestic consumption fell from 1970 to 1975 and picked up thereafter. However, they too were losers on balance for the decade as a whole.

Seventh, if we eliminate the crisis years of 1973-74 and take only years thereafter, the volume of principal exports (coffee, cotton, and sisal) has been declining. The volume of coffee exports fell by 11%; of cotton by 11%; and of sisal by 28% from 1975-76 to 1977-81. In the same years, the trade deficit worsened from $181 million to $342 million (IMF:IFS).

Eighth, although a Task Force of 1983-84 has recommended "heritable leases" of land in *Ujamaa* villages, nevertheless the terms of these leases—which are not alienable and may be revoked at any time—are such as to leave the village authorities, rather than the individual peasants, in charge of decisionmaking.

Drawing on insights from this and other countries, we infer once again that peasants have been responsive to price signals and resistant to coercion. Once again, authoritarian land reform has been one more element in the discrimination against agriculture and the peasantry, which is rampant in the Third World.

References

Bakula, B. B., 1969. *The Effect of Traditionalism on Rural Development: The Case of the Omurunazi Ujamaa Village, Bukoba*, Political Science Paper no. 6, dissertation, Dar es Salaam, University of East Africa.

Bernstein, Harry, 1981. "Notes on State and Peasantry: The Tanzanian Case," *Review of African Political Economy*, May–September: 44–62.

Bernstein, Harry, 1982. "Contradictions of the Tanzanian Experience" in Steve Jones, P. C. Joshi, and Miguel Murmis, eds., *Rural Poverty and Agrarian Reform*, New Delhi, Allied Publishers.

Bezza, Mulugetta, 1980. "Tanzania Country Review Paper," *Land Reform, Land Settlement, and Cooperatives,* no. 1/2, Rome, Food and Agriculture Organization.

Boesen, Jannik; Madsin, Birget; and Moody, Tony, 1977. *Ujamaa: Socialism from Above,* Uppsala, Scandinavian Institute of African Studies.

COPAC, 1980. "Cooperative Information Note: Tanzania," Rome, Food and Agriculture Organization.

Coulson, Andrew, 1981. "Agricultural Policies in Mainland Tanzania 1946-1976" in Judith Heyer et al., *Rural Development in Tropical Africa,* New York, St. Martin's Press.

Coulson, Andrew, 1982. *Tanzania: A Political Economy,* Oxford, Clarendon Press.

Ellis, Frank, 1982. "Agricultural Price Policy in Tanzania," *World Development,* vol. 10, no. 4:263-83.

Ellis, Frank, 1983. "Agricultural Marketing and Peasant-State Transfers in Tanzania," *Journal of Peasant Studies,* vol. 10, no. 4:214-42.

Engas, Zaki, 1982. "The State and Economic Deterioration: The Tanzanian Case," *Journal of Commonwealth and Comparative Politics,* vol. 20, no. 3:286-307.

Finucane, James R., 1974. *Rural Development and Democracy in Tanzania: the Case of Mwanza Region,* Uppsala, The Scandinavian Institute of African Studies.

Freeman, Linda, 1982. "CIDA, Wheat and Rural Development in Tanzania," *Canadian Journal of African Studies,* vol. 16, no. 3:479-504.

Gondwe, Zebron Steven, 1986. "Agricultural Policy in Tanzania at the Crossroads," *Land Use Policy,* vol. 3, no. 1, January.

Government of Tanzania, Marketing Development Bureau, 1981. *Price Policy Recommendations for the 1982-83 Agricultural Price Review,* Dar es Salaam.

Gulliver, P. H., 1971. *Neighbors and Networks: The Idiom of Kinship among the Ndendeuli of Tanzania,* Berkeley, University of California Press.

Hill, Frances, 1974. "Elections in the Local Political Context," in Election Study Committee (University of Dar es Salaam), eds., *Socialism and Participation,* Dar es Salaam, Tanzania Publishing House.

Hyden, Goran, 1975. "Ujamaa, Villagization, and Rural Development in Tanzania," *ODI Review*:70.

Hyden, Goran, 1980. *Beyond Ujamaa in Tanzania: Underdevelopment and an Uncaptured Peasantry,* Nairobi, Heinemann Educational Books.

Hyden, Goran, 1983. *No Shortcuts to Progress,* Berkeley, University of California Press.

IMF:IFS (International Monetary Fund). *International Financial Statistics,* issued monthly.

Jansen, Doris J., 1981. *An Econometric Analysis of Regional Production Price Determination in Tanzania,* Dar es Salaam, Marketing Development Bureau.

Keeler, A.; Scobie, G.; Renkow, M.; and Franklin, D., 1982. *The Consumption Effects of Agricultural Policies in Tanzania,* USAID contract DSANC- 0271, Raleigh, N.C., Sigma One Corporation.

Kleemeier, Lawrence, 1984. "Domestic Policies versus Poverty-Oriented Foreign Assistance in Tanzania," *Journal of Development Studies,* vol. 20, no. 2, January: 171-201.

Kriesel, H., et al., 1970. *Agricultural Marketing in Tanzania,* USAID, Dar es Salaam and Lansing, Department of Agricultural Economics, Michigan State University.

Lochie, M., 1976. "Agrarian Socialism in the Third World: Tanzanian Case," *Comparative Politics,* April:479-99.

Lofchie, M., 1978. "Agrarian Crisis and Economic Liberalisation in Tanzania," *Journal of Modern African Studies*, vol. 16, no. 3:451-75.

Masefield, G. B., 1955. "A Comparison between Settlements in Villages and Isolated Homesteads," *Journal of African Administration*, vol. 7, no. 2:64-68.

McHenry, Dean, 1973. "The Utility of Compulsion in Implementation of Agricultural Policies," *Canadian Journal of African Studies*, vol. 12, no. 2:305-16.

McHenry, Dean, 1979. *Tanzania's Ujamaa Villages: The Implementation of a Rural Development Strategy*, Berkeley, University of California, Institute of International Studies.

Msambichaka, L. A., and Mabeli, Robert B., 1979. "Agricultural Credit and Development of Ujamaa Villages in Tanzania" in Kiword Kim et al., eds., *Papers on the Political Economy of Tanzania*, Nairobi, Heinemann Educational Books.

Mwapachu, Juma Volter, 1976. "Operation Planned Villages in Rural Tanzania: A Revolutionary Strategy for Development," *The African Review*, vol. 6, no. 1:1-16.

Nyerere, Julius K., 1967. "Ujamaa, the Basis of African Socialism" (1962), reprinted in J.K. Nyerere, *Freedom and Unity*, London, Oxford University Press.

PMCCU (Prime Minister's Commission on Re-establishing Cooperative Unions), 1980. Mimeograph Report, Dar es Salaam, Government of Tanzania.

Pratt, Cranford, 1976. *The Critical Phase in Tanzania, 1945-1968: Nyerere and the Emergence of a Socialist Strategy*, Cambridge, Cambridge University Press.

Raikes, P., 1975. "Ujamaa and Rural Socialism," *Review of African Political Economy*, vol. 3:33-52.

Samoff, Joel, 1983. "Bureaucrats, Politicians, and Power in Tanzania: The Institutional Context of Class Struggle," *Journal of African Studies*, vol. 10, no. 3:84-97.

Saul, John, 1971. "Marketing Cooperatives in a Developing Country," in Peter Worsley, ed., *Two Blades of Grass*, Atlantic Highlands, N.J., Humanities Press.

TANU case worker, 1975. "Sukumuland Case Study," in Cliffe et al., eds., *Rural Cooperation in Tanzania*, Dar es Salaam, Tanzania Publishing House.

United Republic of Tanzania, 1982. *Tanzania National Food Strategy*, Ministry of Agriculture, June.

5. Iran

What the Shah Gives, the Shah Can Take Away

To both Western and Iranian observers, the shah's land reform was an outstanding success by the end of the sixties. The shah had sold his own vast lands to the villagers. He was forcing the richest landowners to do the same for substantial portions of theirs and to grant secure tenancy for the rest. Farmayan (1971:100, cited in Savory 1978:105), an Iranian historian, called this the "greatest single piece of legislation in Persian history." Anthropologist Ann Lambton (1969:10, cited in Savory, p. 108) — perhaps the best-known Western scholar of Iran — wrote of the officials of the Central Organization for Rural Cooperation (which administered the land reform): "They have succeeded in gaining the trust of the peasants in which the gulf between government and the governed has seldom been bridged. I cannot speak too highly of their work."

Before he was overthrown in 1978, however, the shah had emasculated his own reform. By pricing and credit policies, he had diverted resources away from the peasants to whom he had distributed lands, undercutting their means of subsistence. He had forced peasants to turn their fields over to agribusinesses and government-run "cooperatives" without a single by-your-leave from those most affected. Perhaps scholarly euphoria was motivated by wishfulness. It was certainly a case of substituting rhetoric and intentions for fact, for had the reform actually been as touted, surely the peasants would have risen to defend the shah when he was threatened by the Khomeini revolution of 1978. They would surely have known that that revolution, in the name of Islam, would return to religion the vast estates that the shah had confiscated from it on their behalf. Yet there was no such outcry of support.

Before the Reform

Land distribution in the fifties can only be approximated, in the absence of surveys or land registration. The traditional village was divided into six parts, called *dongs*; a landlord might own one or more *dongs*. Approximately 2,000 villages were owned by the shah, who had inherited them from his father (Riza Shah, r. 1925–41). Two hundred other families owned more than one hundred villages each (Salamanzadeh and Jones 1981:199). Together, these constituted one-third of the villages in Iran.

Approximately 5% of the population owned 95% of the land (Salamanzadeh and Jones 1981:199). Even this concentration is underestimated in Table 1, which does not distinguish the many owners who held lands in several villages nor the parts of villages held in religious endowments known as *waqf*.

But management was not concentrated along with ownership: landlords were mostly absentees, visiting their villages rarely. Instead, the village headmen was responsible for production, which was actually carried out by *bunehs*, or groups of three to fourteen men.

The *buneh* had originated out of water scarcity (Katouzian 1981b: 298–99). Villagers cooperated to construct and maintain traditional irrigation systems and to ensure equal access to the more fertile fields. Each year in consultation with village headmen, the landlords would appoint *buneh* heads, who would choose their *bunehs* from among those with sharecropping rights in the village. Each head would choose an assistant from among his *buneh* members. Lands were reallocated yearly, so that each *buneh* would have plots of roughly equal quality, albeit in different parts of the village. Typically, a *buneh* would farm 20 hectares with three teams of oxen. The landlord would reward the village headman, the *buneh* head, and his assistant with greater shares of output than team members.

The Reform

By imperial decree in January 1951, the shah announced his intention to sell his royal estates (11,277 whole villages, 706 partial villages) to the peasants who worked them (Lambton 1969:51–53). The distribution would

---

Table 5.1
PERCENTAGE OF IRANIAN VILLAGES ACCORDING TO TYPE OF OWNERSHIP, 1956

Owned in units less than a *dong*[a]	42.0%
Owned in units of a village or more	24.0
Owned in mixed types of ownership	15.0
Owned in units of one dong or more	11.0
Government-owned lands	4.0
Crown lands	2.0
Religiously endowed lands	1.5
Unknown	0.5
Total	100.0%

SOURCE: Jafari 1980:100.
[a]One *dong* is roughly one-sixth of a village.

be implemented by a specially appointed commission, with priority given to those with the means to farm, namely the traditional sharecroppers. The actual distribution was not completed until 1962.

Instead of permitting the peasants to opt or adapt former means of production (such as the *buneh*) once they had been given their land, the government required that a cooperative be established in each reform village, which would both collect land payments and disburse credit. In 1957, these functions were transferred to a new private bank, Bank Omran, which also replaced the commission. Although one author (Denman 1978:259-60) praises the bank highly, others argue that corruption and favoritism abounded (Baldwin 1967:93). It was widely reported that one-third of the land was siphoned off to the shah's relatives on favorable terms. Whereas the shah had originally spoken of giving his land away, apparently he was selling it instead.

The shah had hoped that landowners would follow his example, but few did. In 1960, therefore, he forced a bill into the Parliament to limit the size of landholdings. With considerable opposition—mainly from religious authorities (who did not want to give up their *waqf* lands)—the bill was watered down, with size limits increased to 400 hectares irrigated or 800 dry. The law was passed but was never enforced.

Frustrated in his attempts to induce land and other social reforms by parliamentary means, the shah dissolved the Parliament in 1961 and ruled by decree. He then announced his personal set of reforms, known as the White Revolution (to emphasize that it would be bloodless). Thus occurred the reform law of 1962, so widely hailed both within Iran and outside: "The Shah, on his own initiative, had decided to take action to break the power of the landowning class, which of course included members of the religious classes as well as lay persons" (Savory 1978:105).

The lack of cadastral surveys and land measurements was circumvented by a ceiling of "one village" (of the landlord's choice) for each landlord. Excess land would be sold to the government at values declared for taxes. Most landlords, of course, had undervalued, and now they were caught. The government would resell the land to peasants with sharecropping rights. With landlords electing to keep their best lands, and with exceptions for religious organizations, orchards, and mechanized properties up to 500 hectares, at least half the villages were not reformed at all. By the mid-seventies, peasants were paying only 20% of the amount due, even though that amount was less than they had been paying for rent (Denham 1978:270), and the government was delinquent in compensating landlords.

Phase I (as the 1962 law became known) proceeded rapidly. The land reform agency (in the Ministry of Agriculture) received authority "(1) to survey and requisition land; (2) to make the initial 10% cash payments to landlords and distribute the land; and (3) to form cooperative units" (Platt 1970:52). Arguing that new mechanisms of credit were needed and that political controls were essential now that landlords no longer dominated villages, the government required land recipients to join cooperatives. Staff from the Agricultural Bank were seconded to the cooperative movement district by district. Disputes over land titles were settled by conversation between these officials and village leaders.

The energetic approach of the minister of Agriculture, Arsanjani, won him great personal support in the countryside. Apparently jealous, the shah dismissed him in 1963, ordering that references to land reform should be associated with his royal name. But the pace slowed down in 1963–65. The district-by-district approach had allowed many landlords time to qualify for exceptions, by selling land to relatives or by mechanizing their holdings (Hooglund 1982:55). Many a tractor mysteriously appeared on many a farm.

To counter landlords and meet the high expectations of peasants, the government moved to Phase II in 1964. Ceilings were lowered to between 20 and 150 hectares, depending on geographic region (because of different productivities). Landlords were given different options on excess land: (1) to write thirty-year tenancy contracts (renegotiable every five years) with cash rent; (2) sell to tenants; (3) agree on division of land with tenants; (4) form a joint stock company with tenants; or (5) purchase tenant rights. Once again, mechanized land up to 500 hectares and orchards were exempt. *Waqf* land was also expropriated, with cash rents and ninety-nine-year leases to existing tenants, renegotiable every five years. From this one move, the shah won the undying enmity of religious organizations, causing them to be an implacable foe in the revolution that ousted him in 1978.

Given the options, most landlords chose thirty-year tenancies. Peasants felt betrayed (Hooglund1982:67). Except for a security of tenure not yet tested, their position was not much different from before. To answer their discontent, in 1969 the shah promulgated Phase III, directing that landlords who had chosen thirty-year tenancies should now decide whether to sell the land to tenants or divide it with them. Disagreements between tenants (who wanted the land to be sold) and landlords (who wanted to divide it) slowed this operation, causing the government to decree in 1971 that tenanted land not previously divided must be sold to tenants for ten times the rent (if land payment was made in cash) or twelve times (if made in installments over twelve years). The results of land divisions from 1962 to 1971 are shown in Table 2.

Out of 2.1 million tenants, therefore, a little over 36% became owners under Phase I, another 10% under Phase II, while 92% were owners after Phase III. This high percentage underlies the extravagant praise for the shah's White Revolution, which we examine below.

Despite wide discrepancies for regions, after the distributions most peasants held less land (Table 3) than was required for family subsistence (estimated at 5 to 7 hectares average). Table 4 shows gross and marketable output by size of farm. A small minority appeared to have gained a basis

Table 5.2
LAND REDISTRIBUTION, 1962–71

Total peasants with tenant rights	2,100,028
Peasants acquiring land	
Under Phase I (1962)	753,258
Under Phase II (1964)	
Owner sale to peasants	57,164
Owner division with peasants	156,279
Under Phase III (1969)	
Purchase of 30-year tenancies	738,119
Owner division with peasants	61,805
Totals	1,766,625
Peasants holding 99–year *waqf* leases	172,103
Total beneficiaries of land distribution	1,938,728
Peasants not obtaining land	161,300
Percent of tenants obtaining land	92%

SOURCE: Hooglund (1982:72). Copyright 1982 by the University of Texas Press. Reprinted with permission.

Table 5.3
PEASANT LANDHOLDINGS, 1976

Size of Holding (in hectares)	Number of Peasant Owners (in 000's)	Percent of All Peasants
10.1–50	200	8.6
6–10	434	18.7
3–5.9	545	23.5
1–2.9	342	14.7
<1	801	34.5
Totals	2332	100.0

SOURCE: Hooglund (1982:91). Copyright 1982 by the University of Texas Press. Reprinted with permission.

for greater income, the rest probably not at all. Larger farms sold their output on the cash market, but most peasants appeared to be still subsistence farmers.

Table 5.4
OUTPUT BY FARM SIZE, 1972

Farm Size	Percent of Farm Area	Percent of Gross Output	Percent of Marketable Output
Large 100 ha or more	12	6	77
Medium 450–100 ha 11–50 ha	4 } 46 }	} 36	
Small 6–10 ha 3–5 ha 1–2 ha <1 ha	21 } 12 } 3 } 2 }	41	19
Pastoralists, others	17	17	4

SOURCE: Schulz (1979:83).

This maldistribution of land led Hooglund (1982:98) to argue that the "land reform did not alter the basic character of the pre-redistribution agricultural regime— a system under which a minority of owners derived profit from farming by exploiting the labor of a majority of villagers. [Only] the composition of the minority of owners had changed." He estimated that most holdings over 20 hectares were still owned by absentees, either former landlords or rich peasants.

Because peasants might have benefited from more than one phase of the reform—if they were included statistically in two or more—government data show some duplication. Furthermore, the fragmentation of holdings over villages made calculations difficult. To overcome these problems, Salamanzadeh and Jones (1979) recalculated the lands for 169 villages in the Dez Irrigation project into village equivalents. They showed that 10.8% of the land was distributed to 34% of the peasants in Phase I. In Phase II— when landlords might choose between division and the thirty-year option—only 8% of lands were divided, benefiting 7% of the peasants, while 77% was leased for thirty years to 88% of the peasants. In Phase III, when that 77% had to be divided with or sold to the peasants, 40% (of the original quantity) was sold to 45% of the peasants, while 37% was divided between the landlords and 43% of the peasants.

The State-Run Cooperatives

We have already seen that when the shah distributed his own lands, the government required the recipients to join village cooperatives of the government's making. These were expected to manage the lands just as the shah's private functionaries had done earlier. Denman (1978:280) cites the shah as believing that "the peasant standing alone with no authority beyond himself to guide his thinking and direct his actions would be lost."

Indeed, this paternalistic attitude permeated the bureaucracies. Afshar (1981: 1098) quotes one planner's view of the peasantry:

> The majority of our cultivators . . . do not have much love for labor and hard work . . . and have become accustomed to unemployment or underemployment and are not willing to change their age old habits overnight. . . . The economic viability of holdings which has been one of the major post land reform pitfalls in the West is a problem that should be placed in an Iranian perspective. [Unlike] the West where people are traditionally brought up to be cooperative and help one another . . . in Iran most people argue that if a partner was a good thing to have God would have taken one.

Afshar argues that precisely this attitude systematically undervalued and undermined the peasant as producer. It ignored the historic fact that peasants had successfully provided the basic needs of the nation for 3,500 years, on holdings of 5 to 10 hectares, which they had cultivated in cooperation. It ignored the village headman and the *buneh*.

The government implanted the cooperatives, and later the Bank Or-
mran, rather than permitting the peasantry to form or retain their own
structures, partly because the bureaucrats believed that credit and marketing were beyond the capabilities of "the rustic folk of Pahlavi villages"
(Denman 1978:280) and partly because they needed a mechanism to collect
land payments. Payments would be linked to credit, which now became a
monopoly of the cooperatives. By the time the shah's lands had all been
sold in 1962, the Bank Omran was supervising 629 cooperatives.

With the law of 1962, cooperatives were extended to the entire land
reform. The Central Organization for Rural Cooperatives (CORC), founded in 1963 with initial capital of two billion rials ($26.4 million), would
"provide means for the development, expansion, and strengthening of
rural cooperatives" (Iran, MLRRC 1970). CORC in turn reported to the
Ministry for Land Reform and Rural Cooperatives (MLRRC). The numbers
of cooperatives and their members, amounts of loans, and other basic data
are shown in Table 5.

Government control over cooperatives was extended, beginning in
1968, just as agribusinesses and farm corporations began to be encouraged
(see below). No new cooperatives were formed thereafter, but existing
ones were encouraged to expand membership. In 1969, the Agricultural
Credit Bank became the Agricultural Cooperative Bank, absorbing CORC.
In 1972, at the initiative of the state, cooperatives were consolidated into
several-village units. Thus the number of cooperatives dropped suddenly,
while average membership grew just as suddenly (Table 5, 1972–73 comparison). Many societies had 1,500 members spread over six to seven
villages.

The consolidation, of course, improved the government's ability to
control the cooperatives. While nominally they were managed by demo-
cratically-elected councils, CORC had become a "hierarchical bureaucracy. . . . CORC officials visited villages to explain government policy to
managers and executive councils . . . and inspect whether government
objectives had been followed" (Hooglund 1982:108). Locally initiated projects had to be approved by CORC. Hooglund further argues that this
bureaucratic control explains why cooperatives did not develop beyond
being credit societies.

Moreover, to the extent peasants did influence cooperative decisions,
the larger, consolidated cooperatives increased the power of the few rich
peasants compared with the many villagers. After the consolidation, 6,000
villages ceased to be cooperative headquarters (Hooglund 1982:106).

Each cooperative was required to purchase a share in a cooperative
fund, which was deposited in the Agricultural Cooperative Bank. This
bank was authorized to issue credit at 4% per annum to any cooperative
up to ten times its deposit. Co-ops in turn would lend to members at 6%
interest. In fact, however, at no time did the bank lend more than four
times the paid-in shares of members (Hooglund 1982:106).

Table 5.5

NUMBERS, MEMBERS, AND LOANS OF COOPERATIVES, 1961–74

Year	Number of Cooperatives	Members (000's)	Percent of Members Receiving Loans	Average Loan (in 1959–60 rials)	Average Members per Cooperative
1961	960	352	45	2,788	367
1962	1,292	404	18	2,907	313
1963	2,722	542	28	3,213	199
1964	3,846	645	51	4,191	167
1965	6,067	792	49	4,392	130
1966	7,685	967	58	4,893	125
1967	8,652	1,105	61	5,497	128
1968	8,644	1,278	58	6,155	148
1969	8,377	1,431	59	6,194	171
1970	8,298	1,606	56	6,104	194
1971	8,450	1,854	47	6,537	219
1972	8,361	2,065	56	6,824	247
1973	2,717	2,263	52	7,819	833
1974	2,847	2,488	55	9,520	847

SOURCE: Denman (1978: 282-3, Table 7.4), and author calculations; constant 1959–60 rials calculated from wholesale price index.

NOTE: Beginning in 1969, credit was distributed by the Agricultural Credit Bank (see text).

Three problems immediately emerged. First, the average loan to any member (6,000 rials in 1962-74; Table 5) barely covered production costs for one hectare of dryland wheat (Hooglund 1982:109). While per capita loan amounts increased after 1974, production costs were rising more rapidly than farm output prices. Thus the value of loans in real terms diminished. Second, the program contained no flexibility. Each farmer received a loan on the same day and had to pay it back in exactly twelve months. Since the harvest cycle was nine months, and different crops had different needs, the peasant had no room to maneuver. Since the government applied collective responsibility—a cooperative would not receive fresh loans if a member had not repaid when due—from the individual farmer's viewpoint the cooperative was not a reliable source of credit. Third, credit was unequally available to cooperative members: members closer to headquarters, in larger towns and richer, had easier access. Hooglund (1982:127-8) discovered that the village headman was often on the executive council, which decided on loans.

While kickbacks to council members were frequent, Hooglund believed that close supervision by CORC prevented them from getting out of hand. But Katouzian (1981b:307) had a different perspective:

> The reader must know something about the country in order to understand the full implications (of bureaucratic control) for the distribution of meager credit facilities extended to the traditional sector: the real criteria for selection, the wholesale corruption at every level, the bureaucratic tyranny and blackmail and so forth.

Where research cannot be adequately done, one must accept a view on the basis of its environment. We take Katouzian as probably more accurate than Hooglund because subsidized scarce credit, with inadequate controls over its distributor, inevitably gives rise to an economic rent. We do know that the maximum number of loans granted averaged only 55% of the number of members (Table 5); this fact alone indicates differential access.

For many peasants, village shopkeepers were an alternative source of credit. Shopkeepers did expand their sales on credit, and they purchased small trucks to transport produce to market (Hooglund 1982:95). They also bought crops from poor peasants before harvest at a discount. While Hooglund believes that shopkeepers were siphoning off the surplus formerly taken by landlords, we see a different possibility. Previously, the landlords held *monopolies* over peasant marketing. Now the peasants were dealing with *competitive* shopkeepers *in an environment of increasing output*. Is it not more likely that peasants were increasing their incomes, while the cost of shopkeeper credit (which might have been high) reflected its market scarcity? Furthermore, whatever credit was indeed offered by government cooperatives at subsidized rates would increase the overall supply. Quite possibly, the overall rate of interest was determined by the market, so that when amounts paid to cooperatives were enhanced by bribes, the total may have equaled shopkeeper rates. This, of course, is conjecture, but Hooglund (1982:95) did observe some informal competition between shopkeepers and government cooperatives.

Farm Corporations and Agribusinesses

Impatient with the slow pace of expansion in peasant output, by the late sixties government officials began to believe that increased production of foodstuffs, to satisfy urban development, required largeness of scale. Agribusiness became the darling of the bureaucracy, and the peasants were increasingly forgotten.

Under the "law for the establishment of companies for utilization of lands downstream of dams," passed in 1968, the government handed enormous tax incentives to foreign and domestic investors in agribusinesses in areas served by dams on which the state had already lavished its oil money. More insidiously, the government agreed to acquire this land from the peasants.

Under a second law, which established the legal basis for farm corporations (to be distinguished from the agribusinesses of the preceding paragraph), peasants were encouraged to exchange their land for shares in corporations, which would have exclusive right of cultivation (Najufi 1978:38). The corporation might be established in any area if 51% of the property owners would agree. In practice, however, the Ministry of Agriculture chose the locations and "convinced" the peasants to vote for the corporations (Hooglund 1982:86).

The government also controlled the substance but not the form of the management. In principle the ultimate authority of each corporation was a board of directors elected by stockholders; this board would select a manager from among three persons nominated by the Ministry of Agriculture. But this power of nomination vitiated all possibility of peasant control. In practice, the manager and other government-appointed officials made all the decisions (Najufi 1978:39). By 1978, ninety-four farm corporations and thirty-six agribusinesses had been created, controlling 400,000 and 200,000 hectares respectively.

Government leverage over peasants in all irrigated zones had been gained through the Water Nationalization Act of 1968. All rivers, water basins, lakes, springs, and subterranean water became national property. The Ministry of Water and Power (later, Energy) acquired authority over them all (Amuzegar 1977:37). Peasants in irrigated zones were now hostages to government policy for their water. Farm corporations were now receiving twenty times as much credit as village cooperatives (Table 6).

The takeover of irrigation zones is illustrated in the Dez River irrigation project, in which Salamanzadeh and Jones (1979: 123) surveyed 169 out of 180 villages. In this area, six agribusinesses had affected 100 villages, while four farm corporations had affected 30 villages. In the whole area, 55,000 peasants were evicted with nominal compensation, and their villages were

Table 5.6

DISTRIBUTION OF AGRICULTURAL CREDITS AND GRANTS BY
SECTOR, 1968–75 (RIALS PER HECTARE)

	Total	Per Annum
Village cooperative loans	6,470	808
Farm corporations	122,383	15,297
Loans	(26,839)	(3,354)
Grants	(95,544)	(11,943)

SOURCE: Katouzian (1981b:309; Table 15.2).

bulldozed to make room for eleven agribusinesses, which leased the land for thirty years (Hooglund 1982:85).

Presumably the population in the 100 villages of the Salamanzadeh and Jones study was to be resettled in thirteen new towns. By 1978, however, only five of those towns had been built, housing the people of thirty villages. Of the 68,000 hectares allocated to agribusinesses, only 19,400 were in cultivation by 1973–74. By 1976–77, foreign investors were having a second look (possibly because of the political crisis, but also because losses were surfacing) and began to back out. The Agricultural Development Bank then shored up the financing. By 1977–78, only 43,800 hectares had been actually leased to agribusinesses, and of these only 25,000 hectares were cultivated. The total debt of the four main businesses was $(US) 51 million, of which 61% was owed to the bank. Their cumulative losses—attributed to the indifference of technicians and laborers—ran to $29.4 million. Since the laborers were recruited from among the dispossessed villagers, their "indifference" to the project should not be surprising.

Najufi (1978:39) records gross disparity in the credit/productivity ratio:

> While the contribution of farm corporations to overall agricultural production is negligible, they receive a major share of government grants, credits, and other services. In 1974, 65 farm corporations received 1.7 billion rials and they got another 325 million rials as interest free loans. On the other hand 2.4 million farmers received 35 million rials in loans through cooperatives at 6% interest.

Farm corporations were originally to have been a five-year experimental program (1968–73). A government evaluation report in 1973 gave them a green light, and they doubled (to eighty-five) in the next two years. Despite this optimistic evaluation, no farm corporation was independent of the government financially by 1975 (Najufi 1978:39). They suffered the same problems of low worker morale as the agribusinesses. In the Dez

River area, peasants had given up an average of 10 hectares, on which they realized a dividend of $380 equivalent in 1972–73 (Salamanzadeh and Jones 1981:204–5); they also felt loss of status in being no longer property owners (Hooglund 1982:86).

There is much evidence, furthermore, that the corporate farms produced *less* per hectare than had the peasants. Citing a study by Moghadam (1978), Katouzian (1981b:309) reports that medium-size farms (size not given) showed significantly higher productivity than corporate farms, which themselves performed somewhat better than agribusinesses. *Peasants were performing better even though they had poorer land and less credit than the agribusinesses.* The difference—according to Katouzian—lies between peasants on their own land and peasants requisitioned to labor for others on land that had once been theirs. One of the farm cooperatives studied by Moghaddam (Shams-Abad in Khuzistan) had less output in the mid-seventies than it did in 1960 when the land had been farmed and managed by peasants. Its output was also low compared with surrounding villages (Katouzian 1981b:310).

Government Investment

With funds of its own to invest in agriculture, the government had a choice: it might have supplied technical assistance and credit to others, or it might have invested directly itself. We have already seen that credit was increasingly concentrated in corporations and agribusinesses, to the neglect of peasants. The government also directed funds toward large-scale projects, mainly dams, under its own control. How well did these fare?

Total government investment is shown in Table 7 by plan periods, in

Table 5.7

GOVERNMENT INVESTMENT BY PLAN PERIODS
(IN MILLIONS OF RIALS)

Plan Period	Agriculture/Irrigation		Mining/Industry	
	Amount	Percent	Amount	Percent
First plan; 1949–55	5.7	40.4	4.1	29.1
Second plan; 1956–62	17.4	20.9	7.0	8.4
Third plan; 1963–67	47.3	23.1	17.1	8.4
Fourth plan; 1968–72	41.2	8.1	113.1	22.3
Fifth plan; 1973–78	30.9	6.6	84.0	18.0

SOURCE: Afshar (1981:1101, Table 2). Percentage is of total government investment in each plan period; other sectors account for the remainder up to 100%.

which agriculture is compared with mining and industry. The data reflect a concentration on agriculture during the first three plan periods up until 1967, followed by a sharp shift to industry and mining after 1968.

The investment until 1972 consisted primarily of twelve major dams, very costly and with dubious payoff (Baldwin 1967: 83). In the early sixties, fifty years were estimated for the Dez River dam project to pay off its investment through increased output from irrigation. By contrast, small-scale pump irrigation was showing a payoff in three to four years. After 1967, the government apparently abandoned all hope of promoting peasant agriculture; virtually all its expenditures were directed to major projects.

Terms of Trade for Agriculture

Despite its verbal concern for peasant incomes, the government subsidized urban consumers at the expense of farmers: "From 1970 to 1975 agricultural production costs rose by 300% but farm prices increased by only 50%" (Afshar 1981:1104). In 1974, the government started to subsidize food imports in order to keep urban prices low. The subsidized imports, of course, competed against local peasant output.

Charged with keeping prices stable for consumers, the Cereals Organization turned increasingly to imports in the early seventies (Table 8). By 1974, imports amounted to over 20% of the total wheat supply. Partly because of this, domestic purchases expanded rapidly in 1975, when the organization also purchased 8% of domestic production.

While these imports would compete against peasant production, thus depressing the market price received by peasants, the Cereals Organization was presumably protecting the peasants through the minimum prices it offered. But these prices did not help them, for three reasons. First, the organization would announce prices in mid-harvest, after many poor peasants had sold their crops to wholesalers (who were thus the only ones to benefit). Second, the organization would not buy all wheat offered at the minimum price; in fact, it bought very little (Table 8). Third, during the middle and late seventies, the minimum price was frequently below the cost of production.

Effects on Agricultural Output

Thus the government bias against small-scale farmers surfaced on many fronts: credit was steered away from agriculture into mining and industry, and within agriculture, away from small to larger farms; farm management was taken out of the peasants' hands and given to cooperatives, which the peasants did not control; lands that peasants received in the reform were expropriated and handed over to corporations and agribusinesses, whose productivity turned out to be less than that of peasants;

98

Table 5.8
Total Wheat Production and Purchases by Cereal Organization, 1958–75 (Tons)

Year	Total Wheat Production (1)	Annual Domestic Purchase by C.O. (2)	Annual Import by C.O. (3)	(2) as % of (1) (4)	Stock at Year End (5)
1958	3,040,000	101,119	62,000	3.3	134,363
1959	2,840,000	36,462	13,300	1.3	20,538
1960	2,923,657	12,952	479,000	0.4	37,453
1961	2,869,119	127,353	159,000	4.4	48,304
1962	2,754,740	56,007	133,000	2.0	58,440
1963	2,468,140	133,867	130,000	5.4	110,065
1964	2,622,578	7,061	554,400	0.3	26,461
1965	3,647,713	15,504	239,900	0.4	89,004
1966	4,380,920	196,770	228,600	4.5	232,461
1967	4,618,368	246,270	86,000	5.3	364,637
1968	4,672,000	244,713	500	5.2	302,367
1969	4,200,000	9,331	23,000	0.2	209,638
1970	3,800,000	3,984	650,000	0.1	19,720
1971	3,500,000	5,000	414,500	0.1	na
1972	5,545,700	3,000	156,000	0.1	na
1973	4,600,000	106	800,000	0.0	na
1974	4,700,000	85	1,350,000	0.0	na
1975	5,500,000	450,000	na	8.2	na

SOURCE: Aresvik (1976:144, Table 7.6).

na = not available.

99

government imports competed unfairly against peasants; and government price policy turned against them as well.

According to official data, agricultural output increased at an overall rate of 3.7% from 1959–60 to 1970–72. This average rate even increased after the land reform, from 3.1%, 1959–61 to 1965–67, to 4.4%, 1965–67 to 1970–72 (Aresvik 1976:51, Table 3.8). With population increasing about 2.9% per year, the per capita annual increment went up from 0.2% to 1.2%. Although these increases are far from enough to feed the Iranian people well, they are "par for the course" for the Third World, whose governments are for the most part biased against agriculture. However, it is not an appropriate record for a country with the immense oil income of Iran, which *should* have the means to feed its people well.

Furthermore, there is reason to suspect the data. The jump in output claimed in such a short period is not likely in the absence of unusual events (such as planting of new varieties or changes in weather or climate). Some scholars discount the growth completely, arguing that annual increments remained in the neighborhood of 3.0% (Afshar 1981:1097) throughout the sixties and seventies (until the Khomeini revolution); if that is correct, output was barely keeping up with population growth.

The rapidity with which peasants were migrating to cities provides another reason to suspect the data. Only in rapidly industrializing countries (such as Taiwan and South Korea) do we expect that ever-smaller proportions of the people will feed the entire nation. In other countries, such as Iran, we suspect that an absolute decline in farm labor is associated with either a decline or little increase in farm output. The employment data are shown in Table 9. Numbers in agriculture declined from 3,672 thousand in 1962–63 to 3,200 thousand in 1977–78, while relatively they dropped from 55.1% to 32.2% of the employed population.

Even if the overall data are correct, however, the improvement in yields applies more to luxury market crops (sugar beets, cotton, and tobacco) than it does to basic crops (wheat, barley, and rice), which the peasants grow and from which they take their subsistence. Table 10 shows that the increase in wheat yield, 1965–74, is statistically negligible, that of rice very small, while barley yields fell. The commercial crops whose yield increased are probably those grown on medium-sized rather than small-sized farms. In addition to sugar beets, cotton, tea, and tobacco (shown in Table 10), these would include sugar cane, oilseeds, onions, and other vegetables.

Village Studies

All the above discussion has been of a "macro" style. Do micro-investigations in village economies tell a similar story?

Nasria, Fars Province

Before the reform, Nasria was a comparatively wealthy village of 3,000 irrigated hectares, whose peasants grew mostly wheat, barley, melons,

Table 5.9
Sectoral Distribution of Total Labor Force, 1962–78 (in Thousands)

Sector	1962–63		1967–68		1972–73		1977–78	
	Number	Percent	Number	Percent	Number	Percent	Number	Percent
Agriculture	3,672	55.1	3,861	49.0	3,600	40.9	3,200	32.2
Industry	1,372	20.6	1,947	24.7	2,550	29.0	3,300	33.2
Services	1,584	23.8	2,020	25.7	2,600	29.5	3,379	34.0
Oil	36	0.5	46	0.6	50	0.6	60	0.6
Totals	6,664	100.0	7,874	100.0	8,800	100.0	9,939	100.0

SOURCE: Katouzian (1981b:259, Table 13.2).

101

Table 5.10
YIELDS OF MAIN CROPS, 1961-74
(100 KILOS PER HECTARE)

	1961-65	1965-68	1969-71	1972	1974
Wheat	8.0	8.1	7.5	8.2	8.1
Barley	7.9	9.4	7.8	6.6	6.7
Rice	29.1	31.3	26.9	31.8	30.8
Sugar beets	na	217.9	241.3	280.8	228.8
Cotton	na	13.6	14.7	19.5	18.7
Tea	na	28.8	26.1	na	na
Tobacco	na	10.5	11.5	12.0	na

SOURCE: Arsvik (1976:50).

and sugar beets for the market. Its experience under the land reform was studied by Craig (1978).

Before 1964, two-thirds of the village was administered as *waqf* property, whose authority was in Shiraz, 40 kilometers away. Tenants paid cash rents to that authority through the village headman. The remaining third was owned by an absentee landlord named Saljadi, who received 50% of the output. He appointed the village headman (who also served for *waqf* land).

Under the land reform, which came to the village only with Phase II in 1964, the *waqf* land was assumed by the Ministry of Awqif (i.e., the ministry for *waqf* lands), which signed ninety-nine-year leases with current tenants. Saljadi chose to divide his lands half and half with tenants, he keeping the more productive part (500 hectares). The peasants protested this arrangement with a sitdown strike, but the central authorities—still culturally distant from peasants—sided with Saljadi.

The immediate effect of the reform was an increase in landlessness. Earlier, 95% of the village families had been tenants. But on the half of his lands that he retained, Saljadi dispossessed tenants of their rights to leasehold, taking them back only as hired laborers. This arrangement affected 40% of the families. The average income of these landless peasants was only 4/9 that of those who had obtained land.

The main beneficiaries, it appeared, were the village headman, along with twenty-one of his relatives and friends. This group had previously farmed from 22 to 90 hectares each, whose produce was shared with the landlord. The reform made them outright owners of a total of 500 hectares. Five of them immediately leased their land to landless peasants and moved to the city.

Of course, a cooperative was organized in the village, with each member required to buy shares. Landless peasants were excluded. Shareholders would elect an executive council every three years, which would be directed by the village headman. The cooperative would transport crops; provide agricultural inputs at discount prices; maintain public areas that had previously belonged to the landlord: collect a 2% income tax; provide credit; and arrange for local sale of members' produce. In the event, it could not collect the income tax, nor could it arrange credit. Except for selling inputs at discount prices, it was moribund by 1973. Craig (1978) cites three reasons.

First, he points to little contact between cooperative officials and central government. Second, because the cooperative now acted as village government, a substantial portion of peasants—the landless—were unrepresented in village affairs. Third, and most important, the cooperative was beset by corruption. When it ordered new pipes for the village bath, for example, kickbacks to contractors were widely suspected.

We would argue with Craig's first reason, that the government was too little involved. Our experience is that central government is always too distant to manage effectively a credit and input program on a village level. Possibly, the greater the distance the better, so that the government does not *interfere*. Rather, the problem in Nasria seems to be entirely local: a village bureaucracy was empowered to make vital decisions, and a large portion of the peasants was effectively disenfranchised. These events together opened an opportunity for corruption at the expense of poorer peasants. This opportunity was seized by village elders.

Rahmat-Abad, Northern Kuzistan

In an anthropological study of the village of Rahmat-Abad (substitute name, real village) in Northern Khuzistan, Goodell (1975) discovered that investment had considerably increased after the reform, almost all of it supplied by the peasants themselves. The only aid from the government had consisted of two tractors, replacing oxen. Cropping patterns had changed: spring and summer vegetables, not grown before the reform because of the landlord's whim for watermelons, were now planted in rows. These and other innovations were peasant-initiated.

By contrast, the government-sponsored "agricultural demonstrations" had not succeeded. For example, villagers following "expert" advice to fertilize cucumbers heavily found that although their yields increased, their costs went up more, and they ended up in debt.

Goodell attributed the different successes of villagers to the amount and quality of labor, far more than to capital and land. One of the most efficient farmers, she found, was the one with the least land. She concluded that "size of holding, in itself, as an isolated factor is relatively meaningless" (Goodell 1975:256). Irrigation was conceived as a skilled occupation more than as a supply of capital, requiring a high degree of concentration and conscientious work. The "scientific" application of water to holdings

103

was—in the eyes of the villagers—that last process to be satisfactorily automated.

Family labor was more effective than hired labor, since, Goodell argues, it is easier to "exploit" one's own relatives than it is an outside employee. If there are payoffs in farming from the extra effort of family members, it would be hard for corporations to compete.

What Happened to the Buneh?

Once farming became organized by government cooperatives, corporations, and agribusinesses, the traditional methods of cooperation—such as the *buneh*—diminished. Although Craig (1978) found the *buneh* intact in the areas of his study, Hooglund (1981:202) reported that inequality of holdings had helped it disappear. Previously, the *buneh* was part of the hierarchical ladder that culminated in the landlord. Members shared—unequally—according to their ranks. With the reform, unequal holdings substituted for unequal shares, but the organization associated with the hierarchy was gone. Disputes dissolved many *bunehs*. In areas where landlords divided land with peasants, the latter were often left with subsistence plots, which could be farmed with family labor. The *buneh* seemed no longer needed.

Sometimes the *buneh* survived for a specific purpose, such as to distribute water among neighbors when their turn to use the irrigation system arrived. Isfahan peasants, for example, who had been migrating seasonally to Dezful for thirty years to cultivate summer cash crops in *bunehs* of twelve to fifteen men, contracted with local landholders or even agribusinesses to continue the same work (Salamanzadeh and Jones 1981:207–12). Each *buneh* was well organized, with division of labor and detailed discussion among members concerning methods.

Conclusion

Our glimpses of Iran suggest that agricultural productivity and output would have increased more, and its fruits would have been more equitably divided, if local organizations—such as the *buneh*—had achieved (through their own bargaining) successively greater access to modern marketing and credit, instead of being supplanted by government-sponsored cooperatives, corporations, and agribusinesses.

With its great oil wealth, the Pahlavi government of Iran eclipsed the peasants instead of embracing them. The land reform, so highly touted in the rest of the world, was undertaken by a central bureaucracy that despised the peasants, depreciated their capabilities, and undermined their efforts. When more foodstuffs were needed to feed the burgeoning urban population and artificial new industries, the shah's government looked to foreign sources, both to import the food and to come in and help grow it, rather than the peasants who had supplied Iran—successfully in the terms of each successive century—for 3,500 years.

The Revolution of 1978

Our story leads only to 1978, for in that year the information dribbles away. We do have some reports, however, mainly from Afshar (1981). Naturally, an Islamic government would return the *waqf* lands to the religion from which they had been confiscated. (What the shah gives, Khomeini can take away.) In March 1980, the government announced a policy of "land-to-the-tiller." Nowhere has it been applied, however, except in the case of farm corporations. In most of these, the peasants instantly expelled the management, carving up the land into individual plots. Agribusinesses are still under central government control, but many have been leased to individual cultivators. The two agricultural banks have been merged and instructed not to make loans over one million rials.

Overall, agricultural production has increased slowly, from an index of 107.54 in 1978 (1971-76 = 100) to 112.87 in 1982, while it declined, per capita, from 98.35 to 91.26 for the same period (FAO Yearbook 1983: Table 10). But just as we recall that the increase in output under the shah consisted primarily of luxury crops and not of those of basic needs, we now wonder whether the decrease means a reversal of this trend. Small-scale producers have shifted over to staple production in response to post-revolutionary price rises; thus the production of staples has increased. Ironically, a regime that has paid far less attention to agriculture than the shah's may have achieved an increase in basic necessities far beyond what he could have dreamed.

References

Afshar, H., 1981. "Agricultural Development Policies in Iran," *World Development,* vol. 9, no. 11/12: 1097-1108.

Amuzegar, Jahangir, 1977. *Iran, an Economic Profile,* Washington, D. C., Middle East Institute.

Aresvik, Oddvar, 1976. *The Agricultural Development of Iran,* New York, Praeger.

Baldwin, J., 1967. *Planning and Development in Iran,* Baltimore, Johns Hopkins University Press.

Craig, David, 1978. "The Impact of Land Reform on an Iranian Village," *Middle East Journal,* vol. 32:141-54.

Denman, D. R., 1978. "Land Reforms of Shah and People," in Lenczowski (1978).

Farmayan, Hafez F., 1971. "Politics During the Sixties: An Historical Analysis," in Ehsan Yar Shatar, ed., *Iran Faces the Seventies,* New York, Praeger.

Goodell, Grace, 1975. "Agricultural Production in a Traditional Village of Northern Khuzistan," *Marburger Geographische Schritten,* vol. 64.

Hooglund, E., 1981. "Rural Socioeconomic Organizations in Transition," in N. Kidd and M. Bonine, eds., *Continuity and Change in Iran,* Albany, State University of New York Press.

Hooglund, E., 1982. *Land and Revolution in Iran, 1960-1980,* Austin, University of Texas Press.

Iran, MLRRC (Ministry of Land Reform and Rural Cooperation), 1970. "Central Organization for Rural Cooperatives (CORC): A Summary Report," December.

Jafari, Abdolhamid, 1980. "Social Change and Development in an Iranian Village," Ph.D. dissertation, Claremont Graduate School.

Katouzian, H., 1981a. "The Agrarian Question in Iran," Working Paper, Rural Employment Policy Research Program, International Labor Organization, World Employment Programme, 10/6.

Katouzian, H., 1981b. *The Political Economy of Modern Iran*, New York, New York University Press.

Lambton, Ann K. S., 1969. "Land Reform and Rural Cooperative Societies in Persia," *Royal Central Asian Journal*, vol. 56.

Lenczowski, George, ed., 1978. *Iran under the Pahlavis*, Stanford, Calif., Stanford University Press.

Moghadam, Fatemeh Etemad, 1978. "The Effects of Farm Size and Management System on Agricultural Production in Iran," Ph.D. thesis, Oxford University.

Najufi, Bahaeddin, 1978. "Farm Corporations in Iran: A Case Study," *Zeitschrift für Ausländische Landwirtschaft*, vol. 17, no. 1, January–March:38–45.

Platt, Kenneth, 1970. "Land Reform in Iran," *Spring Review*, Washington, D. C., Agency for International Development country paper.

Puchala, George, ed., 1979. *Food, Politics, and Agricultural Development: Case Studies in the Public Policy of Rural Modernization*, Boulder, Colo., Westview Press.

Salamanzadeh, C., 1980. *Agricultural Change and Rural Society in South Iran*, Cambridge, England, Middle East and North African Studies Press.

Salamanzadeh, C., and Jones, Gwyn E., 1979. "An Approach to the Micro Analysis of the Land Reform in Southwest Iran," *Land Economics*, vol. 55, no. 1:108–27.

Salamanzadeh, C., and Jones, Gwyn E., 1981. "Transformations in the Agricultural Structure of Southwest Iran," *Journal of Developing Areas*, vol. 15, no. 2:199–213.

Savory, Roger M., 1978. "Social Development in Iran during the Pahlavi Era," in Lenczowski (1978).

Schulz, Ann, 1979. "The Politics of Food Self Sufficiency in Iran," in Puchala (1979).

106

6. Egypt

In 14 A.D., with a population of 7 million people, Egypt was not only feeding itself but was exporting grain to most of Italy, with a population of 14 million, and the Roman Empire in Asia, with a population of another 14 million (Clark 1967:65). Although we do not know for sure, it would be reasonable to suppose that Egypt and other states of North Africa were feeding at least 35 million people and maybe as many as 45 million. By the mid-1980s, after two millennia of agricultural technology including the Green Revolution, after the High Dam had been constructed and was operating, and after the discovery of underground water had made new agricultural lands available farther from the Nile, Egypt was having difficulty feeding its own 45 million people. While the population was growing at 2.3% per year, value added in agriculture grew by only 1.7%. In 1970 Egypt imported 1.3 million metric tons of cereal grains and in 1978, 6 million tons, while in the same years, foreign trade in agricultural goods shifted from a surplus of $3 billion to a deficit of $13 billion (Richards 1982:211). Food riots in 1977 caused the government to rescind price increases and to renew subsidies, at enormous cost to its own budget. Why was agriculture so stymied?

No one knows for sure. However, a World Bank study (Ikran 1980) suggested that agricultural pricing policies were partly responsible for the recent stagnation in any event. We will go further, to propose that these policies were but a small part of the massive government intervention that bears the prime responsibility. In 1952, Egypt underwent a thorough land reform, which, with further distributions in later years, has been widely considered one of the world's most successful. Yet this reform became one of the instruments through which the government justified its intervention into the lives and prosperity of Egypt's farmers.

The Land Reform of 1952

The present landowning system is traceable to Muhammed Ali Pasha, Ottoman viceroy (1805–49) who became de facto independent, expropriated all landownings to the earlier Mamluk regime, becoming himself effectively the sole landholder with a monopoly over crop sales. Later, he distributed land and monopolies to his supporters. Except for some sales to outsiders, these and their descendants remained the principal landowners in Egypt right up to the reform of 1952. Inheritances divided the land, however, and considerable fragmentation occurred, especially in the first half of the twentieth century. In 1900, 761,000 farmers held plots averaging 1.46 feddans,* while in 1952, 2,642,000 held plots averaging 0.8 feddans (Richards 1982:211). With population growth, the number of landless households increased from 508,000 in 1929 (24% of all rural families) to 1,127,000 (44%) (Abdel-Fadil 1975:4). Yet large holdings remained. In 1950, 35% of cultivated land was still owned by 11,000 persons, or 0.4 of all landowners (Table 1).

Tenancy increased rapidly during the 1940s, from 17% of the land in 1939 to 61% in 1949 (Richards 1982:172–73). Richards suggests two reasons. First, the government intervened during World War II to ensure adequate grain. Wheat replaced cotton; deliveries were made compulsory. Unable to grow cotton, landlords were less interested in direct control of their estates. Second, the agitation for land reform after the war, with direct attacks on landlords, made the countryside less pleasant for them. Both these reasons induced landowners to rent their properties. Richards also sees a vicious circle: increased cash rents led to more violence, which led to more absentee tenancy subject to cash rental.

Whether this agrarian crisis motivated the Free Officer's Coup of 1952 is questionable (Waterbury 1983:264–65), but the prompt attention paid to land reform is a clear result. The Revolutionary Command Council designated one of its own members, Gamal Salim, to organize the drafting committee for the land reform law, and the first civilian prime minister, Ali Mahir, was dismissed, in part because he had opposed the draft law.

The land reform law of 1952, with its ceiling of 200 feddans per person or 300 feddans per family, destroyed the power of the rural elite. The Agrarian Reform Ministry estimated that 650,000 feddans would be eligible for new ownership. Landlords might choose which land they would keep and might sell their excess privately. Panic sales of 150,000 feddans caused further sales to be prohibited in 1953. By the end of 1956, 462,663 feddans had been expropriated, of which 187,000 were from 112 large holders and 60,000 from the erstwhile royal family (Saab 1967:20).

Still, the holdings of a large group of upperclass landlords had been left intact (Table 1). The authorities did not consider this a problem at the time, since the rent reduction clause would protect the tenants. This restricted rent to seven times the land tax, or a reduction of 20% to 35% of pre-1952 levels (Saab 1967:46). Writing in 1957, Warriner (1962:196–97) saw this as the most effective part of the law in redistributing income. However, by 1958–59, the tenancy provisions were a dead letter "as competition for land intensified and tenants participated to break the law."

Expropriated land was compensated by thirty-year, nonnegotiable bonds at 3% per annum interest. Value was placed at seventy times the

*The principal land measure in Egypt is the feddan, which equals 42.01 acres or 1.038 acres. Readers accustomed to English measures may think of a feddan as approximately one acre. In metric terms, it is approximately two-fifths of a hectare.

Table 6.1
DISTRIBUTION OF LANDOWNERSHIP

Holding Size (in feddans)	Landowners (000's)	Area Owned (000 feddans)	Percent Landowners	Percent Area Owned
Before 1952 Land Reform Law				
< 5	2,642	2,122	94.3	35.4
5–10	79	526	2.8	8.8
10–20	47	638	1.7	10.7
20–50	22	654	0.8	10.9
50–100	6	430	0.2	7.2
100–200	3	437	0.1	7.3
> 200	2	1,177	0.1	19.7
Total	2,801	5,984	100	100
After 1952 Land Reform Law				
< 5	2,841	2,781	94.4	46.5
5–10	79	526	3.6	8.8
10–20	47	638	1.6	10.7
20–50	30	818	1.0	13.7
50–100	6	430	0.2	7.2
100–200	3	437	0.1	7.2
> 200	2	354	0.1	5.9
Total	3,008	5,984	100	100

Table 6.1 (Continued)

Holding Size (in feddans)	Landowners (000's)	Area Owned (000 feddans)	Percent Landowners	Percent Area Owned
After 1961 Land Reform Law				
< 5	2,919	3,172	94.1	52.1
5–10	80	526	2.6	8.6
10–20	65	638	2.1	10.5
20–50	26	818	0.8	13.5
50–100	6	430	0.2	7.1
> 100	5	500	0.2	8.2
Total	3,101	6,084	100	100
Holdings in 1975				
< 5	3,190	2,769	95.0	49.7
5–10	92	617	2.7	11.1
10–20	44	586	1.3	10.5
20–50	23	682	0.7	12.2
50–100	7	520	0.2	9.3
> 100	2	398	0.1	7.1
Total	3,358	5,572	100	100

Source: Parker and Coyle (1981:12–13, Table 6).

land tax, which was probably one-half the market value (Abdel-Fadil 1975:8). By 1958 the reform law had become confiscatory (Saab 1967:24) because of payments spread out over forty years at 1.5% interest.

Between 1953 and 1959, 118,938 farmers, mostly former tenants, were allotted 337,782 feddans (Saab 1967:27), or an average of 2.8 feddans. They would pay the value described above in thirty equal installments, plus a 10% administrative charge. This provision was gradually eased until in 1974 payment was reduced to one-quarter the assessed value, and all government charges were dropped.

The Fifties: Consolidation of State Control

Early in 1953, the High Committee for Land Reform evolved into the Ministry of Land Reform, headed by Sayyid Marei. By paying higher salaries than the regular bureaucracy and by astute public relations, Marei turned his ministry into a personal fief (Springborg 1982:151), with gradually strengthened state control over both reform and non-reform zones. Marei was appointed chairman of the Agricultural Credit Bank in 1953 and Minister of Agriculture in 1957, when the Agriculture and Land Reform ministries were merged. In 1960, full authority over agricultural cooperatives outside the reform zones was transferred to that ministry from the Ministry of Social Affairs. Marei continued in his post until 1961.

Redistribution was conducted slowly, district by district, so that often a number of years passed between expropriation and final distribution. The bureaucracy operated on three levels. On the operational level, blocs of expropriated land of 200 to 1,000 feddans were each assigned to a *zira'at* (agricultural unit), under an agronomist known as *nazir al-zira'a*, appointed by the government. Ten to fifteen *zira'ats* came under a regional administrative center (*mantiga*). The head of the *mantiga*, known as the *mandub*, managed these estates until they were distributed. He was assisted by a large staff of clerks, agonomists, and field workers. Finally, in Cairo, every aspect of estate management and distribution came under the tight financial control of the land reform bureaucracy.

Every *zira'at* was divided into three consolidated plots immediately upon acquisition, with triennial crop rotation. The consolidation was justified by economies of scale and ease in pesticide use, although these were only asserted, not demonstrated. Each prospective beneficiary was assigned one parcel in each plot, so as to have adequate subsistence crops at all times.

In these ways, the bureaucracy became the ultimate managers of Egyptian farming. This control, however, was consolidated through agricultural credit. Credit in both cash and kind (seeds and fertilizer) was extended to all reform beneficiaries by the Agricultural Credit Bank via the *mandub*, on condition (at Marei's insistence) that beneficiaries agree to deliver cash crops to the government marketing centers. The *nazir al-zira'a*

111

and his assistants would see that this in fact happened. Control was facilitated through the compulsory land consolidation.

When beneficiaries received their titles, they were required to agree that: (1) they would follow the advice of the agronomist; (2) they would join the local cooperative; (3) they would sign an agreement to purchase all inputs from the cooperative and dispose of all produce through cooperative channels; and (4) they would settle the entire purchase price before mortgaging or selling their properties. Saab (1967:48–9) observed that these requirements led the peasants to refer to themselves as rent-paying tenants, not landowners amortizing their purchases. Since many of the agronomists were employees of the old landlords, their confusion is not surprising.

Local cooperatives were established in each *zira'at*, each with a board of directors formally elected by all beneficiaries. This board appointed a manager (*mushrif ta'awuni*) as cooperative manager. This manager—usually the former *nazir al-zira'a*—was in fact designated by the central land reform administration in Cairo. In no case was the administration's "recommendation" ever turned down by the local cooperative. Upon land distribution, the *mantiga* became the Agricultural Cooperative Society (ACS), and the *mandub* its supervisor.

The local cooperatives provided agricultural credit, equipment and inputs (fertilizer, seeds, etc.), and marketing. They paid the farmers after deduction for land purchases, taxes, and cooperative loans. They also enforced the crop rotation and maintained the irrigation and drainage ditches. The *mushrif* spent much of his time collecting debts to the cooperative and selling crops. The beneficiaries used the same term to refer to the *mushrif* as they had for the agents of the old landlord.

The ACS under the *mandub* had approximately the same powers and functions as the *mantiga*s before the redistribution. They provided the credit to the local cooperatives; they ran the bulk warehouses for storage of fertilizer and seed; they maintained the main irrigation and drainage ditches; and they sold in bulk for the local cooperatives.

At the national level, the organization became more complex. A General Cooperative Society (GCS) presumably provided local and regional cooperatives with some voice in decisions on the national level, but the Ministry of Land Reform made sure that this representation was nominal.

The GCS had ten separate departments in Cairo, with overlapping responsibilities. "The administrative machinery had become topheavy and inflexible" (Saab 1967:65). Financial operations and transactions were bogged down in paper work and permissions. For example, a cooperative's contribution to funeral expenses took several months for approval.

Marei's campaign to add the non-reform cooperatives to his fief stemmed from an experiment by the Ministry of Agrarian Reform in Nawag—a village in the delta—in 1955. Here the ministry wanted to introduce the same triennal rotation and land consolidation (Saab

1967:149) through revitalization of existing cooperatives. Farmers were lured into the cooperatives with the promise of fertilizer and cotton seed on credit at official prices, which were 30% to 40% below black market prices. Credit would be granted to both landowners and tenants, who would join the cooperative by buying one share for E£1.

Repayment was mainly through sales to private wholesalers under official supervision. Some peasants were asked to sign documents before the tax collector, recognizing themselves as custodians of their own crops. Presumably these documents would diminish the probability of unofficial sale, which would interfere with repayment in kind. In the first year there was no trouble with repayment.

In the 1956-57 crop year, consolidated crop rotation was introduced, but not without difficulty. The incentives for the farmers were threefold. First, they were told that a powerful new insecticide could be used safely only on large blocs of land. Second, ample credit in cash and in kind would be provided. Third, in the autumn at the end of the season, loans valued at 80% of the cotton crop would be available so that farmers would not have to sell at the low harvest price. The difficulty was that small farmers were accustomed to plant food and fodder, for themselves and draft animals, on parts of their plots. The cropland consolidation would frequently place all the land of a farmer in the crop area. The farmers were encouraged to barter land, food, or fodder among themselves to compensate. The yield increase for cotton, 58% in that year, seemed to justify the experiment.

Still, there were some qualifications. The authorities continually complained that peasants resold fertilizer and seed on the black market. To counter this, they declared that insecticide charges would be proportional to the amount of fertilizer and seed loaned in kind. In addition, by 1959-60 the triennial crop rotation had become biased toward cotton, planted on 40% of the land. Finally, lack of storage prevented bulk sales of cotton through the cooperative at Nawag. While recognizing these problems, Saab (1967:196) nevertheless called the experiment a success because of the "dedication and faith of the professional technicians."

Marei gradually absorbed the entire agricultural sector under his personal jurisdiction. Citing the Nawag experiment in cabinet meetings in 1959, he first urged that the same strategy be pursued among cooperatives controlled by the Ministry of Social Affairs and that those cooperatives be transferred to the Ministry of Agriculture. He won on both counts (Springborg 1982:152-53). After the cooperatives had been transferred in the autumn of 1960, the land consolidation program moved into high gear. With Minufiya province selected for the first big push, 103 villages were brought under the program in 1961 (Saab 1967:149).

Marei's plan to extend the Nawag model to the entire country was facilitated by investment of the Agricultural and Cooperative Credit Bank (ACCB) with monopoly powers. In the late 1950s, this bank had started a supervised agricultural credit program. Funds had been allocated to village cooperatives under the land reform, to be distributed to their members on the basis of expected yields; in practice, however, an official of the bank approved the credit allocation made by the cooperatives. In 1959, 2,046 village cooperatives (under the Ministry of Social Affairs) operated under this system. In 1960, the system was further extended, and by 1961 all organized agricultural credit to cooperatives flowed from the Agricultural and Cooperative Credit Bank (Saab 1967:149).

In January 1961, this system was expanded to include the non-land-reform zone as well. Now, each village cooperative was to be headed by a new board of directors limited to resident farmers. An agronomist appointed by the Ministry of Agriculture played essentially the same role as the *mushrif* in the land-reform cooperatives: he would push cooperative marketing and land consolidation, with his salary and bonus depending on his success in so doing.

The village cooperatives were grouped by districts into agricultural cooperative societies (ACS); all the district cooperatives into a central cooperative society for the province; and all twenty-one provincial cooperatives became affiliated with the General Cooperative Organization of the nation. Not surprisingly, the committee heading the last was itself headed by the minister of Land Reform and Agriculture. Since this committee was also responsible for the land-reform GCS, the ACCB, the Fertilizer Price Stabilization Fund, and all training institutes for cooperatives, all the decisions for Egypt's farming, from the most broad supervisory activities down to the last detail of what crop would be planted on what land, and what technology was to be used, in principle fanned downward from the office of one man.

First to be organized under the new plan were the 103 villages of Minufiya Province, where the consolidation had begun. The monopolization of supply of agricultural inputs by the ACCB and its 100% distribution through the agricultural cooperatives caused by a very rapid expansion in their number and membership (Table 2). Thus the cooperation of peasants was more easily obtained. Over the next three years, the crop consolidation program was extended to the rest of the country.

The Land Reform of 1961 and Nasser's Industrial Drive

Nasser's nationalization drive of July 1961 included a "more drastic" land reform (law 127 of 1961). The new ceiling was 100 feddans per person. Saab (1967:175) believes that the new cooperative and credit organizations and the crop consolidation campaigns were preconditions for this reform. Earlier, reform officials had opposed further expropriation for fear that more fragmentation would lead to lower productivity. Without the organizations and the consolidation, Saab argued, it might have been difficult to integrate the smaller properties into cooperatives run by resident *mushrifs*.

But the distributions were not great enough to validate Saab's fear.

Table 6.2
GROWTH OF COOPERATIVES

	No. of Co-ops	Members (millions)
1952	1,727	0.5
1962	4,624	1.78
1965	4,921	2.36
1967	4,879	2.70
1970	5,049	2.83
1972	5,008	3.11

SOURCE: Waterbury (1982:286); Abdel-Fadil (1975:85).

While the per capita ceiling was 100 feddans, a family might own 300 feddans. Only 100,745 feddans were distributed to 48,823 beneficiaries (Abdel-Fadil 1975:10). Additional laws in 1957 and 1962 distributed *waqf* land (belonging to religious trusts), and further expropriations occurred during the 1960s. Still, the combined impact of all activity after the 1952 reform, up to 1978, was to redistribute "about 13% of the cultivated land to about 10% of the rural population" (Waterbury 1983:267). As of 1978 approximately one million feddans had been redistributed (Table 3).

It is not clear whether Marei had initially embarked on a quest for complete power, or whether this just happened once events had been set in motion. Nor is it clear that he had intended to squeeze the agricultural sector. Nevertheless, after Marei had been forced from office in the fall of 1961, the system he had developed became the mechanism by which the peasants paid and paid and paid, to finance Nasser's industrial drive (Springborg 1982:157–58).

The Squeeze System

Thus by the early sixties, the Egyptian government had drawn up a system of complete state control over agricultural inputs, and through this system it had extended its control to the marketing of all traditional crops. It then moved on to cotton, whose trade was nationalized through the State Egyptian Cotton Organization (SECO) in 1961.

The 103 villages of Minufiya Province were the locale for initiating compulsory delivery of cotton (euphemistically known as cooperative marketing) during the 1962–63 crop season. This system was spread to the rest of the country hand-in-hand with the reorganized cooperative system (Table 4). From 1961 to 1964, SECO set the price for ginned cotton from the mills. After 1964, the price was set at the farm before ginning. From 1964 on, SECO was setting targets for type and variety of long-staple cotton produced each year, while the Ministry of Agriculture was allocating

115

Table 6.3

REDISTRIBUTION OF LAND

Law 178 (1952), first land reform	450,305	feddans
Law 152 (1957), taking over public use of land	110,451	
Law 127 (1961), second land reform	214,132	
Law 44 (1962), taking over private use of land	38,336	
Law 15 (1963), prohibition of ownership of agricultural land by foreigners	61,910	
Law 150 (1964), transferring sequestered property to public ownership	45,516	
Co-op purchases of land	25,807	
Land transferred to agrarian reform agency by organizations	25,979	
Law 50 (1969), reducing individual ownership ceiling to 50 feddans	30,000 ?	
Total	1,002,436	
Land returned on legal appeal	72,837	
Net takeover	930,299	
Distributed as of 1967	754,487	

SOURCE: Waterbury (1983:266).

quotas. These quotas were enforced through village cooperatives, which in turn set quotas for members. Penalties were enforced on members not complying (Cuddihy 1980:85). By 1965–66 the entire cotton crop was under central control.

These compulsory deliveries were one of the primary vehicles by which the government has taxed agriculture, although the tax was mitigated by government provision of fertilizer below world prices. Cuddihy's (1980:95–6) measures of effective protection for the principal crops of Egypt from 1965 to 1976 help us assess the burden of the tax, net of fertilizer discounts (Table 5). An effective protection rate of less than 100% is no protection at all; rather, the difference between the (lesser) rate and 100% constitutes a "tax." Thus during the late sixties and early seventies the tax on cotton was approximately 35%. But when the world price of cotton rose in 1973–74, the tax shot upward to between 40% and 60%. The predictable farmer response was to try to escape the cotton quota, by shifting acreage to more profitable crops. The high negative protection in all these years caused cotton acreage to slip from an average of 1.76 million

Table 6.4
PERCENTAGE OF COOPERATIVE MARKETING
(COMPULSORY DELIVERY)

	Cotton	Rice	Onions	Wheat
1962–63[a]	17			
1963–64[a]	42			
1964–65[a]	60		36	
1965–66[a]	100	50	31	
1966–67[a]	100	52	29	
1967–68[a]	100	48	33	
1968–69[a]	100	47	46	
1969–70[a]	100	49	28	1965–70:
1970[b]	100	68	57	Average 27.6%
1971[b]	100	68	57	
1972[b]	100	68	57	
1973[b]	100	68	57	
1974[b]	100	68	57	
1975[b]	100	67	57	
1976[b]	100	65	57	
1977[b]	100	67	57	
1978[b]	100	65	57	

[a]SOURCE: Abdel-Fadil (1975:86–87).
[b]SOURCE: Korayem (1982).

feddans in 1950–54 to 1.59 million in 1965–69; 1.55 million in 1970–74; and 1.30 million in 1975–78 (Table 6). The richer farmers in particular found it profitable to pay penalties rather than plant cotton (Ikran 1980:414).

Because rice was required for urban food subsidies, compulsory delivery quotas were established in 1965–66, with enforcement at the cooperative level. Because of increased irrigation from the High Dam, acreage planted in rice increased rapidly in the late sixties and early seventies (Table 6). However, the "tax" became severe during the mid-seventies (100% minus effective protection rates in Table 5), and leakage onto the black market became uncontrollable. Small farmers suffered especially; after meeting their quotas at confiscatory prices, they had to buy rice at higher (black market) prices in order to feed their families (Ibrahim 1982:205).

Wheat production was not taxed, although compulsory delivery quotas of between 25% and 40% had been imposed (Cuddihy 1980:90–2). The effective protection coefficients imply a slight subsidy during the years studied (Table 6). Various other crops were also subject to compulsory

Table 6.5
EFFECTIVE PROTECTION COEFFICIENTS, 1967–76

	Cotton	Wheat	Rice
1967	0.62	1.10	0.62
1968	0.65	1.30	0.71
1971	0.62	1.10	1.43
1972	0.71	1.10	1.62
1973	0.54	0.80	0.68
1974	0.36	0.80	0.18
1975	0.44	1.30	0.27
1976	0.68	1.30	0.53

SOURCE: Cuddihy (1980; various tables: cotton, p. 88; wheat, p. 92; rice, p. 97).

delivery (sugar, onions, groundnuts, sesame, and more), but vegetables and fruits were exempt (Cuddihy 1980:106; Korayam 1982:177–81). Table 6 shows the consequences, in increased plantings of vegetables and orchards.

Cuddihy (1980:116–17) calculated that for the crop year 1974–75, the compulsory crop and food subsidy systems had transferred E£1,200 million away from farmers, of which E£1,021 million benefited consumers and E£179 million the state (Table 7). Although noting a possible error in his findings, he nevertheless concludes that

> the agricultural sector has been significantly discriminated against and has contributed substantially to domestic savings via state management of the agricultural non-agricultural terms of trade. Yet the social costs of the transfer appear unnecessarily high due to the relative failure of the industrialization program.

Hansen and Nashashibi (1975:193) estimate that the misallocation of cultivated land caused by the price distortions was about 8% of the total. They calculate that this in turn may have decreased the growth rate by one or two percentage points.

Were government price policies or lack of investment responsible for the poor performance of agriculture? Using econometrics to estimate the price elasticity of cotton at 3.75, Antle and Aitah (1986) argue that low cotton prices contributed to the decline in output. Using a systemwide model of production for six governates (52% of crop value), Esfahani (1987a,b) concludes that decreases in investment and drainage are the culprits. Both studies may be right. Either explanation would be consistent with peas-

118

Table 6.6
AREA OF MAIN CROPS (IN THOUSANDS OF FEDDANS)

	Cotton	Rice	Wheat	Berseem	Maize	Vegetables	Orchards
1950–54	1,765	505	1,571	2,184	1,746	70	94
1955–59	1,791	641	1,501	1,362	1,850	104	114
1960–64	1,751	791	1,387	2,444	1,727	149	147
1965–69	1,594	1,028	1,268	2,630	1,510	170	208
1970–74	1,551	1,095	1,362	2,801	1,593	184	255
1975–78	1,302	1,051	1,344	2,801	1,846	214	313

SOURCE: Ikram (1980: 414).

Table 6.7

CONSUMER AND PRODUCER TRANSFERS ON MAJOR CROPS,
1974–75 (NET OF INPUT SUBSIDIES, IN £E MILLIONS AT
PARALLEL EXCHANGE RATES)

Crop	Producer Transfer	Consumer Transfer	Transfer to State
Rice	−562	+518	+44
Wheat	−78	+334	−256
Cotton	−254	+122	+132
Sugar	−400	+40	+360
Maize	−120	+249	−129
Meat	+214	−242	+28
Total	−1,200	+1,021	+179

SOURCE: Cuddihy (1980:117).

ants' responses to a system that constrains their potential profit and individual decisionmaking.

The massive transfer from farmers to consumers and state was made possible by the land reform and the government agencies that followed it; these created central control and monopoly over agriculture. But the agencies also had profound effects on peasant interaction with government, with each other, and with the rest of society, all of them to the advantage of rich peasants and the disadvantage of poor, to which we turn in the next section.

Rich Peasants Favored over Poor

Massive intervention by the central government not only distorted agricultural production away from needed crops and into subsidized ones, but discriminated more against smallholders than against large. The central government shared its political benefits with a local rural élite, namely richer peasants (with holdings of 10 to 50 feddans) who dominated the village cooperatives. Mayfield (1971:163) reported that a single family often dominated all important posts in a village, including the cooperative board. He argues that the revolutionary rhetoric about "feudalism" in the countryside in 1965–66 and the attendant sequestration of land illegally held by this élite (90,000 feddans) is evidence that the élite existed (since the land could be taken from them), while Waterbury (1983:266) argues that the return of all this land to them after the 1967 war is evidence of their power. Before 1969, the intent was that owners of less than 5 feddans would constitute 80% of the cooperative board. However, these small peasants often depended on larger neighbors for the rent or more land and for credit (Richards 1982:182).

In the 1969 law, this ceiling was raised to 15 feddan, and the requirement was added that the peasants should be literate. This requirement is, we argue, another instance of both the cultural arrogance of élites in confusing illiteracy with ignorance, and the use of a literacy requirement to justify assumption of power by themselves.

Among the many ways by which the local élites escaped the constraints of the cooperative was their exemption from crop consolidation. Most of the smaller landowners possessed holdings in only one bloc: 55% to 100% of them, depending on the village, according to Ibrahim (1982:199–200):

> They could not diversify their crops and their sources of income, and they were obliged to purchase many commodities on the open market. . . . [In cotton years] they experienced a shortage of cereals. . . . The low return . . . from cotton cultivation left them with little money to buy cereals. . . . Related is the shortage of winter and summer fodder for livestock. This led to premature sale of calves at considerable loss.

By owning lands in different blocs, the large landowners escaped the onus of crop consolidation. Ibrahim (1982:232, n. 8) confirmed this point in his field study but also presented evidence that it applied throughout the country. Of further advantage to these large landowners was the fact that they might sell cereals and fodder to small landholders who were short.

Large landowners also had differential access to all inputs. An exchange-rate subsidy on farm machinery equipment benefits "large producers who are to dominate the use of cooperative tractors to the exclusion of smaller farmers." Preferential treatment for the former results from a "fixed hire rate (below cost) plus an official gratuity to the driver and the accompanying cooperative official" (Cuddihy 1980:76).

Furthermore, large landowners had easier access to subsidized credit than did smallholders. From 1961 to 1965, no interest was charged on loans by ACCB (Agriculture Cooperative Credit Bank). After 1965, landowners with more than ten feddans had to pay 4% interest, but this discrimination *against* larger holders lasted only two years. After 1965, all holders paid 4.5% regardless of size of holding. Large holders were then favored in two ways. First, the average amount of credit per feddan—at subsidized rates, we recall—increased with the size of holdings, more so in 1978 than in 1960 (Table 8). Second, the incidence of delinquency—always a problem with all groups—was greater for large holders than for small (Waterbury 1983:288).

To gain more central control over both credit and deliveries, in 1967–68 the government denied loans in kind to cultivators with unpaid debts, and in 1975 they were denied for failure to deliver compulsory quotas (Ibrahim 1982:213–14). Each cooperative member was required to buy the recommended amount of fertilizer (subsidized) per cultivated feddan. But poor

Table 6.8
Agricultural Credit by Size of Holding, 1960 and 1978

Holding Category (feddans)	Borrowers		Area Served		Credits Offerd (£E million)[a]	Average Loan per Feddan (£E)
	% of Borrowers[a]	% of Landowners[b]	% of Area Served[a]	% of Total Cultivated[b]		
1960: Agricultural Credits Provided by ACCB						
< 5	68.9	94.4	28.10	46.5	6.36	8.02
5–10	16.6	3.6	15.7	8.8	4.16	9.56
> 10	14.5	2.0	56.2	44.7	16.87	10.77
Total	100.0	100.0	100.0	100.0	27.37	
1978: Agricultural Credit Provided by Banks of Development and AGI Credit						
< 5	93.2[c]	93.4[d]	64.7[c]	49.7[d]	71.07[c]	20.54[c]
5–10	4.4	4.2	14.5	11.1	19.44	25.16
> 10	2.4	2.3	20.8	39.2	35.84	32.16
Total	100.0	100.0	100.0	100.0	126.35	

[a]Source: Ibrahim (1982:212).
[b]Source: Parker and Coyle (1981: 12–13, Table 6).
[c]Source: Ibrahim (1982:219).
[d]Source: Parker and Coyle (1981: 12–13, Table 6, data for 1975).

peasants often had to sell their quotas to the rich in order to supply their immediate consumption (Richards 1982:182).

All peasants tried to shift out of low-return, compulsory-delivery crops, but this shift was more difficult for smallholders than for large. The latter tended to cheat at the margin, by planting vegetable crops between the rows and by transferring to non-approved crops fertilizer designated for cotton (Waterbury 1983:286).

Since credit for orchards would not be granted to landowners of under 5 feddans, large owners could shift more easily (than small) into higher-yielding fruits. The onus of producing vegetables therefore fell more heavily on smallholders (Table 9). The anomalous increase in fruits among holdings of less than one feddan is probably due to the small garden farms around cities (Zaytoun 1982:284).

The power of the rural élite was demonstrated in their successful defeat of a proposed land tax of E£20 per feddan in 1972. The incidence would, of course, have been greater on them than on smallholders (Abdel-Fadil 1975:25; Waterbury 1983: 293).

The terms of trade were a final way in which rich peasants were favored over poor. Table 10 shows the terms of trade for agriculture, separately for rich peasants and poor. These deteriorated for the latter during the early sixties, and during the first half of the seventies they merely recovered (roughly) their pre-1960 status. For the former, on the other hand, the terms of trade also deteriorated slightly in the early sixties but improved almost steadily from the mid-sixties on. One reason for this improvement was the subsidization of fertilizer, which affected rich peasants more than poor.

From all the above, Abdel-Fadil (1975: 25) concluded that

> all significant agrarian policy measures—whether technological or institutional—have tended to shift the center of economic gravity away from the old landed aristocracy and in favor of the new privileged stratum of rich peasants.

Corruption

When official prices are below those of the free market, the excess demand becomes a political commodity. "Insofar as a public institution controls the market, it then has control over this new value (the political commodity)" (Bates 1981:98). According to Bates, the illicit assumption of this value by public officials is financial corruption and its illicit allocation to others, in exchange for support, is political corruption. The quasi-cooperative structure in Egypt and the massive government intervention made both types possible, if not inevitable. We have seen how central government bureaucrats shared this political commodity with rural élites, probably because they had to in order to gain their support.

The many ways in which corruption is manifest are, however, difficult

Table 6.9
CROP MIX BY SIZE OF HOLDING (IN THOUSANDS OF FEDDANS)

Holding Groups (Feddans)		Field Crops		Vegetables		Fruits		
		Area	% Area	Area	% Area	Area	% Area	Total %
≤ 1	1961	380.3	95.7	12.5	3.1	4.8	1.2	100.0
	1977–78	1,447.0	86.8	151.1	9.1	69.5	4.1	100.0
> 1–3	1961	2,066.6	96.7	59.9	2.8	11.4	0.5	100.0
	1977–78	3,432.9	93.6	195.2	5.3	38.5	1.1	100.0
> 3–5	1961	1,748.7	96.4	55.5	3.1	8.8	0.5	100.0
	1977–78	1,926.2	90.8	165.2	7.8	30.8	1.4	100.0
> 5–10	1961	1,897.2	95.7	71.6	3.7	12.4	0.6	100.0
	1977–78	1,228.4	85.7	172.1	12.0	32.8	2.3	100.0
> 10	1961	4,015.0	93.3	186.6	4.3	103.7	2.4	100.0
	1977–78	1,840.5	82.8	231.4	10.4	150.4	6.8	100.0

SOURCE: Zaytoun (1982:284, Table 9.4).

Table 6.10
INDEXES OF TERMS OF TRADE FOR AGRICULTURAL SECTOR

	Poor Farmers			Rich Farmers		
	(1)	(2)	(3)	(1)	(2)	(3)
1960	100	100	100	100	100	100
1961	99	99	101	100	100	101
1962	88	96	68	90	99	70
1963	87	94	70	90	97	73
1964	94	100	78	100	107	83
1965	86	88	79	92	95	86
1966	93	94	89	105	106	101
1967	99	95	115	109	107	121
1968	98	92	120	106	102	124
1969	106	94	123	108	104	126
1970	99	98	104	111	111	111
1971	98	96	103	109	109	111
1972	98	95	109	113	111	120
1973	95	91	109	114	111	125
1974	98	93	116	118	115	132
1975	102	96	124	127	122	146

SOURCE: Richards (1982:206, Table 6.13).

(1) Overall Index of (Prices of Agricultural Output)/(Prices of All Manufactured Commodities).

(2) Index of (Prices of Agricultural Output)/(Prices of Manufactured Consumer Goods).

(3) Index of (Prices of Agricultural Output)/(Prices of Manufactured Inputs).

to describe and difficult to document. But when control over economic decisions that affect the livelihood of others is vested in a few individuals who are not accountable to the constituencies, very little business occurs without an unofficial gratuity (*bakshesh*) for the relevant functionary (Waterbury 1983:288). In this environment, Mayfield (1971:162) finds the *fellah* (poor peasant) and the bureaucracy essentially at odds. The *fellah* wants to maximize profits. To do so within the system of the sixties, he had to trick government officials, fake poverty, work through large landowners, and be unable to "visualize" cooperatives as beneficial institutions (Waterbury 1983:229).

In a major work on political rents—applicable generally (not just to Egypt)—Krueger (1974) argues that the very creation of such rents is inefficient, for resources become diverted into rents rather than the production of real goods and services. Cuddihy (1980:118) concludes that in Egypt

> the use of cooperatives to implement unpopular price administration has effectively destroyed the evolution of a genuine cooperative movement with proven advantages.

Widespread discontent with corruption in the cooperatives and difficulties in the compulsory delivery system forced the government to reorganize in 1976. Compulsory delivery quotas were dropped for almost all crops except cotton. The Federation of Agricultural Cooperatives was dissolved, with credit functions transferred to the 750 village banks of the National Agricultural Credit Bank. Officials of that bank expressed every intention of becoming a commercial bank, with loan repayment mortgaged by property guarantees (Waterbury 1983:285).

Adams (1986:345) shows that this move has only reinforced the power of the rich peasantry. He showed that in one rural district village banks supplied credit only for certain cash crops: sugar cane, cotton, and fruit:

> Such restrictive credit practices serve to bolster the local powers of the rich peasantry at the expense of those of the cooperative bureaucrats. . . . In the absence of any government credit for cultivating the main food crops . . . poor fellahin must still frequently turn to the wealthier village elements for aid.

Whatever the outcome, Egypt's poorer people have already suffered much from the stagnation of agriculture. Not only have the incomes of small farmers fallen, but city dwellers have rioted in recent years because of food shortages. Over a twenty-year period, Egypt's agricultural output per capita has declined (in real terms) at an average rate of 0.4% per year.

References

Abdel-Fadil, Mahmoud, 1975. *Development, Income Distribution and Social Change in Rural Egypt, 1952–1970,* Cambridge, Cambridge University Press.

Adams, Richard H., 1986. "Bureaucrats, Peasants, and the Dominant Coalition: An Egyptian Case Study," *Journal of Development Studies,* vol. 22, no. 2:336–54.

Antle, John M., and Aitah, Ali S., 1986. "Egypt's Multiproduct Agricultural Technology and Agricultural Policy," *Journal of Development Studies,* vol. 22, no. 4:709–23.

Bates, Robert H., 1981. *Markets and States in Tropical Africa,* Berkeley, University of California Press.

Clark, Colin, 1967. *Population Growth and Land Use,* London, MacMillan, and New York, St. Martin's Press.

Cuddihy, William, 1980. *Agricultural Price Management in Egypt,* Washington, D.C., World Bank, Staff Working Paper no. 388.

Esfahani, Hadi Salehi, 1987a. "Growth, Employment, and Income Distribution in Egyptian Agriculture, 1964–1979." *World Development*, September: 1201–17.

Esfahani, Hadi Salehi, 1987b. "Technical Change, Employment, and Supply Response of Agriculture in the Nile Delta: A Systemwide Approach," *Journal of Development Economics*, vol. 25: 167–96.

Hansen, B., and Nashashibi, K., 1975. *Foreign Trade Regimes and Economic Development*, vol. 4: *Egypt*, New York, Columbia University Press for the National Bureau of Economic Research.

Ibrahim, Ahmed H., 1982. "Impact of Agricultural Policies on Income Distribution," in Gonda Abdel-Khalek and Robert Tignor, eds., *The Political Economy of Income Distribution in Egypt*, New York, Holmes and Meier.

Ikran, Khalid, 1980. *Egypt: Economic Management in a Period of Transition*, Baltimore, Johns Hopkins University Press for the World Bank.

Korayem, Karima, 1982. "The Agricultural Output Pricing Policy and the Implicit Taxation of Agricultural Income," in Gonda Abdel-Khalek and Robert Tignor, eds., *The Political Economy of Income Distribution in Egypt*, New York, Holmes and Meier.

Krueger, Anna O., 1974. "The Political Economy of the Rent Seeking Society," *American Economic Review*, vol. 64, no. 3, June:291–303.

Mayfield, James B., 1971. *Rural Politics in Nasser's Egypt*, Austin, University of Texas Press.

Parker, John B., and Coyle, James R., 1981. "Urbanization and Agricultural Policy in Egypt," *Foreign Agricultural Economic Report*, no. 169, September.

Richards, Alan, 1982. *Egypt's Agricultural Development, 1800–1980: Technical and Social Change*, Boulder, Colo., Westview Press.

Saab, Gabriel, 1967. *The Egyptian Agrarian Reform 1952–1962*, London, Oxford University Press.

Springborg, Robert, 1982. *Family Power and Politics in Egypt*, Philadelphia, University of Pennsylvania Press.

Warriner, Doreen, 1962. *Land Reform and Development in the Middle East*, London, Royal Institute of International Affairs (originally published in 1957).

Waterbury, John, 1983. *Egypt under Nassar and Sadat: The Political Economy of Two Regimes*, Princeton, N.J., Princeton University Press.

Zaytoun, Mohaya A., 1982. "Income Distribution in Egyptian Agriculture," in Gonda Abdel-Khalek and Robert Tignor, eds., *The Political Economy of Income Distribution in Egypt*, New York, Holmes and Meier.

7. Bolivia

Countries where peasants are "given the land and left alone" are so rare that analysts must cherish each one, seeking its distinctive characteristics. We dub the Bolivian reform successful: land was divided into individual parcels; peasants formed their own marketing and credit institutions or expanded existing ones; agricultural output and peasant income increased. We do not know why the Bolivian government did not install the same oppressive measures we have seen elsewhere. Our guess is that it was too disorganized to do so. In a macro sense, the peasants have lost, just as all Bolivians have lost from the economic disaster of a disorganized government, but in a micro sense, they have gained from their freedom and mobility.

Although the state did not dominate the countryside after the revolution, some scholars have asserted that the ex-landlords and new middlemen have done so (Graef 1974). However, the influence of these varied with the region, and it was small in the major peasant zones. In the Altiplano, where 70% of the rural population lived in 1950, genuinely new forms of marketing arose. To examine how the peasants resisted ex-landlord influence after the land reform of 1953, we must analyze Bolivia by regions, starting with the years immediately preceding the reform.

The Altiplano: Pre-Reform Agricultural Production and Marketing

Before the 1953 reform, farmland on the Altiplano—12,000 to 14,000 feet high, where 70% of Bolivians lived—was concentrated in haciendas that had encroached on Indian lands in the nineteenth century. They were worked by resident Indians of the *colonato* system. In exchange for farming the central land (hereafter, *hacienda* land) certain days each week with no cash wage, each Indian (*colono*) family received a house and a small plot of land (hereafter *peasant* land), on which to grow its own food. Debt servitude, custom, fear of reprisal, and lack of alternative opportunity combined to make the *colonos* virtual serfs. Sales of haciendas usually included the number of Indian families resident.

Most *hacendados* (hacienda owners) lived in La Paz or other large cities, visiting their estates only for planting and harvesting. In addition to work on the hacienda, each peasant family served a week or two a year in the *hacendado's* city residence. When the *hacendados* bought trucks in the late 1940s, then, because transportation to market had been traditionally the job of *colonos*, the *hacendado* would charge them for their use, *even while they were delivering his own crops.*

Because hacienda land was farmed the same way as peasant land—with seed and equipment of peasants—the *hacendado* spent little cash (Clark 1968:156). Normally, he would leave administration in the hands of a deputy (*mayordomo*). Potatoes, other tubers, high-altitude cereals, and broad beans were grown for subsistence, the major cash crop being barley sold to the brewery in La Paz. The cash part of hacienda produce was sold at the landlord's private store in La Paz, while most peasant produce was consumed at home. Whatever little the peasant might have to sell would be taken to a local village market. Clark (1968:160) estimated that an average peasant family would acquire about $31 (U.S. 1966) worth of goods in the market per year, of which $8 was through barter, $23 in cash. It would buy almost no consumer durables or foodstuffs from other regions.

In the land reforms of many countries, scant peasant participation in the market is often cited as a reason for government assumption of marketing. Therefore, the experience of Bolivian peasants should be telling. Why did they participate so little before 1953?

Clark (1968:160) suggests two reasons. First, under the *colonato* system, almost all the agricultural surplus belonged to the *hacendado*. Second, the *hacendado* prohibited the peasant from producing or selling high-valued products (e.g., eggs) from his own plot. If the peasant did produce any, they belonged to the *hacendado*.

Why was marketing dualistic: one style for peasants, one for the *hacendado*? Knowledgeable observers agree that haciendas on the Altiplano were antiquated and inefficient: the *hacendado* appears not to have improved his income by switching to paid labor and cash marketing, nor to have increased his productivity by investing. Why?

Although the peasants did not market their own goods, they had much experience marketing those of the *hacendado*. Many had delivered hacienda crops to La Paz or Oruro and had worked in the *hacendado*'s store. A small but vigorous core of Aymara Indians (the dominant group on the Altiplano), for example, had long carried on trade with other regions in the country (Heyduk 1974:72–73). These skills were ready to serve an enlarged marketing system. Why was that system not generated long before 1953?

Economists pay little heed to these questions, and economic historians are puzzled by them. Yet they are understandable when we observe that many times in history—the Roman Republic and Empire, ancient Egypt, the eras of Minamoto Yoritomo in Japan and Ivan the Terrible in Russia, for but a few examples—élites had no sense of productivity improvement through investment and political organization. Indeed, such a novelty could come only through radical changes in the political and landholding systems, a concept that was both beyond the horizons of the élites and

130

threatening to their life systems. Until we find evidence to the contrary, we will suppose that the same lack of sensitivity for productivity improvement inhibited the élites of pre-reform Latin America. But for the peasants, it is a different matter. They were inhibited because the hacienda system deprived them of all opportunity, or of all benefit from any of the potential gains.

Cochabamba and the Reform

When reform came, it started in Cochabamba, not on the Altiplano, for a number of reasons, we suspect.

First was the presence of José Rojas, the son of a *colono* who in 1936 had helped found an independent rural union to lease land the *colonos* had worked from the nuns who owned it. Irate *hacendados* forced the nuns to reconsider and called in police to quell the upstarts. Remembering this trauma, Rojas organized an independent peasant union in the Cochabamba Valley in the late forties and early fifties.

Second, Cochabamba is a fertile, semi-tropical valley, which at 2,600 meters offers respite from the cold Altiplano. It is the granary of Bolivia. Densely populated and isolated by difficult transportation on all sides, it forms an entity of its own, sufficiently close to the Altiplano for food deliveries but sufficiently far from the central government for local politics to thrive.

In hindsight, these two conditions—peasant organization and a unified polity that was linked to the nation and yet distinctive—made Cochabamba the tinder spot when a revolutionary spark was prepared elsewhere.

This spark began with the "generation of the thirties," young intellectuals from the cities, who were introduced to the rest of Bolivia and the life of the peasantry during the Chaco War (with Paraguay, 1932–35). Bolivia's economic suffering was so intense, and the leverage gained by soldiers from their service sufficient to demand economic reforms. These led to the progressive government of President Villaroel, 1943–46, which passed legislation to abolish some of the compulsory services of *colonos* (Huizer and Stavenhagen 1974:394).

In 1945, the First Bolivian Indian Congress, with thousands from all over the country, met in La Paz to demand government regulation of agricultural labor and abolition of compulsory service. Despite heavy pressure from the *hacendados*, the government issued decrees to abolish servitude and require schools on each hacienda. But these decrees were ignored, and peasant attempts to enforce them led to evictions and violence. Villaroel was hanged from a lamp post by an irate mob in 1946.

When the succeeding governments—representing the *hacendados*—re-enforced the obligations of the Indians, the *colonos* and miners together invaded haciendas in Cochabamba. Some *hacendados* were killed, but the armed forces quashed the rebellion in 1947, and peasant resistance went underground.

Enter the champion: a middle-class political party, grown out of the "generation of the thirties": the National Revolutionary Movement (MNR for Movimiento Nacional Revoluntario), which had shared power under Villaroel. Their candidate, Victor Paz Estenssoro, had helped sponsor a mild agrarian reform proposal in 1944, but otherwise the MNR was not on record as favoring drastic changes in land tenure. In early 1952, the MNR appeared to win the elections, only to be denied power by the existing government. So they organized armed uprisings into the principal cities, which in turn fueled peasant unrest in the Cochabamba Valley.

Hernán Siles Zuazo led the April 1952 Revolution in La Paz, which recalled Paz Estenssoro from exile to assume the presidency. Sensing their opportunity, peasant unions in the Ucureña area of the Cochabamba Valley started taking over local government functions. Rojas, now a veteran organizer, set up a Regional Peasant Federation, which initiated violent land invasions, prominently helped by ex-miners.

Now sensing its own opportunity, the MNR helped form armed peasant militias throughout the countryside as well as in the mines. Paz created a Ministry of Campesino Affairs (MAC, for Ministerio de Asuntos Campesinos), and the first minister, Nuflo Chavez-Ortiz, established close ties with leaders of the Cochabamba Regional Peasant Federation (Mitchell 1977:45). In collaboration with the labor leader Juan Lechín, Chavez-Ortiz set up roving teams of peasants, ex-miners, and union officials to encourage formation of unions throughout the countryside.

Land reform was decreed by the president in August, 1953. Agricultural property was to be classified into four types: latifundia, agricultural enterprises, medium property, and small property (Graef 1974:8–9). Latifundia, large haciendas worked by compulsory labor in exchange for small plots, were expropriated in full. Peasants were to keep their own plots and receive hacienda land as well. In the other three categories, labor obligations were abolished, and peasants were to own their own plots. Agricultural enterprises were properties run with modern equipment and wage labor. Medium and small properties were haciendas that fell under acreage ceilings that varied across regions. The determination of category was to be made by agrarian reform judges. A National Agrarian Reform Service would help process union petitions and would provide definitive titles.

The classification of properties was not consistent everywhere, and surprisingly, farms tended to be judged latifundia in regions where peasant unions were powerful. Where landlords were powerful, the other three categories were most often declared. There were frequent complaints that political favorites had their properties classified in categories they might keep.

In the Cochabamba Valley, peasants did not wait for official classifications: landlords were expelled and told to stay away. In part, the militancy of peasants was bolstered by ex-miners who flocked home to the valley after government promises of land. Peasant unions stiffened by former miners kept control of two haciendas, whereas a third one, composed of former *colonos*, was classified as an agricultural enterprise (Graef 1974:10–11).

Ironically, because of high rural density, peasants in the Cochabamba Valley benefited less than peasants elsewhere (Heyduk 1974:76). Eckstein (1976:26) quotes a survey by Camacho-Saa in 1966, showing "that mill owners, chicherías (makers of maize beer), and middlemen enjoy a monopoly of liquid capital assets" that allowed them to dominate the valley. But in the lower valley, a new dam, allowing intensive cultivation, made the peasants better off (Eckstein 1976:15). In the upper valley, however, peasants without enough water grew crops of low value. Zuvekas (1977:39) declares that "Cochabamba Valley campesino incomes rose fairly steadily from 1952 to 1967, although afterwards there appears to have been some stagnation."

Did the MNR really intend to sponsor such a radical land reform? To this day, no one can tell. Early in 1953, President Paz formed a commission to study the possibility of land reform, but the peasant unions presented it with de facto reform in many regions. Mitchell (1977:46) argues that the MNR's main motives for organizing the unions were (1) to ensure an adequate food supply to the city when *hacendados* feared to visit their estates, and (2) to use peasants as a basis for political power before other parties beat them to it.

We concur in at least the second of these. Serving in Bolivia in 1959–60, one of the authors (Powelson) had many conversations with high-level MNR officials, including Presidents Paz and Siles, union leader Juan Lechín, and minister (later opposition candidate for president) Walter Guevara Arce. These conversations left no doubt of both the personal integrity of these men and the common cause they saw with miners and Indians. When asked if he had no fear in arming the mining and peasant unions, Paz replied that these unions would never take up arms against the government that had supported them. (He was wrong!) He also believed the peasants wanted to pay for the land they received in the reform, for otherwise they would not fully believe it was theirs: a subsequent government might take it away. Mass incorporations of Indians into the electoral process did allow the MNR to rule longer (twelve years, 1952–64) than any group since then.

Yet the common cause was not to last. Despite its encouragement of unions, *the Bolivian government never controlled them.* Unions were formed and organized from the ranks, an event with both negative and positive outcomes. Negative, because of violent confrontations with government, leading to political instability that suppressed economic progress. In 1960, government officials negotiated with mining unions by radio because the union leaders feared they would be arrested if they went to La Paz, and government officials feared they would be hanged if they went to Oruro (as some had been earlier). Positive, because the farmers were free to organize their own marketing, their own buying, their own credit, and to choose their own technologies. If Bolivian farmers could do this well—and they could—there is little doubt that farmers the world over can do so.

The Reform in the Altiplano

Unlike Cochabamba, the Altiplano possessed no independent peasant unions before 1952. However, the roving teams of activists sent by the government had met great enthusiasm there, partly because of proximity: peasants would be carted into La Paz by the truckload to demonstrate whenever the government needed support. Peasants also made common cause with former peasants now in the city. The active involvement of the Ministry of Campesino Affairs gave the government some initial control over peasant unions. Daily the peasants would be seen congregating on the sidewalk in front of the ministry.

Land distribution on the Altiplano was mainly a refusal to pay labor obligations to the former *hacendado*. Since former landlords and *mayordomos* often feared to go near their properties, peasants gained control. Some authors (Carter 1965:65–83) found that peasants simply retained their small plots without doing labor obligation (with a sample of seven haciendas). But a larger survey (Clark 1968:164) found that in thirty-four cases out of fifty-one, peasants took over hacienda land as well.

The latter results are confirmed by a number of surveys. In ten of eleven haciendas studied by Graef, peasants increased their landholdings. Through legal action, the union in Compi (near Lake Titicaca) obtained most of the hacienda lands in 1957 (McEwen 1975:330), although the *hacendado's* children worked part of them with wage labor until 1961. Surveys and titles were years in the making, but there was little sense that these were urgent. The peasants had the land and would keep it.

In some haciendas, the former hacendado did retain all or part of his land. In seventeen of the fifty-one cases surveyed by Clark (1968:162), this hacienda land remained uncultivated for a time. Sometimes peasants refused to work it; sometimes they were awaiting the outcome of court cases.

In nineteen of the thirty-four cases in Clark's survey where hacienda lands were continuously worked, the peasants delivered the landlord's share to the Ministry of Campesino Affairs, as part of the government's attempt to assure an adequate food supply for the cities. This did, however, confirm the government's initial control over Altiplano unions. In April 1953, four months before the official announcement of the reform, the government decreed that peasant unions were responsible for ensuring the harvest (Clark 1968:165).

134

The Altiplano: Post-Reform Production and Marketing

Land reform redistributed income and wealth massively, albeit unevenly. Land was not earlier distributed evenly among *colonos*, and reform did not affect relative size distribution significantly, but it did cause profits to go to the *colonos*.

The new marketing system did not spring forth fullblown. Ex-*hacendados* often retired their trucks, for fear they would be confiscated by the peasant unions, but the *peasant* marketing system expanded enormously. New fairs were set up, and existing fairs grew. Peasant drivers appeared with trucks (they must have been saving in order to acquire them), to take up the slack of the ex-*hacendados*. In 1966, Clark (1968:167) found that these rural fairs were regularly visited by five to nine trucks on average, but some boasted seventy-five to 150 trucks regularly. Peasants usually had a choice among two to three fairs, so they could play middlemen against each other.

Although fairs expanded with little government regulation, small rural communities did petition central authorities for them. Peasant union leaders saw the importance of fairs and used their power with the MAC to have them located in the vicinity of their unions (Clark 1968:167). These sites often gained population at the expense of older towns, which had been dominated by non-Indian conservatives. Peasants neither felt comfortable there nor expected a fair deal.

Clark calculates that the average peasant family increased its market participation to $100 (U.S. 1966), of which $95 was in cash. Peasants bought more clothing, food from other regions, and consumer durables. Sewing machines and corrugated roofs were popular. Comparing four Peruvian haciendas to four Bolivian ex-haciendas, Burke (1970) found higher labor productivity on the former but greater consumption—better diet and more consumer durables—on the latter. Before the reform, the produce of the Compi hacienda could be driven to La Paz in two trucks, but after the reform eight were required (McEwen 1975:332).

Peasant occupations became more diversified with no decline in agricultural output. Before the reform, peasants had been tied to the hacienda. If they left in the middle of the night, they might be caught, brought back, and beaten. But after the reform, Burke (1971:320) found that one-half of the *campesinos* on four haciendas worked outside at least part time. In Compi, 75% of the *campesinos* had secondary occupations, such as building construction and merchants (McEwen 1975:333). Thus peasants immediately responded to the removal of the labor obligation and the increased mobility.

Although in some places unions atrophied once the land had been secured, for the most part they became de facto local governments (Graef 1974). The secretary-general became spokesman, judge, and advisor to the *campesino* community (McEwen 1975: 375-76). Heyduk (1974: 72-73) sees a continuity of community structures from pre-hacienda times. Even in rent

135

collection, one of the *campesinos* had seen that others paid. The unions successfully opposed government attempts to set up cooperatives on old hacienda land, insisting on small-scale, private ownership. This experience in bargaining turned the unions into the effective representatives of peasants vis-à-vis the government. While the Indians had had local organizations from time immemorial, for the first time since the Conquest they had an effective protector against government intrusion. Provincial and town governments, still dominated by their oligarchies, became eclipsed as government resources flowed instead into the unions.

The Yungas

The Yungas are steep mountain valleys (1,000 to 2,000 ft. elevation) to the north and east of the Altiplano and consist of high jungle rainforests where a variety of tropical plants flourish.

Because of differences in climate and terrain, as well as later settlement, haciendas in the Yungas presented different features from those on the Altiplano. Most haciendas were medium-size, from 11 to 150 hectares, growing coca, coffee or fruits. Almost all owners lived on their land year-round and farmed actively. The *colonato* system was similar to that on the Altiplano but with two crucial differences. First, the *colonos* were growing cash crops as well as subsistence on their small holdings, therefore they had participated in a market economy as long as they could remember. Second, labor scarcity made social stratification slightly less inflexible than on the Altiplano. Whereas on the Altiplano a worker who tried to move would be beaten and returned, in the Yungas he was more mobile. Still, the traditional patron-client system was intact. Indians were addressed as "son." They carefully greeted each *blanco* on the street as a sign of respect.

The marketing system was geared to large-scale production. Coca plants were sold to presses in local towns like Coripata. Around Coroico, the provincial capital of North Yungas, coffee *hacendados* sold directly to processors in La Paz (McEwen 1975:148-49).

Land reform was brought to the Yungas by the MNR government. Graef characterizes the reform as very "official." The MNR formed and dominated peasant unions. Ex-owners suffered little violence, and few central lands were overrun. While most sources (McEwen 1975:148; Heath 1973: 83; Heyduk 1974:74; Léons and Léons 1971:279) agree that the reform was dominated by the MNR and followed official guidelines, there is disagreement on how much the landlords were able to retain central land.

Because of the small size of the haciendas, the properties in all case studies were classified as medium. According to some authors, most landlords were forced off their land. Heath (1973:81-82) writes that around Coroico many moved into town, becoming traders. Ex-owners venturing on to their former lands were "subject to verbal abuse and physical assault" (McEwen 1975:148-49). Around Arapata (halfway between Cori-

136

pata and Coroico), many landlords kept some land but stopped cultivating coca because they could not entice workers with sufficiently attractive wages (Léons and Léons 1971:279). Many resident landlords were trapped in provincial towns, having lost their main means of livelihood (Marshall, cited in Graef 1974:12-13).

But Graef (1974:13) and Heyduk (1974:74-75) disagree with this assessment. Graef argues that most landlords continued to work their land after the reform, while fighting an ongoing legal battle with the unions. They were only worse off in having to pay wages because they had lost the labor obligations of their *colonos*. Often their former *colonos* would have no objection to working for them. Heyduk argues that landlords still controlled much of their central lands.

But the former set of authors appears to us more convincing. Apparently relying on Marshall's work, Graef seems to overstate his case. In his final summary, he concedes that after legal battles, peasants mostly increased their holdings at landlord expense.

The MNR controlled the unions in the Yungas longer than they did on the Altiplano. Peasants were repeatedly told they should thank President Paz Estenssoro for their land (McEwen 1975:150). They were "expected or ordered" to vote for the MNR candidate in the periodic elections. In part this paternalism resulted from the peasant's reliance on official proceedings for ensuring control of the land. Yet the dependency can be overstated. Peasants definitely gained from their association with the MNR. Coroico, controlled by the rural élite, had difficulty getting any funds from the central government, while surrounding *campesino* communities often garnered government resources through their unions (McEwen 1975:151).

As on the Altiplano, the confirmation of *colonos'* right to their existing plots meant a continuation of inequality in holding size among *campesinos*. One hacienda near Arapata had plot sizes ranging from a tenth of a hectare to 11 hectares, with the average around 5 (Léons and Léons 1971:289). Political office in the unions was associated with above-average plot size and greater economic resources. Juan Mendoza (of whom more later), head of the Provincial Campesino Federation, controlled with his brother-in-law 40 hectares of coca land.

The Yungas: Post-Reform Production and Marketing

Just as on the Altiplano, the peasants in the Yungas proved their ability to spawn increased output, increased specialization, and a new marketing system. They began to rely on trade with other parts of the country for their food. In this section we describe separately the marketing structure of coffee and coca, the two main cash crops.

Around Coroico, the most successful marketing intermediary was the *rescatador*, the coffee middleman who both bought for resale in La Paz and supplied peasants with credit in the off season (McEwen 1975:149-50). The peasant, who had much income at harvest and lean months in mid-year, would borrow against the next harvest from the *rescatador*, with whom he had a client-patron relationship. With no explicit interest rate, the *rescatador* earned his profit by using a greater measure for the arroba (25–lb. bag) and quintal (100 lb. bag), then the selling measure in La Paz. McEwen calculated that the real interest rate might be as much as 100% per annum. However, this calculation is suspect, for it includes the return for transportation and marketing as well. The weight differential alone was about 10% to 20%.

Angered by the weight differential, some of the peasant unions tried to find intermediaries who would give full measure (McEwen 1975:150). After a sellers' strike in 1966, the differential was no longer used (Heath 1975:84).

The capacity of peasants to create their own marketing center is demonstrated by Arapata, a new *campesino* town serving small coca producers in the region (Léons and Léons 1971:275–95). What had been a small group of houses by the road in 1950 was a town with a population over 1,000 by 1969. In 1964 there were over thirty-nine stores. The largest storekeepers (Mestizos and Indian peasants from the Altiplano) were both buying coca leaves and extending credit.

While traditional patron-client relationships continued in Coripata, Arapata began to capture new trade with new arrangements. Altiplano-born Indians and *cholos* (Indians mixed with Spanish culture, adopting Spanish dress) became the traders. Léons and Léons (1971:294) estimated that by the late 1960s these buyers had captured as much as 70% of the market in the Nord Yungas.

Still, the peasants did not have a totally clear road in becoming independent middlemen. The government licensed coca merchants in order to tax them. By evading the tax through bribes, established merchants had a competitive edge over newcomers; they also had ways to ensure that newcomers suffered the full brunt of the tax. Furthermore, it was not easy to operate independently of a patron, who might help in disputes with authority, give advice, and protect.

Léons (1977) examined the middleman/patron role in the person of Juan Mendoza, a trader in the Chicaloma area of Sud Yungas whom she believed to represent a new breed that combined political and economic brokerage. Mendoza headed the provincial federation of peasant unions, but he also operated a store, owned a coca farm with his brother-in-law, and bought coca from clients to whom he also supplied goods (not cash) on credit (and who would not think of selling their crop elsewhere). His principal competition came from non-resident Altiplano traders who provided cash credit in return for buying rights. But, Léons discovered, the economic terms imposed by Mendoza on his clients were worse than those of the Altiplano traders. So why did Mendoza have so much of the trade? She concluded that his ability to dispense political favors was part of the calculus. He had access to government services and jobs; he named political officeholders.

While Mendoza surfaces as a cacique, nevertheless his roots appear more in the unions than in land (as was the case for the classic caciques). While writing of patron-client ties, Heath (1973:84–85) argues that few of the new *campesino* leaders wielded arbitrary power. Instead, the union held some check on them, just as it did on the Altiplano. The union mediated disputes over land exchanges, public works, and other community affairs.

Thus the land reform coupled with the weakness of the government (its inability to interfere) left the peasant free to develop his own crops, his own credit sources, and his own marketing structures. If he has chosen new patron-client relationships—and this is not a total pattern—perhaps this choice arose from his conservatism, or the need not to change all aspects of his life at once. The union was effectively controlled by the peasant and his leaders, not by his government.

In the weekly market at Arapata after the reform, one could find many traders from the Altiplano and the lowlands (McEwen 1973:291). They sold fresh meat, tomatoes, corn, rice, and cooking bananas to *campesinos* who could buy these only because they had specialized increasingly in coca, coffee and fruits. It was no longer "worth their while to grow subsistence crops they could buy more cheaply in the market place" (Léons and Léons 1971:291). Regional specialization and a more varied diet were the rewards of the land reform, and of the economics of comparative advantage.

A Loan Program for the Oriente

We have suggested, not proved but argued by illustration, that the government did not co-opt peasant marketing and peasant credit on the Altiplano or in the Yungas or in Cochabamba because it was too disorganized to do so. More succinctly, the benefits would not have repaid the costs. "Costs" included controlling a peasantry whose penchant for rebellion had been demonstrated in Cochabamba; also managing a constituency extending from Lake Titicaca (close to La Paz) in one direction throughout the Beni almost to the Amazon and in the other to Oruro, Potosí, and Tarija near the Argentine border. Some of these constituencies (Oruro, Potosí) included miners whose political leverage arose from the government's need for foreign exchange. A precarious government could not muster the centralized support to confront these far-flung potential troublemakers.

Not so in Oriente Province, however. This section of eastern Bolivia, its capital at Santa Cruz, was a wide open frontier in the fifties and sixties. Despite a paved highway to Cochabamba and a railroad traversing the jungle to connect it with São Paulo in Brazil, Santa Cruz was at the end of "civilization." But it was promising country, and jungle clearing was thought to lead to unlimited, very fertile land. Despite its distance from La Paz—two long days overland—Santa Cruz was virgin territory, sparsely populated. The government sensed, by 1960, that it could develop Santa Cruz as a tabula rasa—little prior population, no peasant unions or other institutions to stand in its way. Another factor was political: the need to defend the east both from infiltration by Brazilians and from a separatist movement.

The main effect of the land reform in the Oriente was to free the labor force on cattle ranches from debt peonage (McEwen 1975: 11–12). At first, these peasants tried to earn their living in subsistence farming. Despite plentiful land, subsistence farming at the edge of the jungle—with little possibility of advancing to the market—is poverty farming, and many drifted back to the ranches as wage laborers. Social stratification remained rigid, and ranchers continued in control of the resources.

Sensing the potential of the Oriente, the La Paz government began pouring in investment in the early sixties. In this, it was aided by the U.S. government, which offered highway construction and "supervised" agricultural credit. This policy was continued and expanded under the military governments of Barrientos (1964–69) and Banzer (1971–78). Cotton, soybeans, and sugar were principally raised. It was hoped that sugar from the Oriente would replace imports from the Grace Company in Peru. The potential for oil was also not neglected.

Unfortunately, few of these prospects would involve peasant farming. There were few peasants. The Indians of the Altiplano did not like the lowlands, at least not at first, although trickles of migrants swelled over the next two decades. A colony of Okinawans was established to fill the needs for small-scale agriculture.

Was it perhaps not curious, then, that from 1964 to 1974 a government smarting from credit scarcity should direct 76.5% of the volume of credit (or 23% of the number of loans) of the Agricultural Development Bank (later the Bolivian Agricultural Bank) to Oriente Province (Ladman and Tinnermeier 1978, 1981)? Because of the intensity of inflation in its early years, the MNR had instituted a stringent stabilization program in 1956, with funds from the United States and the International Monetary Fund contingent on a cap on government spending and controls on monetary expansion. (In 1960, the president of the Central Bank posted a notice in his outer office, "Do not ask for credit; it will be refused.") One might have supposed that a government founded on peasant support in the traditional regions would direct its scarce credit to those constituencies.

Of the $80.9 million loaned by the Bolivian Agricultural Bank in the Oriente region from 1971 to 1978, $45.9 million was advanced in 726 loans to cotton producers. Since multiple loans were made to the same person, the number of borrowers must have been considerably less. Another $4 million went to soybean producers in 118 loans. These two crops alone constituted 41% of the bank's national portfolio in that period and 6% of its loans by number (all data from Ladman and Tinnermeier 1978, 1981).

Largely because of the great distance of Santa Cruz from the principal marketing centers, these projects were not economically justified. The overall delinquency rate on Agricultural Bank loans advanced from 15% in 1971 to 43% in 1978, of which 68% (by volume) was in Oriente Province.

Until 1977, the government applied no pressure for repayment. In June of that year the repayment period was extended from four to twelve years, and the bank issued bonds to stave off backruptcy. Ladman and Tinnermeier (1981:69) argue that even so, only U.S. aid kept it afloat.

Why would a government committed to improving the lot of peasants and miners allocate its scarce credit overwhelmingly to Oriente Province rather than the Altiplano, where the vast majority of peasants were? One suggestion is that the MNR went out of power in 1964, and the succeeding military government was not committed to its ideals. But this suggestion does not hold up to the fact that the program began under the MNR, and the military only continued it. Some (such as Mitchell 1977:46) argue that the MNR was never tied to a peasant base but opportunistically took advantage of the revolution of peasants and miners in 1953. If that is so, then the supposition is reasonable that investors in land, crops, and ranches in the Oriente belonged to the favored élite of both the MNR and its successors, and in final analysis they held the aces.

Conclusion

In one sense, Bolivia constitutes an exception to the dreary pattern of centrally-sponsored land reforms. After initiating the 1954 reform, the MNR government could not control it.

Peasants in Bolivia have shown greater initiative in withstanding their government than have those of other Third World countries. Deprived of the transportation system of the old hacienda, they formed one of their own. Peasants bought trucks and shipped their own products and those of other peasants. Indeed, some became full-time transporters. The number of trucks carrying farm output on the Altiplano increased during the fifties and early sixties.

Without any assistance from government, peasants formed new marketing centers. New towns sprang up at crossroads on the main traffic routes. Peasants also organized their own credit and sales structures.

In some cases, they allied themselves with local bosses, which gave rise to the criticism of monopolistic control. This may have been so, but given the political and strategic environment, this was their choice. With time, they may spring themselves loose from the rural power structure just as did the peasants of medieval Europe and Japan, with the demise of their feudalisms.

Indeed, the initiative shown by Bolivian peasants belies the story so often told, that peasants *need* the paternalistic support of government to grow their products, to buy their inputs, to secure farm credits, and to sell their outputs. When this support is given, the government gains, not the peasant.

Why were the Bolivian peasants exceptions? We do not know, but we can guess. First, in the Cochabamba area where the land reform began, they had already formed local organizations capable of bargaining with the government and exerting leverage upon it. They quickly formed similar organizations in the Altiplano area, around Lake Titicaca. Second, because of the difficult geography of Bolivia, it was hard for the government to send armed forces. While it might have been able to do so in the Altiplano, the lively, growing areas of the Yungas, Cochabamba, Santa Cruz, and the Beni were a different matter. All of these are separated from La Paz by mountains and treacherous roads, and the Beni is accessible only by air.

In another sense, however, the Bolivian farmer has been as much a victim of statism as his counterparts throughout the Third World. In the seventies and early eighties, corruption, extravagant spending, and reckless credit expansion by the La Paz government created an inflation exceeding 20,000% per year by 1986. Much of the economy turned to barter. Seed and fertilizer and all imports were almost impossible to obtain. In these curcumstances, *all* Bolivian output fell off, and the farmer lost out with the rest. Only the coca growers prospered, but their crops were subject to military intervention with the assistance of U.S. troops.

Agricultural output per capita, which had increased on average by 1.77% per year during the sixties, declined by 0.20% per year during the seventies, and by 1.77% per year during the first half of the eighties (Table 19.1). In 1984 it recovered (+20.2%) from a disastrous drop in 1983 (−19.1%), and in 1985 it increased by 6.4%, but in 1986 and 1987 it dropped again by 7.7% and 2.9%, respectively (IDB 1988, with figures adjusted for population growth).

On January 1, 1987, the inflation was stopped in its tracks by a thorough monetary and tax reform. Whether output and income will recover remains to be seen. Nevertheless, the power of the Bolivian peasant vis-à-vis his government—much greater than that of most Third World peasants—augurs well for agriculture.

References

Burke, Melvin, 1970. "Land Reform and Its Effect upon Production in the Lake Titicaca Region," *Economic Development and Cultural Change*, vol. 18, no. 3:410–50.

Burke, Melvin, 1971. "Does 'Food for Peace' Assistance Damage the Bolivian Economy?" *Inter-American Economic Affairs*, vol. 25, no. 1, Summer.

Carter, William, 1965. *Aymara Communities and the Bolivian Agrarian Reform*, Social Science Monograph no. 24, Gainesville, University of Florida Press.

Carter, William, 1971. "Revolution and the Agrarian Sector," in Malloy and Thorn (1971).

Clark, Ronald J., 1968. "Land Reform and Peasant Market Participation on the Northern Highlands of Bolivia," *Land Economics*, vol. 44:153–72.

Eckstein, Susan, 1976. *The Impact of Revolution: A Comparative Analysis of Mexico and Bolivia*, Santa Monica, Calif., Sage Publications.

Graef, Peter, 1974. "The Effects of Continued Landlord Pressure in the Bolivian Countryside during the Post-Reform Era: Lessons to Be Learned," Madison, Wisconsin, Land Tenure Center, paper no. 103.

Heath, Dwight, 1973. "New Patrons for Old Changing Patron-Client Relationships in the Bolivian Yungas," *Ethnology*, vol. 12, no. 1:90–98.

Heyduk, David, 1974. "The Hacienda System and Agrarian Reform in Highland Bolivia: A Re-evaluation," *Ethnology*, vol. 13, no. 1:71–81.

Huizer, Gerritt, and Stavenhagen, Rudolph, 1974. "Peasant Movements and Land Reform in Latin America, Mexico, and Bolivia," in Landsberger (1974).

IDB (Inter-American Development Bank), 1988. *Economic and Social Progress in Latin America, 1988 Report*, Washington, D.C.

Ladman, J. R., and Tinnermeier, P. L., 1978. "Credit Policies and Rural Financial Markets in Bolivia," *Savings and Development*, vol. 2, no. 3:195–223.

Ladman, J. R., and Tinnermeier, P. L., 1981. "The Political Economy of Agricultural Credit: The Case of Bolivia," *American Journal of Agricultural Economics*, vol. 63, no. 1:66–72.

Landsberger, Henry, ed., 1974. *Rural Protest: Peasant Movements and Social Change*, New York, Macmillan.

Léons, M. B., 1977. "The Economic Networks of Bolivian Political Brokers: The Revolutionary Road to Fame and Fortune," in R. Halperin and James Dow, eds., *Peasant Livelihood*, New York, St. Martin's Press.

Léons, Madeline, and Léons, William, 1971. "Land Reform and Economic Change in the Yungas," in Malloy and Thorn (1971).

Malloy, James M., 1982. "Bolivia: The Sad and Corrupt End of the Revolution," *UFSI Reports*, no. 3.

Malloy, James, and Thorn, Richard, eds., 1971. *Beyond the Revolution: Bolivia since 1952*, Pittsburgh, University of Pittsburgh Press.

McEwen, William J., 1975. *Changing Rural Society: A Study of Communities in Bolivia*, New York, Oxford University Press.

Miller, C. J., and Landman, J. R., 1983. "Factors Impeding Credit Use in Small Farm Households in Bolivia," *Journal of Development Studies*, vol. 9, no. 4:522–38.

Mitchell, Christopher, 1977. *The Legacy of Populism in Bolivia from MNR to Military Rule*, New York, Praeger.

Preston, D. A., 1970. "New Towns: A Major Change in Rural Settlement Patterns in Highland Brazil," *Journal of Latin American Studies*, vol. 2:1–27.

Zuvekas, Clarence, 1977. "Rural Income Distribution in Bolivia: A Summary and Evaluation of Quantitative and Qualitative Information," Report no. 4, ERS/FDD, Washington, D. C., U. S. Department of Agriculture.

8. Somalia

Susan Gunn

Somalia is often portrayed as a desperate Third World country—one of the poorest of the poor—locked into economic decline by a spate of drought years, the high cost of oil, falling commodity prices, and a hopelessly backward system of land use: nomadic pastoralism. The country relies heavily on international aid, requiring in 1984 $79.9 million in relief for its "victims of man-made and natural disasters" and in 1982 $162.9 million (IMF:IFS Nov. 1984:427) for general development assistance.

Land reform would seem to be far from the minds of administrators contending with problems like these, but over the years many have become convinced that Somalia must resign itself to mopping up after the inevitable droughts unless it radically transforms its methods of land holding and land use to "drought-proof" itself.

But is nomadic pastoralism, so vulnerable to drought, to blame for current ills? Will changing it to conform to "successful" agrarian models address the country's problems? What happens when massive change of *any* kind is attempted in an arid zone?

In this chapter we examine evidence for an alternative explanation for Somalia's economic and human crisis, one looking critically at conventional assumptions about land in an arid country, one that finds the problem to be more internal, more malleable, and more manmade than many have been inclined to think.

Background

Somalia established its first land tenure policies under the colonial regimes of the British in the north and the Italians in the south. It revamped and regularized them in the parliamentary period after independence (1960) and then launched a formal, full-scale reform after its socialist revolution in 1969. At present, it is dallying with more capitalist approaches but has not changed its laws.

NOTE: This chapter is the result of field work in Somalia during 1981–83. Information not otherwise referenced was gathered on the spot, largely through interviews. I am indebted to Lee Cassanelli and J.D. Von Pischke for their assistance.

As in many African societies, codified law carries little weight in the hinterland. Instead, many of the real changes in land ownership and use have been brought about by development, not by legislation. Land use specifications are inherent in both colonial economic policies and development projects sponsored by government and international donors. Most of the impetus and direction for land reform has come from bilateral (U.S.S.R. and U.S.) and multilateral (World Bank and E.E.C.) donors through programs they have sponsored and policies they have encouraged. Legislation has merely followed suit. This does not mean that Somalis have been only casual observers in this matter; on the contrary, because Somali leaders have consistently chosen policies that depend heavily on foreign assistance, the influence of external agencies has been so great.

Land reform in Somalia differs from that elsewhere in another way: its main purpose is not to restore equity but to replace what seems to be an archaic system—communal tenure and nomadic pastoralism—with one more economically productive and less destructive of the land (Laitin 1976). The consensus among planners has been that Somalia is vulnerable to drought largely because it is locked into a subsistence economy deriving from these traditional patterns. And without an agricultural surplus, the economy can never hope to support a modern state.

Furthermore, Somalia's land reform is more of a process than an event. Obviously it was not intended that way, but results have been slow in coming. To speed it up, the specific strategy has shifted from time to time; the administrative view, however, has remained remarkably consistent.

Rationale for Reform

Starting with the 1947 Glover report on grazing conditions in the Somaliland Protectorate (and likely before), the judgment of colonial administrators has been that the range is overgrazed and agricultural land is overused (Geshekter 1981). In their analysis, three factors are responsible; traditionalism, commercialization, and ignorance.

Traditionalism

As the administrators view the question, communal ownership—the traditional norm in this part of the world—poses the problem that no one has a real sense of responsibility for the land. In the past, elders probably directed that pastures be left fallow, but there is no evidence that they can do so now. The clan ethic of open access to water and pasture, coupled with the "pax britannica/italiana" that reduced inter-clan strife, allowed pastoralists to wander wherever they liked and, in a typical "tragedy of the commons" (Hardin 1968), to bear no responsibility for care and maintenance.

Indiscriminate Commercialization

Although Somalis do not seem to amass herds for the sheer joy of numbers or prestige value, as some African groups purportedly do, they have been accumulating large herds since the 1950s in response to commercial opportunities (Swift 1977). To feed and water the increased numbers, a few wealthy pastoralists and traders are said to be appropriating choice pieces of bottom land for their own use and randomly constructing water tanks that encourage overgrazing in their vicinity.

Ignorance

Ignorance of good veterinary and animal husbandry techniques, in the opinion of experts, has meant that pastoralists keep larger herds than they need as a cushion against epidemics and drought, reasoning that out of a larger number there is a greater chance that some will survive. In the crop sector, the ignorance of fertilizers, pesticides, or any methods of tillage other than the short-hafted hoe has meant that cultivators exhaust the fragile soils quickly and are unable to make more than a bare subsistence living (Whitaker 1982; Haakonsen 1983).

The above analysis reduces to three major premises: (1) as a system of land tenure, communal ownership is environmentally damaging; (2) as a system of land use, nomadic pastoralism is unproductive and static; and (3) traditional institutions, where they exist, are inefficient and outmoded and encourage inequalities. Seen in this way, the direction of development and the needed reforms become "clear": rights of ownership must be defined, of either individuals or the state; the population must be drawn into new occupations (principally settled farming), capable of generating a surplus in demand on the world market or substitutable for imports, which promise stability in the face of Somalia's unpredictable rainfall; and finally, the old kin-based channels for production, marketing, education, and political action need to be replaced with modern institutions under the direction of the government. In the section that follows we will see how these reforms were carried out on the ground.

Reform through Development

Private Ownership

The aim of reform efforts until the 1970s was to make the country (or colony) pay for itself. Both the British in the north and the Italians in the south had mainly strategic interests when they moved in in the late 1880s and probably did not expect to have to subsidize their holdings for the next forty years, as turned out to be the case (Seager 1984). But the British and Italian approaches differed.

The British kept their investment in line with its return; they attempted very little development until the decade before independence, using the

Protectorate primarily as a source of meat for the Aden garrison (Lewis 1981). Then, much of what they did undertake aided in the expansion of agriculture (e.g., water conservation, demonstration plots), and private, registered tenure (Box 1971; Hartley/FAO 1966).

By contrast, the Italians invested a great deal in establishing plantation agriculture along the rivers of the south to export fruit to Italy—an intricate maneuver to prop up their domestic fruit industry with off-season bananas (Karp 1960). Owned by Italians, the plantations used, and sometimes forced, Somali labor. Otherwise, they intervened little in the surrounding economy until the 1940s, when they were obliged to do so under the conditions of the U.N. Trusteeship. Even then the model remained the same: Somalis developed their own plantations, exporting the products through the Azienda Monopolio Banane (AMB), Italy's import monopoly. Because AMB continued to subsidize the fruit, the Somali industry stayed dependent on Italy and was unable to compete internationally (Karp 1960).

Tenure of these plantations has always been ambiguous.* Some land had been "purchased" from local clans, but much was simply appropriated because controlled irrigation promised a higher use-value than the smallholders' subsistence cultivation. Because there were often no formal titles, much less demarcation of boundaries, the plantations tended to expand to suit their "owners."

After independence in 1960, plantation development continued but emphasis shifted to large-scale public projects. The new government had virtually no revenues, so with donor assistance it tried to increase production for export in the fastest way possible, through building ports and roads and by capital-intensive irrigated agriculture. The land tenure legislation proposed in 1960 reflected this commitment to large-scale development by guaranteeing the rights of the developer over traditional users (Jorgenson 1960).

Later in the sixties, when international concern awakened to the importance of the rural producer, Somali development shifted toward upgrading the subsistences sector. Although no tenure laws were enacted, the projects of this era (agricultural extension and livestock) strongly reinforced private ownership. An observer of the Afmadou livestock project, for example, noted: "In order for the project to work at all, the people of a given area . . . have to recognize that water and grazing rights (must) be restricted to a certain small group of people and animals . . . and barred to everyone else" (Mahony 1961). The aim of the project had been to localize and intensify nomadic livestock raising by digging wells, but more significantly by getting people to change from wide-ranging herds of milk-

*Reportedly only twenty-two of the 220 Italian banana growers in 1960 held title to their land (Jorgenson 1960).

148

producing goats and camels to predominantly meat-producing herds of cattle and sheep for sale. This project was just another illustration of how closely economic development strategies are bound up with tenure and how changes in one necessitate changes in the other.

State Ownership

Frustration with this slow style of development and with land-use models that seemed to benefit only government officials and corporate interests supplied much of the momentum for the 1969 revolution. "Scientific socialism" had elements similar to socialist ventures elsewhere (direct economic controls, emphasis on social programs, and parastatal monopolies over marketing, distribution, import/export, and banking), but its hallmark in Somalia was revolutionary change: to galvanize the country for *rapid* economic transformation. Although the strategy had changed from private to public ownership, the goals remained the same as before: the replacement of extensive nomad pastoralism with intensive settled occupations.

Although the land reform law of 1975 appropriated all land to the state, it merely added legal strength to the process already under way of consolidating governmental power over the sectional (clan) and individual interests that had flourished under the previous regime. The law was used as another means of replacing these with new forms of social organization such as settlements and cooperatives. It did this by allowing the latter to acquire large amounts of prime land (and other benefits) while limiting the land leases of private users to 30 hectares for ten years. It was also used to discourage pastoralism. Whereas arable land could be leased, grazing land could not, so that nomads could no longer claim in any way the land they had depended upon. The government hoped that the resulting sense of insecurity would persuade them to join the cooperatives or to become farmers.

Probably the drought, hitting with full force in 1975, put the stamp on this policy. The government was faced with many thousands of people in refugee camps, a rising toll of humans and livestock, and an economy not responding to the socialist measures as strongly as had been hoped. Although drought occurs in Somalia with maddening frequency (at approximately seven-year intervals) (Hunt 1951), the severity of the 1974–75 episode contributed to the feeling that things were steadily worsening and that determined steps must be taken (Cassanelli 1981).

With the nomad sector greatly disrupted, and with aid flowing in to care for refugees, the government made its most ambitious move to date. From the camps in the north, it moved 120,000 refugees to three agricultural and five fishing projects in the south. All available resources were enlisted to teach new skills and attitudes, to provide health care and education, and to feed the people until they should become self-sufficient, which was

149

estimated to occur in four years. It was hoped that those affected would appreciate settled life and would progressively form more collective, land-based production groups.

Even more significantly, these settlements became the model for other development projects (such as irrigation schemes to accompany the proposed Baardheere Dam) and for relations between the government and donor agencies, (e.g., those aiding the refugees from the Ogaden war and the 1981 drought).

Results

In spite of the high level of development assistance over the past thirty years, Somalia is slipping backward. Although it has been one of the most aided countries in the world since 1960 (Berg 1982), its economy has been growing negligibly: the 1% growth over the last decade was fueled only by the aid. Crop production—the object of much of the development program—has stagnated or fallen. Crop exports have declined 63% over the seventies; food imports, conversely, are rising rapidly.

On the ground, projects have been plagued by waste. Poor maintenance and careless use of donated equipment have slowed implementation and in some cases stopped it altogether. Over half the boats of the fishing cooperatives, for example, were derelict within five years, in spite of a fully outfitted expatriate maintenance team (Berg 1982). The Northern Rangeland Project has been particularly hindered by loss and breakdown of vehicles. Wells, pumps, dips, and holding facilities constructed during the development era have not been maintained and have disintegrated, resulting in losses of equipment and time. Public officials spend only a few hours a day at their desks, are unwilling to work in rural areas, and register a high turnover through transfer or leaving for jobs in the Gulf.

These problems make the view from the top not pleasant: there seems to be little hope for a country which, in spite of massive international aid, is still unable to feed itself and shows no sign of ability to do so in the near future. Planners seem to have resigned themselves to the belief that some countries simply lack the minimal resource/land base to survive in an increasingly expensive, competitive world market—regardless of what tenure or administrative system they might choose. Essentially, these countries are welfare cases of the world and must depend indefinitely on the largesse of the more developed, industrial countries.

View from Underneath

No one would deny that the failure of land reform up to the present, and the current dismal state of the economy, have been due, in part, to drought, north-south economics, and cultural conservatism. But these ready-made explanations are too easy, and they absolve us from looking deeper for the real reasons for Somalia's malaise.

Both the capitalist and socialist development efforts assiduously ignored what was going on within the society itself. A good number of planners knew something about the "traditional" Somali system (which no longer really exists), and on this basis they drew conclusions about the desirable course for development: how the "system," presumably static, had to change. However, few took the time to discover the way people today are coping and adapting to changing conditions. And few understood that the strategy for survival of Somalis in the field was not a quaint cultural anachronism but a practical way of dealing with scarce resources.

Strategy for Survival

What make Somalia unique, both in this book and in the experience of most development planners, are its aridity and its nomadic population (66%). Not only is Somali land ownership and use entirely different from that of settled farmers in rain-rich areas, but the whole economy and social structure are geared to maximizing survival in a harsh, unforgiving environment.

With less than 200 millimeters of rain over most of the north and at best 600 in the south—and that only in spates or irregularly scattered—the land will support only a very flexible economy. Somali families have achieved the required flexibility by allocating their members to different occupations so that, should one fail, there are always other sources of support. Although northerners are usually assumed to be nomads and southerners cultivators, a recent study (Haakonsen 1983) shows that 90% of the former and 75% of the latter have "side-lines," e.g., shopkeeping, religious instruction, water services, wage labor. Moreover, there is no strict division between farmers and pastoralists. Almost all Somalis own livestock, and parts of most families are nomadic. Somalis have also managed to live lightly on the land: by choosing mobile occupations, they do not depend heavily on one place. Thus arises the Somali forte of trade, livestock raising, transport, and in certain favored areas, mixed farming.

If aridity mandates an extensive and varied economy, it has also fostered a similar style of society: rather flat (nonhierarchical), far-flung, and autonomous. But this is not to say that Somali society is anarchic, for each person is firmly positioned within a web of blood ties and contractual agreements. These ties identify him or her in the same way that an address does in a sedentary society (Lewis 1981). Therefore, Somali institutions are sometimes described as socially based rather than land-based.

Eight large lineages and their subgroups (clans) hold the land. Unlike in tribal societies, clan territories are not clearly delineated; they are general areas and home wells, with which particular groups are associated. Customary tenure varies with the quality of the land. Where land is suitable only for grazing, the clan as a whole oversees it. Land that produces regularly and dependably (e.g., crops, incense trees, palms), on the other hand, is controlled by individuals from the family, to whom use-rights

151

have been allocated. When they no longer need it or use it improperly, the land reverts to clan stewardship. By custom, land is not alienated. If a person from clan X is allowed to use some of clan Y's land, he or she is adopted into the clan rather than the land being withdrawn from the clan (Luling 1971; Lewis 1969).

With these general observations in mind, let us look again at the premises, discussed above, that formed the basis for planned development and reform, and compare them with what was actually happening in the country.

"Communal tenure is environmentally damaging . . ."

The "tragedy of the commons" may be applicable in some situations—such as England of the sixteenth century—but for Somalia of the twentieth, the tragedy is not the alleged abuse of common land but the removal of land from communal status.

There are good reasons for communal tenure. The climate in an arid zone is erratic. Rain may be heavy here this year, with lush grass, but next year may be totally dry, while an area only 5 kilometers away is drenched. If individuals try to subsist on a specific piece of land, their options are reduced, and they are at the mercy of chance. As part of a larger, mobile group, they can exploit the productive patches of a wide area as an active strategist, greatly increasing the margin for survival. The Somali nomadic system is based not on land *ownership* but on *access* to its assets—a very different concept.

For example, land in a basin can support many people if used extensively. Instead, it is being used intensively by only a few. Customary rule holds that all have access to range and water, but unless they have "improved" it (e.g., dug a water tank), they are allowed use of it for a limited time only—usually three days—after which they must move on and leave it to others. Visitors are expected to reimburse the improver for his or her effort. If land were to be divided as under private tenure, on the other hand, choice places would become the property of a lucky few, with the less fortunate forced to rely on poorer lands. Private tenure works best where all land is of similar quality, an infrequent occurrence in dry areas (Jodha 1982).

Communal tenure systems are not inherently subject to exploitation by all and maintenance by none. The tragedy of the commons occurs only where there is no consensus or leadership strong enough to oversee the interests of the majority. Individual tenure, where land is exploited on a small-scale, localized level, may be especially inappropriate to arid lands, where conservation is best undertaken in large units such as watersheds. Northeastern Somalia affords several examples. Farmers were alternately washed out and dried up when they tried to cultivate the fertile mountain valleys, because the run-off from storms was so rapid that the water had no chance to sink in. Settlement as clan units on clan land was a powerful force to pressure members into the arduous work of constructing gabions (wire and stone retaining walls) and of digging diversion canals.

The tragedy theory can also be challenged for the scant evidence that the converse is true—that private tenure in dry areas encourages better use of land. Faced with the same survival needs but a smaller area, both pastoralists and farmers are even more compelled to use their own land to the limit.

"Nomadic pastoralism is unproductive . . ."

Generations of advisors have viewed pastoral nomadism as a subsistence activity that needs to be modernized along the lines of western ranching. The facts show a much different picture. Livestock is the major export and foreign exchange earner in Somalia (70% to 75% of all exports and 80% to 90% of export earnings), and it is the nomads who produce all the camels and most of the sheep, goats, and cattle for this trade (Berg 1982). Because of them, Somalia is today the number two sheep and goat exporter in the world (after Australia), and its northern port of Berbera was shipping the most livestock per year of any (2 million sheep units) until it was overtaken just recently (Reusse 1982). In addition to its impressive volume, the pastoral production system of Somalia has been durable; the livestock sector has weathered recent droughts better than other sectors, declining only 9% while others dropped over 60% (Berg 1982), and has maintained the value of its exports, even at the height of the 1976 drought, at $340 million—a total of one-sixth of world livestock exports at the time (Reusse 1982).

"Nomadic pastoralism is static . . ."

Prices for livestock in the oil states have not been static—and neither has the Somali pastoral sector. As demand has risen, Somali production has adjusted to meet it. Despite some controversy on this point (Aronson 1980), there is much evidence that this internal development benefits not just a few key traders but a wide sector of Somali pastoral society.

First, the livestock marketing mechanism has become very wide (pulling animals from Ethiopia, Kenya, and even Uganda) and efficient. The herd owner need not even bring sale animals into a market point. Agents of livestock dealers range the countryside, stopping at every encampment (particularly those of their own lineage), urging herders to sell their male and over-age stock. After a sale, it is they who arrange for the collection, trekking or transport, and feed for the animals. Most traders are independent operators, so competition to wring every eligible animal out of the herds is sharp. That they have been successful is seen in field surveys of herd composition. The number of males is down to the minimum needed to service the herd and unproductive females have been culled. Jointly, traders have organized the loading of ships and devised quarantine and vaccination for export animals (Berg 1982; Reuse 1982; Box 1971; Lewis 1962).

In addition to streamlining the purchasing, traders have made the trip from pasture to shipping point more efficient and less debilitating for the stock. Cement-lined tanks, sometimes with auxiliary catchment systems, have been built at intervals (not randomly) where there are no wells to catch and store rainwater. Areas of good quality pasture are enclosed with thornbush fences to reserve feed for the animals while on trek. On the 1,500-meter escarpment above the main port of Berbera, fodder farms have been constructed to provide cut feed for the animals prior to shipping and during the sea journey. Some traders are investigating the purchase of their own livestock carrier. Thus the "indiscriminate commercialization," which administrators deplore, appears on closer view to be a very considered and beneficial undertaking.

Third, pastoralists themselves are improving local stock with foreign breeds, trying new fodder grasses, beginning commercial dairies, and in one intriguing example trying to increase milk yields of camels by confining them and giving supplements.

"Animal husbandry methods need upgrading"

Over the last twenty years, the total market volume of livestock (domestic and export) has risen at an annual rate of "approximately 6.5% and total production at 4.5%"—a "remarkable" increase suggesting steady improvement in production skills. The growth is entirely the result of private efforts; government assistance to the livestock sector is a mere 1.5% of the annual budget (1978) and goes largely for upkeep of holding facilities and other infrastructure (Berg 1982).

One of the reasons indigenous methods have been so effective is that they are labor intensive. The labor of the whole family is divided so as to respond to the specific needs of each species and of each age group. Camels, valued at over $1,000 each for females, receive special care in the wide-ranging camel camps; young animals, near the home tent, are suckled twice daily. Frequent inspection for parasites and signs that might presage disease and keeping animals born at the same time together throughout their lives are techniques that contribute to the low mortality of Somali livestock.

Nomads are frequently criticized because they do not use veterinary medications. In Somalia, this is so since they are simply not available in the amounts required owing to import bottlenecks*—*not* because nomads question their value or have not the money to pay for them.

*Various restrictions and institutions have been created to control private importation of goods so that the limited foreign exchange will be reserved for government priorities.

"Animal husbandry is ecologically destructive . . ."

The forecasts of total and irretrievable destruction of range land by pastoralists rest on very little scientific study and can be questioned for two primary reasons.

First, those who analyze the carrying capacity and rate of deterioration of the range are often comparing the Somali range with pastures they are familiar with elsewhere. Hence, they view, for example, bush encroachment from the perspective of a cattle-raiser rather than that of a camel-raiser: as a negative condition rather than a positive one. Second, without thorough on-the-ground and sequential studies, an admittedly vague concept such as carrying capacity cannot be established for a large and varied range like Somalia's. In 1964, advisors warned that the range was at maximum capacity with 1.4 million cattle, 2 million camels and 7 million sheep and goats, but there are estimated to be over three times that number on the range now, in apparently excellent condition, as judged by veterinary spot checks (Reusse 1982).

Nomads are quite aware of the danger of overgrazing. Elders appealed to have a U.S.-sponsored livestock development scheme halted because they knew that its plan to concentrate new water points within a small area would have a magnet effect on stock and lead to overuse (Mahony 1961).

The Effect of Land Reform on the Livestock Industry

Intensive livestock-raising for sale supports far fewer people for the same amount of labor than does extensive subsistence pastoralism. By encouraging privatization, intensification, and a change in the herd mix, advisors are, in effect, advocating changes that will jeopardize the living of the poorest sector of the society.

Also, emphasizing cattle over small stock and camels leads to greater risk to the range itself. Advisors from both East and West have tended to see livestock in terms of cattle, assuming (erroneously) that the markets preferred beef, or that cattle-raising would allow a more sedentary, modern existence. *But Somalia is the largest camel producer in the world;* the camel is valued for its meat but even more for its volume of milk (350 liters per year compared with 150 liters for cattle in this environment) and for its drought resistance. Camels need water less frequently than cattle (every thirty days if forage is green, every five days in dry seasons; whereas cattle need it every two to three days and calves daily), so that while cattle are confined to grazing near water, trampling or consuming the local grass more quickly, camels can range more widely and browse on a wider variety of herbage. To a camel even a wicked looking acacia thornbush is tasty!

"Settled agriculture is the answer . . ."

If we assume that settled agriculture is indeed the answer to Somalia's inability to feed itself, then we would expect that there is enough arable land, moisture, and labor available to warrant expanding cultivated areas, and that the rate of return would be adequate to sustain them in the future.

No comprehensive survey has yet been done, but detailed studies of two prime areas—the northwest and the Juba River Valley—show that previous estimates of arable land were grossly inflated. Overly optimistic projections have already cost the government much time and money. In one case, over 20,000 people from one of the drought refugee settlements (Dujuma) had to be re-moved when the land was found to be useless for crops. Government estimates place the amount of arable land available for development at 7.35 million hectares (IFAD 1979), but much of this land, although cultivable, is saline, infertile, rocky, or already being used. A much more realistic projection, based on recent sample studies like the above, may be one-fifth of this, hardly enough to justify crop agriculture as the pillar of national economic development.

In addition to bringing new areas under cultivation, the plans for agricultural expansion propose to increase production by modernizing the methods of existing farmers. With traditional agriculture apparently so primitive, new techniques, planners have reasoned, should double or triple production (Jorgenson 1960).

Those who led the U.S.-sponsored agricultural extension program and others like it, however, have had only a sketchy idea of just what these traditional methods were and almost none of *why* they were. A closer look shows that the methods are actually very well adapted to the exigencies of these arid conditions: (1) they conserve moisture (fields are laboriously divided into a checkerboard of small squares four square meters each, with raised edges); (2) they conserve labor (since agriculture is only *one* of a family's resource bases, farms are limited in size to what a wife, young children, and elderly relatives weed; males of the family would likely be herding the livestock or working overseas or in town); (3) they maintain kinship links (farmers preferred longstalked sorghum and maize over the new short varieties because their nomadic kin need the stover for dry season feed, and because, in exchange for this, the children receive milk, — at the time of the year they need it most—and the fields are manured). Farmers appreciate the benefits of pesticides and improved seed and tools. Since state farms and cooperatives have first right to the limited supply the government can import with its minimal foreign exchange, however, there is very little available for private farmers. Fertilizer is a different situation. Under arid conditions chemical fertilizers do not increase the yield enough to justify the expenditure; the very deliberate and long-standing tradition of manuring seems an adequate if not better technique (Luling 1971; Lewis 1969).

The Effect of Land Reform on Agriculture

It is ironic that agriculture—the sector that has received the most development assistance—is the one with declining productivity. The pre-eminent cause has been the government marketing system, with its low producer prices, a now-common situation among the centrally planned economies of Africa. But there are other factors as well, which, if not unique, are more of an issue in dry countries than elsewhere.

Arid-zone farming requires land to lie fallow or rest because soils are thin and not easily replenished. Somalia's 1975 tenure law, like many, takes no account of this; it allows "all land which is not cultivated . . . [to be] taken over by any individual wishing to grow crops there" (Haakonsen 1983). Even though an individual has cleared thorn scrub, leveled the land (extremely arduous work), and rotated the crops so as not to exhaust the soil, under the 1975 reform someone else can claim and plant the part that is resting. Previously, under customary law, a farmer's effort and investment were recognized and protected. (Interlopers, in these cases, were usually people from outside the lineage, such as a newly formed cooperative, or a Mogadishu-based civil servant.)

Overuse of land in this way will be felt over the long term. An immediate effect, however, has been that reforms have increased the scarcity of labor and exacerbated inequalities. Under the traditional system, the farmer whose crop failed would go to work for another until he could build up enough seed to start again or enough money to invest in another occupation, such as livestock (Haakonsen 1983). Working as an agricultural laborer was a temporary condition, often seasonal, with little stigma; it even brought high wages. When wage and price controls were instituted during the 1970s and tenant labor was abolished, agricultural production plummeted. As a result, farmers could no longer afford to hire seasonal help or other farmers whose crops had failed. As incomes fell to below subsistence level, the refugee camp became the only way out. Men left their families in the camps while they went to work for large plantation owners or state farms. Paying less than subsistence wages, the plantations and state benefited . . . at the expense of the most vulnerable farmers. Protection of traditional property rights could have prevented such a descent into poverty.

Perhaps this would not have been so serious if indeed the large schemes were efficient and productive. But this was not the case. In spite of preferential access to machinery, fertilizer, seed, and labor, recent studies (see Hoben et al. 1983) show that state farms have been producing less per hectare than private ones, and large farms were producing at rates equal to

157

or below small ones. These findings suggest that small operations might simply be a much more productive form of agriculture in a dry zone.

And yet large schemes, highly capital- and technology-intensive, have been (and still are) the preferred mode in official Somalia. They were justified on the basis that labor was scarce and time was short, so mechanization was the only answer, and that large farms would be more efficient owing to the economies of scale in procuring inputs and storing products.

These assumptions are incorrect. If labor is scarce, it is because state-set wages are low, and farmers can make more money on their own plots or in other occupations. Those available for longer-term labor are mainly women, children, and the elderly, and these can be better employed in small-scale horticulture than in the heavy work of, for example, cutting sugar cane on the large estates. Time saved by machinery is being used up many times over because infrastructure (roads, spare parts, managerial skill) are far too undeveloped to support ambitious and complex large-scale mechanized farming. The pastoral system plus off- or non-farm occupations are sustainable; "modern" approaches are not.

Moreover, in the haste to implement the large schemes, some of the distinctive agricultural adaptations of smallholders are being endangered; for example, the *deshek* farmers. *Deshek*s are natural or man-made depressions along the two major rivers that, when flooded, provide a source of water and moist, rich ground for planting. Of the six irrigation projects currently existing or planned on the Juba River, apparently none has considered the *deshek* farmers as anything but potential labor for the state farms, and no steps have been taken to safeguard their rights. Where irrigation schemes are planned, wealthier urban-based speculators are forming cooperatives that allow them to procure fifty-year leases to adjacent land. Unaware that their customary usage rights are no longer valid, and unfamiliar with land registration, the small farmers are likely to be alienated from their subsistence base in the whole riverine area. This effective method of using marginal land will be lost.

A potentially more serious effect of the current reform is the destruction of reserve grazing. When water is low during the dry seasons, the riverbeds provide grazing for the herds of southern Somali (roughly 300,000 square kilometers). When severe drought hits, pastoralists from throughout the country look to these areas as the last resort. Until now, the river basins have been "protected" from use by the tsetse fly and flooding during the wet seasons. Now dams are being planned that would restrict the flow of water and allow more intensive cultivation in the basin, ignoring the importance of this land as drought insurance for Somalia's whole livestock industry.

"Traditional institutions are inefficient"

Because their predecessors were allegedly inefficient, the government has now established new marketing, credit, and import/export institutions, along with a new style of group living (settled cooperatives). A more likely reason than inefficiency, however, was that previous forms had all functioned along clan lines, and the clans threatened government sovereignty. A second likely reason was that profits from trade, agriculture, and industry—like those of the livestock industry—were beyond the control of the government. Instead of being taxed, profits were being plowed back into the indigenous economy. In spite of the fact that the new parastatals and cooperatives served political goals more than economic ones, donors have continued to support them in various ways, perhaps not realizing that the indigenous economy has had its own perfectly capable structures.

The livestock industry illustrates one of these. Not only is it an effective production system, as we saw earlier, but it manages imports, exports, and investments efficiently, giving livestock producers comparatively high prices for their stock. Why? First, because producers accept deferred payment. Rather than being limited to the minimum government price of export animals, they agree on a percentage of the selling price in Saudi Arabia. In the meantime, they subsist on profits from their investments in buildings, shops, water tanks, stock, and trucks, or from lending money to relatives or even putting it in the savings bank. Second, the traders would operate on narrow margins in livestock, while making their money on the reimportation of goods. Until 1982, when it was made illegal because of pressure from the International Monetary Fund, the *franco valuta* system allowed the purchase of imports with exchange generated by livestock sales and overseas workers' earnings. Purchased at lower international prices, these imports could be sold more profitably than others acquired in the context of Somali exchange restrictions. Profits would go to the families of the workers, the traders, and the livestock producers.

For organizational efficiency, an even more fascinating example is the *qat* trade. *Qat* is a highly perishable plant, grown in the cool, moist highlands of Ethiopia and Kenya but consumed as a social drug in Somalia and the Saudi peninsula, where it commands high prices. Somalis have developed a highly efficient system of collection, transport, distribution, and sale that ensures that the product reaches its destination, unbruised, within three days of picking! Since it must cross a war zone and as much as a thousand kilometers of open, roadless savannah, the operation relies on considerable prior negotiation and an elaborate back-up system of relay vehicles, fuel, spare parts, mechanics, and food. At central processing points it is divided, repackaged, and sold to middlemen. A recent government study estimated that as many as 200,000 people were employed in various stages of the operation (cited in Cassanelli 1985).

The Effect of Land Reform on Organization

When people live close to the margin, as farmers in the arid zone do, any tampering with the indigenous system can be not only counter-productive but dangerous. Agricultural production declined when the Agricultural Development Corporation (ADC) monopolized marketing, because ADC prices were not high enough to pay for farmers' essential inputs, or to act as an incentive to produce a surplus. Since many farmers experience crop failures (due to lack of rain, flooding, birds, and other natural causes) as often as three years out of five, only their own surplus grain, money from sales, and the assistance of kin tides them over the bad years. When hoarding was prohibited and the prohibition enforced by confiscation, farmers were left with no reserve food. In the next year that crops failed, their only recourse became the refugee camps.

When import was limited to parastatals and the smaller ports were closed to prevent smuggling, the monopoly parastatals could not keep up with the demand for spare parts, small tools, concrete and the like, because scarce foreign exchange was saved for top priorities such as material for the war with Ethiopia. As a result, the proceeds from overseas workers and livestock sales were no longer available for investment in construction (wells, buildings) or for experiments (pumps to open up new land). Instead, they had been diverted to consumer goods. In the 1980s, donors were continuing to provide money for machinery, tools, vehicles, drugs, and pesticides to stimulate development, while even ordinary herdsmen and farmers were insisting that they *had* the money; what they needed was *access* to the goods.

The attempt to reorganize people into land-based production groups — settlement schemes and the agricultural and livestock cooperatives — was supported by scholars and development agencies (e.g., Swift 1977) as an essential step in modernizing and drought-proofing the economy. These attempts categorically failed. In addition to refuge from droughts, nomads used the settlements in the way they used wealthy uncles in town: as places to stay when times were difficult or when there were children to be sent to school.

And the livestock cooperatives were not the "experiment in collective action and new herding methods" they were touted to be. Using the sections of prime pasture that the government had allocated to them from the common lands and their own private dry-season reserves, the thirteen cooperatives continued to run their herds out on the range the rest of the time. It was a fine solution for them, but not for the majority.

Conclusions

Neither the Western nor the socialist methods of reform turned out as planned. Western range conservation projects hastened the destruction of the environment; socialist-style land reform contributed to class formation and strengthened the economic and political statuses of élites. Both committed those who hold land by communal right to more and more precarious conditions. And all advisors, regardless of their political complexion, shook their heads over the "lack of initiative" and "uninspired demeanor" of their Somali co-workers.

Meanwhile in the north, the wealthy livestock owners were elaborating new ways of shipping livestock, investigating the domestication of incense trees, experimenting with paddock-held camels, and diversifying into frozen-fish processing. The poorer livestock owners were joining religious communities that guaranteed food, shelter, and education, or were banding together in loose associations to try mixed farming in new areas. Some placed their families in refugee camps while they went off to build up a survival-size herd.

In the south, the wealthy farmers were buying pumps and pesticides from Kenya, while their poorer kin worked for them, for a short time, at wages twice those of government clerks. Those between the two extremes continued as they had for years—diversified—their family members parcelled out into every occupation that the Indian Ocean littoral could afford.

The view from the bottom—of a society that is vigorous, opportunistic, and aggressive—is totally different from that from the top, where, in the minds of Somali administrators and foreign development agents, the pastoralist is desperately poor, lethargic, and helpless. Tragically, it is the "helpless" view that the world sees, and the only one it will respond to. By focusing on Somalis as victims, development programs have damaged the indigenous economy, have ignored the *real* issues concerning land, and have failed to assist in ways where help is *genuinely needed*.

The Damage Report

In an arid zone, production must be based on minimizing risk, not on maximizing potential profit. Yet most development (both by the state and by individuals) has been of the get-rich-quick variety. It has scorned the prime axiom of arid land survival—that to limit adaptability or restrict movement endangers the life of the society. The developers' single-minded pursuit of land-based, capital-intensive agriculture has had a two-pronged effect. First, it has endangered the industry that the country most depends on, livestock, because it extracts for crops land that is essential for dry-season or drought-year grazing. The overall effect is to replace a multiple-use by a single-use system. The problem is compounded because the single use (intensive agriculture) is heavily dependent on one source of water: the Juba and Shebelli rivers. That these rivers rise in the highlands of Ethiopia and could be diverted through dams or irrigation by their hostile neighbor increases the vulnerability generated by this strategy.

Second, emphasizing a commercial, export-oriented strategy as a way to elicit enough surplus from the people to support a modern bureaucratic state destroys a system by which a larger number of people can feed themselves. Milk is a renewable resource; meat (in the short run) is not. Extensive pastoralism employs more people, feeds more people with fewer animals, and achieves higher levels of productivity per animal than can intensive, commercial methods (Behnke 1980). Dry countries require their own style of polity and economy, demanding fewer resources (less surplus) than the agrarian-based models of northern countries.

The way development has been implemented—fast-paced, expensive, and by government agencies—accounts for the rest of the damage. The indigenous economy ultimately squirms around to achieve some accommodation with new policies—it has to, because people must survive—but when policies shift too quickly (as from private to state to private again), the complex parallel economy cannot adjust fast enough to maintain the interests of the common people. Powerful individuals with international or government connections, however, can move quickly; it is they who gain under conditions of rapid externally directed change.

Projects that call for expensive inputs, machinery for example, reinforce this economic polarization, since only the wealthy few may follow this precedent. In so doing, they further their competitive edge over their kinsmen.

Finally, one of the more serious operational problems in Somali development efforts, waste and apathy, is evident only in government- (or other outside agency-) initiated schemes, not in indigenous ones. One example should suffice (although there are a great number): nobody forgets to change the oil on *qat* trucks!

What Somalis Do Need

The view from the top sells Somalis short. It emphasizes their lacks without considering what is achievable. And it does so for largely political reasons. After decades of aid, which filled in shortfalls and supported unworkable policies, it is more advantageous and more comfortable for donors and recipients alike to continue a relationship of dependency than to search for real solutions. To the extent that Somalis are constrained by outside forces, they do need assistance. The Australians, for example, are commanding a larger bite of the Saudi livestock market, aided by technological advances far outside the reach of Somali traders. Jobs in the Gulf are drying up with the oil glut, closing off an important Somali resource base.

The aid that is needed is not the massive chunks or the monolithic projects that donors find most convenient and cost-effective. Instead donors can assist in removing those structures that stifle indigenous initiative; in discovering where the growing edge of the Somali economy lies; and in judicious support, both monetary and non-monetary (e.g., basic research on local fungal diseases) in all sectors that are indeed innovating.

References

Aronson, Dan, 1980. "Kinsmen and Comrades: Towards a Class Analysis of the Somali Pastoral Sector," *Nomadic Peoples*, no. 7, November:14–23.

Behnke, Roy, 1980. "Indigenous Modernization in Pastoral Cyrenaica," paper presented at African Studies Association, 23rd Annual Meeting, Philadelphia.

Berg, Elliot, 1982. "Encouraging the Private Sector in Somalia," report prepared for USAID, Washington D.C., September.

Box, Thadis W., 1971. "Nomadism and Land Use in Somalia," *Economic Development and Cultural Change*, vol. 19, January:222–28.

Cassanelli, Lee V., 1981. "Drought and Famine in Somalia: Pastoral Strategies through the Twentieth Century," paper presented at seminar on Food Production Systems and Environmental Rehabilitation in Somalia, National Academy of Sciences, Washington, D.C., June.

Cassanelli, Lee V., 1985. "Qat," unpublished manuscript.

Geshekter, Charles L., 1981. "Entrepreneurs, Livestock and Politics: British Somaliland 1920–1950," paper presented at International Colloquium: Enterprises et Entrepreneurs en Afrique, XIXe et XXe siècles, December.

Haakonsen, Jan, 1983. "The Socio-economic Structures of Two Southern Somali Villages: Lama Doonka and Beled Aamin," Somali Academy of Sciences and Arts, March, Report no. 1.

Hardin, Garret, 1968. "The Tragedy of the Commons," *Science*, vol. 162, December 13:1243–48.

Hartley, B./FAO, 1966. *Livestock Development Survey of Somalia: Recommendations Regarding Land Tenure*, unpublished document.

Hoben et al., 1983. *Somalia: A Social and Institutional Profile*, study prepared for USAID by African Studies Center, Boston University.

Hunt, J. A., 1951. *A General Survey of the Somaliland Protectorate, 1944–50*, London, His Majesty's Stationery Office.

IFAD (International Fund for Agricultural Development), 1979. *Report of the Special Programming Mission to Somalia*, Rome.

IMF: IFS(International Monetary Fund), 1984. *International Financial Statistics*, Washington, D.C.

Jodha, N. S., 1982. "The Role of Administration in Desertification: Land Tenure as a Factor in the Historical Ecology of Western Rajasthan," in Brian Spooner and H. S. Mann, eds., *Desertification and Development*, New York, Academic Press.

Jorgenson, Harold T., 1960. *Land Tenure Problems, Republic of Somalia: Land Tenure Reform*, unpublished manuscript, Washington, D.C., U.S. International Cooperation Agency.

Karp, Mark, 1960. *The Economics of Trusteeship in Somalia*, Boston: Boston University Press.

Laitin, David, 1976. "The Political Economy of Military Rule in Somalia," *Journal of Modern African Studies*, vol. 14, no. 3:449–68.

Lewis, I. M., 1962. "Lineage Continuity and Modern Commerce in Northern Somaliland, in P. Bohannon and G. Dalton, eds., *Markets in Africa*, Evanston, Ill., Northwestern University Press.

Lewis, I. M., 1969. "From Nomadism to Cultivation: The Expansion of Political Solidarity in Southern Somalia," in Mary Douglas and Phyllis M. Kaberry, eds., *Man in Africa*, London, Tavistock Publications.

Lewis, I. M., 1981. *Somali Culture, History, and Social Institutions*, London, London School of Economics.

Luling, Virginia, 1971. *The Social Structure of Southern Somali Tribes*, Ph.D. dissertation, University of London.

Mahony, Frank, 1961. "Range Management in the Somali Republic," *Community Development Review*, June: 34–69.

Reusse, E., 1982. "Somalia's Nomadic Livestock Economy: Its Response to Profitable Export Opportunity," *World Animal Review*, no. 43:2–11.

Seager, Andrew, 1984. Personal communication.

Swift, Jeremy, 1977. "Pastoral Development in Somalia: Herding Cooperatives as a Strategy against Desertification and Famine," in M. Glantz, ed., *Desertification: Environmental Degradation in and around Arid Lands*, Boulder, Colo., Westview Press.

Whitaker, R., 1982. *Area Handbook for Somalia*, Washington, D.C., Government Printing Office.

9. Algeria

Bettina Herr

Cooperative farms managed by elected representatives of peasants; one thousand socialist villages; land to those who worked it; no properties greater than necessary for family sustenance; technical assistance, seeds, fertilizers supplied by government agencies: these were the promises of the Algerian land reform of 1971.

Only eleven years later, credit and inputs were scarce and technical assistance virtually nil; prices were controlled by central authority to the disadvantage of the farmer; most cooperatives were earning no profit and could scarcely pay their wages; their "elected" management could make no decisions, for it was overridden by government officials; agricultural output per capita had slipped by 28% (FAO 1983:87). In the early eighties, the government began to loosen the leash on the peasants, in hopes that greater freedom of pricing and markets would stimulate output. The determination to enact this new policy, or its success, is still unclear.

Independence: The "Self-Managed" Sector

French Algeria originates in a slap in the face administered by the dey of Algiers to the French consul in 1830. Partly for revenge, partly to distract Parisian attention from the events leading to the July revolution, and purportedly to end piracy on the Barbary coast, Charles X ordered that Algeria be taken. The history from then until independence in 1962 is one of Algerian resistance interspersed by French take-overs of more and more land, allegedly in punishment for subversion, but clearly also to establish the presence necessary to make Algeria "forever French." By the middle of the twentieth century, almost all the fertile land of northern Algeria was in French hands, while the south was still held largely by Algerians and nomads.

On the eve of independence, several French estates were spontaneously taken over by workers, who declared them to be "self-managed farms." (Quotation marks are used because the term does not describe the reality.) Their action was made legal in 1963, at which time the remaining French farms began to be expropriated and turned over to the workers. By 1964, 21,700 former colonial farms, containing about 2,700,000 hectares, had been regrouped into 2,190 "self-managed" domains (Kielstra 1978). In one

165

way or another, 300,000 to 400,000 hectares "disappeared," appropriated by private Algerians.

The spontaneous process of the workers was itself quickly taken over by the state, which administered the expropriation of French farms, turning them over to the new Office nationale de la réforme agraire (ONRA). These units were large (mostly 500 to 1,000 hectares; 1975 data). But a few, over 1,000 hectares, covered 70.3% of the "self-managed" sector (Trautmann 1979:99). The distortions in size are revealed in Table 1.

The Land Reform

Before 1971, Algerian farmland outside the "self-managed" sector was held in small private units, close to or less than subsistence size. Of these, 73.4% was held in farms of 50 hectares or under, averaging 7.5 hectares (Table 2), while only 4.9% was held in units over over 200 hectares.

Despite the already small size of 95% of the private farmland, the stated purpose of the Agrarian Revolution (*Révolution Agraire*) of 1971 was to

---

Table 9.1

AREA IN "SELF-MANAGED" FARMS (IN HECTARES, EXCEPT COLUMN 2)

Size of Farms	No. of Farms	Total Area	Average Area
0–50	27	625	23.1
50–200	170	22,565	132.7
200 +	1,991	2,309,670	1,160.1
Total or average	2,188	2,322,860	1,066.2

SOURCE: Abdi (1975:33).

Table 9.2

DISTRIBUTION OF PRIVATE-SECTOR LAND BEFORE THE AGRARIAN REVOLUTION

Size of Unit (hectares)	No. of Units	Total Area (hectares)	Average Area	Percent of Total
0–50	570,315	4,287,170	7.5	73.4
50–200	15,645	1,267,310	81.0	21.7
200 +	885	285,180	322.2	4.9
Total or average	586,845	5,839,660	9.9	100.0

SOURCE: Abdi (1975:33).

eliminate exploitation of small farmers by large landowners who had replaced the French. Holdings would be regrouped into larger units—cooperatives—with presumed advantages of scale. Private holdings would be constrained but not eliminated.

Five stages of the Agrarian Revolution would redefine the access rights to land. First, the state collected all public land into the National Fund of the Agrarian Revolution (FNRA), redistributed it to qualifying applicants and grouped them into cooperatives. The second phase abolished absentee landlords and limited private farms to the size that could be cultivated by the family. In the third phase, ownership rights of tribal and communal pasture lands were abolished and these lands turned over to FNRA for grouping into cooperatives. The fourth and fifth stages would redistribute forest lands and reorganize access to irrigation. It is not yet clear whether stages 4 and 5 have begun, and little information is available on them. Therefore, we confine our discussion, below, to the first three stages. Acronyms used in the following pages are explained in the List of Acronyms at the end of this chapter.

First Phase (1971–73)

Lands of the first phase were public, communal, tribal, or religious. Before the Agrarian Revolution, these lands had been mainly rented, the best ones often to large landholders or wealthy peasants, who also owned land. But there were many different sizes, so both small holdings and large were expropriated (Bessaoud 1980:607). While the government may have considered all these lands in the same category, the tribes, communities, and religious organizations probably saw matters differently. Most of this land was mediocre or even marginal, but 800,000 hectares of fertile agricultural land were included.

Data on quantities distributed and grouped into cooperatives are unclear and conflicting. It would seem, however, that half the communal lands were regrouped into cooperatives. By 1973, there were 2,614 cooperatives. These decreased to 2,489 because farms were abandoned, but by the end of 1974 they had increased again to 2,921, where the number stabilized. The respective amounts of land were 730,756, 675,000, and 788,285 hectares (Abdi 1975:34). Abdi further reports that by 1975, 7.7% of the beneficiaries had abandoned their farms. One has the impression of considerable turnover, though this is hard to confirm.

Furthermore, cooperatives continued to be regrouped into larger ones. As of mid-1975, the number of cooperatives had decreased to 2,153 (of which 1,627 were CAPRA, 502 GPMV, and twenty-four GEP),* while average size increased from about 275 to about 289 hectares. We consulted a number of sources (we do not go into details) with differing figures;

---

*A list of acronyms appears at the end of this chapter.

therefore, we enter a cautious note on the data we have selected, which come from Abdi (1975). On average, a cooperative consisted of about eighteen or nineteen farmers, each of whom would be assigned about 14.6 hectares. During the entire first phase, the farming population on these lands decreased by about half.

Second Phase (1973-75)

Although about one million hectares of private land were eligible under the second phase, in fact only about 635,000 were nationalized (Guichaoua 1977:593). Only 3.12% of landlords were deemed absentees (in a re-census the percentage was revised to 2.75%), while those whose holdings were "limited" were only 2.36% (revised to 0.61%). Out of these lands, 1,792 CAPRA were created, along with eighty-three GPMV, and ninety-nine GEP. During both the first and second phases, 555 CAEC and 400 CAPC were also created, though the timing is not available (Guichaoua 1977:592).

Most absentee landlords did not have their lands nationalized because of exceptions applying to farmers over the age of sixty, freedom fighters incapacitated (60% or more) in the war of independence, non-married widows of fallen independence fighters, and descendants of war veterans (Secrétariat 1973). Abdi (1975:37) therefore commented that "the abolition of absenteeism has been a mere exception." Since 1.5 million hectares of this land remained in farms of over 50 hectares (compared with an average size of 32 hectares), and since half of these farms belonged to city-dwellers, Abdi also concluded that the nationalization touched medium owners more than the landed bourgeoisie.

There were some favorable exceptions granted to private properties limited in size. Revenue permitted from these lands could be up to three times the earnings of a farmer in the "self-managed" sector (Secrétariat 1973). Extra-agricultural earnings up to 9,500 DA (Algerian dinars: 4.9 = $1.00) were also permitted (or 13,500 DA for families with children). Thus at best, a family might earn up to 27,000 DA, or six times the income of a permanent worker in the "self-managed" sector (Abdi 1975:37).

Naturally, the government needed a mechanism to control these earnings, so land was divided into "zones of equal earning potential"; presumably farms were allocated in such a way that the limits would turn out the equal probable earnings. Such a feat, however, would be difficult at best, in view of land distributed among different geographical regions, some irrigated and some not. Dry hillsides next to water-rich valleys led to fields of different potential close to each other. The government decreed that non-irrigated farms might vary from 5 to 110 hectares depending on location, while irrigated ones would range from 1 to 5 hectares (Karsenty 1979:97). The organization of such a plan would require a degree of ability, integrity, and cadastral techniques that might have taxed the ingenuities

168

of governments possessing far more resources and skills than those of Algeria.

Yet size limitations did indeed cause land to be lost by the largest holders, for average farm size in this sector became 72 hectares (Abdi 1975:37). Owners who lost their lands were compensated by government bonds at 2.5% interest for fifteen years (Trautmann 1979:220); they were also allowed to keep equipment and machinery. However, sales of large farm equipment to the private sector were prohibited thereafter; thus they were unable to replace equipment or in some cases even to repair it.

Landholders did everything possible to keep their lands. Some understated their holdings to avoid nationalization, others overstated them to receive greater compensation (Michalski 1983:653). They distributed lands among family members. Sometimes only one family member at work was sufficient to avoid being classified as absentee (Abdi 1975:37). Others went to the commissions of appeals, which were sometimes accused of being mere syndicates of large landholders (subject to corruption?). Poor peasants were not well represented in these commissions, having at best two representatives out of thirteen (Bessaoud 1980:610). In some cases, however, the commission did restore poor peasants' land that had been wrongly nationalized (Joensson 1978:51).

Finally, large landowners also encroached slowly on their formerly owned lands, sometimes cultivating them just as if they had not been nationalized, sometimes intimidating the beneficiaries (Michalski 1983:654).

Limitation or nationalization of date palms, the main source of wealth in southern Algeria, offered another target for the Agrarian Revolution. Since the south had not been heavily colonized, these plantations had been mainly Algerian-owned, but income inequalities were severe. Around Tiquedidine, 3% of the farmers owned 25% of the date palms and 33% of the water resources, while 85% of the plantations were below the subsistence threshold (de Villiers 1979:18). Among the medium and large plantations, khammesat (tenancy contract, with 20% of the output for tenants and 80% for landlord) was common (de Villiers 1979:19).

Once again, equal-income brackets were declared. Different varieties of palm trees were ranked according to their "equivalency" to the palm of highest quality: deglet noir. Plantation owners were classified as absentee or working and were treated accordingly. In no case, however, was a small plantation (twenty palm trees or less) nationalized.

Third Phase (1975–Present)

In the third phase, all ownership of communal and tribal pasture lands—estimated at 15 to 20 million hectares—was turned over to the FNRA (Abdi 1975:38). Most of this land pastured sheep, with 50% of the flocks belonging to 5% of the owners.

Limitation and absentee-owner provisions now applied to flocks rather than land, and sheep were distributed to shepherds who had had none. Beneficiaries were grouped into cooperatives (CEPRA), which averaged 1,000 hectares and twenty-six shepherds with 2,000 sheep (Abdi 1975:34). Each beneficiary was entitled to 100 sheep and five rams, or up to half again as many for those with children.

Here the reform was intended to slow desertification, with "green barriers" to be erected by GMV cooperatives. Nomadic herdsmen would be settled, so they might be more easily provided with services to increase their standard of living. Regional service cooperatives (CAPC), for example, would supply wells ands veterinary stations.

Resulting problems are reminiscent of those described by Gunn in Chapter 8. Nomadic families had been using fertile pockets for intensive agriculture during part of the year. But this activity was prohibited, because the soil was presumably too fragile (Trautmann 1982:94). The limitation on transhumance deteriorated the quality of land and vegetation, for want of manure. Nomads had been accustomed to following plants according to season: some plants could be used in springtime only, while others—toxic in the spring—would become available elsewhere in the summer. Only the nomads knew where the appropriate vegetation was at the appropriate times. Limiting their migrations probably led to overgrazing (Schnetzler 1980:68). Farming was limited on marginal lands—which may or may not have protected the lands—but the income of nomads was limited and balance in diets interrupted.

Not all the intervention was necessarily negative, however. Cottage industries were promoted in pilot provinces, including poultry and rabbit raising, as well as weaving (Trautmann 1982:105). We do not yet have reports on the success of these ventures.

Distribution to Individuals

In those few places where farmers could not be grouped into cooperatives, individual titles—for less than 3% of all lands distributed—were awarded to 5,540 beneficiaries by 1975. But the number of individual holders quickly increased from 4% to 13% of all beneficiaries, since some, especially around Algiers, refused to join cooperatives (Abdi 1975:38).

Organization of Cooperatives

In all types of cooperatives, except the "self-managed" sector, governance is theoretically divided between the representatives of the workers and government officials. The general assembly of members elects a Committee of Workers, which in turn elects the president of the cooperative. In the case of fewer than ten members, the president is elected directly. The Ministry of Agriculture then appoints a technical assistant or director, while the Ministry of Finance handles the accounting.

Five managing bodies theoretically shared administration of the "self-managed" sector in its early years. At the lowest level was the General Assembly of Workers (AGT) which elected the Council of Workers (CT), which presumably controlled all cooperative operations through its Committee of Management (CG). The CG would elect the president. Finally, a state director was assigned to the domain to survey technical aspects of production.

Theoretically, the flow of power was from the bottom up; in actuality, several factors interfered. First, the AGT consisted only of permanent workers on the domain, thus part-time workers were excluded from all decisions. But the designation of full-time or part-time was not clear from the functions of a worker; rather it was decided by a few influential families who might use this leverage to their personal advantage or for coercion (Fernandez-Romero 1976:33). Part-time workers received less pay and enjoyed fewer amenities than full-time.

Second, the AGT and CT, which in principle held regular meetings, in fact rarely did so. In some cases, there was no CT, and the AGT rubber-stamped decisions of the CG. Often the CG consisted of powerful families who elected the president from among their numbers, with no reference to the wishes of their "constituents." Fernandez-Romero likened this corruption to the traditional power structure in northern Africa, where the interests of a few families dominated the tribe. The state director, presumably a technical advisor, in fact became the principal decisionmaker.

These excesses provoked the government to pass a number of decrees and laws in 1968 and 1969. Certain measures appeared, on the surface, to favor the peasants: full-time and part-time workers were made equal; the president was to be elected directly by the AGT; no two relatives of first degree could belong to the same CT or CG; and the state director could not be related to any member of either body or to the president. Instead of technical assistant, the state director was made an "advisor," although in fact he retained his veto over major decisions.

Still, the government's idea of protecting the farmers was not to return the decision power to them but to arrogate it to itself. Central government agencies intruded in the cooperative structure. ONRA, which had controlled production, marketing, and credit, was dismantled in favor of the Ministry of Agriculture and Agrarian Revolution (MARA). Credit was taken over by the Central Bank (BNA), while several new national agencies were created to manage the cooperatives. (Kielstra 1978:7). By these moves, the "self-managed" estates became virtually indistinguishable from the cooperatives created by the Agrarian Revolution of 1971.

From the beginning, the "self-managed" farms produced less than the same lands had under the French, a lag that continued at least until 1972. The main reasons usually given for this are the lack of trained managers and technicians and spare parts. Some have argued also that the farms are above optimal size (Trautmann 1982:99). But wage policy must also be responsible. Workers received advances, and later they shared profits.

However, the accounting system was prescribed by accounting "cooperatives" set up by the state and organized by provinces. These "cooperatives" have ruled that after covering costs, part of the revenue of the farmers' cooperative must be devoted to reinvestment and savings (Kielstra 1978:7). Only after that may profits be shared. But many cooperatives run deficits. With no profit to share, the guaranteed minimum wage becomes the maximum earnings of workers (Karsenty 1977:32). Since this minimum was far less than urban wages, workers have abandoned cooperatives, and those who have remained are, in effect, state employees on their own farms.

A further reason for the chronic deficit has been deteriorating internal terms of trade until 1972, dictated by government pricing policy (Karsenty 1977:32). From 1962 to 1971, prices of outputs were almost stable, while prices of farm inputs rose sharply. The cereal price rose 5% during that period, and the wine price 1% from 1966 to 1970. Input prices, however, rose from 38% to 130%, depending on the product (Karsenty 1977:32).

One Thousand Socialist Villages

In the mid-seventies, the Algerian government assessed its rural settlement as fragmented and poorly organized, in dispersed hamlets or loose clusters of houses. This situation was compared with more developed countries, which possessed a varied hierarchy of market places to facilitate commercialization of agriculture (Sutton 1982:247). In addition, rural infrastructure—roads, schools, if not electricity—was deemed to be more easily supplied to clusters than to scattered homesteads—shades of Tanzania and its *Ujamaa* villages (Chapter 4).

Out of 800,000 to 850,000 rural dwellings counted in the 1966 census, 32% possessed only one room, while 42% had two or three; 53% were of solid construction, 23% were of thatch, reed and mud, and 18% were tents. Approximately 50% had a kitchen, 8% electricity, and 10% running water. People per room averaged 3.5 (Boukhobza 1978:32–47).

As early as 1967, the state had attempted to help villagers construct their own houses, but the program had turned out too expensive (Sutton 1982:249). In the mid-seventies, however, the "thousand socialist villages" program was launched, to upgrade rural housing and to create an interlocking commercial network.

Three types of villages were envisioned. The simplest would be the primary village, of 100 to 200 dwellings for 700 to 1,400 people. Each would contain an elementary school with six grades, basic retail stores, and a branch office of the local government. Secondary villages, of 250 to 300 dwellings for 1,750 to 2,400 inhabitants, would have the same basic services, plus schooling up to twelve grades, a post office, a gas station, and a building for the agricultural cooperatives. Tertiary villages would be local administrative centers, of 400 to 700 dwellings for 2,800 to 4,900 people. In addition to all the facilities of the secondary villages, each in the tertiary would have a college, youth club, stadium, public bath, cafe, market, police station, bank branch, city hall, and a multipurpose cooperative (type CAPC) (Sutton 1982:250).

One hundred of these villages were to be built under the first Four Year Plan (1970-74), 300 more under the second Plan (1974-77), and all one thousand were to be completed by 1980. But these aspirations were overly ambitious. Although 402 villages had been planned by December 1979, only 147 had been completed by June 1981.

Many reasons explain the delay. Socioeconomic studies to determine village locations would be needed, but they would have to be carried out by many agencies (provinces, subcontractors, other private groups, and state agencies), which did not coordinate well. Further, the scant constituency for the studies led to their being implemented perfunctorily, with resulting inconsistencies. The village of Oum Teboul, for instance, was built on a flood plain with the only drinkable water 5 kilometers away (Boumaza 1976:44)!

Also, different construction agencies worked at different speeds. Projects endorsed by the army or by a national company were completed with little delay; those managed by provinces—60% of the total—took much longer. Delays occurred for lack for building materials (specifically, cement) and because of shortages of skilled workers and escalating costs. Sometimes, private contractors would go bankrupt and a state agency would assume their functions. Contractors were accused of blocking progress by demanding re-evaluation of costs. One village, Boulhilet, had to be reconstructed because building materials were not solid enough (Boumaza 1976:44).

Although some have argued that completed villages functioned reasonably well and most peasants were content with their houses, there were land complaints. Peasants found themselves with smaller courtyards than before, or with no courtyard at all. Often they lacked space for traditional vegetable gardens. Animal quarters were too small for families accustomed to keeping sheep, rabbits, and poultry for food; for sale to cover emergencies; and lambs for sacrifices required by Islam.

When they lacked a vegetable garden, which would supplement their diet, peasants were forced to buy food on the market, where prices were increasing by more than their wages. Because of price and wage controls, land-reform beneficiaries found themselves having to buy back their own products at more than they had been paid to produce them. As one villager said, "without outside help, you cannot live" (Burgat 1979:58).

House size was also a common complaint, because buildings were set closely together, which did not permit expansion. Such crowding constrained the extended family, still prevalent in rural Algeria (Adair 1982:64). Quality and location were also questioned: ceilings have caved in; villages built on flood plains have been inundated; hasty construction has led to excessive humidity indoors. "The houses are for the outside appearance; inside they are not even good for animals" (Burgat 1979:59).

Authors differ as to whether, on balance, the peasant finds his situation improved in a socialist village over what it had been earlier. A resident nurse, biweekly visits by a doctor, and school are all welcomed (Burgat 1979:59). But would peasants prefer their former dwellings: thatched roofs or tents, with spaces for vegetable gardens and animals, or do they prefer the services despite the sacrifices? Unfortunately, no one that we know of—either the government or the researchers—has taken the trouble to ask them.

Even if the peasants do approve (on balance) of their new situations, two larger questions remain. One is whether the whole program was worth its cost, considering the small proportion of the population that "benefited" from it. With an average of 200 dwellings per village, an average family size of seven, and forty villages inhabited in 1976, we find a total of about 56,000 out of a rural population that in 1977 was estimated at 9,800,000. Even had the full one thousand villages been completed on schedule, at best 5% of the rural population would have benefited. Adair (1982:64) estimates that only 1.5% of rural population was participating in 1980. Lepoul (1977:45) charges that this poor performance is deliberately suppressed in the government news, which falsely touts the state as the great benefactor of vast numbers of peasantry.

The other question asks about motivations of the state. After the state tightened its jurisdiction over the "self-managed" sector, and after it grouped the small, private farms into cooperatives that it also controls, do the thousand socialist villages become but another vehicle of economic and political control, designed to tie the peasants to both the central government and a market economy dependent on the urban industrialization plan?

Though peasants have not been asked, many are voting with their feet. Especially in villages near the major industrial centers of the north—Oran, Algiers, and Annaba—peasants have been abandoning both socialist villages and cooperatives to seek urban jobs. This movement is not *just* the rural-to-urban migration found ubiquitously in the Third World. In most such migrations, rural areas remain at their maximum population density. Farms and homesteads continue to be occupied by remaining family members. In Algeria, however, farms and homesteads have been abandoned by those unable to cope with the terms of trade, lifestyle, and other restrictions imposed upon them by the ever-present state.

The Private Sector

The state has tried to limit the private agricultural sector by subsuming farms into cooperatives. It has also tried to tie the remaining farms into state agencies, which have monopolized and restricted the amount of

174

credit available and have made it more difficult for private farms to purchase machinery such as tractors and even ordinary inputs. As a result, private farm productivity has deteriorated even more than that of the state sector.

Limitation of the private sector was the aim of Phase Two. Before the Agrarian Revolution, 700,000 private farms occupied about 6 million hectares, with (therefore) an average size of approximately 8.5 hectares. These farms were considered two distinct groups. In the "traditional" segment, occupying five-sixths or even more of the total area, 47% of the farmers still used animal traction. The others were the "modern" sector, whose size was not precisely documented but probably fell between 600,000 and one million hectares (Karsenty 1977:33). Despite the Agrarian Revolution, 730,000 farms remained private in 1976, covering 4.7 million hectares, with (therefore) an average size slightly more than 6.4 hectares. Farms of less than 10 hectares constituted 80% of the total. As might have been expected, when the modern portion had been largely converted into cooperatives, the average size of remaining private farms was reduced.

Whereas in most countries of private and collective farming (e.g., Soviet Union, Cuba, Tanzania, Mexico) the productivity of the former outstrips that of the latter, in Algeria the case is reversed. While private farms account for the greatest share of total output—as indeed they should, for they occupy the greatest percentage of land—nevertheless their productivity is somewhat below that of cooperatives and the "self-managed" sector. In 1978, private farms produced 4.91 quintals per hectare, compared with 7.60 for "self-managed" farms and 5.09 for the cooperatives. In barley, the figures were 3.8, 9.18, and 5.38 respectively. In soft wheat the private sector did relatively better, with 5.10 quintals per hectare compared with 4.40 for the cooperatives and 7.22 for the "self-managed" sector.

Why the difference at all? The most obvious reason is that the "self-managed" sector, consisting of former French farms on the most fertile territory, most conveniently located for market, started with a natural advantage. Then, the more favorable private lands were grouped into cooperatives. More insidiously, however, the private sector has been discriminated against in every conceivable way. Credit, for example, was virtually unavailable. Since 1966, "modern" private farms, what was left of them, were not permitted any credit, having to fend for themselves as best they could (Karsenty 1975:120). "Equipment loans" (not crop credit) were permitted the "traditional" private farms. These were offered under quotas, and early permissions were rapidly exhausted. Beginning in 1971, they were limited to the "investment capacity" of a "traditional" farmer—or rather, what the lending agencies presumed that capacity to be—and they fell off sharply. Several authors (Cote 1979; de Villiers 1980) agree that these credits went more to medium-size farms than to small. The drop-off in credits to the "traditional" sector is shown in Table 3.

Table 9.3

CREDITS PROVIDED AND CREDITS USED BY THE "TRADITIONAL"
SECTOR, 1966–73 (THOUSANDS OF ALGERIAN DINARS)

	1966	1967	1968	1969	1970	1971	1972	1973
Credits provided	120.0	115.0	118.0	110.0	90.0	60.0	40.0	60.0
Credits used	85.0	113.0	110.0	102.1	54.0	45.4	22.5	12.2
Percentage used	74	98	93	92	60	75	56	20

SOURCE: Karsenty (1975:138).

Not only did the total amount of credit offered to the "traditional" sector drop off rapidly in the years shown in Table 3, but the share that sector was able to draw dropped from slightly less than 100%, 1967–1969, to only 20% by 1973. These quantities resulted from the tightening that began in the early seventies.

Thus the government's attempt to help the "traditional" sector worsened the conditions of the small farmer. Since all credit was directed toward the medium-size farmer, no other sources were left for the smaller one. Land contracts also discriminated against the small farmer. In one type, the larger farmer would contract the smaller to share-crop on his lands. In another, the larger farmer, having bought equipment with loans from the state, would rent it to the smaller farmer. The latter would end up in debt bondage to the former (Cote 1979:78).

Suddenly, in 1971 the government stopped all sales of farm equipment to the private sector. The impact of this decision is shown in Table 4. From then on, all private farmers would receive most services and rent their equipment from the multipurpose service cooperatives (CAPC). Cote (1979:12) comments that the economic and political condition of the small farmer had remained essentially unchanged by the Agrarian Revolution; the CAPC had merely replaced the absentee landlord.

Probably because of deficiencies in agricultural output, officials in the early eighties began to take a new look at the private sector. Odd perhaps that this phenomenon should occur simultaneously in a number of socialist countries, including the Soviet Union and China. Credit for private farms has eased considerably since 1982 (Harvey 1984:54). Once again, machinery and equipment are becoming accessible. In 1982, more than 60% of the 7,800 tractors acquired went to private farms, as did the same percentage of the 2,000 tractors acquired in 1983 (Harvey 1984:54).

Two questions remain. First, does this new liberalization affect the

Table 9.4
ACQUISITION OF TRACTORS BY THE PRIVATE SECTOR, 1962–73

Year	No. of Tractors
1962–66	4,400
1967	1,830
1968	1,733
1969	1,271
1970	792
1971	62
1972	77
1973	18

SOURCE: Karsenty (1977:33).

poorer peasants or is it once again an approach to the medium size? It is too early to judge. But second, is the turnabout permanent? Or is it merely the mode of the times, by a capricious government, which today sees its advantage in catering to private farms, but which retains the right to change its mind tomorrow? Is it the current decision that counts, or the power to make decisions?

Distribution

Since Algerian independence, in 1962, state agencies have been charged with marketing agricultural products, including imports, exports, and domestic production. But the duties of ONACO, founded in 1962, were broad and vague. When ONRA was formed in 1963, ONACO's responsibilities in marketing were made more precise. Under ONRA's direction, food processing cooperatives (CORA), created in 1964, would buy products of the "self-managed" estates, prepare them for export, and sell the surplus domestically (Bouzidi 1977:505).

But the producer would not receive payment right away, nor indeed would he know the price until the sale was concluded on the final market. Then the cooperatives would receive the balance, net of transport and processing costs. In that way, they ran all the risks, and they swallowed all the inefficiencies and corruption of the government buying agencies. So unsatisfactory was the arrangement that in fact, only about half of the vegetables and three-quarters of the fruit were sold to government agencies, the rest being clandestinely marketed in private channels (Bouzidi 1977:506).

Increasing dissatisfaction led to two reorganizations, one in 1966 and one 1974. But in each case, as has been found in the other case studies of this book, problems resulting from government intervention were addressed by more government intervention. In the first reorganization, ONRA was replaced by UNCAC, which would coordinate distribution under the direct tutelage of MARA. The CORA were still responsible for marketing, while CORE would distribute products locally. Still, most local distribution was done privately, while the new organization was directed mainly at export crops from the "self-managed" sector (Bouzidi 1977:509).

But the proportion of that output marketed through the CORA continued to decline. Instead of in cash, CORA would pay the "self-managed" cooperatives in notes receivable. In September 1968, thirty-seven CORA owed almost 26 million dinars to the production cooperatives. Although the CORA blamed high fixed costs and overemployment for their inability to pay debts, their profits nevertheless amounted to 28 million dinars in 1968 (Bouzidi 1977:511).

Deficient quality control also led to wastage. Fully 40% of the delivered produce in 1967–68 was unfit for export: it either spoiled, was sold internally, or was consumed within CORA. And the producers suffered the losses, for they were paid only for what was sold. Sometimes they did not even cover their costs.

As the government became aware that rural exodus, consumption on farms, and secret sale to private distributors were sapping the product it had intended for itself, it tightened its control with the reorganization of 1974. All cooperatives—in the "self-managed" or agrarian-reform sector—were *required* to sell all produce to the local CAPCS, which would supply local merchants. The CAPCS would sell any surplus to the provincial COFEL, which in turn were required to buy such surpluses. COFEL would balance out local surpluses and shortages within the province and sell any provincial surplus to OFLA, a national agency *required* to buy it. To assure "just compensation" for producers, a 30% global markup was charged for screening, packaging, and distribution. These agricultural output, distribution, and prices became a command economy nationally.

Yet the national distribution machine refused to operate smoothly. Market information would have to be evaluated daily, perishable goods being moved from place of abundance to place of shortage quickly. But the officials did not know which places were which (Kielstra 1978:9). In Mascara in 1966–67, 600,000 quintals of potatoes rotted because neither CAPCS nor COFEL could find a buyer, while at the same time potatoes were in short supply in northern cities (Joensson 1978:55). There are other similar examples.

Furthermore, delivery equipment was not properly deployed. The cooperatives did not have enough trucks to pick up and deliver the product at harvest. So they used private trucking companies, which charged 10% of the produce value—a reasonable margin, perhaps, but one not budgeted. Sometimes the directors of CAPCS would refuse to pick up produce already in abundant supply (Bouzidi 1977:56).

Naturally, cooperatives preferred to sell on the black market rather than

178

let their produce rot. Of course, the artificial scarcities in some places and abundance in others, caused by the state system, increased the arbitrage margin for private distributors, while compressing the profits of peasant producers.

Further, the government agencies did not think of returning containers, nor did they provide adequate storage. Fruits and vegetables would rot for want of either shipping containers or storage bins. Here again, the producers had to turn to private suppliers. Here again, the private companies would overcharge to compensate for the risk of illegal business and the costs of secrecy. Monopolies are vicious for all the reasons economists ascribe to them, but they are even more so when they fail to provide the services that they legally monopolize.

Pricing

All agricultural retail prices are fixed every two weeks by a pricing commission consisting of the provincial director of commerce, the director of COFEL, the president of COFEL, plus one representative of all other interested parties, such as the Union of Workers and the Union of Algerian Women. Their terms of reference are highly motivated. Prices are set:

1. to compensate the producer fairly;
2. to finance distribution organisms adequately; and
3. to harmonize retail sale prices nationally.

Producer prices, on the other hand, are set by MARA every two weeks. Apparently also MARA determines the retail prices, which the pricing commissions rubberstamp. But MARA's methods of calculation remain mysterious; they have never been revealed (Granier 1978:81).

Yet no human being can adequately grasp, much less handle, the vagaries in production costs with different climates, different technologies, different costs of transportation, seasonal variations, and the like. Prices that barely cover the costs of one will produce a substantial surplus for another. Is the inefficiency of one to be condoned, or the profit of the other to be constrained? Those who have harvested in time of surplus, with low prices, and who have had to sell to the private sector, will not have acquired enough funds to buy fertilizer and seed at prices set on the assumption that their produce had been bought by public agencies at higher prices. The manner in which prices have been administered— intended as an incentive to production—has ended up discouraging it instead (Granier 1978:82).

Prices have in fact been set to maximize the profits of the government monopolies to the detriment of peasants. In the province of Setif in 1977, for example, production cooperatives sold their melons to OFLA for 0.75 DA/kg., while OFLA resold them to the consumer for 3.50 to 4.50 DA/kg. While it is quite possible that the margin represented legitimate marketing costs, the lack of accounting for them makes it suspicious. Furthermore, prices of goods sold privately by producers have consistently been greater than those sold to government agencies. In 1975, the discrepancy between private and official prices ranged between 28% for onions and 51% for zucchini (Bouzidi 1977:519).

Reforms of the Eighties

With the election of Bendjedid Chadli as President in 1979, the door to liberalism opened a crack. Beginning in 1980, cooperatives were allowed to sell to private producers (Burgat 1983:87). Price conditions were liberalized in 1982, but to date no one has compiled the new regulations for systematic analysis. On October 31, 1984, Paul Lewis in *The New York Times* was able to report:

> The capital has a dilapidated air. Food and most other goods are scarce, and fruit juice is unobtainable in a country that was once France's orange grove . . . young people gazing at half empty shops. . . .
> Yet beneath the surface, a process of change and relaxation is under way. . . . Housing and farmland seized from the departing French are being sold cheaply to private owners. Efforts are under way to increase production of consumer goods, and private businessmen are being encouraged by the Government. . . .
> The Soviet style centralized economic planning and enormous investment in heavy industry favored by Algeria's early rulers are now recognized as mistakes. So too is the neglect of agriculture, which has produced an explosion in food imports that last year cost the country $2.6 billion, or a quarter of energy earnings.

On November 12, 1988, Steven Greenhouse wrote in *The New York Times* that "Mr. Benjedid's plan to rent 3,500 collectivized farms to private farmers is going smoothly." These tendencies, along with their effects on output and incomes, are all left for future analysis. Observers who favor the market may now be optimistic. But we must remind ourselves soberly that so long as the government is absolutist, in practice if not in principle, and so long as it remains non-accountable to the peasantry, the present stage might be a ruler's whim.

List of Acronyms

AGT: Assemblée générale des travailleurs – general assembly of workers
BNA: Banque Nationale d'Algérie – Algerian National Bank
CAEC: Coopérative agricole d'exploitation en commun – cooperative for the common working of the land
CAPAM: Coopérative de production des anciens moudjahedine – production cooperative of former freedom fighters of the war of independence.

CAPCS: Coopérative agricole polyvalente communale de service—communal multipurpose service cooperative

CAPRA: Coopérative de production de la Révolution Agraire—production cooperative of the Agrarian Revolution

CEPRA: Coopérative d'élevage pastoral de la Révolution Agraire—cooperative for the raising of livestock in the savannah

CG: Comité de gérance—management committees of the self-managed farms

COFEL: Coopératives de commercialisation des fruits et légumes—cooperatives for the marketing and distribution of fruits and vegetables

CORA: Coopératives de rendements alimentaires—cooperatives for the processing of food for sale

CORE: Coopératives locales d'écoulement—cooperatives to distribute agricultural output locally

CT: Comité des travailleurs—committee of workers

DA: Dinar algérien—Algerian dinar. 4.9 DA = \$1

FNRA: Fond national de la Révolution Agraire—national fund of the Agrarian Revolution

GEP: Groupement d'entraide paysanne—grouping of peasants for mutual assistance

GPMV: (also GMV)—Groupement précoopératif de mise en valeur—precooperative grouping to improve the land

MARA: Ministère de l'Agriculture et de la Révolution Agraire—Ministry of Agriculture and the Agrarian Revolution

OFLA: Office national des fruits et légumes—national agency for fruits and vegetables

ONACO: Office national de commercialisation—national agency for marketing and distribution

ONRA: Office national de la Révolution Agraire—national agency of the Agrarian Revolution

RA: Révolution Agraire—Agrarian Revolution

UNCAC: Union nationale des coopératives agricoles de commercialisation—national union of marketing and distribution cooperatives

References

Abdi, Nourredine, 1975. "Réforme agraire en Algérie," *Maghreb-Machrek*, no. 69.

Abdi, Nourredine, 1976. "Réforme agraire et voie algérienne de développement," *Tiers Monde*, no. 67, July–September.

Adair, Philippe, 1982. "Les 'villages socialistes' algériens: 1972–1982," *Economie et Humanisme*, no. 268, November/December.

Bessaoud, Omar, 1980. "La révolution agraire en Algérie: continuité et rupture dans le processus de transformation agraire," *Tiers Monde*, vol. 21, no. 83, July–September.

Boukhobza, Mohammed, 1978. *Aperçu sur les conditions socio-économiques et résidentielles des attributaires avant et apres la révolution agraire*, Secrétariat d'Etat au Plan, Algiers.

Boumaza, Nadir, 1976. "Politique de l'habitat rural et aménagement du territoire en Algérie," *Bulletin*, Société Languedocienne de Géographie, no. 1.

Bouzidi, A., 1977. "Productivité du travail dans l'agriculture algérienne et problèmes dans la commercialisation des produits agricoles," *Revue algérienne de Sciences Juridiques, Economiques et Politiques*, vol. 14, no. 4.

Burgat, Francois, 1979. "Villages socialistes algériens à l'épreuve des réalités," *Maghreb-Mashrek*, no. 86.

Burgat, Francois, 1983. "L'état et l'agriculture en Algérie: vers de nouveaux équilibres," *The Maghreb Review*, vol. 8, nos. 3–4.

Cote, Marc, 1979. *Mutations rurales en Algérie*, O.P.U., Algiers.

deVilliers, Gauthiers, 1979. "Les palmeraies de l'Oued Righ," *Peuples Méditerranéens*, no. 6, January–March.

deVilliers, Gauthiers, 1980. "L'état et la révolution agraire en Algérie," *Revue Française de Sciences Politiques*, vol. 30, no. 1, February.

FAO (United Nations Food and Agriculture Organization), 1983. *Production Yearbook*, vol. 37, Rome.

Fernandez-Romero, Enrique, 1976. *Autogestion y revolución agraria en Algeria*, Zero, Bilbao.

Granier, Jean-Claude, 1978. "La commercialisation des fruits et legumes en Algérie," *Revue des Etudes Coopératives*, no. 194.

Guichaoua, André, 1977. "Politique agricole et transformations socialistes," *Tiers Monde*, vol. 18, no. 71, July–September.

Harvey, Nigel, 1984. "Can the New Plan Match Restructured Vision?" *MEED*, 4 May.

Joensson, Lars, 1978. "La révolution agraire en Algérie: historique, contenu et problèmes," *Research Report*, The Scandinavian Institute of African Studies, no. 47.

Karsenty, Jean-Claude, 1975. "Les investissements dans l'agriculture algérienne," *Annuaire de l'Afrique du Nord*, vol. 14, CNRS, Paris.

Karsenty, Jean-Claude, 1977. "La politique agricole algérienne," *Maghreb-Mashrek*, no. 77.

Karsenty, Jean-Claude, 1979. "Préalable de la révolution agraire en Algérie: La délimitation des zones équipotentielles de revenu agricole," *Hérodote*, January/March.

Kielstra, Nico, 1978. "The Agrarian Revolution and Algerian Socialism," *MERIP Report*, no. 67.

Lepoul, Georges, 1977. "1000 villages socialistes en Algérie," *Maghreb-Mashrek*, no. 77.

Michalski, Edeltraut, 1983. "Die agraren Umgestaltungen im Prozess der nationaldemokratischen Revolution Algeriens —Bilanz und Probleme einer 20 jaehrigen Entwicklung," *asien afrika lateinamerika*, vol. 4, no. II.

Schnetzler, Jacques, 1980. "Où en est l'agriculture algérienne?" *Information Géographique*, vol. 44, no. 2.

Secrétariat d'Etat au Plan, 1973. *La révolution agraire de A à Z*, Algiers.

Sutton, Keith, 1982. "The Socialist Villages of Algeria," *Third World Planning Review*, no. 4.

Trautmann, Wolfgang, 1979. "Entwicklung und Probleme der Agrarreform in Algerien," *Erdkunde,* vol. 33, no. 3.

Trautmann, Wolfgang, 1982. "Zum gegenwaërtigen Stand der staatlichen Umstrukturierungs-massnahmen in der algerischen Steppe," *Essener Geographische Arbeiten,* vol. 1.

10. India/Kerala

Why Is Kerala Different?

What we have seen so far is central power betraying the peasants. If only we might find a federal system, in which the national government was *not* overly powerful in local affairs, *and* in which local political power was *also* not concentrated in landlords, perhaps a land reform favorable to peasants might occur. This was the formula for Kerala, which differs not only from the worldwide pattern but from that of India as well.

Even so, however, we will find that the principal beneficiaries were not the poor but the upper-middle class. The reform did little or nothing for the landless laborers. But it did distribute tenanted land to the tillers, thus widening the scope of landholding.

Coercion was minimal. Farmers were not forced into cooperatives they had not chosen; state farms were not established; nor was there greater state control over credit and fertilizer markets or exportable crops. This is all the more incongruous both because Kerala's government was Marxist—or so it called itself—and because Kerala produces just those export crops that in other countries have been grabbed by the central government for their foreign exchange.

The Cropping Pattern

Kerala's tropical climate, with high rainfall well-distributed throughout the year (despite a dry spell from December to March) is favorable for agriculture. Three geographic zones—coastal lowlands, hilly midlands, and highlands—supply diversified crops. Coconuts are interspersed with other crops on "garden" land in the lowlands, with paddy along the rivers and coastal deltas. Paddy is also found in the narrow river valleys of the hilly midlands, while rubber, ginger, pepper, cashew, cardamom, tapioca, and bananas grow on the slopes (Paulini 1979:89–90). The tropical forest of the highlands has been slowly pushed back by plantations.

This ideal agricultural climate has provided Kerala a comparative advantage in high-value "export" crops (Krishnaji and Raychaudhuri 1981:33), yet with little land left over for its own food, it has faced a chronic deficit (Gwatkin 1979:248). Whereas 76.8% of Indian cultivated land is in food grains, in Kerala this proportion is only 34.9% (Table 1). While Kerala produces 3.2% of India's food grains, only 1.4% of government procure-

Table 10.1

PERISH...

PERCENTAGE OF ACREAGE DEVOTED TO FOOD GRAINS AND
OTHER CROPS ACCORDING TO SIZE OF HOLDING: ALL INDIA
AND KERALA

Size (hectares)	All India			Kerala			
	Food	Other	Total	Food	Tapioca	Other	Total
0.0–0.5	82.8	17.2	100.0	15.8	25.4	58.8	100.0
0.5–1.0	83.2	16.8	100.0	36.8	19.7	53.5	100.0
1.0–2.0	81.5	18.5	100.0	43.3	15.3	51.2	100.0
2.0–3.0	80.0	20.0	100.0	46.2	12.0	41.8	100.0
3.0–4.0	78.8	21.2	100.0	47.7	9.1	9.1	43.2
100.0							
> 4.0	73.6	6.4	100.0	26.1	4.6	69.3	100.0
All	76.8	23.2	100.0	34.9	14.8	50.3	100.0

SOURCE: Paniker et al. (1978:50). Rows 2 and 3, under Kerala, do not add to 100%. Error in source.

ment comes from Kerala, which is indirect evidence of Kerala's deficit in grains.

Food Crops

Kerala is not quite so specialized in non-food crops as might at first appear. Tapioca gained enormously in Kerala during the sixties. Half as expensive as rice per calorie, it is intercropped with other tubers, coconuts, and trees. While acreage devoted to it increased from 209,000 hectares to 318,000 between 1956–57 and 1974–75, output almost quadrupled. Coconut, despite its wide commercial uses (fiber, oil), is also a substitute food. And rice acreage increased from 762,000 hectares in 1956–57 to 881,000 hectares in 1974–75 (Table 2).

Commercial Crops

Coconut is the leading commercial crop in acreage, which expanded by over 50% from 1956–57 to 1974–75, occupying 27.8% of Kerala's cultivated land in 1974–75 (Table 2). But yield per acre declined, partly because of disease. In the mid-seventies, rubber was second to coconut in commercial-crop acreage (Table 2). Rubber acreage doubled between 1956–57 and 1974–75, to 202,000 hectares (Table 2). Production increased more dramatically, to 122,000 tons in the same period. Kerala now produces over 90% of India's rubber (Nossiter 1982:53), but much of it is processed outside the state.

Cashew nuts, both grown and processed in Kerala, account for 47% of the state's factory employment, mostly in one district (Quilon) and mostly

Table 10.2
AREA, PRODUCTION, AND YIELDS OF PRINCIPAL CROPS IN KERALA, 1956–57 AND 1974–75

	Area				Production			Yield			
	1956–57		1974–75		1956–57	1974–75	Index	1956–57	1974–75	Index	Annual %
	000 ha	%	000 ha	%							Increase
Rice	762	41.0	881	32.7	887	1,334	150.4	1,164	1,513	130.0	3.0
Pepper	87	5.0	118	4.4	27	27	100.0	314	230	73.2	−1.72
Cardamom	28	1.5	47	1.7	1	2	162.7	45	44	97.8	0.00
Areca nut	49	2.6	93	3.4	6,617	13,777	208.2	135	148	110.0	0.51
Mangoes	56	3.0	57	2.1	na	na	na	na	na	na	na
Plantains	40	2.1	47	1.7	296	357	120.5	7,350	7,564	102.9	0.16
Cashews	37	2.0	105	3.9	59	118	200.5	1,569	1,122	71.5	−1.85
Tapioca	209	11.2	318	11.8	1,449	5,625	388.3	6,959	17,696	254.3	5.32
Coconut	460	24.7	748	27.8	3,182	3,719	116.9	7	5	71.8	−1.77
Tea	39	2.1	38	1.4	35	49	140.8	871	1,301	149.4	2.25
Coffee	15	0.8	37	1.4	7	16	234.8	434	431	99.3	0.00
Rubber	82	4.8	202	7.5	22	122	561.2	219	601	274.4	5.77
Total	1,864	100.0	2,691	100.0							

SOURCE: Paulini (1979:113).

NOTE: Production in thousands of tons, except cashews and coconuts (in nuts); yields of cashews and coconuts in thousands of nuts per hectare.

Index numbers: 1956–57 = 100.

187

female. But in the late seventies, this source of employment fell off, as nuts were increasingly processed in other states where wages were lower (Nair and Mathai 1983:652).

Coffee, cardamon, and areca (betel) nuts expanded in both acreage and output from 1956–57 to 1974–75 (Table 2). Pepper, which had been the traditional commercial export crop, gained only marginally in acreage, and production stagnated. Tea, grown mainly by one British company on several large plantations with migrant Tamil laborers, increased in yield with no increase in acreage.

In summary, food crops (rice, mangoes, bananas, and tapioca) were losing ground (from 57.3% of cultivated land to 47.8%) relative to commercial crops from 1956–57 to 1974–75:

> The significant shifts in the cropping pattern . . . are largely explained by the increase in the prices of commercial crops; the large rise in rice prices did not influence the acreage changes, partly because . . . the nature of the land brought additionally under cultivation [was not suitable for rice] (Paniker et al. 1978:33).

The Kerala cropping experience is therefore significantly different from what we have discovered in other countries. While the government has procured some export crops at less than market prices, nevertheless Keralan farmers have also been free to respond to price increases in those export crops (relative to food grains), by increasing their output, in most cases in both acreage and yield per acre.

The Cropping Pattern on Small Holdings

It is often believed that food crops for subsistence are grown on small holdings while larger ones grow commercial crops. Though this may hold true in some circumstances, it is hardly an invariant statement. Coffee, tea, bananas, and even sugar are grown on small plots in many countries. Likewise in Kerala, a substantial portion of the smallest holdings are devoted to commercial crops. This fact is of great interest with respect to those countries (for example, Nicaragua, Chapter 17) whose governments have argued that it is necessary to "require" small farmers to produce export crops (through government-supervised cooperatives), because they would not do so if left to their own free choices.

The contrast between Kerala and all of India is shown in Table 1. While the percentage of acreage devoted to non-food crops generally increases with size of holding for all of India, it does not do so for Kerala. Even in the smallest holdings (0–0.5 hectares), 58.8% of the land is planted in crops other than food grains and tapioca. This percentage decreases (and that of food grains increases) with the size of the plot, up to 4 acres, after which the tendency is reversed again. In all of India, by contrast, 82.8% of the land in the smallest holdings (0–0.5 hectares) is devoted to food grains, a percentage that decreases monotonically as plot size increases up to 4 hectares.

Other sources show further evidence of the cultivation of cash crops on small farms. Paniker et al. (1978:52) found in a village survey that small farmers marketed 40% of their coconut crop, in contrast to over 75% for larger farmers. In Table 3, the percentage of commercial crops grown on various size holdings is compared. We find that 56% of coconut acreage occurs on holdings of less than one hectare, as does more than 40% of pepper. Most coffee and rubber acreage is found on holdings of less than four hectares.

In summary, we believe that the ability of Keralan small farmers to defend themselves in land reform is multifeatured. First is the decentralized nature of Indian government, with power to the states (at least over land reform). Second is the fact that small and medium farmers constituted the majority in a political democracy. Third is the existence of a national land reform law that legitimized land reforms of the states. Fourth is the dispersion of crops among farms of all sizes, such that small as well as large farms produced both commercial and food crops. Although the party in power called itself Marxist, the land reform created small, private farms, with no forced collectivization.

The Political Background of 1969 Land Reform

Agitation for land reform can be traced to peasant unions in Malabar (incorporated into northern Kerala) as far back as 1933, after a disastrous drop in the prices of commercial crops (1929–32) had coincided with steady rises in revenue assessment rates (Radhakrishnan 1980:2098). These

Table 10.3

PERCENT DISTRIBUTION OF ACREAGE IN SELECTED CROPS
ACCORDING TO SIZE OF HOLDING

Size (hectares)	Coconut	Coffee	Rubber	Pepper
0.0–0.5	35.4	5.6	1.7	19.8
0.5–1.0	20.5	12.3	5.6	20.8
1.0–2.0	22.0	17.4	19.2	27.0
2.0–3.0	9.1	12.3	15.8	15.1
3.0–4.0	6.7	6.9	11.3	7.1
Over 4	6.3	45.5	46.4	10.3
Total	100.0	100.0	100.0	100.0

SOURCE: Paniker et al. (1978:51).

unions, known as Karshaka Sangham and organized at the village level, began in 1935 to protect tenants from arbitrary actions of landlords. In 1937, the Malabar Karshaka Sangham, formed to negotiate fair rents, terminate feudal dues, and end arbitrary evictions (Jose 1984:52), was crucial to the Congress Party's gaining power in Malabar in that same year.

But lack of attention to peasant affairs eroded the union's support for the Congress Party, and left-wing members—further alienated when that party did not continue its militancy after Independence (1947)—established a separate Communist Party of Kerala. When a 1948 revolt in Malabar, directed at landlord hoarding of rice, was bloodily suppressed by the Congress government, many more peasants shifted allegiance to the Communist Party.

The affinity between peasant unions and the Communist Party did not extend to the rest of Kerala, however. In the south (Travancore and Cochin), the peasants were mainly small owners, not tenants, and the Communist Party was not so successful in organizing them.

In 1957, after the State of Kerala had been organized to unify all Malayalam speakers, the Communist Party secured enough votes to form its first ministry. Under its guidance, the second annual conference of the all-Kerala Karshaka Sangham (KKS) worked out the key provisions of a land reform act passed in 1959. This act was never implemented; instead, it caused the removal of the state government from office in early 1960, by orders of New Delhi. For the next seven years, the Congress Party dominated the government, with an interruption for presidential rule (the national government intervening) in 1964–65. The Congress party passed a watered-down agrarian reform in 1961, which was declared unconstitutional by the Supreme Court. In 1964, it passed another land reform act, calling for security of tenure at fixed rents, ownership ceilings between 15 and 36 acres, and voluntary purchases of land by tenants. However, this act became a dead letter because the government was not interested in setting up enforcement machinery.

In 1964, the Communist Party of Kerala split in two, and so also did the KKS. Most village unions went with the party's left wing, the Communist Party of India/Marxist (CPI/M). In 1967, this party won sufficient strength to lead a coalition government called the United Front Ministry, which included all parties except the Congress. The CPI/M had intended land reform to be part of a larger state effort in the countryside, with features similar to those we have criticized for other countries. These included: (1) nationalization of the wholesale trade in food crops (except for small traders and cooperatives); (2) an increase in the levy on large rice cultivators and in the price of rice on which the levy was placed; (3) state distribution of inputs to farmers and an increase in state organization of peasant groups.

These measures died, however, with the defeat of the CPI/M by the

Communist Party of India, Right Wing (CPI) in 1969. The CPI won as part of a coalition named the Mini Front, whose other members were the Muslim League, the Revolutionary Socialist Party, and the Praja Socialist Party. They were organized with Congress Party backing, specifically to exclude the CPI/M. The CPI/M then became the watchdog of its opponents' efforts to implement the 1969 act. In fact, however, KKS-CPI/M membership was far greater than that of the other federations (in 1974, 200,000, compared with 40,000 for KKS-CPI and even less for the KKC (Congress party affiliates).

CPI/M "watchdogged" through its affiliated peasant unions, by supplying information and advice to tenants pursuing their rights under the 1969 law. This activity encouraged the opposition to do the same, and there was some competition among them (reminiscent of the Gladstone-Disraeli competition for reforms in Britain in the 1860s). Paulini (1979:297) emphasizes the strong political appeal of the peasant unions:

> Whether or not the President of the Indian Union gives his assent to it, whether or not the courts declare it ultra vires, whether or not the bureaucratic machinery helps the landlords to evade the law . . . , the peasants, agricultural laborers, and hutment dwellers of Kerala would deem the legislation to have come into force on January 1, 1970 and assert their rights recognized in the various provisions of the legislations.

The Mini Front, with Achutha Menon (CPI) as chief minister, ran the government by committee in the early seventies. After the 1970 elections, in which the Congress Party gained greater strength, the committee became weighted less heavily toward the parties of the left.

Nossiter (1982:276-68), author of the most complete history of communism in Kerala, asserts that this coalition governed over one of the most corrupt administrations Kerala had ever known. Public employment expanded rapidly, to 40% of all non-agricultural employment in 1970 and 47% by 1975. Landlord influence was strong, and tenants often had to pay bribes to have their cases heard by the local board. Paulini (1979:374) confirms this:

> There is a certain amount of collusion between landowners and land reform officials. This may either result from [social background, material interests such as ownership of land] or from the low salaries of lower land reform officials which provide the material reason for an easy bribery. Furthermore these officials are still in many ways depending on the old masters of the villages, either socially or due to material rewards.

Why, then, did the land reform not lead to much greater state control—with its corrupt bureaucracy—over the countryside? We intend to show (below) that the democratically elected state government successfully provided the necessary restraints. In few other Indian states were the interests of small farmers so well articulated in the political process.

191

The Land Reform of 1969

Section 72 of the Land Reform Act of 1969 (which was legally an amendment to the act of 1964) abolished landlordism. The state government would buy the land from the landlords and sell it to the tenants. The immediate result was that most tenants simply stopped paying rent (and did not pay it to the state either) (Paulini 1979: 353). But in 1975, with a Declaration of Emergency, the law was more speedily implemented. As of February 1981, 1,967,593 acres had been redistributed under this provision to 1.23 million beneficiaries, each receiving two plots of approximately 0.8 acres (Radhakrishnan 1981:A130). Tenants who had themselves hired labor were defined as "cultivating."

Tenants most affected by the act were part-time farmers with plots so small that they had to depend on off-farm income. Surprisingly, they were sometimes richer than their landlords. In fact, wealth did not seem to correlate with landholding. For example, 71.4% of landlords had less than 1,000 rupees annual income, compared with 55.7% for *kudiyirippa* tenants (those without any land at all of their own), 32.0% for other tenants, and 38.1% for owner-cultivators (Table 4). By the same token, tenants constituted a greater percentage of the rural rich than did landlords, and they were not very far behind owner-cultivators as well (Table 5). At the bottom of the scale were *kudikiduppurs* (hired laborers provided with huts).

Because of their non-farm employment, most owner-cultivators and tenants hired labor for most of the farm work (Table 6). As one might expect, the percentage of labor done by hired help increases with the size of farm. For 4 acres and above, it is about two-thirds. "The abolition of tenancy relations was certain to benefit a large number of landholders whose class status was relatively high and whose position in the agrarian hierarchy was relatively privileged" (Herring 1980:A63):

> The real losers were indeed the feudal landlords, the pure rentiers, who were analytically defined in the 1976 survey but were not found in the field; many were financially ruined. Likewise there were significant institutional losers, though the government has guaranteed annuity in perpetuity to such institutions. About 20% of the tenanted land was owned by institutions, primarily . . . temples (Herring 1980:A64).

Losses by the rentiers and gains by the upper-middle classes were confirmed in a survey of seventeen villages by the Indian School of Science (1976), reported by Herring (1980:A64). Capitalist landlords (owner-cultivators who also leased land) had some of their lands expropriated, but they gained more than they lost, or a net amount of 6% of previous holdings (Table 7, Part A). But rich peasants gained an area equal to 36.5% of their previous holdings, compared with only 9.3% for middle peasants, 10.1% for poor peasants, and 19.7% for the mixed class (those who farmed part time). Because the losing rentiers are not included in this

192

Table 10.4

LAND AND INCOME CHARACTERISTICS OF AGRARIAN CLASSES IN KERALA ON THE EVE OF THE 1969 LAND REFORM

	% with Less Than 1 Acre	Leased-in Area as % of Area Possessed	% with Less Than Rs 1,000 Annual Income	Average Annual Income (Rs)
Kudiyirippa tenants	71.2	99.05	55.7	1,137
Other tenants	43.1	68.28	32.0	1,839
Owner-cultivators	65.1	0.00	38.1	4,039
Landlords	1.2	17.8	71.4	4,039
Kudikidappurs	100.0	–	–	–

SOURCE: Herring (1980:A63, Table 1).

Table 10.5

CLASS COMPOSITION OF THE AGRARIAN RICH IN KERALA,
1966–67 (ANNUAL INCOME GREATER THAN 6,000 RS)

	% of Rural Rich	% of Class Belonging to Rich Stratum
Landlords	16.3	8.9
Owner-cultivators	45.7	3.0
Kudiyirippa tenants	9.6	1.2
Other tenants	28.4	33.2
Total tenants	38.0	34.4
Kudikidappurs	0.0	0.0

SOURCE: Herring (1980:A63, Table 2).

Table 10.6

PERCENTAGE OF HOLDINGS WITHIN EACH SIZE CLASS
ACCORDING TO THE NATURE OF LABOR EMPLOYED, 1970–71

Size of Operational Holding (hectares)	By Household Members	Work Done Largely by Household But Also by Others	Largely by Wage Labor	Total
0.04–0.25	70.30	15.47	14.23	100.00
0.25–0.50	51.39	26.55	22.06	100.00
0.50–1.00	37.97	32.09	29.94	100.00
1.00–2.00	28.09	33.18	38.73	100.00
2.00–4.00	19.36	33.49	47.15	100.00
4.00 and up	9.01	23.33	67.66	100.00

SOURCE: Panikar et al. (1978:52).

table, every class shows a net gain. Holders of 5 to 10 acres received almost a quarter of the total distribution, and holders of more than 5 acres almost another quarter (Part B).

The land reform did, however, provide something for the *kudikidappukars*, who were the poorest of the poor—virtual slaves. With support from the agricultural workers' union affiliated with CPI/M, they were allowed to buy from 3.5 to 10 cents (or 1/100 of an acre) of land around their huts, at 25% of market value, on which to grow vegetables. The

Table 10.7
RELATIVE WINNERS AND LOSERS IN KERALA'S LAND REFORMS[a] (ABOLITION OF LANDLORDISM, SECTION 72), RENTIERS (WHO LOST LAND) NOT INCLUDED

A. By Class	Capitalist Landlord	Rich Peasant	Middle Peasant	Poor Peasant	Mixed Class
Area gained as % of total area possessed	7.8	17.9	10.9	11.6	9.1
Area lost as % of total area possessed	5.6	1.0	0.0	0.0	0.0
Net area gained as % of total possessed	2.2	16.9	10.9	11.6	9.1
Households as % of sample	12.2	13.3	11.4	19.1	44.0
Area gained as % of total redistribution	21.3	38.7	9.3	10.1	20.6

B. By Size of Holding	0–1	1–2	2–5	5–10	10–15	15–20	>20
% of households[b]	16.6	33.4	34.2	11.5	2.5	0.6	1.2
% of redistributed land gained	0.9	13.5	21.9	31.5	7.6	10.4	14.3
Net gain as % of total redistributed	0.9	12.7	17.6	23.2	7.1	5.4	11.2

SOURCE: Herring (1980:A64, Table 3).
[a]Based on sample of seventeen villages.
[b]Excludes class of agricultural laborers, some of whom owned less than half an acre.

government paid half of this 25%, leaving the *kudikidappukars* to pay the remaining half in twelve equal installments. The landlords lost the other 75% of value. By February 1980, 269,021 out of 435,555 requests for such purchases had been granted, for 21,522 acres, or 0.08 acre per *kudikidappukar* (Radhakrishnan 1981:A130). Legal regularization was hastened by the fact that many *kudikidappukars* had already occupied the land. Although legitimization was the easiest way to settle the matter, it nevertheless caused tension between the *kudikidappukars* and the new small owners.

Finally, the 1969 law set a land ceiling of 5 standard acres for an unmarried adult, 10 for a family of five, with one additional standard acre for every additional member, up to 15 total. A "standard acre" was defined by its productivity; thus different land qualities were equalized. Tea, coffee, rubber, cocoa, and cardamom plantations were exempt, along with industrial and commercial enterprises (Paulini 1979:294). These exclusions were close to 50% of Kerala's cultivated acreage.

By February 1980, 115,000 acres had been demanded under the ceiling provision, but only 79,000 had been taken; of these, 50,300 had been distributed to 80,825 people, with an average plot of 0.62 acres. Yet the ceiling is generally deemed a failure, for there was no mechanism to assure that landowners declared the required amounts as excess. Most confiscations resulted from agitation and occupation, encouraged by the CPI/M in 1971 and 1972. The government, on the other hand, did not enforce the ceiling any further than necessary, probably because the political support lay with the landowners.

Furthermore, the landowners had had sufficient advance notice so that they were able to divide their holdings among family members or friends, or they underreported. In a study of two villages, Mencher (1980:1789) found many households effectively controlling over 30 acres, which were divided among many names in the land registry.

In sum, the 1969 law deprived the rentier group, consolidated the hold of the rich peasantry on the countryside, and provided some meager security to agricultural laborers.

Agricultural Credit Cooperative System

Before the 1969 reform in Kerala, India's credit cooperative system operated like most of those we have reported, with subsidized interest rates, rampant corruption, loans to the rich, and scarce repayments. After the 1969 reform, it continued to operate that way, *except in Kerala*. Why the corruption diminished and why the repayment rate improved in Kerala are questions yet to be studied. Our informed guess is that as sources became more localized—through investments, deposits, and borrowings—Keralans became aware that the funds that would be corrupted would be their own. With citizen control through a political democracy, they were able to demand accountability on the part of their government.

Although India's cooperative credit system receives funds from the central bank (Reserve Bank of India), administration is done by each state. Primary village cooperatives are federated into a district level bank, which in turn joins a state level cooperative bank. But, notes Franda (1979:45):

> In most states government appointees have considerable power on boards of state and district cooperatives. . . . Because of very close ties between government and the cooperatives, including interlocking directorates and considerable financial dependence, many Indians view the cooperatives as merely an extension of governmental activity.

Overdue amounts at the national level ranged in the neighborhood of 42% (Franda 1979:46). In Kerala before the reform, the percentage was not much different from the national, and it was increasing (Table 8). Nossiter (1982:271–72) summarizes the Keralan cooperatives in the late sixties and early seventies as follows:

> Many societies have passed into the hands of local patrons, frequently protégés of the dominant local party. The conclusions of the All-India Credit Review Committee (concerning corruption and delinquencies) apply with particular force to many parts of Kerala. The intrusion of politics both at the state and the village level has vitiated the working of cooperatives, with the result that individuals who have not ingratiated themselves with particular parties or factions are virtually outside the scope of cooperative credit.

Great changes had occurred by the late seventies, however. The number of societies had decreased through consolidation from 2,160 in 1969–70 to 1,616 in 1978–79, while membership had virtually doubled, from 1,536,000 to 3,004,000 (Table 8). The number of borrowing members and the total number of loans had increased more than proportionately to the increase in membership. But overdues, as percent of loans outstanding, had declined from 24.0 to 18.7. A second All-India Review Committee in 1979 reported that political influence on loan disbursement was endemic everywhere except in Kerala (Tendulkar 1983:131).

Because many tenants had not qualified for loans before the reform—having no land to mortgage—we reason that membership increased largely because of the reform. Paulini (1979:389) found that in Champukalam, membership shot upwards in four primary-level credit societies because the new owners could mortgage their lands. Even some of the *kudikidappukars* joined. Cooperative rates were subsidized at 2% below those of commercial banks.

Not only did memberships and borrowings increase, but borrowings became more widely dispersed among owners of land (but not among the landless). Tenants and landless laborers borrowed very little. Those with less than one hectare held 42% of acreage in operational holdings but

197

Table 10.8
DATA ON PRIMARY AGRICULTURAL SOCIETIES IN KERALA, 1956–79

	1956–57	1960–61	1965–66	1969–70	1974–75	1978–79
No. of societies	2,098	2,336	2,440	2,160	1,787	1,616
Thousands of members	456	806	1,283	1,536	1,962	3,004
Thousands of borrowing members	na	386	499	594	947	1,348
Sources of funds (Rs crores[a])						
Owned	1.6	2.8	6.1	10.7	18.8	32.6
Deposits	0.4	1.2	4.7	8.8	17.0	85.3
Borrowed	na	2.8	10.4	22.3	37.9	59.5
Loans made (Rs crores[a])	1.5	5.1	12.4	25.8	44.5	122.0
Loans outstanding at year end (Rs crores[a])	1.6	5.1	14.6	29.8	52.7	141.9
% overdue	19.8	16.6	24.9	24.0	35.9	18.7

SOURCE: Raj and Tharakan (1983:81).
[a] crore = 10,000,000.

borrowed only 33.1% of the amount advanced. Proportions increased with size of plot (Table 9).

Thus our hypothesis—that control by members, participatory democracy, and voluntarism lead to accountability and efficiency—appears confirmed by the information, although we would like to see further studies of these particular relationships. Certainly credit cooperatives in Kerala are different from those we have studied in other countries, and doubtless they are different from other states in India as well.

Farm Prices: India and Kerala

Kerala is not exempt from inappropriate policies of the central government; India is urban-biased, like most of the Third World. This bias is not easily seen for wheat, since the official price of wheat is higher than the international price, with conversion at the official rate of exchange. But the rupee is overvalued, and at the free market rate the official price of wheat is lower than the international price. For rice, the discrimination is even greater (Table 10). By the same token, effective protection was negative for both rice and wheat during almost all of the same period, when taken at free-market exchange rates, but it was negative for rice only (not wheat) at the official exchange rate (Sukhatme 1984:176, our Table 11).

The government of India has been obtaining about 10% of its rice requirements from Kerala. In this operation, the government behaves similarly to others we have studied, with the procurement price only 50% to 75% of the open market price. Rice thus acquired is sold through licensed retail shops in both urban and rural areas (Gwatkin 1979:249) at prices favorable to the consumer. The Producer Levy Bill of 1969, which specified the requirements and the prices, was probably one cause of Keralans' shifting away from rice and into rubber. In the late seventies, land under paddy decline by about 82,000 hectares (Narayana and Nair 1983:1937–39).

In a statistical analysis, Sukhatme concludes that adoptions of high yielding varieties (HYVs) of both rice and wheat were less than had there been no discrimination against agriculture. He also calculates a social loss of 8.5% (1967–68) and 2.2% (1970–71) of national income originating in agriculture (reduction of producer surplus, plus government loss through subsidies, minus gain from consumer surplus) because of this. He also suggests that the cost from non-adoption of HYVs was greater than the direct social cost of inappropriate prices. Furthermore, although the percentage of rice acreage devoted to HYVs in Kerala increased from 15.57% to 28.38% between 1969–70 and 1973–74, the rate of increase leveled off over the next five years, and the acreage settled at 35% of the total. Possibly because of the same discouragement, rice yields have stagnated. In 1974–75, the average yield was 1,513 kilos per hectare, and in 1980–81 it was only 133 kilos more (Table 12).

Table 10.9
Borrowings by Size of Holdings, Kerala, 1977–78

Category of Borrower	Area under Operational Holdings, 1976–77	Loans and Advances from Primary Agricultural Credit Societies, 1977–78			
		No. of Borrowers	Amount Advanced[a]	Amount Outstanding[a]	Amount Overdue[a]
< 1 hectare	42.3	37.9	33.1	30.6	30.9
1–2 hectares	23.6	21.7	24.5	22.4	23.8
2 hectares	34.1	26.7	34.1	39.3	40.1
Tenants	na	2.2	1.1	1.2	1.6
Agricultural laborers	na	5.8	4.1	3.6	1.6
Others	na	5.8	3.1	3.0	2.4
Total	100.0	100.0	100.0	100.0	100.0

SOURCE: Raj and Tharakan (1983:82).
[a]In crores.

Table 10.10

DOMESTIC AND WORLD PRICES FOR INDIAN RICE (US $ PER METRIC TON)

| | Wholesale Price | | Import | | |
	Official (1)	Market (2)	Price (3)	(1)/(3)	(2)/(3)
1961	82	55	114	0.72	0.48
1962	100	65	119	0.84	0.55
1963	131	91	118	1.11	0.77
1964	119	73	143	0.83	0.51
1965	124	67	173	0.72	0.39
1966	146	80	160	0.91	0.50
1967	116	81	200	0.58	0.41
1968	136	100	179	0.76	0.56
1969	131	91	184	0.71	0.49
1970	135	81	138	0.98	0.59
1971	131	77	156	0.84	0.49
1972	151	108	219	0.69	0.50
1973	158	133	302	0.52	0.44
1974	221	193	362	0.61	0.53
1975	242	211	280	0.86	0.75
1976	160	131	227	0.70	0.58
Average				0.77	0.53

SOURCE: Sukhatme (1984:71).

Of course, like other Indians, Keralans benefit from cheap consumption prices. They hold ration cards that entitle them to purchase specified amounts monthly at the government shops. This grain amounts to approximately 37% of all cereals consumed in Kerala (1971-72) (Gwatkin 1979: 250) and about 15% to 16% of all calories.

Not only were rice prices low in Kerala by international standards, but they were also low relative to cultivation costs and alternative crops. George (1983) found that wage rates rose much more rapidly in the late seventies than did paddy prices. In 1980-81, the index of cultivation costs stood at 603 (1952-53 = 100), while prices received by farmers reached only 480. Narayana and Nair (1983) found that the amount of paddy in Kerala necessary to buy one man day of labor rose from 4.51 kilograms in 1960-61 to 7.49 kilograms in 1978-79 (Table 13).

Column 4 of Table 13, based on column 2, shows how the cost of farm labor rose relative to price of paddy, in 1978-79 reaching over 300% of 1960-61. A conventional comparison might also be between the index for

Table 10.11
EFFECTIVE RATES OF PROTECTION FOR WHEAT AND RICE, AT OFFICIAL COMPARED WITH MARKET EXCHANGE RATES, 1961–76

	Rice		Wheat	
	Official	Market	Official	Market
1961	−36.56	−59.15	9.06	−31.37
1962	−23.96	−52.68	15.99	−30.14
1963	4.75	−30.92	24.43	18.58
1964	−25.52	56.32	46.23	−18.78
1965	−36.41	−67.43	77.23	−16.20
1966	−16.66	−57.15	47.88	−24.99
1967	−49.60	−65.83	47.68	− 4.43
1968	−32.40	−51.53	42.48	− 1.27
1969	−37.23	−57.77	57.27	1.51
1970	−10.12	−49.30	73.21	− 7.38
1971	−24.52	−58.04	51.37	−19.73
1972	−39.24	−57.95	64.57	8.01
1973	−55.06	−62.76	−26.59	−39.66
1974	−46.80	−54.19	−18.47	−30.25
1975	−21.99	−32.97	−31.62	−41.18
1976	−37.73	−50.27	−32.64	−45.53

SOURCE: Sukhatme (1984:176).

NOTE: "The effective rate of protection expresses the margin of protection on value added in the production process rather than on the product price. It is defined as the percentage excess of domestic value added, obtainable by reason of the imposition of tariffs and other protective measures on the product and its inputs, over foreign or world market value added" (Balassa et al. 1971:4). Effective protection can be negative if tariffs or other protective measures are greater on a product's inputs than they are on the product.

the price of paddy and the consumer price index (columns 3 and 5). This would show that the price of paddy rose sometimes by more and sometimes by less than consumer prices in general. However, the comparison is not a fair one, and we have included it only for completeness. Not only is the consumer index based on official prices—kept low because of the urban bias—when unofficial prices might be much higher, but it includes the low price of rice, which is the very problem of the farmer.

Table 10.12
RICE YIELDS IN KERALA, 1956–81 (KG./HA)

1956–57	1,164 kg./ha
1974–75	1,513
1975–76	1,542
1976–77	1,468
1977–78	1,540
1978–79	1,583
1979–80	1,630
1980–81	1,646

SOURCE: 1956–57 and 1979–80 from Table 2; 1975/76–1980/81 from *Monthly Commentary on Indian Economic Conditions*, vol. 24. no. 1, August 1982:74.

Output and Yields

From the scanty data that we have, it would appear that increases in output and yields in Kerala were modest. We could not find data on value added by agriculture in the state nor on overall productivity. Thanks to Paulini, however, we do have a comparison of 1974–75 and 1956–57, which shows the area planted to each crop, the output of each, and therefore the land yield. For the most part, and especially in principal crops, yields increased, although the rate of increase per year was not high by international standards (Table 2). An additional source carries rice yields up to 1980–81, still with modest increases (Table 12).

Conclusion

Kerala land reform redistributed land, away from absentee landlords and in favor of middle- and upper-middle-class farmers. But Keralan beneficiaries were not subject to the same restrictions on their modus operandi as we have found, with some exceptions, in of the other countries of the Third World. We hypothesize that the reason lay in the attenuated power of the federal government vis-à-vis states, the political democracy of Kerala, a peculiar distribution of incomes that does not correlate with size of landholding, and the fact that owners of different size holdings held interests in common. All these situations are rare in the Third World. Thus Keralans were able to keep reasonably good control over their economic behavior with respect to both outputs and fertilizer inputs, but not over the cost of labor. They even participated in cheap credit from the federal government, without apparently the ill effects of such credit that we have seen elsewhere (Adams et al. 1984). Nevertheless, the central government was able to extract a surplus from the rice

Table 10.13

PADDY PRICES AND RELATIONSHIP TO WAGES AND CONSUMER
PRICES, SELECTED YEARS, 1960–79

	Consumer Price of Paddy (Rs/kg.) (1)	Amount of Paddy to Buy 1 Hour of Labor (2)	Price Index for Paddy (3)	Price Index for Farm Labor (4)	Consumer Price Index (5)
1960–61	0.41	4.51	100.00	100.00	100.00
1961–62	0.44	5.00	107.32	101.95	102.31
1962–63	0.41	5.90	100.00	104.67	105.20
1971–72	1.00	5.43	243.90	191.44	194.61
1972–73	1.19	4.86	290.24	201.56	217.34
1973–74	1.87	3.57	456.09	237.35	267.63
1974–75	2.38	3.38	580.49	303.11	308.67
1977–78	1.30	6.67	317.07	320.23	321.19
1978–79	1.20	7.49	292.68	328.40	335.45

SOURCE: (1) and (2) from Narayana and Nair (1983:1939); (3) and (4) calculated from (1) and (2); (5) from IMF (1983:274–75), base year of 1980 converted to 1960–61 and calendar years averaged to equal split years.

production, and we believe that central government policies have lessened the adoption of high yielding varieties and have caused a social loss.

Kerala differs in other ways. It does not have a strong industrial sector divorced from the land: much of the industrial labor force processes agricultural goods for export. Although national economic policies are urban-biased, those of the state are not. Second, literacy statewide stands at about 70%, with little difference between rural and urban areas. Almost all school-age children complete primary school. Possibly a more literate population is able to withstand the paternalistic condescension we have observed on the part of other governments in the Third World. Literacy may also promote articulate political participation, which in turn may limit arbitrary government control.

Clearly, under the Communist Party of India/Marxist, political participation in the land reform act of 1969 was widespread. But the reform could be criticized on egalitarian grounds. It did favor the middle and richer peasants; very small holders benefited less and landless laborers scarcely at all. Despite its "Marxist" nomenclature, the reform itself was a capitalist one: no state farms, no collectives, no cooperatives not joined voluntarily by peasants, only small- and medium-size private farms.

References

Adams, Dale W.; Graham, Douglas H.; and Von Pischke, J. D., 1984. *Undermining Rural Development with Cheap Credit*, Boulder, Colo., Westview Press.

Balassa, Bela, and Associates, 1971. *The Structure of Protection in Developing Countries*, Baltimore, Johns Hopkins University Press.

Franda, Marcus, 1979. *India's Rural Development: An Assessment of Alternatives*, Bloomington, Indiana University Press.

George, P. S., 1983. "Agricultural Price Movements in Kerala," in P. P. Pillai, ed., *Agricultural Development in Kerala*, New Delhi, Agricole Publishing Company.

Gwatkin, D. R., 1979. "Food Policy, Nutrition Planning, and Survival: The Cases of Kerala and Sri Lanka," *Food Policy*, vol. 4, no. 4:245-58.

Herring, Ronald, 1980. "Abolition of Landlordism in Kerala: A Redistribution of Privilege," *Economic and Political Weekly*, June:A59-69.

IMF (International Monetary Fund), 1983. *International Financial Statistics Yearbook*, Washington, D. C.

Jose, A. J., 1984. "Agrarian Reforms in Kerala: The Role of Peasant Organizations," *Journal of Contemporary Asia*, vol. 14, no. 1:48-60.

Krishna, R., and Raychaudhuri, G. S., 1981. "Agricultural Price Policy in India – A Case Study in Rice," *Indian Economic Journal*, vol. 28, no. 3:16-34.

Krishnaji, N., 1979. "Agrarian Relations and the Lift Movement in Kerala: A Note on Recent Trends," *Economic and Political Weekly*, vol. 14, no. 9, March 3:515-21.

Kurup, T. V. Narayana, 1976. "Price of Rural Credit: An Empirical Analysis of Kerala," *Economic and Political Weekly*, July 3:998-1006.

Mencher, Joan, 1978a. "Agrarian Relations in Two Rice Regions in Kerala," *Economic and Political Weekly*, February: 349-57.

Mencher, Joan, 1978b. "Why Grow More Food? An Analysis of Some Contradictions of the Green Revolution in Kerala," *Economic and Political Weekly Review of Agriculture*, December.

Mencher, Joan, 1980. "The Lessons and Nonlessons of Kerala: Agricultural Labourers and Poverty," *Economic and Political Weekly*, special number, October:1781-1802.

Nair, P. A. and Mathai, G., 1983. "Employment and Unemployment in Kerala," in Robinson Austin et al., eds, *Employment Policy in a Developing Country: A Case Study of India*, Hong Kong, Macmillian.

Narayana, D. and Nair, K. N., 1983. "Linking Irrigation with Development," *Economic and Political Weekly*, vol. 18, November 5-6:1935-39.

Nossiter, T. J., 1982. *Communism in Kerala*, Berkeley, University of California Press.

Panikar, P. G.; Krishnan, T. N.; and Krishnaji, N., 1978. *Population Growth and Agricultural Development: A Case Study of Kerala*, Rome, United Nations Food and Agriculture Organization.

Paulini, Thomas, 1979. *Agrarian Movements and Reforms in India: The Case of Kerala*, Saarbrucken, Saarbrucken Press, No. 33, Verlagbreitenbach.

Radhakrishnan, P., 1980. "Peasant Struggles and Land Reform in Malabar," *Economic and Political Weekly*, December 13:2095-2102.

Radhakrishnan, P., 1981. "Land Reform in Theory and Practice: The Kerala Experience," *Economic and Political Weekly*, December:A129-137.

Raj, K. N., and Tharakan, Michael, 1983. "Agrarian Reform in Kerala and Its Impact on the Rural Economy: A Preliminary Assessment," in A. K. Ghose, ed., *Agrarian Reform in Contemporary Developing Countries*, New York, St. Martin's Press.

205

Ratcliffe, John, 1978. "Social Justice and the Demographic Transition: Lessons from India's Kerala State," *International Journal of Health Services*, vol. 8, no. 1:123–44.

Sukhatme, Vasant, 1984. "Farm Prices in India and Abroad: Implications for Production," *Economic Development and Cultural Change*, vol. 32, no. 4:169–82.

Tendulkar, Surish, 1983. "Rural Institutional Credit and Rural Development: A Review Article," *Indian Economic Review*, vol. 18, no. 1:101–38.

11. Pakistan

[A] majority of farmers, because of their rigid belief in the traditional methods and their instinctive aversion towards change, experimentation and risk, would generally be reluctant to make use of modern technology and inputs. However, once they become aware of the resultant increase in their income, they would most willingly accept the change and would help in increasing the output of the agricultural sector. Moreover, the level of education is quite low and the farmers, specially small ones, do not appreciate new innovations. Proper training and educational programmes will enable them to understand and evaluate new ideas and motivate them for adoption (A. Khan 1983:22).

A. Khan, president of an important bank in Pakistan, sets forth four stages to overcome low agricultural productivity. First, a new technology package must be developed every four to five years. Second, each new package must be transmitted to farmers as rapidly as possible. Third, farmers must be "convinced that the new package is economically more beneficial than the one in use." Fourth, the component parts of the technology—credit and other inputs—must be supplied by the government. "Development of appropriate farm technology, its timely transfer to the common farmer, and synchronization in the supply and demand of production inputs, therefore, assume central position under our circumstances . . ." (A. Khan 1983:22).

Khan outlines suggested strategies: he rejects collective farming as contrary to Islam and as likely to upset the "rural masses"; he proposes floors of 25 acres on landholdings so that large farms would not be excessively divided by inheritance; joint stock companies would be established to cultivate large holdings with employed labor. These corporate farms would serve as models of change in each district; the supply of agricultural inputs would be managed by them. Furthermore, he argues, once they are established, the litigation on landholdings that has been crowding the courts would disappear. The fourth strategy concerns land consolidated in each village, so that preparation, sowing, and threshing might be mechanized, while harvesting and irrigation would still be carried out individually "at least for some time more." Next, branch banks would be set up in many villages for small-farmer credit. Finally, although Khan sees many problems with cooperatives, he holds them out "as the major hope of the small peasant."

Along with such an institutional arrangement there should be a pass-book, like a ration card in the possession of every farmer. In this pass-book, on the basis of cropping pattern of the concerned farmer to be adopted in the forthcoming season, the Field Assistant should enter his seed and fertilizer requirements against which the farmer should get a loan. This pass-book should have a pre-entry of the agreement and signatures of an authorized guarantor. . . .

At the "Market level," i.e., in the centre of 6–7 Union Councils marketing and storage arrangements may be provided. Such arrangements will not only help to eliminate the long list of intermediaries but the farmer will feel more at home thus getting rid of city botherations to indulge in which he usually hesitates.

. . . Technical management of cooperative societies may be entrusted for a short period of 5–10 years to professionally well managed institutes such as nationalized commercial banks (pp. 25–6).

We do not imply that Khan's approach is fully endorsed by the government of Pakistan, nor do we know how widely such ideas are held among the Pakistan élite; it is the approach of one influential individual. But it is not inconsistent with the general trend in élite thinking, which is surely toward government control of farming and paternalism toward the small farmer.

The Land Reform of 1972

Upon becoming president in December 1971, Zulfikar Ali Bhutto announced a national, comprehensive land reform, to "bring dignity and salvation to our rural masses who from today will be able to lift their heads from the dust and regain their pride and manhood, their self-respect and honour" (Bhutto, cited in M.H. Khan 1981:171–72).

Martial law regulation 115, promulgated in March 1972, lowered the land ceiling from 500 to 150 irrigated acres (or 300 unirrigated) for an individual (as opposed to a family) holding. As under the earlier (1959) law, Production Index Units (PIUs) were used to determine area equivalence. Bonus PIUs (hence higher ceilings) were awarded owners of tube-wells and tractors.

Although landlords were required to declare excess land and turn it over to the government without compensation, they might choose which land to keep. Existing tenants were given first rights to expropriated land, up to 12.5 acres. Untenanted land would be distributed to small owner/tenants in the immediate vicinity. Neither group would have to pay. Tenant evictions for any other reason than nonpayment of rent were prohibited.

Official data give the appearance of decreased concentration in holdings (Table 1). For the whole country from 1950 to 1976, farms under 25 acres increased from 47% to 64.3% of privately owned area, while those over 100 acres decreased from 31.2% to 12.6% (M.H. Khan 1983:138).

By all appearances from Table 1, the decrease in land concentration was

Table 11.1
Changes in Landownership in Provinces of Pakistan, 1950–76

Farm Size (acres)	Year	Percentage of All Owners				Percentage of All Owned Areas			
		Pakistan	Punjab	Sind	N.W.F.P.	Pakistan	Punjab	Sind	N.W.F.P.
< 5.0	1950	64.4	66.3	29.8	70.3	15.3	15.7	3.6	31.9
	1971	na	60.4	36.7	na	na	20.6	5.6	na
	1976	70.8	69.1	40.3	85.9	24.9	26.1	8.2	40.8
> 5.0–25.0	1950	28.7	28.9	46.0	21.6	31.7	39.0	18.8	25.2
	1971	—	35.6	42.9	na	na	45.7	29.9	na
	1976	25.1	27.4	41.5	12.4	39.4	43.0	30.5	33.0
> 25.00–100.0	1950	5.7	4.1	16.2	6.9	21.8	21.9	23.2	19.7
	1971	na	3.5	17.7	na	na	21.6	40.3	na
	1976	3.5	3.0	15.8	1.5	24.0	21.7	40.4	15.2
> 100	1950	1.2	0.7	8.0	1.2	31.2	23.4	54.5	23.3
	1971	na	0.5	2.7	na	na	12.1	24.2	na
	1976	0.5	0.5	2.4	0.2	12.6	9.2	20.9	11.0
> 500.0	1950	0.1	0.1	0.9	0.1	15.4	9.9	29.1	12.4

SOURCE: M.H. Khan (1983:139).

dramatic. For Pakistan as a whole, farms under 25 acres increased from 47% to 64.3% of the owned area, while those over 100 acres decreased from 31.2% to 12.6%. However, knowledgeable experts argue that the figures are illusory; very little land was distributed. Instead, false reporting by local officials and illegitimate distributions within families led to the appearance of a land reform that, de facto, was minimal.

Even on the basis of official figures, Herring (1979:541) estimates that only 2.5% of the total operated area went to 9.2% of the pure landless tenants throughout the Bhutto period (1972–77). He goes on to suggest that the actual amount was even less because of corruption in reporting the data. Landlords would sign land over to tenants, then reclaim it forcibly. M.H. Khan (1981:180) shows that 73,000 beneficiaries were less than 1% of landless tenants and small owners.

Regulations on tenant rights were completely unenforceable because of the corruption of the Revenue Department and its ties to the local élite. Evictions probably increased during the Bhutto period (Herring 1979:544; M.H. Khan 1981:182), as landowners increased their "areas of self-cultivation."

M.H. Khan (1981:177–79) tells the story by simple arithmetic. Excess lands were expropriated from only 10% of the official owners of more than 150 irrigated acres, even though their holdings averaged 778 acres in Sind and 615 acres in the Punjab. On average, 458 acres (Sind) and 257 acres (Punjab) were expropriated. Thus the actual land ceilings for those affected were 320 acres (Sind) and 358 acres (Punjab).

Complete control of village societies by local notables was chiefly responsible for the failure. Kizilbash (1973:121) describes local government as the lowest rung in a ladder of centrally controlled administration: "No local government popularly chosen and responsible to the local electorate (with broad powers of control in local affairs) has ever existed in Pakistan." Endemic violence in the villages, theft organized by notables, and tenant evictions all keep tenants "in line." Often the landlord owns the residences of both tenants and landless laborers. Hence eviction means loss of livelihood.

Data on operational holdings are perhaps more reliable. Census data show that in both 1972 and 1980 most farm area was cultivated in holdings of 5 to 25 acres, by family farmers in the Punjab and by share tenants in the Sind (Table 2). In the Punjab, farms over 150 acres increased slightly in percentage of total (from 5.7 to 6.4).

M.H. Khan (1983:182) did not combine the census data for 1960 with those of 1972 and 1980 because he believed that different procedures destroyed comparability. We do so, however (in Table 2), partly because others disagree with him on that point (Chaudry and Iqbal 1983) and partly because we have given the reader fair warning. The data show a decrease, during the sixties, in the percentage of area in small farms (under 5.0 acres), 9.4% to 5.3%, a slight increase in middle-sized farms

Table 11.2

Changes in Distribution of Farm and Farm Area in Pakistan, 1960–80

Farm Size (acres)		Percentage Distribution of Farms				Percentage Distribution of Farm Area			
		Pakistan	Punjab	Sind	N.W.F.P.	Pakistan	Punjab	Sind	N.W.F.P.
< 1.0	1972	4.1	4.0	0.4	12.2	0.2	0.1	0.0	0.7
	1980	4.5	4.3	0.6	12.0	0.2	0.2	0.0	0.7
< 5.0	1960	49.5	51.6	25.6	na	9.4	10.9	5.5	na
	1972	28.1	26.1	18.8	55.5	5.3	4.8	4.5	12.7
	1980	34.1	31.7	25.3	61.2	7.1	6.5	6.4	16.5
5.0–<25.0	1960	42.6	40.6	52.2	na	47.9	53.4	51.1	na
	1972	61.0	62.1	73.8	38.0	51.8	53.4	63.7	40.5
	1980	56.7	58.5	67.1	33.6	52.1	53.6	59.8	42.7
25.0–<50.0	1960	5.9	5.4	9.0	na	19.4	20.2	21.1	na
	1972	7.7	8.8	5.2	4.0	18.8	21.2	13.1	14.2
	1980	6.5	7.2	5.3	3.2	17.8	19.3	15.0	13.5
50.0–<150.0	1960	1.8	1.3	2.1	na	13.4	10.6	14.2	na
	1972	3.0	2.7	1.7	2.3	15.0	14.7	10.7	18.9
	1980	2.0	2.3	1.8	1.5	15.0	14.0	11.8	15.8
> 150.0	1960	0.3	0.2	0.3	na	10.0	4.9	8.2	na
	1972	0.0	0.0	0.0	0.0	9.0	5.7	7.9	13.5
	1980	0.0	0.0	0.0	0.0	8.0	6.4	6.9	11.9

SOURCE: For 1960, M.H. Khan (1981:102); for 1972–80, M.H. Khan (1983:141).

211

(50–150 acres), 13.4% to 15.0%, and a decline for very large farms, 10.0% to 9.0%. Despite possible inconsistencies in data collection procedures, we believe the results point toward a remarkable consistency in size of operational holdings from 1960 to 1980.

We turn now to government control over the export trade, commodity by commodity. Table 3 presents the information on major exports, from 1954 to 1983.

Rice

Stinging from the loss of Bangladesh and lucrative jute exports, in 1973 the Bhutto regime established both a Rice Export and a Cotton Export Corporation (REC and CEC respectively), to monopolize the trade in Pakistan's two principal remaining export crops (Tables 3 and 4). Although jute exports had stagnated during the sixties, they were still sufficiently great for their loss to be sorely felt.

The two main rice crops are known as basmati and IRRI (high yielding varieties, or HYVs, developed by the International Rice Research Institute in the Philippines). Basmati, grown mainly in the Punjab, is a fine-grain, fragrant rice preferred by both domestic consumers and Middle East customers. It sells at a premium of 100% or more over IRRI rices. IRRI rices are coarser grains, grown mainly in Sind. The government exports more of these, because the domestic market is slim.

The government had been procuring rice since the fifties (Table 3). A large part of the marketed surplus had been absorbed in interwing trade (between West and East Pakistan), but a large portion (8% to 17%) had also been exported. From 1959 to 1963, the government compulsorily procured rice at a price 30% to 85% below market wholesale for basmati (Islam 1981:90). In the later sixties, rice was included in the Export Bonus Scheme—in which salable import vouchers were paid to exporters—which resulted in monopoly profits for licensed exporters rather than higher prices for farmers. Nevertheless, rice output grew by an average of 6.5% per year during the sixties, mainly because of the new HYVs.

After the civil war, interwing trade diminished, but exports increased enormously, from 195,000 tons (9% of production) in 1971–72 to 789,000 (33%) in 1972–73 (Table 3). Much of this was the old interwing trade now become international. Finding this trade highly profitable and now productive of foreign exchange, the government laid hands on it. Cheong and D'Silva (1984:30–35) have calculated two types of subsidies: financial, or the value of government subsidies through cheap fertilizer and less-than-cost irrigation, less export duties and profits of the export corporation; and economic, or the government procurement price less the market price. In most years, the economic "subsidy" is negative, thereby becoming a "tax," and in the early seventies the financial subsidy was negative as well. The

212

Table 11.3

Major Crop Exports for Pakistan, 1954–83 (Data for East and West Pakistan, 1954–71; West Pakistan only, 1971–83)

	% of Exports			Cotton (000 Tons)			Rice (000 Tons)		
	Jute	Cotton	Rice	Production	Exports	% of Prod.	Production	Exports	% of Prod.
1954–55	51	25	2	281	127	na	838	77	na
1955–56	47	26	4	299	169	na	841	202	na
1959–60	40	6	4	292	80	na	995	117	na
1960–61	47	8	3	301	52	17	1,030	69	7
1961–62	47	7	5	324	49	15	1,227	102	8
1962–63	36	17	8	366	156	43	1,093	181	17
1963–64	33	15	5	419	159	38	1,192	110	9
1964–65	35	12	5	378	129	34	1,350	180	13
1965–66	32	11	5	414	117	28	1,317	145	11
1966–67	30	10	6	463	132	29	1,365	180	13
1967–68	24	14	5	518	223	43	1,499	120	8
1968–69	23	11	5	528	142	27	2,032	138	7
1969–70	23	6	3	536	83	15	2,401	89	4
1970–71	15	8	5	542	110	20	2,200	179	8

Table 11.3 (Continued)

	% of Exports			Cotton (000 Tons)			Rice (000 Tons)		
	Jute	Cotton	Rice	Production	Exports	% of Prod.	Production	Exports	% of Prod.
1971-72	—	28	8	707	256	36	2,262	195	9
1972-73	—	14	13	702	216	31	2,330	789	33
1973-74	—	4	21	659	37	6	2,455	597	24
1974-75	—	15	22	634	200	32	2,314	478	20
1975-76	—	9	22	514	113	22	2,618	782	29
1976-77	—	3	22	435	18	4	2,737	945	32
1977-78	—	8	19	575	101	18	2,950	879	29
1978-79	—	4	20	473	55	12	3,272	1,105	31
1979-80	—	14	18	728	251	34	3,216	1,087	34
1980-81	—	18	19	715	325	45	3,430	951	28
1981-82	—	11	16	748	231	31	3,430	951	28
1982-83	—	9	12	824	109	13	3,445	517	15

SOURCE: Columns 1–4, 6, 1954–57: calculated from *Pakistan Economic Survey, 1972–73:83*, Table 347; columns 5, 7, 1960/61–1982/83 and columns 1–4, 6, 1971/72–1982/83: calculated from *Pakistan Economic Survey, 1982–83:1524–1555; 1983–84:31*.

Table 11.4

Rice Production, Sales, Exports, and Government Subsidies, 1973–74 to 1981–82

	1973–74	1974–75	1975–76	1976–77	1977–78	1978–79	1979–80	1980–81	1981–82
Basmati rice									
Produced	486	602	643	660	560	878	887	980	1,035
Marketed, of which:	316	391	418	429	364	571	577	637	687
Government	216	287	319	201	193	394	387	309	382
% government	68	73	76	47	53	69	67	49	56
Open market sales	100	104	99	228	171	177	190	328	304
Exports	235	184	311	510	298	181	315	410	262
Ratio of government price to wholesale market price	72	95	91	80	66	89	83	74	75
Ratio of export unit cost to export price	46	41	62	98	93	52	55	65	58
Proportional subsidy:									
Financial	−31.2	−14.5	−8.1	−1.4	3.6	6.0	8.4	10.2	4.9
Economic	−96.2	−140.5	−72.2	8.6	9.4	−85.7	−71.5	−43.3	−54.2
Equivalent	−127.3	−150.9	−80.3	7.2	12.9	−79.8	−63.1	−33.1	−49.2

Table 11.4 (Continued)

	1973-74	1974-75	1975-76	1976-77	1977-78	1978-79	1979-80	1980-81	1981-82
IRRI rice									
Produced	1,299	1,107	1,290	1,315	1,671	1,949	1,958	1,796	1,906
Marketed, of which:	585	498	580	592	752	877	881	808	858
Government	288	301	320	430	714	806	742	696	706
% government	49	60	55	73	95	92	84	86	82
Open market sales	297	197	260	162	38	71	139	112	152
Exports	362	294	471	435	582	834	772	834	689
Ratio of export unit cost to export price	23	50	79	88	60	79	59	61	101
Proportional subsidy:									
Financial	−37.5	−5.1	−3.9	0.0	4.1	8.5	12.3	11.7	7.8
Economic	−339.9	−99.7	−27.5	−13.8	−68.3	−27.2	−66.9	−62.6	0.8
Equivalent	−337.4	−114.9	−31.4	−13.8	−64.4	−18.7	−54.6	−50.9	8.6

SOURCE: Cheong and D'Silva (1984:34–35; Tables 14–15), with percentages and proportions calculated by authors.

NOTE: Production and sales in thousands of metric tons. Export unit cost equals procurement price plus incidentals and transportation to Karachi.

"equivalent" subsidy (tax) is the sum of the two. Severe price discrimination during most of the period made the equivalent subsidy negative. For basmati rice, the procurement price averaged only 81% of the wholesale price, while the price paid for exports (including all costs of delivery to Karachi) averaged only 63% of the international price. For IRRI rice, the ratio of prices to farmers (including transport and other costs) averaged only 66% of the international price. In each case, of course, the government pocketed the difference. (Only in 1981–82 did the export procurement price rise to equal the international price.) For the entire period, the average equivalent subsidy was negative 61% of the value of production at domestic prices for basmati rice and negative 78% for IRRI rice. In the early eighties, the government has been increasing the price of fertilizer, to bring it into line with international prices (Cheong and D'Silva 1984:36); thus the financial subsidy will be reduced further.

The Bhutto regime moved quickly to control internal trade in 1972–73. Basmati rice was purchased on a monopoly basis at procurement prices well below internal wholesale prices. Sales of IRRI rice to the government were voluntary in 1972–73, but virtually none was transacted because the price was too low (*Pakistan Economic Survey*, 1972–73:26). When the Export Corporations were set up in 1973–74, rice began to be procured on a monopoly basis in all provinces. In the tradition of the British colonial masters, inter-district movement became illegal, so that stocks might be more easily procured in surplus districts. Dealers and mills were allowed to sell up to 10% of their basmati rice and up to 50% of other varieties in the open market (*Pakistan Economic Survey*, 1973–74:27).

To tighten its hold on the rice crop, the government nationalized 2,113 husking plants in July, 1976, and at the same time, a large number of cotton gins and flour mills; these were all placed under the government-owned Rice Milling Corporation, a move justified as a blow against private monopolies. In a White Paper (1979:29–30), the government characterized this as a one-man decision by Bhutto to strengthen control over the countryside before the 1977 elections. But the government could not implement its intention to process all rice in its own mills because thousands of small hullers were scattered throughout the villages. So in 1976, single-huller units were exempted from the nationalization but were forbidden to operate during paddy season.

Corruption in the newly nationalized mills was immense. In most, the managers – political appointees – had little experience in milling, but they quickly grasped the power of their positions. Farmers were already accustomed to paying bribes for fertilizer or for credit from government agencies, so they were not surprised to discover that rice initially rejected as too wet would be acceptable after payment of a "fee" (Gotsch and Brown 1980:52). Quality also deteriorated, as coarser grains would be mixed with basmati and accepted as pure basmati (Gotsch and Brown 1980:52–53;

White Paper 1979:31–32). Reports of rice being secreted from the mills and sold on the free market were widespread.

Because of these inefficiencies, and to still the public outcry, the Bhutto regime returned 1,500 of the small rice hulling mills to their owners in May, 1977. The martial-law regime that overthrew Bhutto in July of that year quickly divested the rest. Nevertheless, the Rice Export Corporation remains a powerful presence in the eighties. Procurement prices set by government and compulsory sales remain the rule. For 1983–84, the government allowed dealers and mills to sell 50% of their basmati and 25% of their IRRI grains on the open market (*Pakistan Economic Review*, December 1983:71). Two domestic milling subsidiaries of the Rice Export Corporation (REC) supplied from 5–10% of its annual export needs, while government storage facilities—also under REC—could store two-thirds of the annual harvest (*Pakistan Economic Review*, December 1983:14). Although the rice export market has been small and volatile in the early eighties, the government stands poised to take advantage of any upswing.

Cotton

When cotton production soared in 1971–72 and exports more than doubled from the previous year (Table 3), the government stepped in to take its "share," first by imposing heavy duties, then by nationalizing the cotton trade, and in 1976 by taking over 278 gins.

Cotton has always rivaled rice as a principal export (Table 3), for which the government has balanced the conflicting interests of farmers, traders, textile manufacturers, and itself. Because the textile industry produced 48% of the nation's value added by large-scale manufacturing and supplied 27% of the employment of that sector during the seventies (Adams and Iqbal 1983:148), it has been a powerful counterweight to farmer interests as well as to those of the government.

Responding to stagnant production in the late fifties, the government reduced export duties during the early sixties, from rupees (Rs) 115 per bale in 1958 to Rs 25 in 1964–65 (Bose 1972:86) and abolished them in 1967. The response was almost immediate. Production, 281,000 tons in 1954–55 and 292,000 in 1959–60, soared to 414,000 in 1965–66 and continued to rise in the following years (Table 3). So did the rate of growth of cotton production, from 2.3% per annum for the fifties to 6.5% in the sixties (Stern and Falcon 1970:37).

Such a bounty was too much for the government to leave alone. In 1972, it reimposed an export duty, first at 35%, then up to 45% in 1973 plus an additional 35% on the excess of price over Rs 1500 per bundle (Adams and Iqbal 1983:1543).

Such a blatant grab from farmers had, of course, no economic justification, nor any ethical one for income redistribution or economic development. The results were predictable. Cotton production fell year after year, reaching a low of 435,000 tons in 1976–77 (Table 3), followed by minimal recovery in 1977–78 and another drop the following year. Alarmed, the government introduced "support" prices in 1976—one more example of further government intervention to offset previous intervention that had failed. In 1977–78 and 1978–79 the support prices were above the international price, but they fell below them in 1979–89 (Table 5), therefore being ineffective.

Of the 278 gins nationalized in 1976, only one-half were operated. Just as we have seen for rice, the Export Corporation paid a standard price for cotton, regardless of quality. So the cotton available for domestic textiles became of very poor quality. Finally, the Cotton Trading Corporation employed twice the number of workers in half the number of mills, who processed "only 1,878,000 bales of lint cotton in comparison to 2,859,000 bales in 1975–76" (White Paper 1979:32).

Over the protests of existing government banks, the Cotton Trading Corporation extended agricultural credit, much of it to political supporters. Underestimating the intensity of fraud, the White Paper (1979:33) merely commented that "loan recovery has posed serious problems." Martial law in 1977 ended this program.

Table 11.5

COTTON: DUTIES, PROFITS, PRICES, AND EXPORTS, 1974–83

Year	Export Duties (million rupees)	Profits of Cotton Export Corp. (million rupees)	Support Price (1969–70 Rs/40kg.)	Ratio of Domestic to Int'l. Price	Exports as % of Production
1974–75	535	–	–	90	32
1975–76	340	–1	–	102	22
1976–77	1	662	–	82	4
1977–78	–	185	133	117	18
1978–79	–	–	128	130	12
1979–80	–	–	128	130	12
1980–81	500	350	114	87	45
1981–82	150	–	106	113	31
1982–83	462	–	102	95	13

SOURCE: Columns 1, 2, 4, and 5 from Cheong and D'Silva (1984, various tables); column 3 from Government of Pakistan, *Economic Survey*, various issues.

Under the military regime of General Zia ul-Haq, most gins were returned to private ownership in 1978, and export duties were reduced. These acts, coupled with increasing prices of raw cotton compared with both cotton yarn and cotton manufactures (Table 6) and with increased foreign demand, led once again to increased output (Table 3). In the new prosperity, export duties yielded greater revenues even at lower rates (Table 5). Production grew at an annual rate of 16.56% from 1978-79 to 1981-82 (Cheong and D'Silva 1984:4).

In a comparison of domestic to international prices, Cheong and D'Silva find that price distortions for cotton lint (not for growers) were least among the four main crops (wheat, rice, sugar, cotton). But the improvement in the ratio of raw cotton prices to those of both yarn and manufactures disappeared, 1978-79 to 1980-81 (Table 6). Although raw cotton was clearly better off, relative to yarn and textile manufacturers, in the early eighties than in the early seventies, the trend at that time was no longer clear.

Pakistani cotton over the past two decades exemplifies again that the

Table 11.6

RATIOS OF RAW COTTON PRICES TO PRICES OF YARN AND
COTTON MANUFACTURES, 1971-72 TO 1980-81
(1969-70 = 100)

	Ratio of Raw Cotton Prices to	
	Cotton Yarn	Cotton Manufactures
1971–72	126.4	124.0
1972–73	96.7	139.3
1973–74	124.1	123.0
1974–75	136.6	94.4
1975–76	143.6	108.6
1976–77	126.9	118.5
1977–78	149.9	125.5
1978–79	158.9	153.7
1979–80	139.9	131.5
1980–81	141.7	139.3
Comparison of three-year averages:		
1971–72 to 1973–74	115.7	128.7
1978–79 to 1980–81	146.8	141.5

SOURCE: Adams and Iqbal (1983:158); three-year averages calculated by authors.

market "works." The Zia regime was not so unfriendly to growers as had been the Bhutto regime, but the future is unclear. The very ability of a government arbitrarily to make polar switches in duties, support prices, and rules on compulsory sales creates an uncertainty scarcely reassuring to farmers.

Wheat

Largely because of the green revolution, which produced HYVs, Pakistan's wheat production has grown prodigiously over the past twenty years. Whereas growth from 1949–50 to 1959–60 had averaged only 1.1% per year, that rate that jumped to 5.2% from 1959–60 to 1968–69. Once again, there was an opportunity for the government to fill its coffers, and once again, the predictable response. Table 7 shows government increasing its procurement from 3% of production in 1972–73 to 35% (or 79% of marketed output) in fiscal year 1982.

The government justified its intervention by saying that the existing market structure could not handle the increased volume. Were the market to fail – they went on – a catastrophic fall in wheat prices would have discouraged the spread of HYVs (Qureshi 1974). Let us evaluate this claim by examining the market structure since 1947.

Partition (1947) marked a fundamental break in Pakistan's market structure. Earlier, credit and markets had been in the hands of merchants and moneylenders, typically Hindu or Sikh; with partition, most of these fled to India. The following results are catalogued by Qureshi (1974:282). Debts were wiped out. New people were attracted into newly opened lucrative spots. Because of their different backgrounds, the newcomers formed no cohesive group, therefore did not collude. Finally, the three functions – moneylending, produce-buying, and merchandising – previously combined into a single person, were now divided among many. Hence, moneylenders were unlikely to "reap monopoly profits."

Transportation was vastly improved during the fifties and early sixties (Table 8). From 1950 to 1965, rail freight and hard-topped roads both doubled. The stock of trucks increased from 3,020 in 1950 to 31,230 in 1965–66 (Table 8). Possibly this infrastructure overexpanded during that period, for the increases tapered off to zero or almost zero during the five years – 1965–1970 – when the green revolution brought forth the amazing increase in marketable wheat. But the number of tractors did multiply fourfold during that half-decade.

By examining daily and monthly prices in village markets from 1965 to 1967, Qureshi found agricultural marketing to be highly competitive. Marketing margins correlated with transportation costs (with high statistical significance). While poor and indebted cultivators sold immediately after harvest, "no evidence was found . . . that prices in village markets were unduly low." He concluded that "the private marketing sector was

221

Table 11.7

WHEAT PRODUCTION, MARKETED OUTPUT, GOVERNMENT PROCUREMENT, AND IMPORTS, 1966–83
(THOUSANDS OF TONS)

Year	Production (1)	Marketed Output[a] (2)	Gov't. Procurement (3)	(3)/(1)	(3)/(2)	Imports
1966-67	4,096	na	86	0.02	na	–
1967-68	6,317	na	91	0.01	na	–
1968-69	6,513	na	793	0.12	na	–
1969-70	7,179	na	906	0.13	na	–
1970-71	6,374	na	1,017	0.16	na	285
1971-72	6,782	na	341	0.05	na	690
1972-73	7,325	na	208	0.03	na	1,359
FY1974	4,639	3,357	1,342	0.18	0.40	1,288
FY1975	7,674	3,376	1,253	0.16	0.37	1,164
FY1976	8,691	3,824	1,236	0.14	0.32	1,167
FY1977	9,144	4,023	2,376	0.26	0.59	499
FY1978	8,367	3,681	1,842	0.22	0.50	1,035
FY1979	9,950	4,378	1,086	0.11	0.25	2,236
FY1980	10,805	4,745	2,376	0.22	0.50	602
FY1981	11,473	5,048	2,955	0.26	0.59	304
FY1982	11,420	5,025	3,989	0.35	0.79	360
1982-83			3.8 million			

SOURCE: Chaudry and Iqbal (1979:76–77), for 1966–73; Cheong and D'Silva (1984:33) for 1974–82.

[a]We follow Cheong and D'Silva (1984) in assuming marketed output, after 1974, to be 44% of production. Before 1974, no reasonable estimate can be made. Probably the proportion marketed was only about 10% in the early sixties (before the impact of the green revolution).

Table 11.8

TRANSPORT FACILITIES IN RURAL AREAS OF WEST PAKISTAN, 1947–70

	Rail Freight (millions of ton miles)	Road Mileage (concrete surface)	Stock of Trucks	Tractors
1947–48	2,349	5,053	823	na
1950–51	2,718	6,150	3,020	na
1955–56	3,506	8,083	14,004	na
1960–61	5,074	8,827	20,472	na
1965–66	5,599	10,934	31,203	5,059
1969–70	5,175	10,306	34,871	20,715

SOURCE: Condensed from Qureshi (1974:283, Table 1).

doing an efficient job of assembling agricultural produce at the stage where farmers participate in the market" (Qureshi 1974:304–05). Thus we are suspicious of government claims of a need for central intervention in the market (for "efficiency").

Throughout the sixties, the government of General Ayub Khan procured wheat at 62% to 66% of the international price (Chaudry and Iqbal 1979:64). Only in the final years of that decade did domestic prices rise above international prices.

The Bhutto regime (1972–77) increased the government presence in the wheat market enormously through the Pakistan Agricultural Services and Storage Corporation (PASCO), established in 1973. During PASCO's first three years, 30% to 40% of marketed wheat was procured by the government. Flour mills were nationalized in 1976 (at the same time as cotton gins and rice hulling units). To supply them, the government stepped up its procurement to 59% in 1976–77 (Table 7).

Despite the great increase in domestic production, demand so outstripped supply that in the early and mid-seventies, the government was importing wheat at high international prices (Table 7). It mixed the imported with the domestic supply, but chapatty (a thin griddle-cake) made with this flour did not have the consistency to which consumers had been accustomed. Government procurement of domestic wheat at less than international prices constituted a negative economic subsidy ("tax") on the farmer, similar to those we saw in rice. Cheong and D'Silva's calculations are shown in Table 9.

Just as with rice, the negative equivalent subsidy ("tax") was more severe during the Bhutto regime of the mid-seventies than in the early eighties, but no decreasing trend appeared in the latter period. Unlike rice,

Table 11.9

FINANCIAL AND ECONOMIC SUBSIDIES FOR WHEAT, 1973–82

	1973–74	1974–75	1975–76	1976–77	1977–78	1978–79	1979–80	1980–81	1981–82
Production, of which:	7,629	7,674	8,691	9,144	8,367	9,950	10,805	11,473	11,420
Marketed	3,357	3,376	3,824	4,023	3,681	4,378	4,754	5,048	5,025
Gov't. procured	1,342	1,253	1,236	2,376	1,842	1,086	2,376	2,955	3,989
Ratio, prod. to market	0.40	0.37	0.32	0.59	0.50	0.25	0.50	0.59	0.79
Imports	1,288	1,164	1,167	499	1,035	2,236	602	304	–
Ratio, imports to procurement	0.29	0.59	0.59	0.72	0.62	0.63	0.59	0.68	0.60
Ratio, proc. price to wholesale	0.86	0.89	0.96	0.93	0.76	0.88	0.91	1.02	0.87
Ratio, proc. price to import unit cost	0.29	0.59	0.59	0.72	0.62	0.63	0.59	0.68	0.60
Proportional subsidy:									
Financial	2.9	5.5	10.2	2.8	9.1	17.7	24.0	21.8	17.3
Economic	– 211.0	– 58.5	– 64.4	– 34.3	– 37.9	– 45.2	– 60.8	– 49.6	60.5
Equivalent	– 208.2	– 52.9	– 54.2	– 31.5	– 28.8	– 27.6	– 36.8	– 27.7	43.2
Imports	1,288	1,164	1,167	499	1,035	2,236	602	304	–
Ration of imports to procurement	0.29	0.59	0.59	0.72	0.62	0.63	0.59	0.68	0.60

SOURCE: Cheong and D'Silva (1984:33, Table 13).

the financial subsidy was positive during the entire period, 1973–82, because no taxes offset the subsidies of fertilizer and water. Although these positive subsidies did increase during that period, they would be expected to lessen later, with the government increasing fertilizer prices to international levels by 1985.

So, what of the wheat market in the eighties? We found it quite efficient before the increased intervention of the Bhutto period. As Zia raised the procurement price to approach the wholesale, even reach it in 1980–81, did the private market retain its efficiency? We believe so. In a detailed study of the wheat market in 1980–81, Cornelisse (1984:70) describes the trade pattern:

> Procurement depots—which absorb . . . 3/4 of the marketed volume dominate the whole market in the Punjab . . . [so] the procurement price strongly influences the price in wheat transactions among private actors. Normally this price is determined by deducting handling charges from the procurement price where charges appear to vary positively with distance to nearest depot and negatively with batch size. In other words, price formation by private traders is of the retrograde type. Further traders hold very low stocks and use little credit. . . . They aim at maximization of turnover speed.

("Retrograde type" means that the government procurement price rules. Private traders set their buying prices by what they know they can obtain in the government centers.)

Although wholesale prices are in this way affected by the government price, nevertheless—because procurement is not compulsory—both prices are strongly influenced by the market, and private trade has continued much as before. A network of specialized categories (which the government could not duplicate)—from village shopkeepers to large wholesalers buying primarily from other traders—continues to function similarly to the market structure of fifteen years earlier, as studied by Qureshi.

We conclude, therefore, that the Bhutto government's reasons for intervention—to preserve efficient marketing—were instead a cover for a greater take by the state. The Zia government has reduced that take, by higher procurement prices and therefore a lesser negative subsidy (Table 9). Possibly because of this increased liberalism, Pakistan again achieved an exportable surplus of wheat in 1982–84. Even so, the remaining intervention assures that the government will be a principal beneficiary. Once again, the government's *ability* to intervene hangs heavy over the farmers and traders.

Sugar

In its quest to save foreign exchange, the government of Pakistan has always looked to sugar production, to substitute for imports. During the sixties, government procurement prices were significantly above world prices, far more than necessary to induce production. In 1966, farmers earned three times as much growing sugar as they would have with cotton, their most profitable alternative (Islam 1981:167). Thus cane output grew from 11.6 million tons in 1960–61 to 26.3 million in 1969–70, at an annual growth rate of 7.7% (1959–60 to 1968–69) (Stern and Falcon 1970:37).

But procurement prices are ruled by fiscal necessity and the caprice of the government. While averaging 2.73 constant Rs per 40 kilo bag in the three years 1969–72, they were raised to 3.53 Rs in 1972–73, then decreased over the next six years to a low of 2.12 Rs (all in 1969–70 Rs; Table 10). The rate of growth fell to a 0.44% annual average, 1969–70 to 1979–80 (Cheong and D'Silva 1984:8). Part of the decline reflected a diversion of cane into gur (a local kind of sugar) in response to low procurement prices. Cane crushed by the mills declined from 29.8% of total output in 1977–78 to 22% in 1978–80 (*Pakistan Economic Review*, March 1983:45).

To hold down the import bill, the Zia government has intervened directly in sugar production, requiring sales to the government (which had earlier been optional). It established cooperative societies and district

Table 11.10

PROCUREMENT PRICES OF AGRICULTURAL COMMODITIES,
1969–83 (IN 1969–70 RUPEES PER 40 KG. BAG)

	Wheat	Rice (basmati)	Paddy (basmati)	Sugar Cane	Cotton (desai)	Seed Cotton (desai)
1969–70	18.22	37.50	na	2.95	na	na
1970–71	17.19	38.42	na	2.78	na	na
1971–72	16.41	36.10	na	2.45	na	na
1972–73	18.69	39.37	na	3.53	na	na
1973–74	15.98	38.86	na	2.66	na	na
1974–75	18.79	45.71	na	2.67	na	na
1975–76	17.31	42.12	na	2.69	na	na
1976–77	15.55	42.67	21.85	2.42	na	50.43
1977–78	14.63	37.56	21.95	2.27	132.47	52.20
1978–79	16.63	40.65	22.34	2.12	127.50	49.52
1979–80	15.77	37.19	20.28	2.37	118.30	45.31
1980–81	16.16	38.16	20.89	2.69	114.03	43.45
1981–82	14.72	38.07	21.57	2.45	106.24	42.13
1982–83	15.61	37.56	21.46	2.35	102.20	40.98

SOURCE: *Pakistan Economic Survey* (1982–83, Table 9), converted to 1969–70 rupees by authors, using wholesale price index, p. 116.

councils "to coordinate and implement policies covering everything from vertical improvement to farm credit and guaranteed price levels" (ISO 1983, vol. 3:30; we presume by "vertical improvement" they meant "vertical integration"). In the Punjab, which grows two-thirds of Pakistan's sugar, a Cane Control board allocates zones among mills, which must each purchase all the cane in its zone. Growers may keep 20% for seed. It is illegal to produce gur and other sugar-cane derivatives in the mill zones.

In non-mill zones, however, where sales are not compulsory, "growers . . . find it economic to manufacture gur . . . because of more demand for gur and higher prices." From this one judges that government prices in the mill zones are not attractive without compulsion.

Although the mills are privately owned, their profitability depends on shifting government policy. In the 1970s, the government paid slightly more for sugar produced in new mills, thus encouraging start-ups. But in 1983, when the government decided to de-ration sugar, mill profitability became questionable, as retail prices fell 20%.

Apparently, Pakistan's comparative advantage does not lie in sugar, and both its production and long-run benefit to farmers are questionable.

Fertilizer

> During some periods, the number of vendors was sufficiently small to create monopoly positions in the countryside. . . . For a small farmer to purchase fertilizer on credit in this situation required (1) a payment to the revenue official (patwari) to secure an official affidavit certifying land ownership or tenancy, (2) a payment to the bank official to obtain the loan, and (3) the payment of so-called "black market" prices to the fertilizer vendors. As a result of this combination of payments, the real "price" of fertilizer to small farmers was often substantially above its official price. For larger farmers the actual price was much closer to the official price (Gotsch and Brown 1980:51).

Government control of fertilizer distribution—intensified during the Bhutto administration—was clearly the cause of the situation described by Gotsch and Brown. In the 1960s, fertilizer had been sold partly by government and partly by private firms. But in November 1973, provincial government agencies were given a monopoly in distributing imported fertilizers, and private producers were required to sell 50% of their output to those agencies (White Paper 1979:26). Distributors who were not also producers were forced out of business. The number of fertilizer distributors decreased, and fertilizer production and consumption—which had been increasing—leveled off during the next two years (Table 11).

In 1975, private firms were again allowed to distribute imported fertilizer, receiving it from provincial agencies, which maintained their monopoly over imports. Although production stagnated for the rest of the seventies, consumption increased dramatically, beginning 1975–76, and more

227

Table 11.11
PRODUCTION AND CONSUMPTION OF FERTILIZER, 1965–83
(THOUSANDS OF NET TONS)

	Production	Consumption
1965–66	47.43	70.49
1966–67	51.46	111.83
1967–68	52.50	190.43
1968–69	81.14	244.64
1969–70	133.42	307.70
1970–71	144.64	283.20
1971–72	220.00	381.93
1972–73	282.74	436.50
1973–74	304.26	402.68
1974–75	326.90	425.49
1975–76	326.70	553.83
1976–77	325.70	631.30
1977–78	327.80	717.23
1978–79	365.50	879.81
1979–80	441.70	1,044.05
1980–81	644.80	1,079.33
1981–82	783.60	1,081.14
1982–83	1,044.60	1,243.59

SOURCE: Government of Pakistan, *Pakistan Economic Survey* (1983–84:33).

than doubled by 1980. The resulting rise in imports led to new private urea plants in the early eighties.

In those years, fertilizer production, imports, and distribution were divided among one large public company, the National Fertilizer Corporation (NFC), the provincial agencies established in 1973, and three licensed (favored) private companies. NFC was the largest producer, manufacturing urea, ammonium sulphates, and phosphates; all of its output was marketed by a subsidiary. But provincial agencies began to monopolize the distribution of imports. As of late 1983, however, this monopoly had lost some of its importance, since nitrogenous fertilizers were no longer imported because home supply had become sufficient. According to Sadiq (1983:41), they were to serve as "fertilizer controllers in their provinces, suppliers of imported fertilizer to marketing organizations, and as competitors to private marketing."

Urea is also produced by three large private companies: Exxon, Dawood, and Fauji. Although presumably they gained their positions by ordinary competitive techniques—advertising and contacting potential customers—the strong role of government among such principal customers as sugar would open the possibility for collusion. Sadiq (1983:40) finds that when Fauji began business, it gained its market not only through "legitimate" techniques, but also through contacts with officials in the sugar-cane industry.

Agricultural Credit

Perhaps the chief virtue of the government's agricultural credit system is that at no time did it forbid credit by the traditional sources of a traditional society: friends, relatives, and large numbers of private moneylenders. So long as the government does not tap these sources, it is possible that official credit will be an increase in the total, and if it is misallocated, the small farmer may at least not lose.

But even this is not certain, for consequences may be hidden. We are never sure that government credit has not diminished the amount available through the traditional sources. Real credit is scarce; it can be increased only through an increase in real resources, or through their diversion from other purposes. If this diversion should somehow suck in the real resources of traditional suppliers (as it might do through inflation), then we cannot be sure that small, unfavored farmers are not worse off than before.

We have already seen that upon independence, many of the traditional sources fled to India. Thereafter, most rural smallholder credit came from friends and relatives. In 1960, the government created the Agricultural Development Bank of Pakistan (ADBP), to supply credit for "progressive" landowners (Alavi 1983:61). In addition, cooperatives were loaning funds that they received mainly from the State Bank of Pakistan. (We do not have good information on how the cooperatives were formed.) In real terms, however, the state system provided very little credit during the sixties and early seventies; only in 1972–73 did this source begin to swell (Table 12). The initial spurt in Pakistani agricultural output occurred during the sixties without much assistance from government credit.

Before 1973, commercial bank lending for agriculture had been negligible. In that year, President Bhutto nationalized the banks, demanding that a certain portion of their portfolios be allocated to small farmers for production loans. Because of these, commercial banks rapidly caught up with the ADBP, and from 1975–76 on, their loans have been persistently greater than ADBP, except in the 1982–83 estimated data (Table 12). The martial law government under Zia, beginning 1977, decided to funnel additional funds to small farmers through the state-run cooperative system. From then until 1981–82, the number of cooperatives doubled. Both cooperative and commercial-banks loans have been difficult for small farmers, however, since they require cumbersome procedures and dealing with many officials and interim merchants (M. H. Khan 1983:151).

Table 11.12

AGRICULTURAL CREDIT DISBURSED (IN MILLIONS OF 1969-70 RUPEES), 1959-83

	Agricultural Development Bank	Taccavi[a]	Cooperatives	Commercial Banks	Total
1959-60	33	24	59	–	116
1960-61	39	19	73	–	131
1961-62	54	15	117	–	187
1962-63	54	13	109	–	175
1963-64	59	15	87	–	160
1964-65	47	35	66	–	148
1965-66	80	15	61	–	156
1966-67	107	12	89	–	208
1967-68	112	14	63	–	188
1968-69	84	12	49	–	145
1969-70	91	11	53	–	155
1970-71	87	10	52	–	149
1971-72	72	8	35	–	115
1972-73	131	8	33	66	238
1973-74	243	39	84	167	533
1974-75	187	6	39	247	479
1975-76	232	11	40	353	636
1976-77	250	5	37	358	663
1977-78	159	3	51	476	689
1978-79	144	4	143	476	707
1979-80	224	3	224	501	951
1980-81	297	2	314	510	1,125
1981-82	395	2	279	618	1,294
1982-83	548	3	422	503	1,477

SOURCE: *Pakistan Economic Survey* (1982-83:34, Table 7), deflated by author using wholesale price index, p. 118, and *Pakistan Economic Survey* (1973-74:42, Appendix Table 23), for wholesale price index used to inflate 1958-60 through 1968-69.

[a]Emergency loans in time of flood, drought, or other crop failure.

Meanwhile, M. H. Khan (1975:107) reports that ADBP focused its lending on farmers with holdings of more than 25 acres. As this bank expanded its lending, a greater percentage went into tractors, tubewells, and other heavy equipment, for which only larger farmers might supply collateral (M. H. Khan 1983:151). In order to validate Khan's assertion, we examined the data for ADBP loans by size of holding (Table 13) and by use (Table 14). Here we encounter a curious inconsistency. While Table 13 reveals a distribution favoring small farmers (5 to 20 hectares), Table 14 shows that most loans were made for tractors, power tillers, and attachments, which are not common to farmers of such small size. Furthermore, the agricultural machinery census in 1975 reported that 83% of tractors were owned by farmers with holdings above 12 hectares (Salam et al. 1981:95). While the evidence is not enough for a "conviction at law," it appears to us highly probable that the data in Table 13 have been modified. Landowners do not have any reason to report their holdings accurately, when a smaller number will make it easier to secure a loan, and the ADBP also has incentive to report that its loans favor small-scale farmers. No one that we know of verifies the accuracy of their data. With such inconsistencies, we tend to believe Khan's findings that ADBP does favor larger, capital-intensive farming.

We now return to the passbook system proposed by A. Khan (1983:25) at the beginning of this chapter. This system was indeed installed by the Bhutto administration (*Pakistan Economic Survey*, 1972–73: 26), and it is, to the best of our knowledge, still in force. Passbooks, issued by revenue officers only to landowners, are required for receiving bank loans. The amount and value of the farmer's cropland is inscribed. Since loans are subsidized, landowners have the incentive to pay small bribes to revenue agents for passport validation. With the Zia administration's 1980–81 deci-

Table 11.13

AGRICULTURAL DEVELOPMENT BANK LOANS BY SIZE OF HOLDING, 1973–74 TO 1981–82 (IN PERCENTS)

	Landless Tenant Project Loans	Size of Owners' Holdings			
		< 5 ha	5–20 ha	20–40.5 ha	> 40.5
1973–74	47.7	24.0	11.8	8.7	7.8
1974–75	13.6	11.4	46.3	21.4	7.3
1975–76	10.2	8.7	47.9	24.2	8.8
1976–77	17.1	17.8	49.9	20.5	3.7
1977–78	10.7	6.5	56.6	23.3	2.7
1978–79	3.7	9.9	66.0	17.2	3.2
1979–80	15.4	10.2	21.2	36.4	16.8
1980–81	16.2	9.5	57.1	9.6	7.6
1981–82	8.5	17.6	53.5	18.3	2.1

SOURCE: *Agricultural Statistics of Pakistan* (1982:153).

Table 11.14

AGRICULTURAL DEVELOPMENT BANK LOANS BY USE, 1973–74 TO 1981–82 (IN PERCENTS)

	Seeds	Fertilizer	Tractors, Tillers, etc.	Tubewells, Pumps, Engines	Draft Animals	Poultry and Dairy Farming	Other
1973–74	3	27	20	12	8	7	23
1974–75	3	20	35	22	5	2	13
1975–76	1	13	66	9	2	*	9
1976–77	2	22	52	4	4	*	16
1977–78	1	10	75	3	3	*	9
1978–79	1	10	75	3	4	*	7
1979–80	2	8	66	1	2	1	20
1980–81	2	10	60	1	3	4	20
1981–82	3	12	57	1	5	5	17

SOURCE: Percentages calculated by authors from *Agricultural Statistics of Pakistan* (1982:151, Table 86).

*Less than 1%.

sion to extend more credit to many more smallholders, the system was expanded (*Pakistan Economic Survey,* 1980–81:30).

For want of adequate field studies, we are unable to quantify the workings of agricultural credit. Indeed, our information is scattered and sometimes suspect. We can point only to possibilities, not to actualities. Surely the system is pregnant with possibilities to ignore the smallholder, leaving him no better than before, still dependent on his traditional sources, or else to deteriorate his position through diversion of real resources (via inflationary creation of money credit) away from smallholders and into the hands of larger farmers, whose production — like that of sugar — may be less efficient.

Later Events

Land reform in Pakistan was a creation of the Bhutto government (1972–77), so most of the events in this chapter refer to that period. After Bhutto had been overthrown in 1977 (and executed in 1979), his successor General Zia ul-Haq showed little enthusiasm for reform. Indeed, he "established an advisory council, nearly half of which was composed of wealthy landlords, and used foreign assistance to hasten adoption of modern agricultural methods and to increase farm production" (Weisman 1986:108).

In this, he achieved a questionable success. From its low base of 95.41 in 1975–77 (1979–81 = 100) as a result of Bhutto's policies, agricultural output per capita increased only to 104.29 in 1984–86 (FAO 1988:50), or by slightly less than 1% per year on average. Compared with Third-World countries with freer markets, this is not a great achievement.

Zia's death in an air crash in 1988 led to a return of the Bhutto regime in the form of Benazir Bhutto, daughter of the late President, appointed as Prime Minister. Her platform remains obscure, with her public statements confined to assertions that she will reinstate the populist policies of her late father. If she indeed does so, the future of agriculture and the peasant is anything but bright.

References

Adams, John, and Iqbal, Sabiha, 1983. *Exports, Politics, and Economic Development: Pakistan, 1970–1982,* Boulder, Colo., Westview Press.

Alavi, Hamzla, 1983. "Class and State," in Gurdezi and Rashid.

Ali, K., ed., 1982. *Pakistan: The Political Economy of Rural Development,* Lahore, Vanguard Books.

Bose, Swadesh, 1972. "East-West Contrast in Pakistan's Agricultural Development," in Griffin and Kahn.

Chaudry, M., and Iqbal, 1979. "A Quantitative Analysis of Procurement Price Policy," *Pakistan Economic and Social Review,* Autumn/Winter.

Cheong, K., and D'Silva, E., 1984. *Prices, Terms of Trade, and Role of Government in Pakistan's Agriculture,* World Bank Staff Working Paper no. 520, Washington, D.C., World Bank.

Cornelisse, Peter, 1984. "Wheat Market Flows in the Punjab," *Pakistan Development Review*, vol. 23, no. 1:65–67.

Darling, M. L., 1925. *The Punjabi Peasant: Property and Debt*, New York, Oxford University Press.

FAO (Food and Agriculture Organization), 1988. *Agriculture Yearbook, 1986*, Rome.

Gotsch, C., and Brown, B., 1980. *Prices, Taxes, and Subsidies in Pakistan, 1960–1976*, World Bank Working Paper no. 387, Baltimore, Johns Hopkins University Press.

Government of Pakistan, 1979. *White Paper on the Bhutto Regime*, vol. 4.

Government of Pakistan, 1983. *Pakistan Economic Survey*, various years, Ministry of Finance, Economic Advisor.

Griffin, K., and Khan, A. R., eds., 1972. *Growth and Inequality in Pakistan*, London, MacMillan and New York, St. Martin's Press.

Gurdezi, Hassan, and Rashid, Jamal, eds., 1983. *Pakistan: the Roots of Dictatorship, the Political Economy of a Pretorian State*, London, Zed Press.

Herring, Ronald J., 1979. "Zulfikar Ali Bhutto and Eradication of Feudalism in Pakistan," *Comparative Studies in Society and History*, vol. 21, no. 4:519–57.

Islam, Nural, 1981. *Foreign Trade and Economic Controls in Development: The Case of United Pakistan*, New Haven, Conn., Yale University Press.

Khan, Abdul Jabbar, 1983. "Planning Strategy for Agriculture," *Pakistan Economic Review*, March:20–28.

Khan, M. H., 1975. *Economics of the Green Revolution*, New York, Praeger.

Khan, M. H., 1981. *Underdevelopment and Agrarian Structure in Pakistan*, Boulder, Colo., Westview Press.

Khan, M. H., 1983. "Classes and Agrarian Transition in Pakistan," *Pakistan Development Review*, vol. 22, no. 3:129–62.

Kizilbash, H., 1973. "Local Government: Democracy at the Capital and Autocracy in the Village," *Pakistan Economic and Social Review*, vol. 11, no. 1:104–21.

Qureshi, Sarfrez, 1974. "The Performance of Village Markets for Agricultural Produce," *Pakistan Development Review*, vol. 113, no. 2:280–306.

Sadiq, Mohammed, 1983. "Promotion by a New Company Entering the Fertilizer Field in Pakistan," *Agrochemical News in Brief*, December:38–41.

Salam, A.; Hussain, M.; and Ghayur, S., 1981. "Farm Mechanization, Employment, and Productivity in Pakistan's Agriculture," *Pakistan Economic and Social Review*, vol. 19, no. 2, Winter:95–114.

Stern, J., and Falcon, W., 1970. *Growth and Development in Pakistan*, Cambridge, Mass., Harvard University, Center for International Affairs.

Thobani, Mateen, 1979. "Wheat Prices and Incomes," *Pakistan Development Review*, vol. 18, no. 4:282–90.

Weisman, Steven R., 1986. "The Return of Benazir Bhutto: Struggle in Pakistan," *New York Times Magazine*, September 21.

Wizerat, Shahida, 1981. "Technological Change in Pakistan Agriculture, 1953–54 to 1978–79," *Pakistan Development Review*, vol. 20, no. 4:425–39.

12. South Korea

Unlike other countries discussed in this volume, except Taiwan, South Korean land reform was comprehensive and egalitarian; it did not squeeze the farmers, nor, for the most part, did it lead to ever-greater government intervention. Some observers have seen these happy outcomes as the result of government astuteness and refusal to tolerate inefficiency. Our perspective will be somewhat different. On a number of occasions, the government did impose its own prices, sometimes to the detriment of farmers. It has also employed direct controls. Why did these interventions not blossom into virtually total government control over agriculture, to the detriment of both farmers and, ultimately, the economy as a whole? In short, why is South Korea different from most of the countries studied in this volume? That is the question we will address in this chapter.

Korea is different in two ways, both unusual. First, many of the largest landowners were tainted by their collaboration with the Japanese. After they were discredited and made politically impotent, no strong rural élite remained to co-opt government institutions. Second, central control over input markets occurred much later than the land reform and did not directly follow from it. Already, the peasantry had attained a certain capacity for political defense. Their resistance to the Japanese—especially the Japanese in defeat—sharpened their ability to resist landowners and the central government.

Background

The political education of Korean peasants was stimulated by the Japanese occupation. In their constant search for rice, the Japanese greatly improved Korean agriculture before World War II. They surveyed the land, formed credit and cooperative institutions, and promoted education. By the late thirties, half the rural population was literate (Ban et al. 1980:311).

Not all their activities were serendipitous for the Koreans, however. As rice exports (to Japan) increased dramatically in the twenties and early thirties, so did the rents of the landlords. In the balance of payments, one offset the other and little was left for the Korean farmer. More and more, Japanese landlords took over the land. The increasing tenancy (Ban et al. 1980:27) created the need for land reform after the war.

Agricultural output increased greatly after the Korean War (3.5% per annum from 1952 to 1971; 3.8% from 1971 to 1982, and almost 2.0% per capita in the latter period). It has also diversified. To be sure, rice still occupies 60% of cultivated acreage, but it has lost relatively. Barley is a distant second, with only 8%. But a study of farming by region (Keidel 1980:126) shows that "as the structure of the Korean economy has shifted away from agriculture, so has the structure of agriculture itself shifted away from the cultivation of rice."

Increased output of livestock and vegetables, resulting from rapid urbanization, has led to greater regional differentiation. Keidel divides livestock increases into two phases: countrywide from 1945 to the mid-sixties, mainly in pigs, chickens, and rabbits; and thereafter, concentrated in dairies in Kyonggi Province surrounding the rapidly growing metropolitan area of Seoul. Vegetable production increased in areas close to urban markets. These shifts have caused farmers' incomes in "the northern and dry field regions" to rise above those in the "traditionally good grain regions" of the south (Keidel 1980:146). Thus the south (of South Korea) has been more affected by government intervention (because it centered on rice) than has the north.

Migration out of agriculture has been so high in postwar years that total farm population started to decline in 1969, even though overall population was increasing by 2.1% per annum. Agriculture's share of total population fell from 58% in 1960 to 38% in 1975.

In response to rapid urbanization and rising incomes, grain imports increased dramatically, from 490,000 metric tons annually in 1956-60 to 2,560,000 in 1971-75 (Table 1). This increase gave the farmers further leverage upon their government. Fearful for its balance of payments, government officials dramatically reversed their pricing policy to increase domestic output of grains. In the late sixties, producer prices were raised above market, while consumers were still subsidized.

Table 12.1

GRAIN IMPORTS, 1955–75 (ANNUAL AVERAGES, THOUSANDS OF METRIC TONS)

	Wheat	Rice	Barley
1955	42.3	0.8	3.5
1956–60	277.3	41.1	171.9
1961–65	491.2	23.5	149.9
1966–70	879.2	360.9	56.6
1971–75	1,623.0	563.0	383.9

SOURCE: Ban et al. (1980:29, Table 13).

The Land Reform

Tainted by their cooperation with the Japanese, at the end of World War II Korean landlords received no sympathy from the U.S. military government. This government set quotas for grain delivery and landlords received their rent in grain, at official low prices. Therefore, rents averaged only 7% of annual output (Ban et al. 1980:439). But landlords receiving any rent were the more fortunate. The market value of farmland in 1948 had fallen to one half its annual output, primarily because in many places tenants were refusing to pay any rent at all (Ban et al. 1980:288). This breakdown in the social hierarchy not only paved the way for land reform but helped shape the form it would take.

There were, in fact, two land reforms: the official and the unofficial. The former included the confiscation and sale of Japanese-owned land by the U.S. military government, which set up a temporary public corporation to manage both the process and the land. Under the Land Reform Act of 1949, the South Korean government distributed 240,000 hectares of this land, primarily to former tenants. The tenants were to pay the government 20% of their annual output for fifteen years. That worked out to a price of two times the annual yield, with later payments discounted at 10% (Ban et al. 1980:288).

Also as part of the official reform, in the new constitution the South Korean government promised land-to-the-tiller. The Land Reform Act of 1949 (amended 1950) decreed that all rented land, plus owned land above 3 *chongbo* (one *chongbo* = 0.992 hectare), would be purchased by the government and sold to tenants. Compensation to landlords was to be in government bonds valued at 1.5 times the annual output. Tenants were to pay the government 30% of their yield for five years. By 1952, 330,000 hectares had been distributed.

The unofficial land reform was the sale of 550,000 hectares of rental land by owners to tenants. Although these sales bypassed the official reform, the government encouraged them both verbally and—perhaps unwittingly—by setting up conditions favorable to them. First, the government was slow in redeeming the bonds created for the official reform; their market value fell dramatically, to approximately 3.5 *sok* of rice per *chongbo*. Tenants' obligations to the government for land distributed in that reform had a present value of approximately 19 *sok* per *chongbo*. As Perkins points out (Ban et al. 1980:290), these extremes left much room for private negotiation. Second, the "effective" ownership of the land by tenants refusing to pay rent in the late forties encouraged the landlords to sell.

The fact that peasants had genuinely bought much of their land, as opposed to countries where land was "given" to them, or "sold" at concessions that converted sales into virtual gifts, also distinguishes the South Korean from other post-World War II reforms. Regardless of the advantages caused by the circumstances, it was the *peasants* who bargained for their land in the informal reform. The government did not set the terms for them.

Whereas owners were only 13.8% of farm households in 1945, in 1964—after the reform—they had become 71.6% of farm households (Table 2). The 4% of farm households holding more than 3 *chongbo* in 1945 owned 26% of the cultivated acreage. In 1960 the 0.3% of farm households who held more than 3 *chongbo* had only 1.2% of the cultivated acreage (Tables 3 and 4). One-half of the land had been redistributed to approximately two-thirds of the rural population.

Because the size distribution was much the same—very little land was broken up, and mostly the same farmers tilled the same soil—the government did not fear for a decrease in productivity. Here is another contrast.

Table 12.2

OWNER-TENANT DISTRIBUTION OF FARM HOUSEHOLDS FOR SELECTED YEARS, 1913–65

	1913–17[a]	1928–32[a]	1938[a]	1945	1947	1964	1965
Owners	21.8	18.4	19.0	13.8	16.5	71.6	69.5
Part owners	38.8	31.4	25.3	34.6	38.3	23.2	23.5
Tenants	39.4	50.2	55.7	48.9	42.1	5.2	7.0
Farm laborers				2.7	3.1		

SOURCE: Ban et al. (1980:284, Table 118; 286, Table 120).
[a]These columns do not include farm laborers.

Table 12.3

FARM HOUSEHOLDS BY LAND UNDER CULTIVATION, 1945–70 (IN PERCENT)

Farm Size (hectares)	1945	1947	1953	1960	1965	1970
0–0.5	72.1	41.2	44.9	42.9	35.9	31.6
0.5–1.0		33.3	34.2	30.1	31.7	31.7
1.0–2.0	23.8	18.8	16.5	20.7	25.6	25.8
2.0–3.0		5.3	4.3	6.0	5.6	5.0
3.0	4.1	1.4	0.1	0.3	1.2	1.5
Noncrop farms						4.4

SOURCE: Ban et al. (1980:295, Table 123).

238

Table 12.4
Cultivated Area, by Size of Farm, 1945-70

Farm Size (hectares)	1945	1955	1960	1965	1970
0-0.5	10.4	18.0	16.7	12.4	10.7
0.5-1.0	29.2	27.9	26.7	27.8	
1.0-2.0	40.0	35.9	37.0	40.5	40.6
2.0-3.0	15.9	17.3	15.3	13.6	
3.0	26.4	1.0	1.2	5.1	7.3

SOURCE: Ban et al. (1980:296, Table 124).

In other countries, officials (improperly, we believe) decided that peasants would not know how to farm their new holdings without government supervision.

Why was the South Korean reform so successful? We cannot say for sure, but we are intrigued by four features, all of which militate toward more effective political power by the peasants than has been the case in other countries we have studied. First, the reform did not lead to new government institutions in the countryside. The grain procurement program was already in effect. While the additional grain collected for land payment was a severe burden on the beneficiaries, it was part of the existing system. It may have been the more acceptable because it formalized the peasants' de facto holding of the land. Only eight years later—in ways we will describe below—did the government attempt to consolidate its control in the countryside, and then its actions were not linked to the land reform. Second, the land reform effectively destroyed the rural élite without creating a new class of rich peasants. Thus any non-market allocation of resources would be less likely to be distorted by inordinate political power. Although endemic in the early sixties in the cooperatives, corruption was not biased in favor of one sector of the farm community. Third, tenants' intransigence on rent in the late forties and their active negotiation in private transfers of property reflected a certain political power, to which the government had to yield. Fourth, value added in agriculture grew at a respectable rate of 4.0% per annum in the eight years after the reform (Keidel 1981:36). The fact that the peasants could achieve this "on their own" (without massive intervention) doubtless enhanced their power vis-à-vis the government.

Credit

Nevertheless, Korea has a long history of rural credit institutions, in which central control has been associated with the drying up of credit. During Japanese colonial rule, in 1933, the Korean Federation of Financial

239

Associations was authorized to raise loanable funds by issuing debentures. These associations functioned effectively during the thirties. During World War II, however, the Japanese authorities co-opted their resources, and farm credit was exhausted. After the war, the associations were the main government agency in the countryside, handling the compulsory grain procurement and rationing. In 1949 they took over distribution of fertilizer. In the same year, the government extended credit to the associations, to be retailed to farmers. This renewed intervention in the rural credit market was disrupted by the Korean War of 1950.

After that war, the government tried to pre-empt both rural credit and control over cooperatives. In the mid-fifties, approximately 75% of rural debt was owed to private sources (Morrow and White, 1972:5) and interest rates ranged from 40% to 60%. Finding these rates usurious, in 1956 the government reorganized the cooperatives (Financial Associations) into the Korean Agricultural Bank, channeling additional funds through it. In 1958 the bank became the only public agency dispensing agricultural credit. Thus the government separated the credit function of the cooperatives from the other functions.

In 1961, however, the Park military government recombined the Korean Agricultural Bank with the local cooperatives, forming the National Agricultural Cooperation Federation (NACF) (Ban et al. 1980:213). The formal structure of the NACF was highly centralized and became more so during the sixties. The president of the NACF is appointed by the president of South Korea for a three-year term; he in turn appoints the presidents of the county and special cooperatives. Presidents of the local village or township cooperatives are elected by the board of directors (of the local cooperative), which contain the only popularly elected officials in the cooperative structure. Both the county and local cooperatives are chartered by and registered with the Ministry of Agriculture and Forestry. The consolidation of cooperatives was justified as an efficiency measure: small village cooperatives were deemed not financially feasable, for they lacked economies of scale.

Table 5 shows the employment levels of NACF in June 1972, by hierarchical level. Because the major cooperative functions are carried out at the county level, a large percentage of employees is found there. The centralized nature of the county cooperative is emphasized by Morrow and White (1972:22):

> The county cooperatives represent the major contact point with the farmers and they engage in a wide range of activities such as purchasing, marketing, storage, distribution of consumer goods and agricultural inputs, processing, bank credit and insurance.

Farmers have to go to the township cooperative headquarters to obtain credit. Local cooperative presidents forward a list of potential credit bene-

Table 12.5
EMPLOYMENT IN NACF BY LEVEL: JUNE 1972 EMPLOYEES

National level	
Directly employed	1,832
2 city cooperatives (Seoul and Puson)	807
138 county cooperatives	6,446
Local level (1,283 township and 1,803 village cooperatives)	6,589
Special cooperatives (by product)	2,358
Total	18,032

SOURCE: Morrow and White (1972:18).

ficiaries to the county cooperative, recommended according to credit-worthiness. Each beneficiary must be a member, must have a surplus to sell through the cooperative, and must have a good record in filling market contracts with the cooperative. The actual decision on credit is made at the township level (Morrow and White 1972:24).

Although the reconsolidation of cooperatives in 1961 was to be accompanied by a major expansion of public agricultural credit to replace private credit, this did not occur until 1969 (Table 6). In real terms, the absolute amount of agricultural lending by NACF decreased from 1961 to 1965; only in 1967 did it reach a higher level than in 1961. Why?

One reason was that during the early sixties NACF was paying very low or negative real rates of interest on savings deposits. Before 1965 it was allowed to pay only 8%–15% on savings deposits (Lee et al. 1977:1185) even though the consumer price index was rising at an average rate of 17% from 1961 to 1965 (IFS Yearbook 1983: 322). After the interest rate reform of that year (which raised rates to 24% for six-month deposits, to encourage savings), NACF started attracting more deposits, even though its rates were still lower than in the private market. But NACF's savings deposits were partially compulsory (Morrow and White 1972:24), in that each township was required to meet a quota. The township cooperatives used a variety of techniques to do so, such as requiring a savings deposit to be set up before any loan was made or that a certain portion of loan repayments should be placed in a savings deposit.

A second reason was the competitiveness of private savings and loan associations. The "Ke," a mutual savings society, had long been characteristic of rural villages. A group of more well-to-do villagers would pool

Table 12.6

AGRICULTURAL LENDING THROUGH KOREAN AGRICULTURAL BANK AND NACF, 1957–70 (IN BILLIONS OF 1965 CONSTANT WONS)

	Agricultural Loans and Fertilizer Credit (1)	Agricultural Lending by KAB 1957–60 and NACF 1961–70 (2)	Percent of (1) + (2) That Was Government Funded
1957	23.4	19.3	50.0
1958	24.8	20.7	35.0
1959	24.5	21.4	35.0
1960	30.9	27.8	55.0
1961	38.3	34.5	51.3
1962	40.4	33.9	60.1
1963	35.5	25.1	68.9
1964	32.0	24.9	53.0
1965	34.0	23.3	51.2
1966	35.4	24.0	47.6
1967	35.7	27.5	46.9
1968	na	37.7	35.7
1969	na	53.9	36.8
1970	na	58.9	32.6

SOURCE: Column 1, Cole and Lyman (1971:148, Table 7.9); Columns 2 and 3, Ban et al. (1985:208, 222).

their savings, lending them at very high rates. Loans made in the spring would be repaid with 50% interest after the fall harvest. In a survey of seventy-five South Korean villages in 1969, the value of the Ke's assets were found to be four times those of the local village cooperative (Morrow and White 1972:13). Private credit decreased steadily until 1960–64. Cole and Lyman (1971:149) believe that the private credit market reached its low point in 1962 with the instigation of the counter-usury program, to be discussed below. A 1964 survey estimated that 70% of farm households used private credit. For 40% of those households, private credit constituted 80% of total debt. The source of these funds were: other farmers 60%; relatives and friends 28%; traders and moneylenders 12% (Morrow and White 1972:29). Brown (1973) estimates that in 1965 NACF supplied 25% of total farm family credit while in 1969, after the interest rate reform, it supplied 66%. Morrow and White (1972: 38) report NACF as supplying 30% of total rural credit in 1971.

The private credit system was, however, hampered because land received under the reform law of 1949–50 could not be mortgaged. In 1970 farmers were permitted to mortgage their land but only to an agricultural cooperative.

The counter-usury program was designed to combat the private credit market. The government established local debt liquidation committees, to which all debts with interest rates over 20% were to be reported by both debtors and creditors. Creditors were required to exchange their claims for Agricultural Finance Bonds issued by the NACF, to be retired over five years at 20% per annum. Debtors were to repay the NACF over five years at 12% (thus an $8 subsidy). Bonds were issued to cover 781,766 loans.

Ban et al. (1980:215–216) point out two problems with the program. First, it caused the private lending market to dry up more quickly than public funds became available to replace it. Second, NACF did not "retire on schedule the Agricultural Finance Bonds that it had issued to creditors." This also may have aggravated the credit shortage in the countryside, since private sources were deprived of funds.

During the sixties, therefore, the government provided a limited amount of agricultural credit at a subsidized interest rate. But the low official rate thwarted its attempts to control the private market. In the early years, cooperative officials routinely charged an additional personal fee to process a loan application (Ban et al. 1961:274). Even though anti-corruption campaigns and the interest rate reform of 1965 combined to lessen this practice, nevertheless government funds rapidly decreased as a percent of NACF's total lending in the late sixties. The expansion of the agricultural credit program thereafter was due to the rapid increase in savings deposits at NACF and not to an increase in government funding.

The delinquency rate on NACF agricultural loans never exceeded 8%, another way in which South Korea is distinct from much of the Third World. This low percentage is probably due to NACF's discrimination in making loans rather than any attempt to improve the efficiency of small farmers. Morrow and White (1972:6) report that the NACF has always shown preference in lending to farmers considered "viable" (those with more than one-half hectare). Approximately 30% of farms do not qualify under that criterion, and the exclusion of these small farms from credit sources may help explain both the financial health of the NACF in the seventies and the rapid rate of migration to the cities.

By the seventies, finally, the government had emasculated the private credit market, at the expense of some credit shortages and difficulties for some farmers in obtaining credit. But the biggest disadvantage to farmers is that they are dependent on a single source for credit—government—

whose reliability is questionable. So far, this source has worked tolerably well. But will it continue to work?

Fertilizer

Korean farmers have long been familiar with the benefits of chemical fertilizer, the principal non-farm input. During its colonial rule, Japan promoted chemical fertilizers to help turn Korea into its "rice bowl," and after the Korean War, the use of chemical fertilizer increased rapidly.

Table 7 provides information on fertilizer use per hectare and the annual growth rate for three subperiods. Before 1962 fertilizer sales were not completely controlled, although government had tried to regulate prices. The division of Korea in 1945 had left all fertilizer plants on the northern side of the 38th parallel. The vast majority of nitrogenous fertilizer in the period 1955–61 was therefore imported, with AID financing. But supplies must have been inadequate, or government distribution inefficient, because black market prices were two to three times the controlled price. The amount of AID financing appears to have been the limiting factor. Foreign exchange was rationed, and fertilizer was not a priority.

Thus we cannot compare a "free market" (pre-1962) with a government-controlled monopoly (post-1962). Ban et al. (1980:101) credit AID financing for the rapid expansion in fertilizer use, 1955–61. This is so, but it is not our main issue. Rather the private market was never given a chance to respond to demand. Ban et al. (1980:108) acknowledge that "government management was so chaotic that farmers seldom received fertilizer at the proper time or the proper place."

Because of this, AID recommended expanding private distribution in the early sixties. Instead, the government awarded a monopoly to the NACF. Domestic production had begun in 1960 with the first government-owned plant; the second followed in 1963, and by 1968 the country's entire consumption of nitrogenous fertilizer was supplied by domestic plants, mostly government-owned, at a price covering cost plus a return. Because the government subsidized storage and distribution, however, fertilizer was sold below its total costs (Brown 1973:127).

Did government control speed up fertilizer adoption? Brown says no, that "many observers feel that it has been supply and availability of fertilizer, not its price, which has limited its use in Korea." Clearly the government is responsible for that.

Because soil scientists had been arguing that potassium and potash were needed for soil improvement, the government used its market control to force these fertilizers upon the farmers. But this paternalism had its costs. In the sixties and seventies, fertilizer had always been sold as a mixture by the cooperatives. In the late seventies, one of the principal farmer complaints against cooperatives was their prescription of the mixture in fertilizers (Cho 1981:200).

Table 12.7
CHEMICAL FERTILIZER CONSUMPTION, IN KILOGRAMS PER
ARABLE HECTARE, AND GROWTH RATE PER PERIOD

	Chemical Fertilizer Consumption (kg./ha)	Growth Rate Annual Average
1955	92.0	
1956	110.7	
1957	109.6	
1958	121.0	
1959	111.6	1955–62, 6.9%
1960	138.0	
1961	151.8	
1962	149.2	
1963	175.1	
1964	167.7	
1965	174.2	
1966	184.6	1963–69, 6.1%
1967	210.4	
1968	206.4	
1969	231.4	
1970	243.0	
1971	266.0	
1972	288.9	1970–75, 8.6%
1973	353.9	
1974	373.8	
1975	395.7	

SOURCE: Column 1, Ban et al. (1980: 102–3, Table 38); Column 2, author's calculations.

Chemical fertilizers were big business to the NACF. In 1970 they were 75% of its sales to farmers (Morrow and White 1972: 9). Furthermore, prices (1957–68) did not seem out of line with world prices.

Fertilizer was among the first items of import substitution in the sixties. In terms of cost, it competed well with imports, but production increase outstripped storage and distribution, and much fertilizer was wasted "due to . . . rapid deterioration" (Khil and Bark 1981:64). In 1968, for example, 433,000 metric tons were produced, compared with 286,000 consumed and 11,000 exported. The difference was more likely spoiled than stored. With a dramatic decrease in imports and increase in exports over the next few years, supply and demand became more closely aligned. The problems of the meantime, however, had occurred because of NACF's monopoly.

The Output Markets

The Japanese instituted a complete rationing system during the war. Unlike in Japan, however, farmers were paid a low price for confiscated grain; little incentive was left for production. After a brief period of a free market and another one of price controls, the American occupation authorities reverted to the Japanese system. The new Korean government, set up in 1948, at first continued the American policy, but its low official price did not attract sufficient grain production. So a free market was permitted in 1949. Even so, the government forced some purchases at below market prices, for rationing to the armed forces, government employees, and critical industries. This dual system has persisted ever since.

With the Grain Management Act of 1950, the government assumed the right to control the grain market completely. It may export and import, buy and distribute, and intervene in the free market. From that point on, it has used a number of programs to collect rice.

In the fifties, government relied mainly on the farmland tax. At first, it also purchased rice directly, but later in the decade it emphasized its rice-lien program. Loans were made to farmers at harvest time, so they would not be forced to sell at seasonally low prices; the government retained a lien on rice, by which repayment was made. In the sixties direct purchase was reinstated, along with a rice-fertilizer barter program that became a significant source of government rice. Toward the end of the sixties, government imports of rice increased substantially.

Government collections of rice were minor during most of the fifties and sixties, less than 10% of production. Low purchase prices constituted an implicit tax. But in the seventies, as government sought to increase the rice crop to combat the import deficit, it stepped up its purchases, and at higher prices.

The earlier discouragement of production through low prices had been made possible (or at least politically feasible) by imports from the United States under the foreign aid program (Public Law 480). From 1956 to 1960, these equaled 9% of grain production (Ban et al., 1980:239). While lip service was paid by the Park military government to "fair farm prices," extensive intervention in the grain market during the early sixties was unfavorable to farmers.

Indeed, the freezing of commodity prices was an early act of the new Korean government. Almost immediately, however, all price ceilings were lifted except on rice, wheat, and barley (Moon 1977:21). When the crop failure of 1962 led to an extensive black market in grain, even these ceilings were removed. But price controls were again instituted in 1963. The ratio of government purchase prices to market prices was

0.589 for 1962 and 0.594 in 1963. These ratios proved unenforceable, and price controls were quashed in 1964.

Responding to complaints of low farm incomes, to the concern over rising rural-urban income differences, and to the cutoff of U.S. grain under Public Law 480, the government increased its official purchase prices, in 1968, but without practical effect until 1970 (Moon 1977:31). Rice constituted 57% of food expenditure in 1965 but only 41% by 1970. The shift in urban tastes away from rice, caused by higher incomes, released the government from having to extort from rice farmers to cater to its urban constituency.

The story of government intervention—and its ill effects—is therefore confined to the fifties and sixties. During this period, cooperatives were a principal means of extracting grain. As far back as 1949, the financial associations were required to collect, store, and distribute government grain (Ban et al. 1980:202). Although that function was eliminated during the fifties, it was restored by the Park regime (Brown 1973:114). While government collection was never more than 10% of output during the fifties and sixties, it "usually represented 15% to 18% of rice marketed by farmers during any year" (Brown 1973:113). At harvest time government purchases were about one-third of the marketed total. Hence farmers were well aware of the connection between "their" cooperatives and the central government.

What was the impact of government price policies on rural real incomes and income distribution during those two decades? We have no information for the fifties. In the sixties, the policy appears to have had little effect. Rural real incomes fell as the terms of trade moved against the farmers. According to Brown (1973:120), however, this decrease was not caused by government price policies:[*]

> . . . The principal effect of government rice procurement appears to have been to support the price of rice and hence farm income levels at harvest time, thus probably helping to improve the income distribution and bring (harvest) prices closer to annual equilibrium level.

In the seventies, however, the government price policy pushed rural real incomes higher (Table 8). Whereas in 1968 the government purchase price to cost of production ratio was 1.234, in 1974 it was 1.98, and the rural real income index had risen from 91.9 to 147.1.

In both 1965–70 and 1970–75, increases in agricultural incomes (in part due to government rice price policies) reduced the rural-urban income gap. At the same time these increases caused greater rural income inequal-

*Brown's summary ignores the 1963 and 1964 price ratios. His data reflect a much lower market price for rice in 1963 and 1964 than did Ban et al., whose data, collected by Moon, an agriculture specialist, appear more reliable, and which we use.

Table 12.8

GOVERNMENT RICE PRICE POLICIES AND AGRICULTURAL TERMS OF TRADE, 1948–74

	For Rice		Terms of Trade (1970 = 100)		Index of Rural Real Incomes
	Gov't. Purchase Price ÷ Cost of Production	Gov't. Purchase Price ÷ Market Price	All Farm Products	Rice	
1948	66.3	34.8			
1949	39.9	20.2			
1950	103.6	31.4			
1951	–	41.5			
1952	61.0	44.8			
1953	60.6	57.3			
1954	93.2	53.1			
1955	46.6	40.1			
1956	93.4	66.6			
1957	76.5	80.8			
1958	81.6	91.5			
1959	81.4	77.4	70.2	72.6	
1960	80.7	62.8	78.6	82.0	
1961	112.6	87.7	85.7	94.4	
1962	116.3	58.9	85.2	90.3	
1963	149.7	59.4	113.6	129.8	100

Table 12.8 (Continued)

| | For Rice | | Terms of Trade (1970 = 100) | | Index of Rural Real Incomes |
	Gov't. Purchase Price ÷ Cost of Production	Gov't. Purchase Price ÷ Market Price	All Farm Products	Rice	
1964	153.3	89.3	112.2	127.2	104.6
1965	117.9	92.1	100.8	106.8	83.6
1966	132.5	88.2	95.4	97.3	86.8
1967	131.2	83.7	96.5	94.5	88.1
1968	123.4	81.7	94.3	92.9	91.9
1969	144.8	89.0	97.7	104.6	103.0
1970	150.8	97.9	100.0	100.0	106.0
1971	186.9	88.9	106.1	109.8	131.4
1972	161.7	101.6	113.3	122.2	141.8
1973	173.0	93.4	114.7	117.2	149.1
1974	198.0	88.4	112.0	126.1	147.1

SOURCE: Columns 1, 2, 3, 4: Ban et al. (1980:240, 244); Column 5: Lee (1979).

ity (Kim 1978:183). The price supports benefited large farmers more because a larger portion of their income was from agriculture and a larger portion of their agricultural income was from rice (the primary price-supported crop). In addition, the percentage of crop sold increases dramatically with size of holding (Lee 1979: 502).

In summary, the South Korean government in the fifties and early sixties, like many less developed countries, followed low-price food grain policies. These were made possible, without undue political consequences, by the import of PL 480 grain. Moon (1977) believes that had it not been for PL 480, the government would have had to reconsider its pricing policy. When market prices were rising rapidly in the early sixties, the government attempted price controls. Only in the late sixties, with the rapid growth of industry and urbanization, did it become necessary to shift the terms of trade in favor of agriculture. Even then, the government chose to absorb the increase itself rather than pass it on to the urban consumer.

Conclusion

While South Korea is an authoritarian state, with control over agriculture centralized, its land reform was egalitarian, and government intervention not so severe as in other countries. This intervention worsened the conditions of both peasants and the nation's economy in the fifties and sixties and probably improved both in the seventies and eighties.

Two forces distinguish South Korea from the "archetypical" state of countries in other chapters. First is its peculiar condition as a liberated Japanese hostage (a status shared only by Taiwan), which destroyed the rural élite. Second was the political power already gained by the peasantry before the reform, which gave them leverage against their government.

South Korea (and to some extent Taiwan as well; see next chapter) demonstrates that an authoritarian government can and sometimes does introduce decentralized decisionmaking, and that when it does, an efficient economy results. Agricultural output per capita has increased steadily for the past quarter century, although there is a slight slowdown in the early eighties (Table 19.1). Still, a threat remains, for the government may possess the power to take away what it has given.

Yet there are signs that that power is waning. For example, the government has long enforced antilabor laws that limit unions and prevent strikes. It has hired thugs to beat up workers and send them to the hospital (Gaer 1987). But protests of students and laborers forced humiliation and a public apology upon former President Chun Doo Huan in 1988.

While peasants and workers have both shown signs of defending themselves, their power to do so has not been put to a real test. Until that test comes, South Korea remains an exception to the betrayal of land reform that we have found in other countries.

References

Ban, Sung Hwan; Moon, Pal Yong; and Perkins, Dwight, 1980. *Rural Development: Studies in the Modernization of The Republic of Korea, 1945–1975,* Cambridge, Harvard University Press.

Brown, Gilbert, 1973. *Korean Pricing Policies and Economic Development in the 1960's,* Baltimore, Johns Hopkins University Press.

Cho, Haejong, 1981. "A Study of Changing Rural Communities in Korea," *Korea Journal,* vol. 21, No. 6, June: 18–25.

Cole, David C., and Lyman, Princeton N., 1971. *Korean Development: The Interplay of Politics and Economics,* Cambridge, Mass., Harvard University Press.

FAO (Food and Agriculture Organization). *Annual Review Fertilizers,* Rome.

Gaer, Felice D., 1987. "Seoul's Anti-Labor Policies," *The Wall Street Journal,* August 19.

Keidel, Albert, 1980. "Regional Agricultural Production and Income," in Ban et al.

Keidel, Albert, 1981. *Korean Regional Farm Product and Income, 1910–1975,* Seoul, Korean Development Institute.

Khil, Young Whon, and Bark, Dong San, 1981. "Food Policies in a Rapidly Developing Country: The Case of South Korea, 1960–1978," *Journal of Developing Areas,* vol. 16, October:47–70.

Kim, Daemo, 1978. "Sources of Overtime Changes in the Rural-Urban Gap and the Intrafarm Inequality of Income in Korea," *Journal of Economic Development,* vol. 3, no. 1, July:173–85.

Lee, E., 1979. "Egalitarian Peasant Farming and Rural Development: The Case of South Korea," *World Development,* vol. 7:493–517.

Lee, T. Y.; Kim, D. H.; and Adams, Dale, 1977. "Savings Deposits and Credit Activities in South Korean Cooperatives, 1961–1975," *Asian Survey,* December, vol. 17, no. 12:1182–94.

Moon, Pal Yong, 1977. "Evolution of Rice Policy in Korea," in Kim, Chuk Kyo, ed., *Industrial and Social Development Issues,* vol. 2, Seoul, Korean Development Institute.

Morrow, Robert, and White, Paul, 1972. "Farm Credit in Korea" in *A.I.D. Spring Review of Small Farmer Credit,* vol. II, Washington D.C., U.S. Agency for International Development, February.

13. Taiwan

By ordinary standards, Taiwan's land reform has been a great success. In 1953, all tenanted land above three *chia* (2.874 acres) was expropriated and sold to the tenants on easy terms; landlords were compensated; agricultural output increased. One-quarter of the cultivated acreage became owned by former tenants, almost one-half the farm households. Three experts—Ladejinsky (1964), Jacoby (1966), and Manzhuber (1970)—agreed that the reform was positive-sum all around: for landlords, government, and tenants. Following Smith (1972), in an earlier work (Loehr and Powelson 1981:252) we have pointed out that in fact the landlords lost.

What the landlords lost, both the government and the tenants gained. The government gained because it bought the land for paper—securities that promptly depreciated with inflation—but sold it to tenants for real value: crops and cash. The tenants gained because the price they paid the government was less than market value. Even after the land distribution, however, the government went on gaining by a number of devices that, when added up, constituted a very high "tax." They also discouraged rice production.

Background

Tenancy and high rents, rather than unequal distribution, were the fundaments of the Taiwanese land reform. Despite significant increase in agricultural output during the Japanese occupation (1898–45), the percentage of land cultivated by tenants (about 56%) and the percentage of farm families that were tenants (around 40%) changed little over the half century. On the other hand, land ownership, while skewed, was not nearly so skewed as in much of the Third World. Farm sizes were small, more than 70% of the agricultural surface being in farms of less than five *chia*, or 14.37 hectares (see Table 1). Seven percent of the owner-cultivators held 41% of the land in plots of over three *chia* (8.62 hectares), while 70% of the owner-cultivators farmed plots of less than one *chia* (2.874 hectares). The average tenant operated a farm of approximately $1/2$ chia ($1^1/2$ hectares) (Yang 1970:196).

Taiwan is blessed for rice, its principal crop. Fifty-five percent of the cultivated area (873,962 hectares) was irrigated in the early fifties (Ho 1978:353). Under such favorable conditions, three or four crops a year are possible through intercropping young and mature plants. The first crop is in the ground from February to June, the second from August to October.

253

Table 13.1
LAND DISTRIBUTION IN TAIWAN, 1952 AND 1960

Size of Holding	Distribution of Owner-Cultivator Households		Distribution of Land (percent)	
	1952	1960	1952	1960
0.5 *chia*	47.3	0.7	9.9	5.2
0.5–1	23.3	45.9	15.1	30.5
1–2	16.9	15.3	21.1	19.3
2–3	5.7	14.8	12.3	30.3
3–5	3.9	2.7	13.2	10.2
	3.4	0.6	28.4	4.6

SOURCE: Ho (1978:183).

On dry land, one crop is planted in the rainy season, but there is often a different winter crop, such as sweet potatoes, peanuts, or green manure (Koo 1968:353).

Implementation of the Reform

Arriving in Taiwan in 1949 with almost a million refugees, the Nationalist government needed two things from agriculture: food and rural stability. While the government had resisted land reform on the mainland, the shock of its defeat jarred it into awareness that the same appeal of land hunger that had swelled the communist ranks could appear on Taiwan (Yang, 1970:12–14; Apthorp 1979:521). It was to these needs that the land reform of 1949–53 was addressed.

Land reform was carried out in three stages: rent reduction in 1949, sale of public land (formerly held by Japanese) in 1952, and expropriation ("land-to-the-tiller") in 1953. While official panegyrics treat these as part of one planned program, probably instead the impetus of one step led to the next.

The Rent-Reduction Program

Shortly after retreating to Taiwan in 1949, the government ordered rent to be reduced, from about 50% to 60% on irrigated paddy to a ceiling of 37.5% of expected yield. Provided rent was paid, tenancy was made secure for six years. Within one year (1949), farm values dropped precipitously, much more for tenanted than for owner-occupied land. Clearly, rent reduction had affected the market more than fear of expropriation (Koo 1968:33–34).

To settle the growing number of disputes over enforcement, in 1951 a presidential decree established Farm Tenancy Committees, consisting of five representatives for tenants, two for the local government, two for the landlords, and two for owner-cultivators (Tai 1974:400–1). These committees had been recommended by Wolf Ladejinsky, an American advisor who had seen them operate successfully in Japan. (In Japan, however, the tenants had elected a majority of the committee.) Whereas in Japan tenant representatives had held a majority of votes, in Taiwan the tenants were allocated only five memberships out of eleven. These committees settled 62,645 disputes between 1952 and 1956.

The Sale of Public Land

Twenty percent of rural households were allowed to buy public land. Started in 1948 by the provincial government, these sales were suspended during the rent reduction drive and continued in 1951. Seventy thousand *chia* (approximately 173,000 hectares) were sold to existing tenants for 2.5 times the annual yield, payable in kind or in cash in twenty semiannual installments. Since total payments (purchase price and land tax) were less than the 37.5% of yield previously paid in rent, the tenant was better off. The average amount purchased was 0.5 *chia* (1.437 hectares), which frequently supplemented other land already held. Thus the average holding of the purchaser was 1¹/₈ *chia* (3.233 hectares) (Yang 1970:83).

Land-to-the-Tiller

Urged by President Truman, "land-to-the-tiller" was conceived in 1951, when the Joint Commission on Rural Reconstruction conducted a detailed ownership classification survey. It was "joint" because the American and Taiwanese governments participated; it was "reconstruction" after the Rural Reconstruction Movement started in China some thirty years earlier by Dr. Y. C. James Yen, whose interview with Truman had helped bring about U.S. support. The law was announced in 1953.

Every landlord with more than three *chia* (8.622 hectares) was required to sell the excess to the government, which would resell it to the tenant for 2.5 times the annual yield. The landlord would be paid in full money value, 70% in land bonds and 30% in stocks of government enterprises. The former would be redeemable in twenty semi-annual installments at 4% interest, with payment in either rice or sweet potatoes, depending on the land sold. The new owners would also pay in twenty annual installments at 4% interest. For irrigated rice lands, payment would be in kind, for dry rice lands in cash.

The township government implemented the law, but farm tenancy committees checked that no land or landlords were overlooked. All levels of the Kuomintang Party were ordered to give full attention to the reform, which was completed by the end of the year. The total amounts of lands affected by all three programs (rent reduction, public land sale, and land-to-the-tiller) are shown in Table 2.

Table 13.2

AREA AND HOUSEHOLDS AFFECTED BY LAND REFORM

Area Affected	Reduction of Farm Rents	Sale of Public Land	Land-to-Tiller Program	Total Redistribution
Thousands of *chia*	256.9	71.7	193.6	215.2
% total area cultivated	29.2	8.1	16.4	24.6
Farm households affected (000)	302.3	139.7	194.9	334.3
% of total	43.3	20.0	27.9	47.9

SOURCE: Ho (1978:163).

Initial in-kind payments were made to landlords by early 1954, along with the stocks in government enterprises. Probably, the *money* value was adequate, if one accepts as "adequate" the lower market value of tenanted land because of the rent-reduction program. However, many landlords, distrustful of the value of government-enterprise stocks, sold these at an average value of $7.325 compared with $10 par (Smith 1972). Even those who held them until 1969 lost out, for in that year the value was only $11.38 (or a money return of 0.9% per year) while inflation ran at 6.1% (Loehr and Powelson 1981:252). By the same inflation, they lost out on their government bonds, which, at 4%, yielded a negative real interest. If this is compared instead with the nominal interest rate of 30% to 50% (Ho 1978:167), the opportunity costs of the expropriated landlords were enormous. Since these losses were gains to the government as issuer of the bonds and enterprise stocks, *the expropriation constituted a transfer of real value from the landowner to the government.* The tenant, *who had to pay the government in real crop value,* gained only in so far as he may have received the land at less than its true market value.

Postulating a real value of land equal to five times the annual yield, Ho (1978:166) estimates that in fact the tenant did gain. Compared with the amount he had to pay (2.5 times annual yield), he received one-half the value of the land as an outright gift at the time of redistribution. By combining the impact of rent reduction and land-to-the-tiller, Ho estimated that land reform redistributed wealth equal to 13% of Taiwan's gross domestic product of 1952. Thus roughly 50% of the total value redistributed went from owner to tenant and 50% from owner to government. The tenant paid for his 50%, but the government's payment (landlord's loss) was discounted by the depreciation of government bonds and stocks through inflation.

Lee (1971:75) has estimated that the percentage share of net farm income for both tenant and government increased after the reform (Table 3) at the expense of the landlord: the cultivator from 67% before the war to 81% in 1956–60 and the government from 8% to 12%. The government's relative share seems great when thought of as a 50% increase, yet 12% is relatively moderate when thought of as an income tax on agriculture. However, Lee's calculations included only the overt tax. We will see below that a hidden tax—through compulsory sales, price controls, and monopoly— increased the government's take much more, while reducing that of the peasant.

Land ownership certificates were given to the former tenants on payment of the first installment in kind to the Taiwan Provincial Food Bureau. When all payments had been made, the certificate was inscribed to that effect. By the end of 1964, all land distributed under the land-to-the-tiller act—193,000 *chia* (554,682 hectares), or 16.4% of the cultivated acreage— had been paid for by 194,900 households, or 27.9% of all farm households (Table 2).

257

Table 13.3
Percent Distribution of Farm Income, 1931–60

	Net Farm Income	Landlords/ Moneylenders	Cultivators	Government and Public Institutions
1931–35	100	25	67	8
1936–40	100	25	67	8
1950–55	100	10	77	13
1956–60	100	6	81	12

SOURCE: Lee (1971:75).

Table 4 compares land distribution by size of holding after the redistribution (1955) with that of before (1952). The percentage of owner-cultivated land had increased from 61.4% to 84.4% (Yang 1970:83). In 1955, 59% of farm households were owner-cultivators, compared with 36% in 1950. The percentage of pure tenants had decreased from 38% in 1950 to 17% in 1955 (Table 5).

Table 13.4

CHANGES IN SIZE OF LAND HOLDINGS BEFORE AND AFTER LAND REFORM

Farm Size	Pre-reform (1952)		Post-reform (1955)	
in hectares	No. of Farms	%	No. of Farms	%
< 0.5 ha	67,511	10	92,146	14
0.5–1.0	102,577	15	146,042	21
1.0–3.0	227,890	33	285,627	42
3.0–10.0	175,064	26	124,113	18
> 10.0	108,108	16	31,642	5
Total	681,150	100	679,570	100

SOURCE: Kuo (1983:29).

Table 13.5

PERCENT OF FARM HOUSEHOLDS BY TYPE OF TENURE, 1925–70

	Owner/Cultivator	Part Owner	Tenant
1925	29.0	30.1	40.9
1930	29.1	30.7	40.2
1935	31.4	30.6	38.0
1940	32.0	31.2	36.8
1945	29.8	29.5	40.7
1950	36.0	26.0	28.0
1955	59.0	24.0	17.0
1960	64.0	21.0	15.0
1965	66.7	20.6	12.6
1970	76.4	12.3	10.9

SOURCE: Ho (1978:355).

Farmers' Associations

Taiwanese farmers' associations were descendants of compulsory organizations set up by the Japanese. In 1900, the Japanese colonial administration formed a farmers' association in a village near one of its agricultural experiment stations that functioned as an all-round service cooperative, providing fertilizer, tools, seeds, and extension service (Tai 1974:397–8). Finding the prototype successful, the Japanese organized associations in every district in Taiwan over the next few years. While the local magistrate served as head of each association, all were kept under strict control by the occupying government. Rural credit cooperatives followed. They grew rapidly, from thirteen in 1913 to 443 in 1940 (Ho 1978:63). By then, the cooperatives and banks, both public and private, provided half the rural credit. Finally, small-group educational units were set up in most villages to assist with agricultural extension. All these organizations together employed about 40,000 people in the early 1930s.

In 1938, the Japanese made membership in the cooperative associations compulsory, and by 1940, 609,817 farmers belonged (Yang 1970:407), more than the number of farm households in Taiwan. During World War II, the Japanese used the associations for compulsory rice collection, as well as for solidifying political control.

After the war, local landlords replaced Japanese leaders (Wu 1971:151–55). But to replace the associations, the Nationalist government formed the Taiwan Provincial Farm Bureau, whose first task was to collect a land tax in kind and rent on public land. In that year, these together yielded only 5.2% of total rice production (Table 6). Even before 1949, the provincial government was under pressure to find food for the great number of refugees streaming in from the mainland. Beginning in 1947, it decreed compulsory rice sales at official prices, which in most years averaged between 60% and 75% of the wholesale price (Table 7). Beginning in 1948, a rice-fertilizer barter program provided fertilizer to farmers in exchange for rice. In 1950, the Nationalist government grabbed a monopoly of chemical fertilizer, so that the barter program became the *only* source of this input for farmers, at an official price similar to the one used in the compulsory sale program. In all of these ways together, the government acquired 25% of the rice crop in 1950 (Table 6), the year of the great final tide of refugees.

In 1952, the farmers' associations, the rural credit cooperatives, and small agricultural units (organizations on a more local level) were all unified into a Provincial Farmers' Association. ("Provincial" refers to the Province of Taiwan.) On the township level, the farmers' associations were converted into agencies of the government rather than representatives of their constituencies vis-à-vis the government. They were assigned the collection of rice for the Taiwan Provincial Farm Bureau's programs, the operation of the rice-fertilizer barter system, and the management of

Table 13.6

Compulsory Government Rice Collection (thousands of metric tons of paddy), 1946–65

	Land Tax	Compulsory Purchase	Rent on Public Land	Land Cost Repayment	Refund for Land Bond	Rice-Fertilizer Barter	Net Gov't. Rice Collected	Total Rice Production	Percent Collected
1946	51	–	7	–	–	–	58	1,117	5.2
1947	76	78	15	–	–	–	169	1,249	13.5
1948	71	73	15	–	–	61	220	1,355	16.5
1949	77	79	18	–	–	91	270	1,519	17.8
1950	95	81	22	–	–	247	445	1,776	25.1
1951	92	78	20	–	–	256	446	1,856	24.0
1952	91	78	16	–	–	389	574	1,962	29.3
1953	91	77	9	135	84	369	597	2,052	29.1
1954	90	76	9	122	90	359	566	2,118	26.7
1955	82	20	9	111	97	406	581	2,018	28.8
1956	89	74	10	132	98	458	665	2,237	29.7
1957	93	77	10	132	98	465	679	2,298	29.5

Table 13.6 (Continued)

	Land Tax	Compulsory Purchase	Rent on Public Land	Land Cost Repayment	Refund for Land Bond	Rice-Fertilizer Barter	Net Gov't. Rice Collected	Total Rice Production	Percent Collected
1958	90	75	13	126	98	477	671	2,367	28.4
1959	81	70	9	114	98	496	672	2,320	29.0
1960	83	69	9	113	98	480	656	2,390	27.4
1961	89	75	9	114	98	480	669	2,520	26.5
1962	113	73	10	267	98	501	866	2,641	32.8
1963	104	66	8	75	na	533	786	2,636	29.8
1964	118	75	9	34	na	548	784	2,809	27.9
1965	124	10	20	na	na	496	728	2,935	24.8

SOURCE: Wu (1971:161); percent collected calculated from Wu data.

Table 13.7
RATIO OF OFFICIAL PURCHASE PRICE OF RICE TO WHOLESALE PRICE, 1949–65

Year	Ratio
1949	35%
1950	72%
1951	73%
1952	53%
1953	68%
1954	80%
1955	72%
1956	72%
1957	70%
1958	75%
1959	63%
1960	62%
1961	72%
1962	78%
1963	76%
1964	76%
1965	78%

SOURCE: Wu (1971:154, calculated from Table 5–13).

credit for members. In August 1953 Chiang Kai-shek declared that the reorganized farmers' associations were vital to the success of the land reform.

Formally, the associations are democratic, with officials elected by members (Tai 1974:398ff.). The most local office is a Small Agricultural Unit (SAU) in each village. The chairman and vice chairman of each of the 5,035 SAUs help bridge the gap between the farmer and the township association. Each township association elects an assembly from among its members, and this assembly in turn chooses from its members both the governing Board of Directors and a Board of Supervisors for financial auditing. This assembly also elects representatives to the county association, where the same procedure is followed. Representatives chosen by the twenty-two county associations govern the umbrella provincial association.

Yang (1970:408) explains why a household would join the association:

> . . . Because of the great number of farm-related functions performed by the associations, and the degree and variety of ways in which farming and farm life are involved in, or affected by, the associations' activities, no

263

farm household today can be a going concern without having some relationship with the farmers' associations. . . .

Even though internal governance appears to be a democracy, in fact the association remains the instrument through which the government controls a significant part of the marketable surplus, and the individual farmer has little choice but to join and to comply. The close association with the land reform is reflected in the fact that associations were the means by which land payments in kind were collected under land-to-the-tiller.

The program probably did not cause tenants to join the associations, however. A survey by Yang (1970:357–58) shows that 64% of former tenants belonged to the associations before the program and only 68% afterwards. Yang is surprised that the first percentage was so high. Whatever the reason for that, it is likely that many had simply continued their membership from Japanese days or had joined at the time of the rice-fertilizer barter program.

In 1954, the government collected 566,000 tons of rice, or 26.7% of rice production (Table 6). Since almost half of the rice produced was consumed on the farm, it therefore controlled close to 50% of the amount marketed. The largest part of this, 359,000 tons, came to it through the fertilizer barter program. The next largest, 122,000 metric tons, was from payments for land under the land reform, some of which had to be turned over to former landlords. The land tax brought in 90,000 metric tons, and compulsory sales, 76,000 metric tons. The government used this rice primarily to feed its army and civil servants. Only very indirectly, if at all, could the agricultural surplus be interpreted as a transfer into industry, in accordance with the models of Lewis (1955) or Fei and Ranis (1964).

These payments were supplemented by a "hidden" rice tax, consisting of two parts: (1) the difference between the official price and the wholesale market price, and (2) the excess price that the rice farmer was required to pay for fertilizer under the fertilizer-rice barter program. The first of these is shown in Table 7.

The second part of the hidden tax—on fertilizer—comes from the government monopoly. Taiwanese farmers pay higher prices than they would have on the world market. The government buys high-cost fertilizer from domestic producers and low-cost imported fertilizer, and by selling both at an in-between price, the government comes out in the black, and the farmers indirectly subsidize the domestic fertilizer producers.

Not only have the farmers been heavily taxed, but the high price of fertilizer has reduced its use and therefore decreased rice production (Ho 1978:187). Rice fell from 50% of total value of agricultural output in 1952 to 29% in 1971 (Kuo 1983:24). To determine whether this decrease resulted from a change in tastes or other factors, Kuo ran a regression, which showed that the hidden rice tax was the most powerful independent variable affecting relative share.

Other distortions arose from the rice-fertilizer barter program. First, since bartered rice was given priority for fertilizer, 70% to 80% of the total available went to rice in the 1950s, and little was left over for other crops. Second, farmers had no choice over the mix of fertilizer. We have seen in other contexts (e.g., Goodell's chapter on the Philippines) that farmers often have better judgment than the government on their fertilizer needs, and we see no reason why this should not be so in Taiwan. Third, the distribution system frequently did not have fertilizers in the right place at the right time (Ho 1978:181). Since fertilizer represented 35% of the average farm family's production expenses in 1960, these were no minor problems. (Wu 1971:155 fn.2). Fourth, the government fertilizer monopoly precluded the farmers from establishing integrated marketing cooperatives with economies of scale. Instead of using the same vehicles to carry inputs and outputs, truckers would ride empty one way.

Kuo (1983) has estimated the amount of "hidden rice tax" for selected years between 1952 and 1965, by multiplying the difference between the official price per metric ton and the market price by the total amount of rice collected from compulsory sales and fertilizer barter. The ratio of the total hidden tax (high for most years) to the total amount of income tax collected is shown in Table 8. Kuo also concluded that this tax amounted to approximately 25% of the value of all rice produced. Since half of rice produced is consumed on the farm, the hidden rice tax probably therefore takes in about 50% of the value of all marketed rice. When added to all the direct taxes, this proportion constitutes a very heavy burden upon the rice farmer. (The decline shown in Table 8 for the later years is due primarily to the increase in income tax collected, as the economy prospered.)

Most puzzling is the fact that this hidden tax—so heavy upon the farmer—amounted to no more than 10% of visible government revenues. By increasing its other revenues by only 10%, therefore, the government might have avoided the burden inflicted upon the farmer, as well as the distortions to agriculture caused by departures from market pricing.

Conclusion

The land reform of Taiwan was far more than a simple redistribution of land; its very implementation transferred value from landowners to government more than from landowners to tenants. All tenanted lands greater than three *chia* (8.622 hectares) were required to be sold to the government, with payment in bonds and stocks in government enterprises, the bonds to be redeemed over ten years. The lands were then sold to tenants at the same price, also payable over ten years. However, the government bonds depreciated because of inflation, and the stocks did not yield a return commensurate with inflation. But the tenants made their payments in kind, hence there was a transfer of real value from owners to government. Because the price was less than probable market price, there was also a transfer of real value from old owner to new owner.

Table 13.8
RATIO OF VALUE OF HIDDEN RICE TAX TO INCOME TAX COLLECTED, 1952–71

Year	Ratio
1952	107.2
1953	204.1
1954	82.8
1955	106.1
1956	84.9
1957	105.4
1958	83.2
1959	71.5
1960	104.6
1961	129.1
1962	118.4
1963	100.7
1964	83.5
1965	82.5
1966	83.4
1967	74.5
1968	52.0
1969	21.6
1970	14.3
1971	8.5

SOURCE: Kuo (1983:36, Table 3.9).

Once the reform had been completed, the government intervened in the agricultural markets in several ways. First, it required farmers to barter rice for fertilizer, at terms favorable to the government (compared with free market prices). Second, it required sales of rice to the government at prices lower than free market. Third, it taxed the farmers, with payments in kind. Through all these ways, within ten years after the reform the government was garnering approximately 50% of marketed rice. Since it used this rice to pay its civil servants and army, this was no "agricultural surplus" available for investment in a Lewis or Fei and Ranis model of development. Chinese writers have estimated that both the income and production of farmers suffered from these requirements.

Both the reform itself and the various ways by which the government extracted the surplus were implemented by farmers' associations. Although in principle membership was voluntary and election of officials democratic, nevertheless the manner of operation—with complete acquiescence to government wishes—would indicate that these were not robust representatives of the interests of farmers, bargaining for their rights, privileges, and economic advancement.

References

Apthorp, Raymond, 1979. "The Burden of Land Reform in Taiwan: An Asian Model of Land Reform Re-analyzed," *World Development*, vol. 7, no. 4/5:519–30.

Fei, John C. H., and Ranis, Gustav, 1964. *Development of the Surplus Economy*, New Haven, Conn., Yale University Press.

Ho, Samuel, 1978. *Economic Development of Taiwan, 1860–1970*, New Haven, Conn., Yale University Press.

Jacoby, Neil H., 1966. *U.S. Aid to Taiwan: A Study of Foreign Aid, Self-Help, and Development*, New York, Praeger.

Koo, Anthony, 1968. *The Role of Land Reform in Economic Development: A Case Study of Taiwan*, New York, Praeger.

Kuo, Shirley, 1983. *The Taiwan Economy in Transition*, Boulder, Colo., Westview Press.

Ladejinsky, Wolf, 1964. "Agrarian Reform in Asia," *Foreign Affairs*, April.

Lee, T. H., 1971. *Intersectoral Capital Flows in the Economic Development of Taiwan, 1895–1960*, Ithaca, N.Y., Cornell University Press.

Lewis, W. Arthur, 1955. *The Theory of Economic Growth*, Homewood, Ill., Irwin.

Loehr, William, and Powelson, John P., 1981. *The Economics of Development and Distribution*, New York, Harcourt Brace Jovanovich.

Manzhuber, Albert, 1970. "The Economic Development of Taiwan," *Industry of Free China*, vol. 33, no. 4, May.

Smith, Theodore Reynolds, 1972. *East Asian Agrarian Reform: Japan, Republic of Korea, Taiwan, and the Philippines*, Cambridge, Mass., Lincoln Institute of Land Policy, research monograph no. 2. (The monograph bears no date; 1972 is inferred.)

Tai, Hung Chao, 1974. *Land Reform and Politics: A Comparative Analysis*, Berkeley, University of California Press.

Wu, Rong-I, 1971. *The Strategy of Economic Development: A Case Study of Taiwan*, Louvain (Belgium), Vander.

Yang, Martin M. C., 1970. *Socio-Economic Results of Land Reform in Taiwan*, Honolulu, East-West Center Press.

14. Peru

Peru's land reform of 1968 is unique in two ways. First, it is the only such reform so far undertaken by a military government in Latin America. For some decades, the military in many Latin American countries had been casting off its image as protector of the rich and admitting soldiers of modest origin to officer status (Johnson 1964; Lieuwen 1960). Now a general risen from those ranks challenged the "landed aristocracy." By 1970, informed observers agree, the political hold of Peru's aristocracy had been broken. Second, the government announced a "Peruvian-style" reform not modeled after any other country. Of course, this slogan has been heard often, in many countries, but the institutions spawned in the new Peru did bridge capitalism and socialism in original ways.

A decade and a half later, the experiment was in shambles. Increases in agricultural output did not keep up with population growth (Table 1), and the drop in per capita output from an index of 115 in 1961 to 80 in 1983 (1974–76 = 100) is alarming: an *average drop per year of* 0.79% from 1961–63 until 1971–73 and 2.39% from 1971–73 until 1981–83. Some were estimating that income distribution had worsened because small, independent farmers who used to work part-time on haciendas had been squeezed out of the new cooperatives (Loehr and Powelson 1981:249; Berry 1972). Instead of yielding power over land and its management to peasant cooperatives, as had been the plan, the state controlled all levels of pricing, crop, and other decisions, so that the peasants were released from being serfs of hacienda owners only to become serfs of the state. Thus the peasants on whose behalf the government had addressed the reform were striking against it. In 1981, the government was returned to the same president (Belaunde) who had been overthrown, and in 1985 the APRA* candidate (García) was elected. A new guerrilla movement (*Sendero Luminoso*) is now destabilizing both society and government. Although the reform was not reversed – it had gone too far for that – most of its uniquely Peruvian institutions have been dismantled, and politics and agriculture are thrown into an abyss of uncertainty, from which no easy escape is apparent.

What happened? To explore this question, we study the years leading up to the reform and the reform itself. We turn then to the methods of state control and the reasons for their failure. As an illustration of what

*American Popular Revolutionary Alliance.

Table 14.1

INDEXES OF OVERALL AND PER CAPITA FOOD PRODUCTION FOR PERU, 1961–83 (1974–76 = 100)

Year	Overall	Per Capita
1961	76	115
1962	79	115
1963	80	114
1964	83	115
1965	83	112
1966	87	113
1967	87	110
1968	83	102
1969	88	105
1970	96	111
1971	98	108
1972	97	105
1973	99	105
1974	102	104
1975	98	98
1976	100	98
1977	102	96
1978	100	93
1979	103	93
1980	95	83
1981	100	85
1982	103	85
1983	100	80

SOURCE: Food and Agriculture Organization Yearbooks; data for 1961–72 (1961–65 = 100) spliced onto data for 1971–83 (1974–76 = 100) at overlap years, 1971–72.

"might have been," we examine the hacienda of Vicos, where a group of anthropologists from Cornell University had attempted a land reform in the fifties.

Background

Both ongoing processes and one-time events appear to have made some kind of land reform inevitable in Peru. The former are those facing all of Latin America. Industrialization requires more deliveries of food from farm to factory; yet central policy, with a push toward industry, has neglected the farm. The stagnation of agriculture is blamed on the hacienda; more and more, old forms are declared obsolete. Rural to urban migration has shifted the political balance away from the aristocrats of land. The one-time events will be treated in the body of this chapter.

The Bias against Agriculture

Food production in Peru was already stagnating in the fifties and sixties. Data for the fifties are extremely poor, but Thorp and Bertram (1978:275) cite indirect evidence that there were no significant gains. Data for the sixties are more reliable (Table 1). Since most food (other than rice) is produced in the sierra, low output means stagnation of the highland rural economy.

Since 1959, Peru's development program had been one of import substitution industrialization (ISI). The Industrial Promotion Law exempted equipment and intermediate goods from import duties and permitted tax-free reinvestment of profits. In 1964 and 1967, duties on virtually all consumer good imports except food were raised. The collective impact of these policies was to increase prices of manufactured goods relative to food, which turned the internal terms of trade against agriculture.

But ISI was not the beginning of the bias against agriculture. In the forties the government had begun to control food prices in Lima. In 1942, the Agriculture Bank started buying food at fixed prices. In 1943, the government dictated minimum food crop acreage of 40% instead of the 10% required before. Although in the fifties the only official price was for bread, still the government closely monitored food prices in Lima. In the sixties again, attempts to keep food prices at official levels were launched, but enforcement was sporadic. The downward trend in agriculture's terms of trade since the late forties reached its nadir in the early sixties, with scant improvement thereafter (Thorp and Bertram 1978:280).

Incipient Support for Land Reform

The twins of ISI and agricultural stagnation contributed to the high rate of migration from village to city and from sierra to coast. In 1940, only 35% of the population was urban; in 1972, 60%. In 1940, 64% of the population lived in the sierra and 29% on the coast; in 1972, 47% and 43% respectively (Falaris 1979). The massive influx fed back on agriculture in two ways: the government tried to assure cheap food in the city to minimize urban unrest; and even urban politicians began to think the unthinkable: land reform.

All three major presidential candidates favored land reform in 1956, but none cited equitable income distribution as a reason. In 1959, Conservative President Manuel Prado appointed a commission to make recommendations about "property" problems in both country and city. Pedro Beltran, prime minister from 1959 to 1961 and long-time editor of La Prensa, a prestigious Lima daily, headed the commission. The Beltran Commission recommended that the government try to make the title rights of poor urban squatters secure and encourage colonization of the eastern jungle. It acknowledged the skewed distribution of agricultural land, but it felt that expropriation should be a last resort, and then only with full cash compensation.

But events in the countryside outpaced the political recommendations. By the late fifties, migrants to the coast were beginning to return to their home communities, politicized by their experiences. They recalled how haciendas had continually encroached upon their community land throughout the twentieth century and even before, leading to a highly skewed land distribution (Table 2). Previously, they had had little recourse: their marginalization—with different language, customs, and dress—had left them no access to the legal system serving those of European descent.

Thus began the invasions of haciendas by their workers. Their force led Thorp and Bertram (1978:282–83) to comment that "the landowners of Peru entered the 1960s with the expectation that their properties would be sooner or later subject to expropriation either formally or informally."

Table 14.2
LAND CONCENTRATION IN PERU, 1961

Size of Holdings (hectares)	Number of Units	Percent of All Units	Hectares	Percent of All Hectares
1	290,000	34.1	127,869	0.7
1–5	417,357	49.0	926,851	5.0
5–20	107,199	12.6	879,385	4.7
20–100	24,628	3.0	980,058	5.3
100–500	8,081	0.9	1,624,643	8.7
500–1,000	1,585	0.2	1,065,157	5.7
1,000–2,500	1,116	0.1	1,658,636	8.9
> 2,500	1,091	0.1	11,341,981	61.0
All holdings	851,057	100.0	18,604,500	100.0

SOURCE: Comité Interamericano para el Desarrollo de la Agricultura (CIDA), Tenencia de la Tierra y Desarróllo Socio-económico del Sector Agricola en el Perú, Washington, D.C., Pan American Union, 1966. Reprinted in Cleaves and Scurrah (1980:32).

The Belaunde Presidency

In this climate, the election of Fernando Belaunde Terry to the presidency in 1963—with a campaign promise of comprehensive land reform—seemed the last chance for a legal political solution. In 1962, Haya de la Torre's APRA party had won a plurality that seemed to assure him the presidency. This once radical leader, whose support lay mainly among unionized sugar workers of the northern coast, had moderated his position over time in exchange for a share of the political pie. Nevertheless, the military's traditional animosity for APRA caused it to invalidate the election on the charge of fraud. Before Haya could assume office, the military took over, declaring a new election, which was won by Belaunde and his Partido de Acción Popular.

As Belaunde toured the countryside promising land-to-the-tiller and distributing symbolic bags of soil, the military put down a peasant rebellion in La Convención Valley with both stick—a show of force—and carrot—a special land reform for that valley. These and similar events convinced them that only a comprehensive land reform would prevent internal conflict. Within ten months of his election, Belaunde pushed a weak land reform (law 15037) through an opposition-controlled Congress. Farms greater than 150 hectares, other than sugar plantations, would be expropriated. However, the legal holding size of public corporations was large: 150 hectares multiplied by the number of stockholders. Despite loopholes and endless judicial delays, 795 units totaling a million and a half hectares were expropriated in the four years of the law, and 570,000 hectares were allocated to 19,820 families.

Nevertheless, organized land invasions intensified, sometimes in anticipation of formal expropriation and sometimes to force it. The army was not called out to halt them until 1965, when a small guerrilla band formed in La Convención Valley. This latter experience, of the army once again upholding a feudalistic order, helped convince General Juan Velasco Alvarado to lead a bloodless coup in October 1968, dissolve Parliament, and form an all-military cabinet. His principal objectives were nationalization of Peruvian oil and land reform.

The Military Government and Reform

On June 23, 1969, the military government announced Decree Law 17716, harbinger of a fundamental change in ownership of Peruvian agriculture. Although communal ownership was intended for expropriated land, by 1979, when 7.8 million hectares (40% of cultivated acareage) had been adjudicated to 337,662 families, 13% was assigned to individual peasant proprietors despite no provision in the law for so doing (Cleaves and Scurrah 1980). Another 35% to 40% of the land, nominally under common ownership, was probably farmed individually. But the greatest proportion of expropriated land was assigned to two types of communal organization, the Agrarian Production Cooperative (CAP) and the Agricultural Society of Social Interest (SAIS). The rationale for these communal farms requires a flashback to the pre-reform agrarian society.

The Physical Situation and the Type of Tenure

Peru divides geographically into three regions: the coast, the sierra (highlands), and the selva (the eastern jungle). The coast is a long strip, mainly of river valleys where sugar, cotton, and rice are grown on large plantations. These were dominated by twelve highly capitalized sugar cane units (85,000 hectares), farmed by permanent wage laborers who had been unionized during the sixties. Their wages and benefits were at least double the average rural income. These plantations possessed some of the highest yields in the world; usually half their annual production was exported.

Communal ownership and collectivized production made economic sense in these plantations, because of the highly technical production process. The cotton and rice plantations, on the other hand, often consisted of a central area cultivated by tenant-laborers, as well as plots individually farmed by tenants. The rationale for common ownership here depended on the belief of civilian technicians—not adequately demonstrated—that common production was more efficient.

In the sierra, expropriable units fell into two types. The first was haciendas specializing in food crops, such as potatoes, barley, and beans, sold mainly in regional markets although a small part was trucked to cities on the coast. Usually the central area (hacienda land) was a small portion of the total. The remainder (peasant land) was rented in exchange for labor on the hacienda land or for cash.

The second type of unit was large ranching haciendas, mostly pasture. Their expansion over the last century had often been at the expense of Indian communities. The land reform, therefore, brought much pressure to restore this land to the communities. Instead, the government set up SAISs to achieve the advantages of large-scale ranching, while the Indian communities were presumably benefited.

Agrarian Production Cooperatives and Agrarian Societies

Decree 240–69AP, November 1969, set out the legal form of the Agrarian Production Cooperative (CAP). Each CAP was a unit, governed by its owners, who were previously tenants or permanent laborers. Private plots were not recognized. In accepting the property, the new owners contracted a debt to the land reform agency, to be amortized over twenty years, in consideration of the government's payment to expropriated landowners ($2,000 cash maximum, the rest in bonds). Until the debt had completely matured, the ministry would appoint the general manager of the CAP from a slate of three candidates proposed by members. In a general

274

assembly, the membership would elect an administrative council to supervise the general manager.

In the Agricultural Society of Social Interest the workers and tenants formed a service cooperative that elected delegates to a general assembly dominated by those Indian communities deemed to have a fair claim to hacienda land. Each SAIS had an administrative council as well. The Indian communities were to benefit from membership through a share of the profits.

The Land Reform Agency studied each property in detail, deciding what form the new agricultural enterprise would take: CAP or SAIS. The members had no choice. Between expropriation and adjudication, a Provisional Administrative Commission of government technicians made the major production decisions, giving the members no opportunity for participation. They often contracted loans for equipment. The members had no choice but to assume this debt as well.

Once having determined this form, moreover, the state—again without consulting the peasants—decided on centrally planned and centrally implemented operations. It trained cooperative members. Since land could not be mortgaged, the Banco Agropecuario de Fomento (the state's Agrarian Bank) became the only institution through which loans might be received. The numbers of state employees making agrarian decisions increased.

Official Rationale for Cooperatives

Cooperatives had not been discussed by the committee drafting the land reform law. Rather, civilian advisors who wanted to emphasize redistribution of income and wealth persuaded the military government, citing five reasons. First, production might fall if large-scale units were divided. Second, economies of scale would occur in several areas of operation: marketing, finance, technical assistance, and management. Third, the man-land ratio was so low that division would leave every plot with less than subsistence for a family. Fourth, they argued that cooperatives might provide health and education. Fifth, "collective ownership and labor (were expected) to overcome peasants' traditional isolation and (help) establish more socially oriented attitudes and behavior" (Cleaves and Scurrah 1980:222).

The emphasis on cooperatives was strengthened by the so-called "parcelling controversy." To permit quick action, Title 9 of Decree Law 17716 allowed property owners to parcel their estates into nonexpropriable units of less than 150 hectares, to be distributed among workers. When owners used this clause to give the land to family members plus just a few workers and tenants, the ensuing protest led the government to insist that if the owners chose parcelling, the family-size plots had to be provided for all workers. Since the owners then had little incentive to parcel, the cooperative model took over by default.

The Mechanisms of State Control

Bank Credit

Adequate provision of credit and its more equitable distribution were touted as among the expected results of land reform. Previously, credit had reflected the highly skewed distribution of land (Table 2), the lion's share going to the export crops of the coast. This was so whether the loans came from the state bank (BAF, for Banco Agropecuario de Fomento) or from commercial banks.

Table 3 shows data on BAF loans by number and value for three years before the 1969 reform, by geographic region. In all of these years, 75% by value went to the coastal area. Table 4 shows the amount loaned by BAF in 1965–66 by farm size and region: almost 50% went to coastal enterprises of over 100 hectares. Virtually all *minifundistas*, by contrast, received their credit from informal moneylenders. To "free" peasants from these moneylenders was one of the purposes of the land reform.

Since large private farms were expropriated, agricultural credit from commercial banks disappeared. Even had commercial banks been willing to extend credit to coastal cooperatives, they would not have competed with the negative real interest rates—arising out of low nominal rates combined with rapid inflation—offered by the BAF. BAF loans doubled in real terms between 1970 and 1976, while the proportion going to CAPs producing export-oriented crops on the coast gradually increased from 40% in 1970 to 50% in 1978. In sum, while access to moneylenders was denied the farmers on the sierra, state credit did not effectively replace them, precisely when credit was desperately needed to overcome the decapitalization occurring on many estates before expropriation. On the other hand, the state was subsidizing the coastal export cooperatives with cheap credit in real terms—farms which by their prosperity were the least in need.

McClintock (1987:104) testified to the continued geographic concentration during the 1980s:

> While only 15% of Peru's rural population resided on the coast in 1980, coastal agriculturalists received over 70% of all agricultural credit in the 1960s and 1970s. . . . The percentage declined slightly under the Belaunde government to about 60–65%; but the differential was allocated to Peru's jungle region rather than the poorer highlands area. . . . The needy highlands with about 68% of the rural population in 1980 received only 10 to 17% of total agricultural credit between the early 1960s and the early 1980s.

Production and Marketing of Fertilizer

As with credit, the government's intervention in production and marketing of fertilizer antedates the reform of 1969. The state had licensed a private firm to mine guano (bird droppings on the coastal islands, highly

Table 14.3

Banco Agropecuario de Fomento (BAF) Loans, 1963–66

	1963–64		1964–65		1965–66	
	Number	Million Sales	Number	Million Sales	Number	Million Sales
Coast	11,693	1,271	11,780	1,418	11,328	1,549
Sierra	9,440	160	7,989	162	8,676	235
Selva	5,112	143	4,617	183	5,611	250

Source: USDA (1968:49).

Table 14.4

BANCO AGROPECUARIO DE FOMENTO (BAF) NUMBERS OF
CROP LOANS, BY FARM SIZE AND REGION, 1965-66

Farm Size	Coast	Sierra	Selva	Total
Small (average 4 ha)	283	132	111	484
Medium (25-100 ha)	297	61	56	309
Large (> 100 ha)	969	42	83	987
Total	1,549	235	250	2,034

SOURCE: USDA (1968:50).

valued as fertilizer both in Peru and throughout the world) after the turn of the century. The government had held some shares in the firm from the start, but in 1963 it bought out the private investors to establish a public company, CONAFER, to mine guano and to distribute it and other fertilizers as well. This firm was placed under the Ministry of Agriculture from 1968 to 1970 and (with the name changed to SENAFER) the Ministry of Industry and Commerce from 1970 to 1974. It received exclusive rights to import fertilizer in 1973. In 1974, it became an autonomous public enterprise, ENCI, which greatly expanded its role in the sale of fertilizers toward the end of the decade.

ENCI monopolized fertilizer sales from 1975 to 1982, charging a common price anywhere in the country. From 1975 to 1977 this price was 30% to 45% below the cost of production, with the government subsidizing the difference. But the financially pressed government could not continue the subsidy. From 1978 to 1982 the price of fertilizer rose more rapidly than the rate of inflation, and consumption declined. In 1982, the Belaunde government ended ENCI's monopoly, and transportation costs were again reflected in price (McClintock 1986:90-91). The new García administration in 1985 again cut fertilizer prices, and consumption rose dramatically.

It is not clear how these policies affected regional consumption. Attempts to subsidize fertilizer and to maintain a uniform price, regardless of transportation costs, may have helped redress the imbalance felt by the sierra. But the policy was withdrawn. Any subsidy is questionable if a hard-pressed government may rescind it at any time, and thus inflict capricious behavior on its beneficiaries.

Imports and Exports of Food

McClintock (1981:262), who did an intensive study of two small coastal CAPs and one large sierra SAIS, reflects the popular view of the moneylender, which we have been criticizing:

278

Most Peruvian agricultural enterprises sold their products not directly to the consumer but through middlemen. These intermediaries included large private and cooperative firms as well as peasants, such as prosperous coastal ex-sharecroppers and wealthy comuneros. Only these intermediaries had the necessary storage, transportation, and/or processing facilities. And, thus, the middlemen were able to squeeze producers economically, in many cases leaving them with less than $1/3$ of the selling price of the good.

Her study, furthermore, does not reveal what portion of the selling price represents marketing costs.

Less than two weeks after the announcement of the land reform law, D.L. 17716, the military government set up a centralized agency to control all public enterprises in the food industry. The goal was to gain some control over food prices by competing with private firms in both wholesale and retail marketing.

The Empresa Publica de Servicios Agropecuarios (EPSA) was most successful in controlling the import and export wholesale market. The government simply made EPSA the sole legal food importer and exporter. Initially, EPSA imported on the basis of public bids, but it later gained the right to purchase without public bidding.

But EPSA did not have the same success in competing with the private sector in the countryside, for the following reasons (Cleaves and Scurrah 1980:206). First, private middlemen were often the main source of credit to a farmer, so that EPSA's specialized service held little appeal. Second, relationships between middlemen and farmer had been built up over the years, whereas no one farmer had any guarantee that EPSA would be back again next year. EPSA did try to tie into the land-reform cooperatives, but its rigidity on product prices and its "collect now, pay later" approach was resented. Finally, "many middlemen offered higher prices for quality food products that they could easily resell in Lima."

EPSA sold at low, official prices through its own supermarket chain. It also sold to 2,000 small grocery stores at less than official prices. Naturally, demand was greater than supply, stores ran short, and EPSA survived only with large subsidies (Cleaves and Scurrah 1980). On the other hand, many foodstuffs could be bought at much higher prices in traditional markets, but the government harrassed the sellers in these markets with arrests and fines.

While believing the stereotype that middlemen are exploitative, Guillet (1979:191) summarized the marketing experience of the TUPAC AMARU II cooperative to show that EPSA's services have been insufficient:

> The cooperative is still subject, however, to the same exploitative marketing channels as found during the period prior to the agrarian reform. The intermediaries continue to be the major vehicles for the marketing of agricultural products. . . . EPSA . . . is involved in only a partial mar-

keting of the potato production of the cooperative. Most products are sold to the same middlemen who purchased goods from the hacienda.

Marketing the product of the sierra has always been difficult because of poor roads and inadequate storage. McClintock (1981: 272) estimates that only a third of all cooperatives were tied into an active central cooperative or a state marketing agency; the rest "bought and sold as isolated entities in a competitive marketplace."

Nevertheless, by 1974, when EPSA still controlled one-quarter of the country's food marketing, its immense subsidies attracted political attention. In search of a scapegoat, the authorities indicted approximately one hundred top EPSA officials for embezzlement. During two years (1974–76) of dragging investigation, charges were reduced or dropped for most officials. Possibly the government would have preferred to dissolve EPSA, but it is far harder to liquidate a public entity than it is to set it up. From this point on, one senses rivalry among a number of government agencies for the privilege of importing, exporting, buying, and selling foodstuffs.

EPSA's functions were transferred piecemeal to others. In 1973, the Ministry of Commerce took over food imports and exports, leaving EPSA mainly in control of basic domestic foodstuffs. In 1978, ENCI assumed the marketing of cotton, wheat, corn, sorghum, soy, barley, milk products, and meat products, but in 1979 it was merged with EPSA. For twenty years before land reform, the government had bought all domestic rice through the Banco de la Nación, for sale to private retailers at fixed prices. But after the reform the rice CAPs had to sell to EPSA. In the late seventies, the growers—acting through a central organization ECASA—gained control of all sales of domestic rice. These growers were mainly middle-sized (c. 50–100 hectares) farmers, with considerable political power, who were able to influence decisions of ECASA.

The only major challenge to government-organized marketing of foodstuffs that we have uncovered was an attempt, in 1975, by the National Agrarian Federation (CNA) to establish a rival, cooperative marketing network. The CNA had been set up by the military government, shortly after its take-over to counteract the Communist Party's peasant federation (CCP). Later, the Indian communities came to dominate the CNA, acting increasingly on their own initiative. Not interested in a truly independent agrarian sector, however, the government at first ignored CNA's attempt at marketing, and then, in 1978, disavowed it completely.

Still subsidizing rice consumption in January 1981, the post-military government under Belaunde has been trying to loosen the EPSA/ENCI monopoly. By July 1981, ENCI lost its exclusive rights to import feed grains, but, despite firm protests by farmers and cooperatives, it still controlled all cotton marketing. Cleaves and Scurrah conclude that EPSA was one more mechanism by which the government subsidized the urban consumer at the expense of the countryside.

Tariffs and the Terms of Trade for Farmers

In its policy to favor industrialization over agriculture, in the post-reform period the Peruvian government has persistently turned the terms of trade against farmers and in favor of urban areas. Billone et al. (1982) showed that the terms of trade for cotton and corn worsened from 1973 on, although not for sugar and potatoes. The terms for rice actually improved (Martinez 1986:498). Taking into account the relative importance of these crops, however, Billone et al. (p. 94) calculated the net transfer out of coastal agriculture as approximately 19,511 million 1973 soles, of which 18,211 million went to industrial suppliers.

Valdes (1985, 1986) and Franklin, Leonard, and Valdes (1985), cited in Carter and Alvarez (1986), document the post-reform negative impact on agriculture of overvalued exchange rates, tariffs on industrial imports, and subsidies for imported food. While the military governments directly taxed coastal cooperatives, peasants on the sierra suffered mainly from the subsidy on imported wheat (McClintock 1987:100).

Ferroni (1980:3) has suggested that the subsidies to the cities overcame less poverty there than they created in the countryside. The farmers, of course, paid the real cost of those subsidies:

> Despite the strengthening of real incomes of non-subsistence consumers originating from cheap food, caloric deficiency associated with low incomes is frequent in urban areas. Hence, the ex post alleviation of poverty through cheap food would appear to be less extensive than the poverty which low food prices create ex ante in the rural areas and which is exported to the cities through migration.

The Sugar Cooperatives

Twenty-four thousand permanent workers in the twelve large sugar plantations gained the most from land reform, as owners of the new self-managed cooperatives. Far from backing the military regime solidly, however, they became one of the centers of active resistance.

One day after President Velasco announced Decree Law 17716 on June 23, 1969, stating the conditions under which land would be expropriated, troops seized the large sugar plantations. Why so fast? First, the government wanted the plantations to remain productive, since sugar was a major earner of foreign exchange. Second, it saw an opportunity to lure the unions of the north coast away from APRA, its long-term opponent. Third, owners had been among the most powerful of the traditional oligarchy, whom the military had to challenge to secure their own power. (By contrast, Belaunde's land reform law had exempted the sugar plantations.) Fourth, almost half of Peru's sugar was produced by two foreign-owned companies, Guildemeister and W. R. Grace. Their expropriation would confirm the military's nationalism. Finally, the government feared that if it did not move quickly, the former owners would decapitalize their lands by removing machinery and other valuables.

From July 1969 to April 1970, the government appeared content to start the sugar plantations on the road toward worker-owned and -managed cooperatives. In November 1969, Decreto Supremo 240–69AP made the Agrarian Production Cooperative a single unit of land owned by the field workers in common.

But we have seen that the government's control would continue as long as the debt to the Land Reform Agency (to reimburse ex-owners) had not been paid. So from the start, the government intervened in management. Besides the right to select the general manager from the slate of three picked by the CAP, the state authorities would specify the percentage profits to be allocated to a number of funds: reserve, social, investment, and the like. Aside from these provisions, the internal governmental structure would presumably be democratic. A general assembly of 100 to 200 members would be elected on the basis of one member, one vote. The general assembly would elect the administrative council (to decide on policy with the advice of the general manager) and a vigilance council (to act as a watchdog on the administrative council). Elections were set for May and June of 1970.

The first serious government intervention occurred to stave off unions. Increasingly fearful that APRA-based unions would control the assembly and the councils, in May 1970 the government barred any union leader from any office in the cooperative for as long he had been a union official. In addition, field workers could have only a minority representation in the general assembly and might name only two out of nine members in the administrative council. The unions countered with agitation and strikes over the next two years. They forced the government to back down in early 1972. The decrees of May 1970 were withdrawn, and secret fair elections were held for the assembly and council. In many of the cooperatives, former union leaders were elected.

Despite these initial struggles, the first five years of the reform were seen as successful. While production did not increase dramatically, high international sugar prices and good weather led to large profits for most of the cooperatives. Horton (1977: 201) cited the following reasons for success. First, the plantations had already been single production enterprises, with decisions made by central management. Second, the workers, unionized, were accustomed to taking directions and to routine systems of work. Third, the estates were profit-making units that had not been decapitalized by their owners.

But worker control was not to last. In 1969, the government took control of water, the lifeblood of Peruvian sugar. Before the reform, irrigation works had been managed by the plantations even though the government had financed their construction. Now the state assumed ownership, announcing that water would be allocated according to "perceived need." Initially, this did not hurt the cooperatives, which had priority, but it did give the authorities potential leverage. Also, credit, essential to cooperatives, was now monopolized by the BAF. Previously, the plantations could choose among commercial banks. In addition, a separate military organization, SAFCAP (system of advice and control of agrarian production cooperatives), consisting of a colonel and civilian research associates, was set up on each sugar cooperative to monitor its financial health. In December 1973, the general assembly of the small sugar cooperative Cayalti was told that if it wished to retain access to public sector credit, it should formally request the state to "intervene" in the running of the cooperative. (It did so.) Finally, all sugar cooperatives were required to belong to a central marketing cooperative, CECOAAP, the exclusive agent for marketing sugar and setting prices, in consultation with the Ministry of Agriculture. Through these organizations, the state was poised to exert greater control when problems arose.

And problems did arise. International prices of sugar increased wildly up to 1974, then they took a sharp drop to approximately the level of the late sixties. The impact of this drop was compounded by a drought from 1978 to 1980, which caused a severe decline in production (Kay 1982:155). A traditional exporter of sugar, Peru was converted into an importer by 1980, and by 1981 its exports had dropped to zero (Table 5).

State management became part of the national development plan. The plan for each cooperative was then drawn up yearly by the general manager with technical assistance from CECOAAP (Stepan 1978:212–13). The administrative council might suggest revision, after which the plan was voted on by the general assembly. It then went to the national headquarters of SAFCAP, to be checked against national criteria for investment. SAFCAP might return the plan for redrafting. Thus the final say over cooperative investment and financing lay firmly with the government, not with the "worker-owners."

Decree Law 21585 in 1976 authorized the Ministry of Agriculture to set maximum wages and salaries and to supervise work conditions and effort. In early 1977, Decree Law 21815 abolished the representative government of the cooperatives, and government functionaries were put in charge of four of the sugar CAPs. Because of the drought, CECOAAP was $84 million in debt by June 1981. With government permission, three of the sugar CAPs withdrew from CECOAAP, and the government in desperation permitted six others to market their sugar domestically on their own. In 1982, CECOAAP collapsed completely due to its financial burden, and the remaining sugar cooperatives were freed to sell on the market.

In 1988, the government forgave the sugar cooperatives the debt remaining from the period of intense government control (*Latin American Monitor, The Andean Group*, June 1988:3).

The drought and an increase in internal consumption conventionally explain why Peru no longer exports sugar. But the drought has now been

Table 14.5

SUGAR PRICES, PRODUCTION, EXPORTS, AND IMPORTS, 1968–81

	International Price[a] in U.S. cents/kg. (1979 $)	Production[b] (metric tons)	Exports[b] (metric tons)	Imports[b] (metric tons)	Value of Exports[c] (billion soles)
1968	13.56	752,132	454,419	0	2.43
1969	22.63	632,810	267,611	0	1.52
1970	23.58	770,764	403,165	0	2.56
1971	26.67	882,496	428,611	0	2.74
1972	39.10	899,415	480,932	0	3.04
1973	42.60	897,634	407,011	0	3.41
1974	107.37	992,464	462,171	0	6.04
1975	64.07	963,657	421,841	0	11.77
1976	35.70	929,651	284,000	0	5.09
1977	23.34	900,350	411,832	0	7.37
1978	19.48	856,472	265,891	0	7.86
1979	21.30	695,283	180,790	0	7.93
1980		537,375	52,816	50,005	
1981		478,500	0	157,622	

[a]SOURCE: *World Bank Commodity Trade and Price Trends*, August 1980.
[b]SOURCE: *World Sugar Economy*, 1982, ISO: 90.
[c]SOURCE: IMF, *International Financial Statistics*, January 1981:314.

over for several years, and Peruvians could hardly increase their consumption to supplant all exports. No, the reason lies squarely in the decline of production, which Scott's (1979:85-6) review of labor conflicts politely attributes to "the changing balance in the struggle between aspirations of cooperative members for effective self-management, the imperatives of the world market, and the requirements of the Peruvian state for financial resources."

Parcelization on the Coast

Some cracks in government domination of the land appeared with the return of democratically elected presidents in 1980. President Belaunde had always favored small peasant plots rather than collective farming. His government therefore legalized the division of land of coastal CAPs among their members. For the first two years (1980-82), parcelization was slow. But it accelerated thereafter, and by 1986 almost all coastal CAPs, other than the giant sugar complexes, had been parceled out. Wage laborers had been turned into peasant proprietors.

Why? McClintock (1987:93) believes that external economic forces were the main cause:

> Peruvian cooperatives were beset by such adverse terms of trade (1981-83) and such tight credit restrictions that bankruptcy was virtually inevitable; ironically many of the previously most successful cooperatives, which had enjoyed ample credit during the 1970s, were the hardest hit as they had the largest debts. Bankrupt or nearly so, the cooperative enterprises were then unable to resist pressures of the Agrarian Bank in their area for parceling out the land.

Possible by coincidence—though we would like to think not—after two decades of stagnation, agricultural output in Peru began to increase right after the successful parcelization of land of coastal CAPs. We do not yet have the regional information that would tell us whether the increase was concentrated on the coast. After a decline by 10.8% in 1983, agricultural output increased by 11.8%, 3.1%, 4.5%, and 5.1% in the years 1984 to 1987, respectively (IDB 1988:488).

Carter and Alverson (1987) and Mehmed and Carter (1988) agree that external economic forces drove the CAPs to parcelization, but they add another reason: unresolved problems of internal discipline. They ascribe the period of delay (1980-83) to a wait-and-see attitude, as some held back to watch the experience of others.

Organizations of *parceleros* have formed to protect individual rights. Since some parcelization took place without all legal formalities, titles may be clouded. These organizations are expected to help if possession is challenged.

Large Commercial CAPs

> For the average worker with scant education and few friends in leadership posts, the incentive to work hard was small. The hope of promotion was slim, the threat of being fired was infinitesimal and neither wages nor profit remittances for "basic labor" were pegged to work achievement. Work quotas were pegged to quantity rather than quality (McClintock 1981:230).

Here McClintock wrote about the other large coastal cooperatives—formerly commercial farms or haciendas producing cotton, rice, maize, or fruits for the market—which averaged 400 to 500 hectares and had 100 to 150 members. She also found (pp. 241–43) that work commitment varied with the size of the cooperative and its financing. At La Estrella CAP, for example, where wages and profits were high, members worked seven hours daily on cooperative work, whereas at Marla CAP, where wages were low and losses incurred, they spent only four hours on the cooperative, devoting other time to private economic activities. These choices are highly rational.

The Livestock SAISs and CAPs

The livestock SAISs and CAPs of the high sierra operated without significant incident for at least seven years (peasant invasions came later). These were the former haciendas whose owners had encroached on the common land of peasant communities over the preceding hundred years, and against which many land invasions had been directed.

In the SAIS format, peasants of a former hacienda joined a service cooperative that had one vote in a general assembly of similar, neighboring cooperatives. In principle, the peasants controlled both the service cooperatives and the general assembly. In fact, the assembly—authoritarian and under strict government supervision—suppressed the initiative of the cooperative. From the start, therefore, interests of the cooperatives differed from those of the general assembly: the former wanted higher wages and a greater distribution of profits to individuals; the latter, responding to the "higher" interest of the society, wanted lower wages and more profit distribution to the communities, which under law would be spent on projects that they would manage. With no clear definition of powers, the peasants were uncertain whether they had the choice to allocate their income between consumption and community investment.

In hopes of increasing their influence, some members of cooperatives formed unions, thereby defining themselves as adversaries rather than as owners. The conflicts became so intense that in a number of SAISs the government stepped in to manage directly. Now conflicts were between peasants and the SAIS—an odd spectacle for visionaries of peasant empowerment through land reform—with government usually taking the side of the SAIS, whose management (and resources) it was more able to control. Many SAISs showed no profit at all, and in the few that did, the government looked upon profits as a substitute for spending its regular revenues on community improvements.

Dissatisfaction with these conditions led to a new wave of land invasions in the late seventies and early eighties, along with informal parcelization of many of the livestock SAISs. Ironically, the SAIS structure had been designed to halt this very process.

Amortization of the debt for the land led to early financial problems in the SAISs. McClintock (1981:222) estimates that the share of profits allocated to debt amortization in the early years was 75% at SAIS Huanca, 22% at CAP Marla and 11% at CAP Estrella. As inflation took hold, however, the real debt diminished, and in 1979 it was canceled.

Backward Haciendas of Highlands

The reform touched haciendas of all types, including small units in the highlands where tenants held rights to individual plots in exchange for service on hacienda land. These farms were converted into non-commercialized CAPs. The government had little success in encouraging tenants to collectivize their plots for joint farming. One might have supposed that the hacienda land would be cultivated collectively. Instead, the better-off peasants chipped away at this land, which became their private property de facto. Shades of sixteenth-century England! But there was no Ke's Rebellion here. Employed part-time on the plots of influential farmers, smaller tenants did not dare offend their patrons by opposing enclosures. Preoccupied with production, the government paid little attention to these CAPs. Combined with continued farming of individual plots, this parcelization of hacienda land destroyed the rationale for a production cooperative.

What Happened to Vicos?

Could the peasants have succeeded on their own, had the government done nothing more than expropriate the land and turn it over to them? Such a question is not a total "might-have-been." We do have an example.

In order to examine the impact of direct socioeconomic change on a community, in 1951 a group of anthropologists from Cornell University, acting jointly with Peruvian colleagues, rented the highland hacienda of Vicos (Holmberg 1960). There they began a program of "guided change." They dismisssed the non-resident manager (mayordomo) and vested management (including finance) instead in the Indian elders (mayorales).

Once Vicosinos became aware that hacienda profits belonged to them, for distribution or investment, production increased dramatically. In some cases, the potato crop (staple of the region) was up by 400% Presumably the Indians were working harder. But the improvement may have been in distribution as well as production. Before the Cornell reform, Indians doing forced labor on hacienda land had been accustomed to pocketing a part of their crop surreptitiously; therefore it would not have been included in the marketing data. After the reform, when community members made all decisions on planting and harvesting, on accounting, and on who would drive the trucks to market, communal profits increased enormously.

Welfare of members improved in other ways as well. The community elected its own president and officials, who controlled de facto and not just in name. Even though a primary school already existed, the anthropologists were unable to find a single child who could read or write. Furthermore, parents seemed little interested in sending their children to school, for literacy was not a necessary part of their everyday living. With the introduction of a lunch program—in a community where hunger was endemic—the school quickly filled up. When the hacienda was remodeled to include administrative offices and the national flag was raised, many members wondered what it was. They had not been aware they were Peruvians; the anthropologists wanted to establish a sense of national identity.

In a chronological table of events, Doughty (1982:14), one of the original anthropologists, writes the following:

> 1951-56. CPP (Cornell Peru Project) operates manor, conducts research and introduces changes in consultation with Vicos community: peonage abolished, giving Vicosinos social freedom and right to make employment choices as available; new agricultural practices and crops, political reorganization of community, school constructed and staffed, health studies and program begun. Peruvian agencies begin work at Vicos.

The Cornell group has been roundly criticized for paternalism. Some have argued that Vicos' success would never have been possible without significant funding and leverage from outside. In 1961, U.S. Senator Edward Kennedy nudged the Peruvian government into providing a loan to assist the community in its purchase of the hacienda. (From that point on until the land reform of 1969, the hacienda was owned by its former peons.) Doughty has documented the various criticisms, while defending the initial concept as a success, since Vicosinos did indeed take charge of their own economic lives and, until the land reform, succesfully managed their economy. He (1982:16) continues his chronology:

> 1969. New Military Revolutionary government classifies Vicos as an official "Peasant Community" and decrees organizational change in Vicos to conform with new laws governing all such entities; Vicos resists imposition of changes; government officials call Vicos backward and impossible; government attempt to rig Vicos election fails, but new organization is imposed.
>
> 1969. Regional potato blight sharply lowers production causing severe economic problems in Vicos and in region; potatoes from region embargoed from national markets. . . .

288

1973–75. With the urging of former . . . employees now with the Ministry of Agriculture, the community reassigns school land use from vocational gardening practice, to community feed lot use as part of projected dairy development. Protesting teachers are expelled from the community and replaced, community support for school diminishes; subsequently, Vicos victimized by incompetent Ministry of Agriculture dairy cattle program at great financial loss; community government discredited and morale low.

Vicos presents a dilemma. What else could the Cornell anthropologists have done? Probably nothing that would have prepared the community to withstand the assault by the government. We have heard that the Vicosinos did indeed turn back the first government agents to arrive (telephone call, Powelson to Doughty, 1984) but that they succumbed on a later round. Suppose the Cornell anthropologists had not "guided" the choices of Vicosinos—for a school through the lunch program; in methods of accounting and marketing—but had done nothing more than turn the land over to them and leave them alone? We cannot say. Whatever its successes, and we believe Doughty has defended them well, this "reform by grace" did not leave the peasants with much more leverage upon their government than the members of enforced cooperatives possessed all over Peru. Vicos is now a reformed hacienda, operated and controlled by the government, just like all the rest.

Sendero Luminoso

Interviews by Berg (1987) in the highland areas provide some evidence that the hated, mysterious movement of *Sendero Luminoso* ("Shining Path") may have been caused, in part, by government domination of the land reform. SAIS haciendas have been a favorite target of this movement, which started in the early 1980s.

Sendero Luminoso had been a splinter group from the University of Ayacucho (San Cristóbal de Huamanga) of the early 1970s. Antonio Díaz Martinez, a leader of that group, was a professionally trained agronomist who had become disillusioned with the top-down nature of reform in the highlands. He believed that peasant communities would evolve only if peasants themselves were in charge. Lack of peasant participation in the military land reform convinced him of the need for a violent mobilization (Harding 1988:68–69).

Berg's interviews revealed much peasant hostility toward highland cooperatives. The state had expropriated haciendas in this area only after peasant seizure in 1974. The state's response was a massive show of force (Berg 1987:173), which let the peasants know that the state was not on their side. Berg reported that peasant interviewees did not express dismay when a cooperative was attacked by *Sendero Luminoso*. Instead, their conversation turned to how cooperative leaders had siphoned off funds while ordinary workers gained little.

In 1985, the year of Berg's interview, *Sendero Luminoso* had penetrated but little beyond the southern highlands. By 1988, it was a powerful guerrilla force, with sympathizers widely spread in Peruvian society. In mid-1988, President García publicly admired its courage and ideals, while calling for renewed efforts to fight it.

By mid-1989, *Sendero Luminoso* had become powerful enough to control the eastern slopes and exclude an increasingly impotent and almost bankrupt government. It cooperated with and taxed farmers who had "deforested most of a fragile cloud forest known as the 'eyebrow of the jungle' and destroyed an area estimated at well over 500,000 acres of tropical forests" (Brooke 1989:1) to grow coca for distillation into cocaine and export into the world's drug market.

It is too big a jump to attribute Peru's deterioration—economic, political, ecological, and agricultural—to the land reform alone. Yet all these are part of a process of the failure of a government whose overall reform policies were developed with little or no understanding of or communication with peasants in all parts of the country.

Conclusion: The Vicious Circle

Poor agricultural performance and increased state intervention fed one upon the other, each leading to an increased round of the other. Whereas the original dream of the Velasco administration had been a model uniquely Peruvian, in which all property would be social, widely held by self-managed cooperatives, this dream was not implemented from the start. Peasants had no choice about their agrarian structures. The dream then melted away into state-organized production centers, images of similar centers throughout the Third World. Every error, every mishap, whether natural or human-induced, afforded the pretext for further government intervention. Another reason, not uncommon in the Third World, was that the plans of the individual cooperatives had to fit in with the overall national development plan.

The farmers' debt, arising from required purchase of the land by cooperatives, was the principal weapon for state intervention. The motto—that the land had originally belonged to the Indians and ought to be returned to them—proved shallow. Price controls, production controls, and credit restrictions added their cumulative force. Urban bias—low prices of foodstuffs to benefit city workers—was implemented through price ceilings, while government-induced inflation made manufactured goods more expensive: the very capital goods on which the rural cooperatives depended for modernization. Low tariffs on imported foods and high tariffs on manufactures contributed to these distortions. These inefficiencies combined with natural disasters, such as drought, to justify the state in assuming management.

The formal ownership of land by the landless, whether through cooperatives or private plots, is sterile if the new owners are squeezed in their earnings, deprived of decisions over production and marketing, and treated as serfs of the state. Until the parcelization of coastal cooperatives began to show some hope for individual farming, land reform in Peru gave land to the state instead of to the peasants. Parcelization conforms to the liberalization movements now found in several countries where forced collectivization of agriculture has failed, such as China and the Soviet Union. Let us hope that it will spread in Peru.

References

Berg, Ronald, 1987. "*Sendero Luminoso* and Peasants of Andahyaylas," *Journal of Inter-American Studies and World Affairs*, vol. 28, no. 4:165–96.

Berry, Albert, 1972. *Land Reform and the Agricultural Income Distribution*, Center Paper No. 184, New Haven, Yale University, Center for Economic Growth.

Billone, Jorge; Carbonetto, Daniel, and Martinez, Daniel, 1982. *Términos de Intercambio Ciudad-Campo, 1970–1980: Precios y Excedente Agrícola*, Centro de Estudios para el Desarrollo y la Participación, Lima.

Brooke, James, 1989. "Peruvian Farmers Razing Rain Forest to Sow Drug Crops," *The New York Times*, August 13.

Carter, Michael R. and Alvarez, Elena, 1987. "Changing Roads: The Decollectivization of Peruvian Agrarian Reform Agriculture," in W. H. Thiesenhusen, ed., *Agrarian Structure and Reform in Latin America*, forthcoming.

Cleaves, P., and Scurrah, M., 1980. *Agriculture, Bureaucracy, and Military Government in Peru*, Ithaca, N.Y., Cornell University Press.

Doughty, Paul, 1982. "What Has Become of Vicos? The Aftermath of a Classic Program," paper presented at the 1982 meetings of the Society for Applied Anthropology.

Falaris, Evangelos M., 1979. "The Determinants of Internal Migration in Peru: An Economic Analysis," *Economic Development and Cultural Change*, vol. 27, no. 2, January:327–42.

Ferroni, Mario, 1980. "The Urban Bias of Peruvian Food Policy: Consequences and Alternatives," Ph.D. dissertation, Ithaca, N.Y., Cornell University.

Figueroa, Adolfo, 1984. *Capitalist Development and Peasant Agriculture in Peru*, New York, Cambridge University Press.

Franklin, D.; Leonard, J.; and Valdes, A., 1985. *Consumption Effects of Agricultural Policies. Peru: Trade Policy, Agricultural Policies, and Food Consumption: An Economy-Wide Perspective*. Report prepared by the Sigma One Corporation for the Agency for International Development. Raleigh, Sigma One.

Guillet, David, 1979. *Agrarian Reform and Peasant Economy in Southern Peru*, Columbia, Mo., University of Missouri Press.

Harding, Colin, 1988. "Antonio Díaz Martinez and the Ideology of the *Sendero Luminoso*," *Bulletin of Latin American Research*, vol. 7, no. 1:65–73.

Holmberg, Allan R., 1960. "Changing Community Attitudes and Values in Peru: A Case Study in Guided Change," in Richard R. Adams et al., eds., *Social Change in Latin America Today*, New York, Harper & Row, for the Council on Foreign Relations.

Horton, D., 1977. "Haciendas and Cooperatives: A Study of Estate Organization, Land Reform, and New Reform Enterprises in Peru," Ph.D. dissertation, Ithaca, N.Y., Cornell University.

IDB (Inter-American Development Bank), 1988. *Economic and Social Progress in Latin America: 1988 Report*, Washington, D.C.

Johnson, John J., 1964. *The Military and Society in Latin America*, Stanford, Calif., Stanford University Press.

Kay, Cristobal, 1982. "The Peruvian Agrarian Reform," *Journal of Development Studies*, vol. 18, no. 2, January.

Lieuwen, Edwin, 1960. *Arms and Politics in Latin America*, New York, Praeger.

Lipton, Michael, 1977. *Why Poor People Stay Poor*, Cambridge, Mass., Harvard University Press.

Loehr, William, and Powelson, John P., 1981. *The Economics of Development and Distribution*, New York, Harcourt Brace Jovanovich.

Lowenthal, A., ed., 1975. *The Peruvian Experiment: Continuity and Change under Military Rule*, Princeton, N.J., Princeton University Press.

McClintock, Cynthia, 1981. *Peasant Cooperatives and Political Change in Peru*, Princeton, N.J., Princeton University Press.

McClintock, Cynthia, 1986. "After Agrarian Reform and Democratic Government: Has Peruvian Agriculture Developed?" in F.L. Tullis and W.L. Hollist, eds., *Food, the State and International Political Economy*, Lincoln, University of Nebraska.

McClintock, Cynthia, 1987. "Agricultural Policy and Food Security in Peru and Ecuador," in B.A. Yesilada, C.D. Brockett, and B. Drury, eds., *Agrarian Reform in Reverse: The Food Crisis in the Third World*, Boulder, Colo., Westview Press.

Melmed, Jolyne S., and Carter, Michael R., 1988. "The Economic Viability and Stability of Capitalized Family Farming: An Analysis of Agricultural Decollectivization in Peru," Xerox.

Scott, C., 1979. "The Labour Process, Class Conflict, and Politics in the Peruvian Sugar Industry," *Development and Change*, vol. 10:57-89.

Stepan, Alfred, 1978. *The State and Society: Peru in Comparative Perspective*, Princeton, N.J., Princeton University Press.

Thorp, Rosemary, and Bertram, Geoffrey, 1978. *Peru, 1890-1977: Growth and Policy in an Open Economy*, New York, Columbia University Press.

USDA (U.S. Department of Agriculture), 1968. *Peru Agricultural Situation Report* (annual), Washington, D.C.

Valdes, A., 1985. "Exchange Rates and Trade Policy: Help or Hindrance to Agricultural Growth?" Paper prepared for 19th International Conference of Agricultural Economists, held in Malaga, Spain.

Valdes, A., 1986. "Trade and Macroeconomic Policies' Impact on Agricultural Growth: The South American Experience," Washington, D.C., International Food Policy Research.

Webb, Richard, 1975. "Government Policy and Distribution of Income in Peru, 1963-1973," in Lowenthal.

15. Indonesia

Charles W. Howe

The Origins of Sugar in Java

Ever since the Dutch first occupied Java in the seventeenth century and even to the present day, Javanese smallholders have been required to devote significant portions of their land to growing sugar for the authorities, on the terms of the authorities, which have never been advantageous to the peasants.

Sugar growing for export, which changed the lives of the Javanese in the seventeenth century, has therefore vitally affected them ever since. By the end of the seventeenth century, the Dutch East India Company operated about one hundred estates around Batavia—now Jakarta, the capital of Indonesia. Although the company plantations were assumed by the Dutch government in 1799, the foreign rulers continued to encourage sugar growth. Under the so-called culture system (Geertz 1963) of 1830–70, villages were required to grow cane on their own land while the government owned and ran the mills. Villagers were also compelled to labor in the mills.

Under the culture system, sugar production increased from 40,500 tons in 1830 to 405,000 tons in 1870, mainly because of intensive cultivation and efficient milling and because the companies could requisition the best village lands. They also helped to build better irrigation systems for both their own and village lands. Their research institute developed superior seedlings, which were disseminated widely.

The culture system was replaced by the Agrarian Law of 1870, under which the East Indies government began to transfer the plantations to private (Dutch) ownership. In fact, however, this law changed things very little. Forced cultivation gave way to compulsory leasing of peasant lands to the sugar mills, which continued to use compulsory labor. Villages were required by their leaders and civil servants to sign twenty-one-year leases with the mills under which roughly half the wet rice lands (*sawah*) were put into some stage of cane cultivation. The mills supervised the conversion of land from sawah to cane, as well as cane cultivation and harvesting. After about eighteen months, the land would be returned to the peasant farmer for his own purposes, until the next cycle should begin.

By 1928, Java was second only to Cuba as world sugar exporter

(Mubyarto 1969: 37). One hundred seventy-eight mills, harvesting about 200,000 hectares, produced 3 million tons, comprising 75% of Java's total exports. With the collapse of world prices during the depression, however, the cultivated area fell to 35,000 hectares in 1935 and production to only 500,000 tons. It increased thereafter until World War II. During the Japanese occupation, sugar growth was not encouraged, and much land reverted to rice.

Company efforts to restore production after the war were countered by the desperate need of Indonesians for food, which competed for the land. In 1957, the mills were taken over by the newly independent Indonesian government.

Indonesia in Control: 1957-75*

During the Dutch period, foreigners (both companies and individuals) had not been allowed to own land; thus the sugar mills had to "rent" (in some form) from the peasants. These compulsory rentals were resented, and frequent conflicts erupted over the rental rate, which was generally not sufficient to cover the opportunity cost to the peasant farmer. Farmers always strove to minimize the quality and quantity of land rented to the mills and to delay the turnover of control.

Although the rental system continued after independence, systems of greater freedom for peasants were increasingly considered. Such systems, it was hoped, might increase the managerial and farming skills of the peasants. Below we discuss four systems practiced from 1957 to 1975 and cite the problems of each.

Postwar Systems

As the old rental system continued, villagers leased their land for a fixed period, with rent prepaid in cash. The amount was decided by the Minister of Agriculture, in consultation with mill managers and with farmers' representatives. Rental rates changed slowly and did not keep up with inflation. They were set for large production areas without regard to fertility, water supply, and distance. Thus rental incomes lagged behind what might have been earned on wet rice and other crops. Sometimes the farm family could sell its labor elsewhere for extra income, but such opportunities were limited. Because of the lag in land rents (Table 1), farmers would submit to leasing only under continued compulsion.

Second, under the "farmers' sugar cane crop system," peasants planted cane on their own land but had a choice between selling to the government refining mill or to local traditional mills producing brown sugar. With help from Farmers' Sugar Cane Cooperatives, they would sign sale contracts, usually before land preparation. These frequently specified that the mill would help supervise the planting and would provide certain

*This section relies heavily on Gunawan (1977).

294

Table 15.1

COMPARATIVE RETURNS BETWEEN WET RICE AND SUGAR
LAND RENT, 1967–74

	Net Value of 2 Crops Wet Rice (rupiah/ha)	Sugar Cane Land Rent for 16 Months (rupiah/ha)
1967	22,028	15,000
1968	72,276	17,500
1970	85,200	60,000
1972	120,107	80,000
1974	210,471	185,000

SOURCE: Gunawan (1977:15, Table 1.3). Since the mid-1970s, it has been possible to get at least three wet rice crops from the land over a sixteen-month period; hence the advantages of rice over sugar are even greater than shown in this table.

inputs and working capital. This tended to keep production high and reliable for the mills. At the end of the crushing season, the farmers received 50% of their output in kind, from which they had to repay the mill for various expenses.

With this system, farmers appeared more willing to devote land to cane, partly because payment in kind was a hedge against severe inflation. The mills for their part were assured of cane without having to attend to cultivation, harvesting, or delivery. But the cane was usually inferior to that grown by the mills on rented land.

Third, a "sharecropping" system known as SK.4/1963, designed to resist inflation through partial payment in kind, was really a modification of the rental system. Farmers received 25% of the sugar produced on their land, of which 60% was paid in three installments: at lease time, when they needed cash for other cropping operations, and after harvest. Farmers might choose to work the mills' assembled lands for wages, thus getting supervised training.

Because of partial payment in cash, the system did not fully compensate for inflation. Furthermore, the farmers had no say in determining the shares paid to them, and they could not verify the production figures. For the mills, the multiple-part payment scheme meant bookkeeping complexities and problems based on the government's policy of keeping basic food prices low.

Fourth, under true sharecropping—labeled SK.3—each landowner did all cultivation, harvesting, and delivery, in exchange for 60% of the value: 12% in kind and 48% in cash. In these areas, cooperatives provided technical assistance to farmers and useful liaisons for mills. But because the cooperatives lacked technical expertise and sufficient financing, they often called on the mills for help. This resulted in a diffusion of authority over field operations, as well as confusion and resentment.

The characteristics of these four systems are summarized in Table 2.

Problems of Sugar Production and Land Tenure: 1957–75

By the late sixties, the sugar industry was in trouble. Total production and yield per hectare had fallen to less than half their pre-war levels. Java was able to meet only about two-thirds of Indonesia's demand for refined sugar. The nationalized industry incurred large losses in 1967 and 1968 (Mubyarto 1969:37).

The main problem was a steep decline in the yields of both the lands owned by the mills and those rented from smallholders. Mubyarto (1969:38) attributes this to the poor return provided farmers for committing their land to cane which, in turn, was partly caused by the government policies of keeping the retail price of sugar low and taxing sugar heavily. In addition, the lack of managerial skills following the Dutch departure still plagued the industry. Table 3 shows the long-term trends.

Since independence in 1957, refined sugar has been classified as a "basic commodity," the prices of which have been controlled at levels considerably below equilibrium market prices. Thus the price of sugar paid by the government logistics agency to the mills was kept low; in turn, the mills were forced to limit the rentals they could pay farmers. Thus compulsion had to be exerted to get the farmers to put their best lands into the program.

Not only are retail prices fixed low, but sugar is heavily taxed—a strange carryover from the Dutch, who tried to *raise* the domestic price to discourage consumption so there would be more for export. The taxes (imposed at the mill) depress further the prices that can be paid the farmers. There are also certain "funds" to which the mills must contribute according to their production. The names of the funds are shown in Table 4, but their purpose and disposition have not been clarified in the literature. Table 4 shows that all these add-ons constituted a large part of the total "production" costs.

While our information happens to be for 1966, that year was not necessarily typical. In 1967 and 1968, contributions to the "funds" diminished noticeably. Marketing costs were steady, however, for these arrangements were highly centralized under a General Management Board that built up a huge bureaucratic superstructure, which absorbed a large part of the proceeds (Table 4).

Because many of the farmers were compelled to rent land to the mills, they also began certain tactics to reduce their losses. Whole villages would allot only their poorest lands to the mills. They also offered scattered plots rather than contiguous sections, as had been enforced in the past. Farmers

296

Table 15.2
Four Systems of Sugar Cane Growing on Farmer-Owned Lands in Java

Characteristic	Regular Rental System	Farmers' Sugar Cane Crop System	Share-cropping SK.4	Share-cropping SK.3
1. Control of land	mill	farmer	mill	farmer
2. Planting and harvesting	mill	farmer and co-op	mill	farmer and co-op
3. Form of rent or payment	cash	sugar @ 50% output	75% sugar 25% cash	40% sugar 60% cash
4. Role of local government in obtaining land	great	little	great	little
5. Role of farmer	passive	active	passive	active
6. Role of co-op	none	great	none	great
7. Opportunity to develop farmer skills	small	great	small	great

SOURCE: Gunawan (1977:108, Table 3).

Table 15.3
INDONESIAN SUGAR TRENDS, 1928–75

Year	Area (000 ha)	Production of Sugar (000 tons)	Sugar Yield (tons/ha)
1928	194.9	2,923	15.0
1932	171.6	2,560	14.9
1935	29.5	509	17.3
1937	85.7	1,379	16.0
1940	91.8	1,583	17.2
1958	76.2	728	9.5
1960	72.7	652	8.9
1966	79.5	601	7.5
1970	81.7	713	8.7
1975	82.9	890	10.8

SOURCES: Mubyarto (1969:41, Table 1); Mubyarto (1977:31, Table 2).

also delayed the delivery of land, to get in one more non-cane crop; because of this, the cane would frequently miss the optimal initial growing period.

By the early seventies, it had become necessary to restore incentives to growers and mills alike. Mubyarto (1969:58) felt the most important step would be greater decentralization of decisionmaking, with autonomy to individual mills in rental-purchase policies and marketing. This was attempted through a big change in sugar policy in 1975, which seems in retrospect to have been a natural evolution from earlier policies, although it startled observers at the time. It is called the Tebu Rakyat Intensificasi Program (intensified smallholder cane program, or TRI).

The TRI Program*

TRI was established by a Presidential Instruction (Inpres 9/1975) of April 1975. Specifically, its objectives were: (1) to raise the total production of sugar; and (2) to get rid of the rental system in favor of one that would allow the smallholder to manage his own affairs. Since smallholder productivity has, on average, been lower than that of land fully managed by the mills, these objectives were quickly seen to conflict.

To offset the likely decrease in production per hectare, the area under cultivation was to be increased substantially, while cultivation was being intensified through better rootstock, fertilizers and pesticides, to be pro-

*This section relies heavily on Brown (1982) and Mubyarto (1981).

298

Table 15.4
COMPONENTS OF THE RETAIL PRICE OF REFINED SUGAR, KEBON AGUNG MILL, DECEMBER 1966

		Rupiah/100 kg.	Percentage
1. Cost of production ex-mill		465	27
2. Contributions to funds:			
Development	150		
Rehabilitation	75		
Special	155		
Management fee	65		
Estates department	10		
		455	26
3. Taxes:			
(a) excise (19% on 1 + 2)			
(b) sales (20% on 1, 2, and 3a)	294	17	
4. Bags		80	5
Selling price ex-mill		1,294	
5. Marketing and distribution		431	25
Retail price		1,725	100

SOURCE: Mubyarto (1969:49, Table 5).

vided by the mills to the smallholders. The mills were also to advise on farming techniques while they took responsibility for cutting and transporting the cane. Funding of these inputs was to come from credits extended to the smallholder through the rural credit bank, Bank Rakyat Indonesia (BRI), to be repaid out of cash received after crushing was complete.

Somehow it was hoped that long-standing conflicts between mills and smallholders would be reduced under this system. However, one of the old practices under the rental system was to be retained and even expanded: administrative determination of which lands were to be planted with cane. Farmers were given no voice.

To make the system seem attractive to the smallholders and the public, overly optimistic, biased farm budgets were projected. Table 5 shows one of these projections.

If this promise could be achieved, smallholders would be much better off under the program, and their complaints could be expected to stop.

The area cultivated by smallholders increased steadily, 1975–80, under the TRI program, although the percentage increase in cane output was only half that of the acreage increase, while the increase in sugar production was only half again. These are shown in Table 6.

The lower increase in sugar output and the overall drop in output per hectare are partly due to the decreasing quality of land being planted at the margin, the lack of technical cropping skills by the farmers, and an apparent failure of the mills to advise farmers to the degree required. On the positive side, mills have been able to operate more closely to their design capacity than in earlier years.

Table 15.5

NET RETURNS ON VARIOUS CROPS CALCULATED UNDER ASSUMED CONDITIONS OF THE TRI PROGRAM AT A LOCATION IN CENTRAL JAVA

	Rupiah/ha
1. Farmers' sugar cane	418,000
2. Two wet rice crops plus one peanut crop	227,997
3. Two wet rice crops plus one soybean crop	221,357
4. Two wet rice crops plus one maize crop	205,780

SOURCE: Gunawan (1977:121, Table 3.8). Data originally from Djamasri and Hussein (1975:275–76).

NOTE: In 1975 (approximate year of these estimates), the market rate for the rupiah was 415.00 to the dollar. Therefore, the return on sugar cane was predicted at something above $1,000 per hectare.

Table 15.6
SUGAR PRODUCTION, 1975–80

	Area Harvested (000 ha)	Sugar Production (000 tons)	Sugar per Hectare (tons)
Java smallholders			
1975	21.5	128.4	6.0
1976	31.3	204.7	6.6
1977	50.1	392.5	7.9
1978	78.4	522.8	7.1
1979	104.4	755.0	7.2
1980	131.9	903.0	6.8
All Indonesia			
1975	104.8	1,023.4	9.8
1976	116.1	1,061.1	9.1
1977	124.4	1,124.4	9.0
1978	148.2	1,288.6	7.7
1979	178.1	1,288.6	7.2
1980	188.6	1,250.0	6.6

SOURCE: Brown (1982:42, Table 1).

Continuing Mill-Smallholder Conflicts

Yet conflicts continued between mill and smallholder, the main ones being over time and method of cutting. These activities, along with speedy processing, are crucial in determining the sugar yield. If cane is cut at twelve months, its sugar content is likely to be 10% or 12%, while at sixteen months it will yield 14% to 15%. Since most of the sugar content is in the lower part of the stalk, too high cutting will waste large amounts of sugar. After cutting, processing delays of more than forty-eight hours will substantially reduce the yield.

Because the mills determine when the harvest is to take place and then cut the cane and transport it for processing, individual villages feel they have been treated unfairly in the mills' harvesting decisions. There have been frequent complaints of favoritism; there is even a consensus that some areas are favored over others. The author knows of mills that have simply refused to buy cane because of plant overload or equipment failure. When the farmers lack alternative outlets for sale, these refusals can deprive them of their livelihood. During the extended May-December drought of 1982 in Central Java, one could see large areas of uncut dry cane that was later burned.

Taxation and the Smallholder

TRI farmers continue to be taxed more highly than those producing other crops. Sugar taxes averaged 15% of the ex-mill price through 1979, while those on rice production averaged only 1.9% of its value. Under current conditions heavy excise taxes seemed unjustified, since the producers affected are no longer wealthy foreign-owned companies, but Javanese smallholders.

Rattooning

One of the first things to strike a new observer of Javanese sugar culture is that rattooning (taking a second or third cutting before replanting) is almost never practiced. In other large sugar areas, such as Brazil and Hawaii, a second cut is always taken. Once cane has been cut, only about twelve months are needed for it to grow again to harvest maturity. Since the heavy investment of materials and labor has already been made in the original land preparation and planting, very little added work is needed to grow the rattoon crop. And although the sugar content declines on second and later cutting, most sugar-growing areas find the rattoon crop very profitable.

In the absence of rattooning, heavy labor costs of *two* land conversions are incurred for each crop: one from paddy to cane field and the other back again. Anyone who has watched this process carried out manually can attest to the labor involved.

The landowner would rattoon in many areas if he perceived it to be in his interest. In some places, poor drainage and plant disease prevent rattooning, but in most cases, we infer that the typical farmer is so unfavored in sugar that he wants to get out of it as quickly as possible, and go back to rice or other traditional crops.

Impact of the TRI Program on Smallholders

> Through implementaion of the TRI program, sugar production has been increased and the transfer of cane production from the mills to the smallholders largely completed. To the extent that these were among the Government's goals in establishing the program, it has been successful. But these successes must be measured against the costs of the program, *especially those borne by the smallholders.* It is not at all clear that farmers' incomes have risen as a consequence of their involvement with the program; indeed, there is evidence that at least until 1981, many farmers suffered a decline in income attributable to the program. . . . The experience of the first five years of the TRI program shows that individual *smallholders have frequently not received the full benefits of the program* to which they are entitled (Brown 1982:59, emphasis added).

An exhaustive study undertaken by the Faculty of Agriculture of Gadja Mada University in 1966–67 shows that out of the fifty-five sugar-producing regions of Java, in only four areas did the farmers believe that cane was the most profitable crop. Various newspaper accounts support this belief. In Cirebon, West Java, during the 1978–79 season, TRI farmers averaged a net income of rupiah (Rp) 350,000/ha for the sixteen-month season. Growing rice, they could have netted Rp 500,000/ha for a five-month season. In Lumajang, East Java—a showplace of TRI cultivation—farmers netted just over Rp 500,000/ha from cane, while they could have netted Rp 675,000/ha from local varieties of rice and Rp 1,350,000/ha from high-yielding rice varieties. In Bantul, Central Java, farmers cleared an average of Rp 480,000/ha/year compared with Rp 900,000/ha/year growing a highly favored variety of local rice.

Table 5 shows the intended *higher* profitability of cane under the TRI program, but from the data of the preceding paragraph we infer that only compulsion is keeping many smallholders in sugar cane. What happened?

The intention of the program was that the farmer would promptly receive the full cash proceeds from his cane after crushing and would be aided through credit by Bank Rakyat Indonesia. These transactions were to be facilitated by the village cooperative unit (Kooperasi Unit Desa, KUD) and by the smaller farmers' groups (kelompok tani) that had to coordinate the areas and operations of the individual farmers. The effectiveness of these groups in aiding the farmer depends on the groups' leadership.

The directors of KUDs are appointed by the provincial and district governments. They manage the distribution of root stock, fertilizer, and pesticides. The head (*ketua*) of the farmers' groups is supposed to be a local farmer elected by his fellows. However, very often the village head (*lurah*) has become the *ketua*. Even if the village head is close to his constituency, he may be pressured by higher officials and the mills.

Thus, the leadership of those groups intended to assist the local farmers is frequently assumed by persons not sharing the farmers' interests. The KUD official and the *ketua kelompok* are in positions to skim large benefits intended for the farmers. Through the control of inputs, especially credit, and of the sugar proceeds back to the farmer, these officials channel large sums into personal coffers. They frequently divert all the bank credit intended for the farmers into investments in small businesses or to the purchase of farmland. But the farmer still is the one who is responsible for successful cultivation:

> . . . Some farmers seem to have been reduced to the status of wage labourers on their own land, hired by the ketua kelompok and paid with TRI credit originally intended for them. In such cases, the ketua kelompok has taken on the functions of a contractor, managing the cane cultivation and enjoying the main benefits from it, but at minimal risk or cost to himself (Brown 1982:51).

Conclusion

The TRI program of 1975 was intended to place more responsibility on the small farmer, while providing him greater returns, better inputs, and adequate credit for the sixteen-to-eighteen-month growing period. But the program was made compulsory: farmers are required to devote part of their land to cane growing. Even if their returns drop below what they could earn on other crops, they cannot drop out of the program.

The organizations that were to have worked on the farmers' behalf, the village cooperative unit and the farmers' group have fallen under the control of the village heads and wealthier landowners who are able to divert inputs, credit, and income from the farmers to themselves. Given the hierarchical structure of Javanese society and the willingness of the lower social strata to accept their fates stoically, this form of exploitation continues almost without protest.

References

Brown, Colin, 1982. "The Intensified Smallholder Cane Program: The First Five Years," *Bulletin of Indonesian Economic Studies*, vol. 18, no. 1, March.

Djamasri, Adenan, and Hussein, M., 1975. "Kemungkinan Keprassan dan Perluasan Potensiil Terhadap Supply Tebu di PG Pesantren," in Proceedings of Seminar Tebu Rakyat.

Geertz, Clifford, 1963. *Agricultural Involution: The Process of Ecological Change in Indonesia*, Berkeley, University of California Press.

Gunawan, Sumodiningrat, 1977. "Prospect of Sugar Industry in Indonesia," Master's thesis (English language), Thammasat University, Bangkok, Thailand, July.

Mubyarto, 1969. "The Sugar Industry," *Bulletin of Indonesian Economic Studies*, vol. 5, no. 2, July.

Mubyarto, 1977. "The Sugar Industry: From Estate to Smallholder Cane Production?" *Bulletin of Indonesian Economic Studies*, vol. 13, no. 2, July.

Mubyarto, 1981. "Tebut Rakyat Intensivikasi: Prospek dan Masalahnya," *Prisma*, vol. 10, October.

16. El Salvador

Amid passions, distortions, insufficient information, and violence, the world renders judgments—differing vastly one from another—on the land reform in El Salvador. Our format for the present chapter will be different from that of previous ones, for two reasons. First, the Salvadoran reform has been conducted in the midst of a war. Judgments must be more tenuous, partly because data are missing and partly because the experience has been recent. Yet we see some of the characteristics of reforms in earlier chapters developing in El Salvador despite these qualifications. Second, we turn attention not only to the reform but to its supporters and its critics, whose arguments, we believe, influence how land reforms are shaped, probably more than economic logic does. Critics on both sides emerge as paternalistic, so sure of their own judgments that the peasants need not be consulted. We summarize our conclusions as follows:

The deficiencies of the land reform in El Salvador are similar to those of other countries where reform is undertaken in an authoritarian, centralized manner: bureaucrats do not know how to farm, yet they co-opt decisions as if they did; the government monopolizes credit although it does not know how to ration it well and is financially unable to disburse it well; the state distorts the input and output markets by its control over prices, buying, and selling; above all, civil servants are corrupt.

Furthermore, critics of the Salvadoran reform, whether pro or con, tend to judge it not in terms of the deficiences just mentioned (or similar ones), but with reference to some form that exists in their imaginations. We know of none—other than ourselves—who criticize the Salvadoran reform with reference to other reforms already undertaken. Is this reform somehow better or worse than others, or is it just par for the course?

Finally, most critics judge the reform in the light of their political ideologies. If the critic is sympathetic to the guerrillas or to Marxism, then the reform is judged harshly. Some critics believe failures were premeditated: the government feigned a reform it did not want, just to forestall a "true" revolution. (We do not believe the government is well enough organized for such fine-tuning). On the other hand, if the critic favors the government, then the reform is praised, and it "would have worked" had it not been for the war. We believe the reform should be judged on standard criteria, apart from one's ideology and, as far as possible, apart from the war. We try to do that in this chapter.

Sources of Information

The war makes our sources of information scarcer and less reliable. The usual reporting agencies cannot cover agricultural output in military zones. Observers selectively perceive what promotes their ideologies. But even ideological reporters sometimes tell the truth, and when truth is scarce, we seek all sources. Therefore, we are hard put to decide what is true and what is fancy. We divide our information into four groups.

First, information from the governments of El Salvador and the United States (except the Inspector General) is biased in favor of the reform. In the same class are reports of the American Institute of Free Labor Development (AIFLD) and its consultants and staff who helped prepare the reform and therefore have a stake in it. Much of the information from these sources we take as true but selectively perceived. We are also skeptical of the judgments of these observers.

Second, information from ideological critics is highly charged and selectively perceived (on the opposite side from the governments and AIFLD), but some of it may be true. Here, however, observers report on what they have seen and been told or what they have *felt*; they tend to believe that their experiences and their inspirations reflect the generality. If they are told that peasants favor the reform, or if those whom they meet favor it, or if they *feel* the peasants should favor the reform, they report categorically that peasants do favor the reform. Nevertheless, these sources contain some elements of truth, which may be founded through careful sifting. Among these sources we include the EPICA task force, Oxfam, and the American Friends Service Committee.

Third, we take *The New York Times, The Washington Post, The Wall Street Journal,* and *Latin American Newsletters* (London) as largely unbiased but anecdotal sources. Our belief in their lack of bias stems from two observations: (1) our interviews with ideological critics reveal that each side believes these media are biased in favor of the other; and (2) the editorial positions taken by these media criticize the government and the rebels indiscriminately (with the possible exception of *Latin American Newsletters,* which appears more inclined to criticize the government than the rebels). Anecdotes in these sources, for example concerning visits to peasant cooperatives, have a ring of truth in that they represent the reform as not all evil nor all good, but beset by problems and violence.

Fourth, we rely heavily on the Inspector General of the United States (hereafter IG), who examined all aspects of the reform on the site, taking reasonable samples and seeking information according to usual (statistical or auditing) procedures, and whose report is critical in ways the governments have not admitted. In brief, instead of a political bias in favor of its own government, the report bears a stamp of independent professionalism found in none of our other sources.

The information and judgments in the rest of this chapter represent the best "truth" we can find, under very difficult circumstances.

Background

El Salvador's political crisis took root a century ago. In March 1980 the government ruled that all *ejido* land should become private property. Laws enacted during that decade, at the time of the great international coffee boom, suppressed communal land ownership and paved the way for concentration of land in the hands of the '14 families.' Peasants were evicted to work on the large estates, and a rural police force was created to make sure they did so (LARR 3/21/80:5).*

Even earlier than a century ago, land use was inequitably distributed in El Salvador as in all of Central America: *ejido* communal property was subject to rule by tribal elders, and Spanish haciendas were encroaching upon Indian lands. We must, in fact, go back to the time when lands were abundant before we find any semblance of free occupation or equitable distribution, and those times—centuries ago—are not well recorded by historians.

Continued evictions of peasants, poor working conditions, and increased concentration of land ownership in the late nineteenth and early twentieth centuries led to a rural rebellion in 1932, in which 10,000 to 30,000 peasants died (different observers guess different numbers). Following this revolt, the government established a land reform agency, whose purpose was to buy land for distribution to peasants and to colonize the outer areas. From then until 1975, some 67,000 hectares were acquired (IG 1984:1), of which 80% was adjudicated to 10,700 families.

Despite these attempts, the 1950 census reported that "slightly more than 1% of the *farms* occupied one-half of the farm land, while 80% had less than 5 hectares and 94% had less than 20 hectares" (IDB 1961:114–5). Some attempts at colonization, made by the *Instituto de Colonización Rural* in the fifties and sixties, were thwarted by the small size of the country, poor lands in outlying areas, and high population density. The rural landless labor force grew from 30,000 in 1961 to 166,000 in 1975, or from 11% to 40% of all peasants (LARR 3/21/80:5). In 1975, the government created the Institute of Agrarian Transformation (ISTA) to provide land, technical assistance, and credit, and in other ways to increase farm productivity. This same institute administers the land reform today.

In October 1979, a group of young officers, after overthrowing the

---

*The number "14" is traditional; it refers to the small number of élite landowners who presumably "run" the country. The actual number of families may differ, and the degree to which they "run" the country depends on definition.

military government, declared land reform to be their major plank. They instituted the reform in March 1980. By then, however, the country had been plunged into civil war.

The Reform of 1980

In January 1980, the government of El Salvador appointed Rodolfo Viera, secretary general of the *Unión Comunal Salvadoreña*, the largest organization of peasant farmers, to head ISTA and therefore to direct the land reform it was already planning. In his work with the peasant union, Viera had come to respect AIFLD, which had provided technical assistance on labor organization; he therefore requested that AIFLD be appointed as technical advisor to the land reform. (Critics have argued that this appointment was an indication of lack of sincerity in reform, since AIFLD had no prior expertise in this field.) AIFLD in turn appointed Roy Prosterman, professor of law at the University of Washington, and Michael Hammer of the AIFLD staff, as consultants. (Viera and Hammer, together with Mark David Pearlman, another U.S. consultant, were assassinated in January 1981.) With this assistance, ISTA drew up the reform proposals, which—with financial help from the United States (through the Agency for International Development, AID)—were enacted into law by Decrees 153 and 154, dated March 5, 1980.

The reform was intended to be implemented in three phases. In Phase I, all farm lands over 500 hectares would be expropriated from about 200 families and organized into cooperatives, to be farmed primarily by the peasants already working on them, but outsiders would also be assigned. Compensation to landowners would be made in interest-bearing bonds, but some small holdings would be reimbursed in cash (Gist, 11/80). The expropriations were begun on March 6. At the same time, the government took 50% of the stock of local financial institutions. Covering the expropriation of one hacienda (Los Logartos), *The New York Times* reported (3/10/80):

> The peasants, some still carrying their machetes, others accompanied by their wives and children, were stunned. Many had lived and worked here for decades and could not grasp the enormous significance of the announcement. "Will we get paid next week?" José Fuentes Beltrán, a 73-year-old peasant, asked nervously.

In Phase II, farms of 100 to 500 hectares were to be expropriated and also placed into cooperatives. The owners of this size group, rather than those of the large estates, turned out to have the most political clout, and they were able to postpone this phase continually, until it was repealed in June 1984.

In Phase III, tenants on farms less than 100 hectares would become owners of the lands they tilled, up to a maximum of 7 hectares each. If a tenant held more than 7 hectares, he would continue to farm all the land until the harvest; thereafter the excess land would be assigned to another beneficiary.

Progress of the Reform

Phase I: Peasant Cooperatives on Large Farms

By June 1980, all farms larger than 500 hectares, numbering about 376 and covering about 224,000 hectares, had been seized by the government and converted into peasant cooperatives. *The New York Times* (3/7/80) reported that these farms represented "60% of the country's best farmland." This land included the most fertile and most productive—although it also included less fertile land—but we do not know the *Times'* definition of "best," without which the figure 60% means little. Substituting for owners, government technicians urged the peasants to continue to work normally.

Writing for Oxfam, Simon and Stephens (1981:32) reported that the beneficiaries included two classes: employees (managers, clerical workers, tractor drivers, etc.) and *colonos* (peasants living on the land), the latter far more numerous than the former. But Oxfam, in apparent expectation of total democracy with executive positions held by the humblest, criticized the cooperatives for being administered by the former managers, even though the *colonos* had in fact elected them. It is because of statements like this that we believe Oxfam criticizes the government for failing to achieve an idealized rather than a practicable reform.

By the fall of 1982, the dream had begun to fade. Reporting (anecdotally) on El Parajal, a cotton farm, *The Wall Street Journal* (9/1/82) stated:

> The peasants can't get enough credit from the bank, and production has fallen by half in the past two years. Last year the co-op lost $60,000. Wages have been slashed 50%, and Mr. Rezinos [one of the peasants interviewed] says it is getting harder and harder to feed his five children.

The same issue of *The Wall Street Journal* goes on to report that many cooperatives are bogged in bureaucratic mire, and there are right-wing officials who do not want the reform to succeed. Elements of mismanagement that might be expected under sudden-change conditions include cooperative managers' being duped by farm-supply companies, missed planting dates, and starving livestock. *The Wall Street Journal* also reports that forty cooperatives in areas occupied by guerrillas cannot be farmed at all, although we wonder how they know this. In the same article, the United States Embassy is reported as saying that out of 328 cooperatives, ninety-five are solvent, ninety-five more have problems that may be resolved, while another ninety-five are "beyond hope." A member of El Angel cooperative reported that guerrillas had burned 40% of the previous year's sugar crop, with a loss of $320,000.

Yet optimism was also expressed in some quarters. One peasant stated: "We know we can make it if they'll just leave us alone." A similar statement will be found coming from a Turkish peasant except that for him "they" referred to the government; here the guerrillas are cited.

Almost a year later, *The New York Times* (7/3/83) reported that many Phase I cooperatives were not receiving credit on time; that low prices for output and lack of technical assistance were blamed for the fact that only one-third of the cooperatives were profitable. In many cases, the former owners had burned or removed the farm equipment. Other sources say that equipment was frequently sold in Guatemala or Honduras, and the cooperatives had had to start from scratch.

In January 1984 IG (1984:8) reported that:

> Most Phase I cooperatives are not producing sufficient income to be viable organizations. Income is deficient in part due to the poor quality of lands and excessive membership in the cooperatives. Most Phase I cooperatives have little chance to recover on their own.

IG found that neither AID nor ISTA possessed a complete listing of cooperatives; that the cooperatives had been "structured without fully considering the basic ingredients necessary for profit-making productive enterprises"; and that "many Phase I cooperatives had (1) massive capital debt, (2) no working capital, (3) large tracts of land that were nonproductive, (4) substantially larger labor forces than needed to operate the units, and (5) weak management" (IG 1984:13).

Poor quality land may surprise those who have been led by the media to believe that the most fertile land of El Salvador was encompassed in these expropriations. The media were right, but the expropriated farms *also* contained much land of poor agricultural quality. El Salvador is a mountainous country, and good land is intermixed with poor. In 1974, the Organization of American States took a census of El Salvador's land resources (cited in IG 1984:19), placing them into seven standard classes according to quality: I, II, and III suitable for intensive crops (383,645 hectares); IV good for limited cultivation (128,410 hectares); and V, VI, and VII difficult because of steepness, erosion, and rocks (1,189,975 hectares) (but VI, with 385,000 hectares, acceptable for forestry). IG (1984:21) reported that in seventeen cooperatives studied, 43% of the land (4,439 out of 10,341 hectares) was nonproductive.

Decree 153 (to set up the reform on March 5, 1980) had stipulated that "preference was to be given to those peasants who earned all or part of their incomes from the property prior to the reform" (IG 1984:23). Nevertheless, in its zeal to find land and occupation for as many peasants as possible, ISTA apparently brought in peasants from elsewhere as well, placing far more on the cooperatives than had worked the same lands earlier or than the lands could reasonably support. IG further reported that in one such cooperative (La Labor), the previous owner had maintained approximately 2,000 full-time employees to operate three farms with a total of about 5,100 hectares. After the reform, one of these farms alone was formed into a cooperative with 2,100 members for only 2,300 hectares. As a result, most members would work only two or three days a week. Even though each of these farmers earned less than in pre-reform days, the cooperative was running at a loss. It simply could not support that number of employees.

By February 1984, *The New York Times* was reporting (2/5/84) that large expanses of farmland had been abandoned, and that about $1 billion of funds had been taken from the country since the land reform began.

In addition to problems of finance and excessive membership, IG listed the following areas of weakness: lack of capable managers; lack of technical assistance; state of the worldwide economy; low productivity; the civil war; and lack of institutional capability.

Phase II: Middle-Sized Farms

Uncertainty over Phase II was felt early in the reform. *The New York Times* reported (3/15/81) that owners were delaying investment because of fear of expropriation, and that agricultural output was harmed thereby. In May 1982 Phase II was suspended for one year by the Constituent Assembly elected in March (NYT, 5/24/82). Membership in this Assembly was split (thirty seats held by right-wing parties led by Roberto d'Aubuisson, and thirty by the Christian Democrats). With some pressure from the United States, in April the Assembly elected Christian Democrat Alvaro Alfredo Magaña as provisional president. Although the Christian Democrats had asked President Magaña to veto the legislation suspending Phase II, he did not do so. Members of the Assembly argued that El Salvador needed grain production critically at this time, and the risk of interruption through change in ownership of the large number of middle-sized farms was too great. Other observers have suggested that this middle group of landowners—by sheer numbers—was now more politically powerful than the "14 families," and their opposition swung the vote. Some tenants on these farms told reporters that they believed the Assembly merely suspended Phase II instead of annulling it, because the government feared a cutoff of American aid. Nevertheless, Phase II was aborted by the Assembly in June 1984.

The election of the Constituent Assembly marked a swing to the right, and landowners found more basis for opposing government reforms. In September, a leader of the peasants' union reported to *The New York Times* (9/25/82):

> The real problem is that we have two governments: the President and the Armed Forces, which support the reform, and the Constituent Assembly, which is not interested, dominated by the right wing and the oligarchs.

311

Phase III: Small Farms

Phase III, or "land-to-the-tiller," was put into effect by Decree 207 of April 28, 1980. This decree provided that all tenants of lands less than 100 hectares were now the owners of 7 hectares and might cease to pay rent. Specification of properties and adjudication of titles would follow in due course. The suddenness with which the decree was announced, only one month after Phase I, surprised most observers; it was generally taken as a dramatic response to the guerrillas. A year later, Prosterman (AIFLD consultant et al. 1981:37) waxed enthusiastic over Phase III:

> Almost overnight, more than two-thirds of the landless peasants received the land they were tilling—44 percent of the nation's cropland. Over one million acres, previously owned by 7,000 mostly absentee families, are now owned and operated by those farms' 210,000 peasant families—one and a quarter million peasants. . . . All of the country's 150,000 farm tenant and sharecropper families, on whatever size farm, are now legally the owners of their previously rented land. They have eaten or sold their first harvest and are growing their second.

If these authors really meant to convey the idea of the above paragraph, their naïveté is astounding. Experienced observers would suspect that nowhere in the Third World would such a massive transformation occur so quickly and so smoothly as is implied. In fact, several realities stood in the way. First, the land had to be surveyed and titled. When families were tilling more than 7 hectares, the excess had to be adjudicated to truly landless families. (Which ones?) Second, peasants had to apply for provisional titles, which would be held while they awaited final titles. In fact, many peasants hesitated to apply, fearful that the law would not be enforced and that, instead of receiving land, they would be evicted by former owners.

These fears were quickly realized. President Magaña wanted to exempt cotton and sugar land from Phase III, for fear a land transformation would reduce output of export crops. The Constituent Assembly added grain and cattle to this exemption (WSJ, 9/1/82). As rumor spread that the reform was over, former owners attempted to evict peasants, sometimes employing thugs or private armies to do so. In January 1983, *The New York Times* (1/22/83) reported that 4,791 such peasants had been evicted in the last three months.

By March 1983, about 50,000 peasants had filled 63,000 applications for Phase III land, for which about 35,000 provisional titles had been received (NYT, 3/2/83). IG (1984:25) reported that those who were actually working the land "were in a position to substantially improve their economic and social positions" (although no data were given). At the same time, IG pointed out that approximately 50,000 of the 117,000 eligible peasants had not filed applications. "They were not working the land because they had been threatened, evicted, or had disappeared." The army, however, was trying to reinstate these peasants.

By June 1984, 62,692 peasants had received 95,500 hectares under Phase III (NYT, 6/30/84). Once again, the deadline for filing application for provisional title—often extended—was now running out. This time, despite pressure from Christian Democrats to renew once more, the Constituent Assembly voted not to extend. Further land distribution under Phase III was dead.

Credit

We know of no studies of informal credit agencies (moneylenders) for El Salvador, except that Tun Wai (1977:304) mentions their existence in 1970 with average interest rates of 25%. These sources are undoubtedly used by small farmers; however, the large farms received their credit from modern banks or abroad. When these farms were converted into cooperatives, it was not expected that the same banks would continue to offer the same credit to the same farms. Furthermore, sources of credit for small farms subject to Phase III were likely also to be disrupted.

In 1973, the government founded the Bank for Agricultural Development (BFA), to pay special attention to small farmers. IG reported that before the reform, it performed its functions well and maintained a strong capital position. We infer this to mean simply that it was in sound financial condition, not that it played a major role in getting credit to small farmers at less than the informal rates. With the land reform, however, IG (1984:28) reported that

> demands for credit expanded enormously. From December 1979 to September 1982, BFA's loan portfolio increased from $56 million to $176.4 million, over a threefold increase. This increase in lending activities strained the Bank's resources causing high operating costs, low rates of recuperation, and inadequate loan supervision. As a result, BFA's financial condition was precarious. The delivery and supervision of agricultural credit to the Bank's agrarian reform clients was less than satisfactory. It appears that the Bank's financial position improved during 1983 due to the infusion of AID funds, improved rates of loan collections, and actions by the Government of El Salvador. The Bank's financial position, however, still is a matter of concern.

IG (1984:29–32) found three main deficiences in the credit system: high operating costs, poor rate of loan recuperation, and weak accounting controls.

High Operating Costs

By diverting demands for credit from the former sources (private internal and external), as well as by promising more credit from the formal sector than was heretofore available, the agrarian reform generated an

313

enormous demand on BFA. As a result, its administrative costs rose by about 43% (from $6.2 million to $8.4 million) from 1980 to the end of 1983, while financial costs rose by about 250% (from $3 million to $10.6 million). To meet the increased demand, it had to borrow from the Central Bank, at high cost because of the Central Bank's efforts to control inflation. Thus the cost for BFA to borrow on short term increased ninefold, from $1.1 million in 1978 to $10.6 million in 1981; net losses from banking operations increased from $1.1 million to $3.5 million in the same period.

Loan Recuperation

In 1980, the loan recuperation rate was only 40%. On September 30, 1982, $22.9 million (about 18%) of its outstanding loans of $128.7 billion were more than one year overdue. Since BFA does not carry a reserve for bad debts or write off delinquent loans, IG estimated that its equity capital was overstated by $48.4 million.

Accounting Controls

IG also reported that BFA did not possess a uniform accounting system or internal auditing controls, which would be essential for determining that funds had not been used irregularly. Its data processing system was judged obsolete, producing "such untimely and inaccurate results that it had no management utility." Finally, IG found that approximately $1.4 million of AID funds had been used in an unauthorized manner, and it recommended (naively, perhaps) that the AID office in El Salvador take immediate steps to recover them.

Effect on Output

Some reports, during the first year of reform, showed that output and wages might have increased on Phase I cooperatives. Wages on the El Peñón cooperative jumped from $1 to $3 per day (NYT, 1/15/81) and in Los Lagartos from $2.08 to $2.40 for men and from $1.86 to $2.08 for women (NYT, 3/16/81). Basic medical care and tortillas continued to be free, as they had been before the reform. Of course, newspaper reports are anecdotal; investigations on individual farms may or may not reflect the generality for all farms. However, we believe this information is reliable for the farms concerned. But it is not clear that wages were increased because the farms could afford to pay more.

In February 1982, the Washington-based consulting firm Checchi and Company issued a report commissioned by AID, showing that in the first year, average yields of coffee, cotton, sugar cane, rice, and beans were all higher on Phase I cooperatives than the national average (NYT, 4/19/82). The study team, directed by Don Paarlberg, a professor emeritus from Purdue and a respected agricultural economist, visited twenty-two farms in six states (NYT, 2/13/82). However, the Center for Documentation and Information at the University of Central America disputed the results, preparing its own figures which compared production before and after the reform. Selections from the two sets of data are shown in Table 1. Both studies have their deficiencies. It is always precarious to compare two single-year crop figures, as the university did, because of differences in weather, rainfall, and other chance factors. The Inter-American Development Bank (IDB) data on value added by agricultural production (Table 2) show an all-time high in 1979; the university figures therefore may have

Table 16.1

AVERAGE YIELD OF SELECTED CROPS: COMPARISON OF
CENTRAL AMERICAN UNIVERSITY AND CHECCHI STUDIES
(MILLIONS OF POUNDS)

| | University Study | | Checchi Study, 1980–81 | |
	1979–80	1980–81	National Average	Cooperative Farms
Coffee	769	749	687	750
Corn	3,156	2,952	1,598	2,901
Beans	727	662	669	661
Rice	2,489	2,711	3,186	2,722
Sugar cane	na	na	60,247	75,349
Cotton	na	na	1,767	2,008

SOURCE: NYT, 2/19/82.

Table 16.2

VALUE ADDED BY AGRICULTURE, 1975–82
(MILLIONS OF 1980 DOLLARS)

1975	842.6
1976	775.9
1977	804.1
1978	885.6
1979	904.5
1980	860.3
1981	773.2
1982	716.0

SOURCE: Years 1975–78, from IDB (1979:408). Original data were in 1978 dollars; these have been multiplied by 904.5/728.9, since IDB reported 1979 value added as 904.5 million in 1980 dollars and 728.9 million in 1978 dollars. Years 1979–82 are from IDB (1983:348).

improperly compared the first year of the reform with an extraordinary preceding year. Furthermore, bad weather did decrease the production of coffee (and possibly other crops) during the second year. On the other hand, the Checchi comparison is also dangerous. The soil and growing conditions vary greatly over El Salvador, and output deviates from region to region. Cooperative farms may have possessed more favorable conditions than the national average. We have included Table 1, not because it gives us a definitive story, but because it illustrates degrees of divergence among experts.

Prosterman et al. cite data showing that agricultural production was approximately the same in the first year after the reform as in the year before (Table 3). They do not give their source, but presumably they have used official data.

They attribute the small decline in coffee production to the weather, and the decline in cotton to the uncertainties facing Phase II farms not yet reformed, where the bulk of cotton production takes place.

Whatever may have happened during the first year on the cooperative farms, production and exports for the country as a whole declined both in the first year and thereafter.

The International Monetary Fund (IMF:IFS Supplement on Trade 1982:13) reports that total value of exports declined 12.4% from 1979 to 1980 and another 26.2% from 1980 to 1981 (data on volume not reported).

It is, of course, not possible to tell how much of the decline was due to the inefficiency of institutions, or to the administration of the land reform, or to the destruction of the war, or other causes.

The Critics

We have already seen the extravagant statement by Prosterman et al. on Phase III. The statements by the United States government and its consultants have been optimistic but sometimes cautious. Bob Dougherty, the executive secretary of AIFLD, was reported by *The New York Times* (1/6/81) as saying:

> We've changed their title from feudal serf to freeman. This is a revolutionary approach, not only in terms of numbers involved but in the way it's done. More than a million people are now individual private capitalists in a way whose only parallel is the Homestead Act in the early days of our own country.

Among the adverse critics, Oxfam (Simon and Stephens 1981) is highly perceptive in some ways, yet extremely biased in others. They declare that "the land reform program is a 'top-down' model solution imposed on the government and people of El Salvador by agencies and advisers under contract to the U.S. Government" (p. 70). Since the junta had announced the land reform before both the civil war and consultation with the United

316

Table 16.3
PRODUCTION IN EL SALVADOR, 1979–80 AND 1980–81
(THOUSANDS OF METRIC TONS)

	1979–80	1980–81
Corn	521	520
Dry beans	47	41
Rice (paddy)	57	53
Sorghum	160	162
Tobacco	3	3
Coffee	170	150
Cotton	65	34
Cotton seed	106	58
Sugar cane	2,857	2,800
Livestock (cattle)	40	40
Pork	14	14
Milk	348	350
Eggs	38	38

SOURCE: Prosterman et al. (1981:47).

States, and since AIFLD had been freely invited by Viera, who had known its performance in the past, this statement by Oxfam appears to us excessive. The true part is that the reform was paternalistic, top-down; however it was imposed not by the U.S. government but by the military junta. (Later on, as the reform was implemented, the U.S. government put pressure on the Salvadoran government not to abandon it.) In addition, Oxfam declares that "the peasantry, Church, academics, and agrarian experts of El Salvador have been excluded from the design, planning, and implementation." Our own interviews with persons close to the scene make us believe this part of the statement is also true.

While perceptive in its discovery of paternalism, the Oxfam report is naive in at least two ways. First, the authors seem unaware that with only a few exceptions, all land reforms of the twentieth century are paternalistic. Imposed by authoritarian governments, they are designed to extract the surplus from the peasantry. Why, then, did Oxfam choose to judge El Salvador instead of the many other countries available? We suspect it was because they wished to criticize the U.S. intervention. We ourselves (the authors) personally condemn the U.S. intervention, but this judgment should not be confused with a dispassionate analysis of land reform.

The Oxfam report also hints that if the reform had been undertaken in a collective (socialist?) manner, it might have been more successful. For example, in a critical tone Simon and Stephens (1981:62) report: "Land-to-the-Tiller is based on individualistic competition rather than collective cooperation—an aspect which flatly contradicts advice and concepts of the first Junta." In this brief statement, neither supported nor elaborated, they imply that socialist reforms are more successful than those based on private farmering, a hypothesis contrary to our findings in earlier chapters.

Prosterman et al. quite properly chide Oxfam (Simon and Stephens 1981) for criticizing "Prosterman's model for non-Marxist social change [as] based on the belief that humanitarian concerns and long-term U.S. interest require support for land reform through *existing* regimes":

> The real objection of Simon and Stephens to El Salvador's land reform slips out between the lines at one revealing point. Our belief that land redistribution can be carried out peacefully through existing regimes is described by them as an "idealized view" of "grass roots" democracy and social change. The implication clearly is that violent revolution alone can alter developing country agrarian structures.

Unabashedly, Marxist rhetoric appears in a report of EPICA (Wheaton 1980), which criticizes the government for undertaking a "counter-revolutionary" reform oriented toward private property. The idea that the reform is a sham undertaken to thwart a "popular" movement, but that it contains its own contradictions, is expressed in paragraphs such as the following (Wheaton 1980:13):

> A second concern in the implementation of the Agrarian Reform was the issue of public reaction to the question of private property raised by the expropriation of land. Because the Reform had the dual goals of eliminating the landed aristocracy while at the same time preventing the peasantry from joining the popular forces, the Reform could not be a charade nor restrict itself to a pilot project. The stakes were too high. Thus the Reform would have to carry out the expropriation of significant tracts of land which in turn raised the question of how far the military might go. On the one hand, the drafters of the Agrarian Reform decree didn't want to deny the philosophy of private property and thus stated from the outset: "Private property is recognized and guaranteed as a social function." On the other hand, the Decree made it quite clear that the *latifundia* system was to be replaced.

To our thinking, such imaginative and adventurous forays into the motives and thinking of others—carrying with them assumptions about the unity of purpose of the government (as if it is far more consciously directed than we believe it to be)—subtract from the credibility of such reporting. We therefore set it aside as not offering useful contributions toward understanding the land reform.

Writing for the American Friends Service Committee, Berryman (1983) states the following about the Salvadoran land reform:

318

Not only has the land reform not worked—it cannot work under the existing regime. To work it would have to provide access to land to a significant proportion of the landless rural population, and in order to do that it would have to include a much larger area of agro-export land, that is, expropriate the oligarchy's landholdings. In its present shape the land reform is little more than a public relations effort which serves to legitimate the regime in the eyes of U.S. public opinion.

Like those of Simon and Stephens and Wheaton, Berryman's judgment is not based on examples elsewhere of what land reform is likely to accomplish in its initial stages. In fact, the Salvadoran reform in its first few months had distributed far more land (in percentage of total agricultural land available) than any other land reform in Latin America, including those of Mexico in its revolution, Cuba under Castro, and Allende's Chile, and probably more than any twentieth-century land reform in the world, including the People's Republic of China. It seems to us that in Phase I, the Salvadorans did indeed "expropriate the oligarchy's holdings." The statement on not "providing land to a significant proportion of the landless rural population," unsupported by any data, therefore appears to us an improper (and at worst, untrue) impression of what might reasonably be expected of any land reform. Quite the contrary, the reform put *more* people on the cooperatives than they could logically hold. In addition, the doomsday judgment that the reform "cannot work under the existing regime" is contradicted by similar land reforms undertaken by military governments, such as that of Peru in 1968. To us, this statement of impossibility is tantamount to an endorsement of violent revolution.

Without endorsing the government's reform, we are more impressed by Singer's (1981) argument:

> . . . But they [the guerrillas] fail absolutely and utterly [to justify the war] because the violent counterrevolution of the Left began before the [government of the junta] was three months old. No one can justify starting a brutal and destructive war, resulting in thousands and thousands of deaths, and increasing the possibility of an eventual victory by the extreme Right, on the suspicion of what the revolutionary junta might do despite its promises. A minimum respect for human life would have given the new revolutionary government at least six months to see whether it would deliver on its promises of reform and democracy.

Recent Events

El Salvador's agricultural production decreased by 4.74% per capita per year during the first half of the eighties (Table 19.1). In 1986 it decreased by 3.6%, but in 1987 it increased by 2.0% (IDB 1988:408, data adjusted for population growth). Surely this sad performance is caused mainly by the war, but just as surely it is aggravated by agricultural policy and corruption. In the later eighties there are no more official reports on land awarded to peasants under Phase III, so we must conclude that these awards continue to be foraged by former owners. The cooperatives of Phase I continue to operate inefficiently.

In an article entitled, "Land for Salvador's Poor: To Many, Bitter Victory," Lindsey Gruson (NYT, 9/28/87) describes the trials of a peasant farmer:

> "It's bad land," said Mr. Cruz, who is 35 years old and has four children. "Every year it produces less. I don't have enough money to buy fertilizer. I don't have enough to pay the mortgage. My life isn't better, it's worse. I've been working that piece 11 years and I'll have to leave soon."
>
> Mr. Cruz's plight is an example of the problems that have led to a sharp decline in agricultural production and a surge in discontent with the land program in El Salvador, the backbone of the United States-supported attempt to bring social stability to a country racked by civil war.

Mario Rosenthal agrees with this assessment in an article in *The Wall Street Journal* (6/10/88):

> The Duarte government, with the blessings of the State Department and with massive assistance from the U.S. taxpayer, has implemented a radical program rarely equaled in the West. Coffee, sugar, cotton and coconut plantations have been expropriated: so, too, sugar and coffee mills. . . .
>
> U.S. rationale for supporting these policies was to undermine the Marxist guerrillas by giving the *campesinos* (peasants) what the communists offered—all subsidized by the U.S. taxpayer. But widespread corruption and inefficiency left the *campesinos* worse off than before. Though Agency for International Development and State Department audits reported widespread corruption and economic failure, they were rarely made public; misuse of AID funds was covered up by classifying the audits.
>
> The victory of the Republican National Alliance (ARENA) in the presidential elections of March 1989 marks a further deterioration of the land reform. President Alfredo Cristiani has announced his intention to dismantle the Phase I cooperatives and divide their lands among member-farmers. If he were indeed to do so, this liberalization might be a step forward. At present writing, however, no plans for implementation have been announced, and because of their political leverage upon ARENA, it is widely predicted that former owners will simply occupy the cooperative lands (Kandell 1989; Gruson 1989).
>
> The continued occupation of Phase III land by militarized former owners marks a further retrenchment from land reform. Since Phase II did not happen, and Phases I and III are in process of reversal, it is almost as if the land reform had not occurred. Almost, that is, except for the deterioration of agricultural output that it caused in the meantime.

Conclusion

The Salvadoran agrarian reform is among the more tragic cases covered in this book.

First, it has become the political football of opposing sides in a civil war. It is not *whether* to have a land reform; it is a question of *power*. Each side proclaims land reform. In a peaceful democracy, the opposing sides would sit down with each other, determine their commonalities, and compromise on their differences. In the current Salvadoran context, this is impossible.

Second, the land reform has become a pawn in the cold war between East and West. While Gorbachev and Bush are tending toward political conciliation on higher levels, their two countries are violently at odds over policies toward El Salvador and Nicaragua as well.

Third, in none of the scenarios by either side does the farmer figure in policymaking. In an effort to promote "democracy," the government of the United States has contributed to reform "from above" that involves forced "cooperatives" and unenforceable land titles, without a whit of intellectual input from the peasant. Pricing and production controls are similar to those in many Third-World countries.

It is hard to be optimistic about El Salvador on any count.

References

Berryman, Phillip, 1983. *What's Wrong in Central America, and What to Do about It,* Philadelphia, Pa., American Friends Service Committee.

EPICA: *See* Wheaton.

Gist. One-page statement of policy issued periodically by the U.S. Department of State.

Gruson, Lindsey, 1987. "Land for Salvador's Poor: To Many, Bitter Victory," *The New York Times,* September 28.

Gruson, Lindsey, 1989. "Change and Its Record in El Salvador," *The New York Times,* March 26.

IDB (Inter-American Development Bank). *Economic and Social Progress in Latin America* (annual).

IG (United States Agency for International Development, the Inspector General for Audit), 1984. *Agrarian Reform in El Salvador: A Report on Its Status,* audit report 1-519-84-2, January 18.

IMF:IFS (International Monetary Fund). *International Financial Statistics,* published monthly.

Kandell, Jonathan, 1989. "Conservatives' Victory in El Salvador Signals End to Land Reform," *The Wall Street Journal,* March 22.

LARR. *Latin American Regional Reports, Mexico and the Caribbean,* London, Latin American Newsletters, Ltd.

Oxfam: *See* Simon and Stephens.

Prosterman, Roy; Reidinger, Jeffrey M.; and Temple, Mary N., 1981. "Land Reform in El Salvador: The Democratic Alternative," *World Affairs*, vol. 144, no. 1, summer.

Simon, Laurence R., and Stephens, James C., Jr., 1981. *El Salvador Land Reform, 1980–1981: Impact Audit*, Boston, Oxfam.

Singer, Max, 1981. "Can El Salvador Be Saved?" *Commentary*, December.

Tun Wai, U, 1977. "A Revisit to Interest Rates Outside the Organized Money Markets of Underdeveloped Countries," *Banca Nazionale del Lavoro Quarterly Review*, no. 122, September.

Wheaton, Philip, 1980. *Agrarian Reform in El Salvador: A Program of Rural Pacification*, Washington, D.C., EPICA Task Force.

17. Nicaragua

Class struggle can be seen either from the point of view of hate or from the point of view of love. State coercion is an act of love. (Tomás Borge Martínez, interior minister of Nicaragua, quoted in *Time* Magazine, 4/16/84.)

For those unfamiliar with history and economics, Sandinista Nicaragua may seem a promising adventure. For centuries, Nicaraguan land had been in the hands of the few and powerful, whether they were Indian chiefs or Spanish settlers or Nicaraguan plantation owners. In 1934, the Somoza family owned no land. By becoming president in 1937, General Somoza established his family as the ruling dynasty. By 1946, that family held almost a monopoly on coffee and beef exports and domestic milk production. By the 1970s the Somozas possessed forty-six coffee farms, seven sugar plantations, fifty-one cattle farms, 400 tobacco farms, 60% of all beef packing plants in the country, and the fishing and cigar industries (Deere and Marchetti 1981:46). We will refer to the years 1937 to 1979 as the Somocista period. (When the Somozas did not themselves hold the presidency because of a constitutional provision against succession, they named puppet presidents.) In July 1979, a revolutionary army, known as the Sandinista Front for National Liberation (FSLN), overthrew the next-to-the-next-to-the-last fiefdom in Latin America, confiscating the businesses and the lands of the Somoza family as well as of families associated with them. All this was done in the name of the people.

The Land Reform

Above all else, the poor majority in Nicaragua yearned for land—land to feed themselves, land for security, land to free themselves from the humiliation of having to sell their labor and even that of their children to a *patrón* (Collins 1982:79).

Pressured by the Alliance for Progress, the Somocista government in 1963 established the Nicaraguan Agrarian Institute (IAN) to promote the agricultural use of lands not then serving a social purpose (Deere and Marchetti 1981:46). Instead of confiscating much land, however, this program primarily settled peasants on unoccupied national lands. In 1970, the Institute of Peasant Welfare (INVIERNO) was organized to provide credit

323

and technical assistance for small growers of basic grains. This institute was generally conceded to be a sop to American aid, however, not effective in promoting credit and agriculture.

In June 1979, as the Sandinista revolution began to roll, peasants invaded large estates in areas of the Province of León controlled by the revolutionary army (Kaimowitz and Thome 1980:6). With the help of the Sandinista forces, they organized these into communal farms known as Cooperativas Agrícolas Sandinistas (CAS).

With its victory in July, the landholdings encountered by the Sandinista government were even more of a study in contrasts than in most Latin American countries. Thousands of peasants were either landless (working on the larger estates) or owned plots averaging 3.5 hectares, while estates of the Somoza and associated families—including cotton, sugar, coffee, rice mills, and slaughterhouses, almost 80,000 hectares—constituted over 23% of farm land (Deere and Marchetti 1981:51). There were other large family holdings as well; for example, the Pellas family owned 6,000 hectares, producing 52% of the country's sugar in its mills (NYT, 7/19/83).

Upon assuming power, the Sandinista National Front decreed that all the Somoza and Somoza-related lands would be converted into fifty-three state farms, which became known as the Area of People's Property (APP). Since these were highly productive units primarily for export, it was not deemed wise to divide them into smaller farms. Other private lands, no matter how large, were not expropriated if they were productively used. However, rented land and fields not in production were divided among the landless or families with holdings too small to support themselves. Titles have been given to these families. These and other smallholders were encouraged to combine their lands into cooperatives. Thus the main patterns for Sandinista Nicaragua emerged: state farms, large private productive farms, and smallholder cooperatives.

On a number of occasions, the government of Nicaragua has maintained that it presides over a mixed economy, partly socialist and partly private property. In 1988, however, it confiscated a sugar farm that was the nation's largest private business (NYT, 7/15/88), asserting that "the owners were not investing enough money to maintain the adjacent refinery." When the state intervenes in decisions on how much to invest and confiscates property without judicial process, the economy is state-dominated and can no longer be termed "mixed."

In this massive Sandinista reform, new organizations were set up, new names appeared. IAN became the Nicaraguan Institute of Agrarian Reform, which managed the state farms. In January 1980 it was merged with the Ministry of Agriculture, to become the Ministry of Agricultural Development and Agrarian Reform (MIDINRA). In September 1980, MIDINRA entered into an agreement with the United States foreign aid program (USAID) and the Land Tenure Center of the University of Wisconsin, to engage in research for MIDINRA's Center of Research and Studies on

Agrarian Reform (CIERA). This agreement lasted until U.S. aid was terminated two years later.

Too Early to Judge?

Sandinista land reform supporters argue that the drops in productivity and output are to be expected when a nation's landholding system is radically reordered, and that they will be corrected with experience. They also argue that continued low production is explained by the civil war, nurtured by U.S. government support to the rebels (known as Contras). But when the reform is taken in historical context and is compared with similar land reforms elsewhere, it is not too early to arrive at a prognosis.

Unfortunately, we see in Sandinista Nicaragua a repetition of problems in Egypt, Tanzania, the Philippines, Mexico, and other countries covered in this book. We are struck, as we were in El Salvador, that neither the government of Nicaragua nor its admirers or critics appear (from what they say and write) to have read the history of land reforms elsewhere.

We now summarize our own position, which the reader will quickly see follows not mainly from the present chapter but from those that have preceded it. The following are generalizations that will be supported as details are elaborated in the remainder of this chapter.

Despite its rhetoric to the contrary, the Sandinista government is centralized and authoritarian. The major agricultural decisions—those over pricing, production, and technology—are tightly controlled, albeit within a framework that *appears* decentralized. Many decisions are made by cooperative committees freely elected by peasants. But these are not the *basic* decisions (on how land tenure is to be structured, what prices to charge for output, where to buy inputs and how much), and even the less basic ones are made within a framework highly constrained by central authority.

Who will make the best decisions? We argue that on prices, production, and technology, the peasantry is likely to have more expertise than the government. Therefore, such decisions are best made locally, and if so, they will differ from place to place. Instead, the junta, highly paternalistic, believes it is the peasants who need to be educated. It rules from Managua as if it had complete knowledge and total moral authority. Centralized decisions on prices, interest rates, rents, wages, and the like cause inefficiencies: scarce resources are improperly used, and output is not as great as it might be. In a poor country like Nicaragua, this waste cannot be afforded.

The junta, as well as its literary adherents, appear to have little knowledge of economics (or interest in it). To them, interest rates are not a means of allocating resources among efficient uses; but a lever for converting from one agrarian structure to another. The exchange rate is not a means for determining what resources should be designated for exports and what for supplying the local market but a way to redistribute income and wealth. Prices are not a means of determining which goods should be produced and which technologies used for them; like exchange rates, they are a way to transfer income from one group to another. However laudable these transfers may be, the managers are left with no guidelines on what to produce, what inputs to use, and where to sell the output. Without these guidelines, they are making ruinous mistakes.

None of the above in any way questions the integrity or purpose of the Sandinista government.

Parcelization

In land reforms all over the world, at any time in history, peasants have, with rare exception, opted for private rather than collectivized land. The rare exceptions include those with religious fervor, such as members of Israeli kibbutzim or Hutterite communities (Dorner 1977). Now we are told, by Sandinista admirers, that peasants in Nicaragua are of a different breed; unlike their counterparts everywhere else, they prefer cooperative farming.

Goverment Reasons for Opposing Parcelization

Joseph Collins, who spent three years in Nicaragua interviewing peasants, government officials, and others, while experiencing life on state farms and cooperatives, cites (1982:60) the following reasons given by the government for not dividing land up into small parcels to be owned and managed by individual farmers. First is the fear that productivity would drop. To break up the Somoza farms might have lost the advantages of mechanization and advanced technology. Second, jobs may be created more easily on large farms than on small. Third, parceling would inevitably be unjust.

On its face, the first appears to be a good reason. Historically, however, the experience is opposite. As has happened frequently elsewhere, both productivity and output have dropped substantially on the Nicaraguan state farms. On the private farms in Bolivia after the reform, on the other hand, they increased instead, while private farms of the Paraguayan agrarian reform achieved the greatest productivity increases in all of Latin America over a whole decade (see Chapter 7 and 18). Furthermore, it is not clear that the mechanization of Somoza farms was efficient and worthy of preservation, especially with abundant labor available. From this it follows that the second reason makes little sense. Productive jobs may be found *more* easily on small, de-mechanized farms than on Somoza-type plantations. If the Soviet Union and China are good examples, state farms tend to be repositories for surplus, unproductive labor. Finally, to judge the injustices of dividing up farms into private properties against the injustices of assigning workers to different jobs in a cooperative and of determining how the wages shall be apportioned appears to us a precarious balance.

What Do the Peasants Want?

Collins and other Sandinista supporters argue that cooperatives and state farms are what the peasants want. Since they have never been allowed a plebiscite, and since opposition newspapers are controlled, we wonder. In between the lines written by supporters, we find evidence that Nicaraguan peasants are not a breed apart; they do want private land. The first hint is that the government had to induce the peasants to form cooperatives by offering them cheap credit, which was denied to those who did not join. (Why was this necessary if the peasants preferred cooperatives anyway?) Furthermore, when the unused lands of large holders were expropriated and distributed among peasants, preference was given to those who agreed to form cooperatives. (Why was this preference necessary, if cooperatives were what peasants wanted anyway?)

"The Sandinistas also feared that spontaneous land takeovers would result in thousands of tiny plots, too small ever to produce efficiently" (Collins 1982:80). If they feared this, it must have been a threat. But the argument misses the point. If the worker population is so large that it leads to thousands of tiny plots, then cooperatives and state farms are no answer either. The ratio of workers to land cannot be changed by the organizational form selected for farms. But the most revealing citation from Collins (1982:80) is the following:

> Reinforcing all this pragmatic reasoning was the belief of many Sandinistas at the start of the revolution that a wage-earning ("proletarianized") labor force represented historical progress. They felt it laid the foundation for eventual worker-management. *Thus increasing the number of peasants, especially individual small owners, would be a step backward.* "There have been many agrarian reforms that in one stroke have handed over the land," Jaime Wheelock (minister of Agriculture and Agrarian Reform) stated in 1979. "But this type of land reform destroys the process of proletarianization in the countryside and constitutes an historical regression." (Emphasis added.)

Now we find a high Sandinista official arguing for state farms on philosophical grounds, not because they are the most efficient form or because the peasants want them. "Proletarianizing"—the accusation flung by Marx upon the capitalists—is now made virtuous when done by the state. Of course, Wheelock is also wrong in his assumption. After studying many agrarian reforms, we can find very few (Bolivia, Paraguay perhaps) that "in one stroke handed over the land" without encumbrances.

Furthermore, Wheelock's statement was apparently made in response to peasant threats to seize for their private use land in state farms or cooperatives. Collins (1982: 80) goes on to describe the reaction of the peasants:

Not surprisingly, the landless were confused. A Chinandega campesino summed up the bewilderment of many a few days after the July 19 triumph: "I don't understand it at all. One minute seizing the land is revolutionary and then they tell you it is counterrevolutionary."

Collins cites other expressions of peasant desire for private property as well. On many cooperatives, farmers insisted on receiving small pieces of land of their own. When they got their way—the government complained—they would spend so much time on their own land that they would shortshift the "gran producción" of the cooperatives (Collins 1982:76). As peasants continued to resist forming cooperatives (Collins 1982:82,103), the government was forced into a number of measures. They allowed peasants to "borrow" unused land on state farms. They also used the Union of Peasant Workers (more on that below) to pressure peasants into forming cooperatives. These anecdotes recall the experiences of both the Soviet Union and China, in which state farms, failing generally, are giving way to more productive, private plots.

Below is another example cited by Collins (1982:104):

> As soon as the hacienda (El Sol) was taken over by the ministry (and turned into a state farm), the workers began demanding land to grow food for themselves. At first the ministry resisted; but then it realized that if it did not relent, the workers would simply seize the land and divide it up among themselves. To prevent this, the ministry offered to lend the land on the condition that it be farmed cooperatively.

In short, the ministry wanted a state farm; the workers wanted private plots; and they compromised on a cooperative.

Deere (1982:21), also a strong supporter of the Sandinista regime, nevertheless reports that "many of the production cooperatives were functioning in name only. Tenants, for example, often rented land collectively, but they continued to cultivate that land on an individual basis."

At the time of the November 1984 elections, Kinzer of *The New York Times* (11/5/84) reported:

> Voters in several towns said that they belonged to cooperatives that receive raw materials from the Government, and hence it was wise to vote. "They control the distribution, so we want to stay in their good graces," said a potter in the artisan village of San Juan del Oriente.

In summary, peasants were never allowed any choice about whether the Somoza lands that they had tilled would be put into state farms. Although ostensibly they agreed to form cooperatives on other expropriated lands, nevertheless the pressures to do so were great, even irresistible. We will describe these pressures further in the section on credit below.

Credit

Imagine yourself a peasant with six acres of land on a Nicaraguan hillside, four days by mule from the nearest town. One afternoon in early 1980, you suddenly hear the thump-thump of a helicopter. A few minutes later the helicopter lands fifty yards away and a young fellow steps out saying he is from the Agrarian Reform ministry. He offers you a loan to produce more corn and beans. The interest rate? 11 percent—one third the rate of inflation. Is this a dream? Is this the revolution? (Collins 1982:51).

Collins does not say whether the above is a true story, but it represents the spirit with which the new government approached credit. Before the revolution, credit had been monopolized by the few large owners. Now it was to be distributed instead to peasants. A little farther on, Collins explains that this strategy did not work. Much credit was extended to farmers who could not use it because they were too far from markets, or who did not want to use it productively and spent it on consumption instead.

All this could happen because the commercial banking system was nationalized in August 1979 (Deere and Marchetti 1981:58). Instead of different banks' setting interest rates competitively, the government now had a monopoly on all credit.

The Real Counterpart of Money Credit

Nothing in the Sandinista literature reveals an understanding that credit—a money phenomenon—has a real counterpart. There is a certain amount of goods (fertilizer, seed, machinery) that can be made available, either by local production or by borrowing abroad. Credit represents a money claim upon those goods. By creating money, as the government did, to distribute credit, it re-allocated those claims but did not increase their real value.

"Real credit" is the goods that "money credit" can buy. Who can use it best? The state farms? Peasants on cooperatives? Private largeholders? Private smallholders? In a free market, the interest rate would allocate real credit among various forms of enterprise. Suppose that private smallholders use credit more efficiently than cooperatives. (There is some evidence, cited later, that Nicaraguan peasants—like farmers everywhere—work harder and longer hours on their own plots than on cooperatives, thus produce more per worker.) If a market interest rate made the choice, the scarce real credit would go primarily to private smallholders, who could afford to pay higher rates because they were producing more. By channeling it instead into cooperatives, the government is denying it to private smallholders; thus its use is wasteful. Once again, this kind of waste is not affordable in a poor country.

In Nicaragua, however, the credit allocation depends not on the productiveness of the activity but on the type of enterprise. As of 1981, members of production cooperatives (CAS) were paying 7% on agricultural loans, while members of credit and service cooperatives (CCS) paid 8%, and smallholders not in cooperatives 14% (Deere and Marchetti 1981:57), at a time when inflation was running about 25% (IMF:IFS). The differences in rates among types of enterprise indicate a political rather than an economically efficient allocation.

Furthermore, an interest rate lower than the rate of inflation constitutes a subsidy. If (say) the interest rate is 8% and the inflation rate 25%, a borrower of 100 córdobas for one year pays back córdobas worth only 80% (or 100/125) of what he borrowed. If he pays the interest at the end of the year, he pays a real value of 8% of 80%, or 6.4%. Thus he has repaid a total real value of 86.4% of what he borrowed, so he has been subsidized to the tune of 13.6 córdobas at last year's price level, or 17 córdobas at this year's price level. But the calculation need not be exact. Roughly, we say that the *real* rate of interest is the *nominal* rate of interest (8%) minus the rate of inflation (25%), or approximately negative 17%. Such a subsidy means, in effect, that the borrower is being paid (17%) to receive funds instead of paying for the privilege.

Now, the Sandinistas boast that they increased credits to smallholders (mainly in cooperatives) by 600% (Deere and Marchetti 1981:58) in the first year. The fact that they did so attests more to the astuteness of the peasant (in figuring out the real interest rate) than to that of the government. Who would not want to borrow when the real value to be repaid was less than the amount borrowed? Furthermore, the fact of a sixfold increase in such a short time is *prima facie* evidence of waste, for it could not have been made with careful attention to the uses and productivity of credit.

The government assured the private sector that it would receive the same level of credit as before (Deere and Marchetti 1981:58). We do not know the seriousness with which this promise was made, but if it was sincere, then it reflects lack of understanding of the limits of the real credit supply. If the government drastically increases real credit to the cooperatives, real credit to those outside cooperatives must be reduced. Of course, the same *nominal* amount might be continued, but if so, the outsiders lose by inflation.

Repayments

Repayments are a classic problem when governments lavish funds on their favored constituencies. We have found this to be so in other countries. When a loan is given for political reasons (such as for joining a cooperative), the government is in the borrower's political debt. The borrower for his part perceives the loan as a gift; after all, the government has been extending other forms of largesse, so why not money?

Deere and Marchetti (1981:62) perceived the problem for Nicaragua, but nothing in their article suggests recognition that it is a classic situation applicable to many countries:

> The big question of the moment concerns whether the loans will be repaid. The rapid dispersal of the credit made it difficult for INRA to assure the availability of sufficient agricultural inputs in rural areas and few loans were actually tied to the purchase of inputs. Much of the credit may have been used to increase consumption and, thus, the standard of living of rural producers.

Austin et al. (1985:21), also supporters of the Sandinista regime, agree that "the 1980 'spilling of credit in the countryside' led to repayment problems that were not quickly resolved. . . ."

Deere and Marchetti go on to report that the Peasant Workers' Union asked "the banks to pardon the debts of small grain and coffee producers if they joined cooperatives." Apparently the development bank (BND) hesitated, partly because the request would undermine fiscal responsibility, the very point we ourselves would emphasize. But it undermined fiscal responsibility through the back door and settled for a rescheduling of debt for those who would join cooperatives. With negative real interest rates because of inflation, however, a rescheduling is tantamount to forgiveness over time.

Price and Wage Policies

> Studies of the first two years showed that better credit was not the best way to increase production. Raising guaranteed prices to producers was tried instead. (Collins 1982:112).

For many countries (e.g., Mexico, and Zambia), when the government intervenes to address one economic disequilibrium, it usually creates another (or several more), which calls for new intervention. Ultimately, a huge bureaucracy is created, absorbing large amounts of real resources and creating more disequilibria than it has solved. Collins's quotation is a case in point, although he seems not to share this perception. Credit was channeled to cooperatives to solve the disequilibrium in land ownership; the distortion of credit contributed to the shortage in food output, for which guaranteed prices were then prescribed.

Prices

But as Collins (1982:134–6) points out, apparently without seeing a general principle, the guaranteed prices led to further disequilibria:

> Government subsidies on food staples have been fundamental to . . . the food security of the poor. . . . [But] paying higher prices to motivate the producers further increases the subsidies. . . . Not only is the subsidy

331

enormous, but it is not targeted to the poor. If anything, the poor are discriminated against by programs that market low-priced foods through workplaces. . . . [So the Sandinistas now want to work out] subsidies that discriminate in favor of the poor. . . .

The next step, of course, was for the government itself to get into the business of selling food. We will return to that below and show the enormous disequilibria that that created.

Wages

In Sandinista philosophy, workers and employers are considered partners in an enterprise, able to discuss differences philosophically and to agree on wage rates that maximize social benefits. With deep religious commitment, such cooperation (e.g., the Hutterites, and the Society of Brothers in the United States) is successful. More often, however, religious commitment is previously lacking, and the "cooperation" becomes imposed. Then disputes over wages and working conditions are not resolved with religious love but because one group sets the philosophy and another conforms. This is the case in Sandinista Nicaragua.

Shortly after its victory, the government boosted the minimum wage 30%. Since this wage had not been paid in the past, the average may have been increased by 60% (Collins 1982:70). With inflation of 25% to 30%, however, within two years the gain was wiped out. In explaining to workers why wages could not be increased further, the same Tomás Borge Martínez quoted at the beginning of this chapter argued that increased money wages would lead to inflation, which would further wipe out the benefits. Of course, he was wrong. Increased money wages fail to help the worker only when they are the *only* source of inflation. When subsidized credit and other reasons for government deficits cause the inflation, then increased money wages will help workers regain what they have lost.

That wages have been in contention is clear. In 1980, when labor for the harvest was short, workers tried to increase wages. Deere and Marchetti (1981:63) tell of workers destroying coffee trees or harvesting cotton "dirty" in order to protest wages. Workers do not have unions of their own choice. Rather, there is a "company union," described below. Other than "discussing" wages with their higher-level comrades, the workers have no organization through which to make their demands known.

The government, furthermore, has provided health care, meals, and housing in the cooperatives; it also imported great quantities of food for consumption in cooperatives. In these ways, it has diluted the wage demands of workers in the cooperatives, while leaving those outside to suffer from the inflation caused by this largesse. Collins (1982:77) quotes a conversation with Augusto Zeledón, administrator of a coffee cooperative, who had been explaining the farm's balance sheet to the workers: "At first there was a lot of disorientation. Workers were coming two, three hours late and going off early to work their own plots. But now they are working practically a full day. What has made a difference is that I have spent a lot of time talking to the workers in the fields."

Clearly more research is needed in this fundamental matter, but we are not inclined to accept Zeledón's statement at face value, as Collins apparently did. Had the suggestion come from the workers that they perceived the problem by themselves and would willingly sacrifice, then we might believe that a truly revolutionary change had occurred. Since the need was explained to the workers by their boss, and the workers were said (by the boss) to have agreed, we are more inclined to see a paternalism that became acceptable only because the workers had no other choice.

We close this section with another quote from Collins (1982:77): "[The leadership] is determined to work out a mix of non-coercive means of motivating the workers." Why a mix? Why not just higher cash wages (or profits on individual smallholdings), determined according to productivity, and not dependent on whether workers join cooperatives or not?

Unions

> The organization of the ATC (Asociación de los Trabajadores del Campo, or Rural Workers' Association) was the product of several years of organizational work by the FSLN and closely tied to the progressive role of various church groups in the rural areas (Deere and Marchetti 1982:48).

Deere and Marchette explain that because of Somoza's intense repression, "only religious groups had the freedom to carry out organizational work in rural areas" and for that reason they associated themselves with the Sandinista Front (FSLN). However, once the war had been won, the FSLN did not disengage itself and leave the workers to regroup into whatever unions they chose.

Indeed, to have done that would have been most atypical, for in virtually all Latin American countries unions are closely associated with the government. Government sets the rules and organizes the negotiation between labor leaders and employers. Sometimes (as in Argentina) it sets the wage that will be "negotiated." In most of Latin America, however, three groups participate: government, unions, and employers. In Sandinista Nicaragua, where the government is also a major employer because of state farms and nationalized enterprises, the trilogy breaks down. Even on cooperatives, government is really in charge—making all the major decisions, including wages—and therefore the trilogy does not apply there either. In short, ATC is a "company union," organized by employers who leave employees no alternative of their own choosing. Company unions are often planned with the cooperation of employees, as is the case here, when they know they have no other choice.

Deere (1982:18) refers to ATC as autonomous and points out that it "has

333

assured that state policy be responsive to the demands of rural workers and peasants as well as that they be active participants in the process of socio-economic transformation." She shows that "ATC unions have now organized workers for the first time to assure compliance with the payment of a minimum wage" as well as to enforce regulations requiring private landlords to rent unused land. Certainly company unions can help employees. But both of the enforcements cited here fall well within government guidelines. From all this, we judge that ATC serves the interest of peasants and workers provided those interests do not conflict in a major way with state policy. We know of no instance in which ATC has confronted the state on a major policy issue, and we doubt that one would ever occur.

The role of government is illustrated in the formation of the Unión Nacional de Agricultores y Ganderos (UNAG, or national confederation of farmers and cattle ranchers). To derail the possibility that small- and medium-sized producers would join UPANIC, the union of larger cattle ranchers, the government organized UNAG in 1981. Our judgment of paternalism is supported by Thome's (n.d.:6) observation on this, that "government plans . . . would be easier to implement through a friendly and collaborative association of producers."

Cooperatives

Collins provides reasons why the government preferred the cooperative form of agriculture instead of small, private farms (1982:97–8): "Some (reasons) are philosophical: working together is morally superior to working alone," but for the most part, he says, they are practical. Among these is the "isolation and extreme deprivation of the Nicaraguan campesinos. Campesino families often live miles from other families. With few and very poor roads, many have no access to schools, clinics, churches, or even the simple pleasures of social life among friends. Thus cooperatives are seen as one way of drawing people together to make possible at least a better, more social, life."

Had we not written Chapter 4 on Tanzania, we might be persuaded by this argument. But we recall that the TANU government had substantially the same reasons for establishing *Ujamaa* villages. It turned out, however, that the villages were created only with great difficulty and in some cases by force. Apparently the Tanzanian peasants preferred isolation on their ancestral lands and were not impressed by the attractions of schools, clinics, churches, and social life. The impact on agriculture of the *Ujamaa* villages was disastrous, as we have already seen. Crops declined in the traditional areas without being replaced in the villages. We now have over twenty years of experience with Tanzania and only a few for Nicaragua. But the experience of those few is quite consistent with that of the twenty.

Collins's (1982:100) descriptions of cooperatives are fraught with paternalism that he sometimes sees as a problem, but not, as we do, as a degenerative condition. "The farmworkers' association, the ATC, was charged with organizing . . . credit and service associations." But who charged it? Are not unions self-charging? He goes on to show that "many campesinos have mistrusted ATC organizers with urban student backgrounds. Organizers were rushing things—trying to accomplish everything at once, one campesino told me."

Curiously, the same facts are seen in quite opposite ways by supporters of the Sandinistas and by skeptics like ourselves. For example, Austin et al. (1985:23) view the following developments as positive:

> The cooperative movement was characterized by important variations in the breadth and degree of cooperativization between 1979 and 1983. Cooperative membership increased from 1% in 1979 to about 60% in 1980, but MIDINRA's emphasis on consolidating the APP and maintaining the national unity limited government emphasis on cooperatives in the next 2 years.

We see the same paragraph as threatening to peasant integrity. First, such a sharp increase in membership within a single year smacks of coercion. Characteristically, people do not anywhere join cooperatives so massively and so suddenly of their own volition. (More time would be needed for unpressured persuasion.) Second, we interpret the "emphasis on . . . maintaining the national unity" (a reason for slowdown thereafter) as reflecting peasant opposition. Finally, the tenor of the paragraph reveals that the total operation was managed by MIDINRA and not by the peasants.

Likewise, what Collins reports as matter-of-fact events, we see as frightening implications for an economy. For example, he shows how cooperatives were growing "faster than the government could provide them with the basic services." Therefore (Collins goes on), "the ministry and the leadership of UNAG (the government-sponsored union of small farmers) decided to select 150 cooperatives—half CAS and half credit associations—and strengthen them by making sure they were properly supported, especially with technical assistance and machinery" (1982:105). Collins seems unaware of how such discrimination might demoralize cooperatives not selected. Technical assistance and machinery are scarce, and what is supplied to one group of cooperatives is denied to another. We would argue that the government is far less likely than the free market to choose those units that can make most productive use of those inputs.

Finally, we note the following from Collins: "The CAS members were asking the ministry for barbed wire to fence off their land from the cattle. But the ministry fears a fence would de facto make the land concession permanent." We are appalled that farmers in Nicaragua must apply to the government for a common item that most farmers throughout the world buy at the local hardware store. We are even more appalled that the request was turned down. But we are most appalled that Collins makes no particular comment on this event, apparently regarding it as one of the routine operations of the day.

Food First

Joseph Collins, whose observations on Nicaragua have been cited many times in this chapter, is, along with Frances Moore Lappé, one of the authors of *Food First* (1979), which proposes that the top development priority for less developed countries (LDCs) should be food to feed their hungry peoples. All other elements of development should come later. The Sandinistas and Lappé and Collins appear to have influenced each other: food first is one of the principal tenets of Sandinista rhetoric.

Had Lappé and Collins confined themselves to the priority expressed in the preceding paragraph, not only would we agree with them, but they might have done great service to the thinking of development economists. Throughout the LDCs, agriculture has been discriminated against, exactly as Lappé and Collins have argued, and this book has shown how land reform has been an instrument of this discrimination. Many (probably most) LDCs could feed their poor well if they devoted greater resources to agriculture.

Lappé and Collins erred, however, in the proposition that food for local consumption should replace plantation crops for export. In some cases—Nicaragua is an example—this would be a formula for poverty. In a classic case of comparative advantage, countries adept at plantation agriculture (exporters of sugar, coffee, tea, cotton, etc.) can feed their poor *better* if they export these crops and buy basic foodstuffs with the proceeds, than if they grow the basic foods themselves.

The problem is not one of which crops to grow—exports or home consumption—but one of increasing the income of the poor. All fields devoted to export crops might be planted instead in beans and corn, and the poor would still go hungry if they did not have enough land or if the landless poor did not have enough income to buy beans and corn. Land reform might help correct this condition, for lands distributed to the poor would increase their incomes. But income is what counts, not whether the poor grow beans to eat at home or coffee to export.

One of the Sandinista arguments against parcelization was that if the poor were given their small plots, they would produce beans and corn instead of sugar, coffee, and cotton for export. The government argued that Nicaragua vitally needed the foreign exchange that exports would bring, hence the Somoza and allied lands should remain large plantations of export crops.

All over the world, however, *smallholders* produce for export. Coffee is grown on small holdings (as well as large) in almost any coffee-producing country; so also is tea. Witness Kenya, Uganda, and Tanzania. Bananas for export come from small farms in Ecuador and northern Africa. Cotton is grown on small holdings in Egypt, cocoa on small farms in Ghana and Nigeria, and sugar on small farms up and down the west coast of Latin America (as well as on large ones).

But Nicaragua is different. Probably smallholders would produce coffee and bananas for export, but cotton and sugar are questionable. Central American cotton is a high-technology crop grown since the fifties on large plantations. While sugar may be grown on small plots, the transportation from field to mill requires large-scale planning.

The popularizing of DDT (invented in 1874, but insecticidal qualities discovered only in 1939) and other pesticides in the fifties not only cleared Central America lowlands of malaria but opened the way for cotton in areas where it would previously have been destroyed by insects (Avery 1985:72). Rich, volcanic soils near the coast—not only in Nicaragua but in El Salvador and Guatemala—permitted cotton varieties developed in the United States to grow stronger and faster than they would in the United States. As banana production was reduced by disease (and higher costs of boxing and shipping the new, disease-resistant varieties), landowners turned increasingly to cotton. In Nicaragua, the opportunity was seized by the Somoza and related families. With mechanized planting and harvesting, with herbicides replacing labor for weeding, fewer workers were needed. Since alternative opportunities for employment were not developing fast enough in Somocista Nicaragua, unemployment and poverty spread.

Because of high humidity, high temperatures, and high rainfall in the growing season, cotton in Nicaragua requires liberal, well-controlled applications of fertilizers and pesticides. Only in countries where pests are easier to control can cotton be grown on small farms: in the United States because winter kills them; in Egypt and Peru because they do not thrive on semi-arid or irrigated desert farms. In Central America, where pests have no natural enemies, high technology is required, which can be applied most efficiently on large-scale plantations.

Thus the Sandinistas established large-scale cotton plantations for the same reason that Somoza did. They also face the same dilemma: little employment. The optimal quantity of labor is determined by technology, not by whether the government is capitalist or socialist. Confronted by fiscal restraints, as they have been, Sandinistas are not sharing the foreign exchange proceeds with redundant workers. Unemployment and low incomes are therefore just as much a problem in Sandinista Nicaragua as they were in Somocista, and this is why we believe the conditions of the peasantry may not have been improved.

The apparent dilemma lies between equity and efficiency. (1) Parcel the land to peasants, and they might grow beans and corn, which would give *them* higher incomes but would not maximize the nation's product. (2) Keep the land in plantations to maximize output, but the peasants will be the poorer, whether under Somoza or the Sandinistas.

We see a possible alternative, but it would be experimental: to parcel the land among small-scale farmers, who might, if they so chose freely, combine into cooperatives organized by themselves to buy the technology, the management, and the inputs to run a modern cotton plantation. Technical assistance could be made available to them. While this arrangement would not bring full employment, at least farmers would share the operating profits—which they do not now nor did under Somoza—as a cushion while some of them acquired new skills. By selling their cooperative interest after a few years, redundant workers might finance new enterprises with new employment for themselves.

Similarly with sugar. Sugar requires high capital investment in a mill, a scheduling of harvest to provide the necessary flow of cane to the mill, a transportation system from field to mill, and a planted area to provide cane with logistic efficiency. Judged by performance in other countries, the small farmer can figure all this out; he might become prisoner of the mill, however, owing to lack of competition among buyers of his crop.

The analogous outcome for sugar might still be small-scale production, with a cooperatively owned mill: a genuine cooperative, not one established on government terms. In this way farmers would set their own prices according to the wider market and determine for themselves whether sugar or other crops were profitable. Alternative crops might be coffee, bananas, and foodgrain, which can be grown successfully on small farms.

We argue that agriculture would be most efficient, as it has been in other parts of the world, if by owning their own land outright, small farmers may choose both crops and markets. If cooperatives are profitable because of advantages of scale, the farmers will organize them on their own terms. Because, instead, "cooperatives" have been imposed by the Sandinista government on its terms, not only are they less efficient than if managed by farmers, but the government can skim off any profit to cover inefficiencies or corruption elsewhere, or to wage war.

The National Food Plan and the Nicaraguan Basic Foods Company

In March 1980, the Sandinista government set forth the National Food Plan (PAN) as an efficient system for distributing foodstuffs. It was to be chaired by a vice minister of MIDIRNA and administered by representatives of high-ranking ministries and autonomous institutions (Thome n.d.:6). The entire government apparatus—state farms, cooperatives, credit institutions, and labor unions—would be part of this system. State stores joined it later on. In this way, the government created a bureaucracy, to be centrally controlled, that would perform those tasks that elsewhere are done through price signals.

It is often argued that market prices are historic means by which the wealthy feed their power. But the market can also be used for equitable distribution among the poor, as it has been in many countries. So long as the incomes of the poor are increased, and the Sandinistas averred they would do this, the market becomes feasible and the heavy bureaucratic apparatus unnecessary. Even more, because a small group at the top is unable to comprehend the intricate interactions of a total economy, centralized rationing, price control, and bureaucratic restrictions are a drag on economic growth and a principal cause of the crisis.

The Sandinistas did succeed in increasing the plantings of basic grains during their first year. In 1980, bean land had increased 26% and corn land 20% over 1978. But this was at the expense of cotton and coffee, whose plantings were considerably less then envisaged in the national plan (Deere and Marchetti 1981:64). This shift illustrates market principles: when land and credit are made available cheaply for beans and corn, and less so for export crops, then more of the former and less of the latter will be grown. But the statistics do not show whether the incomes of the poor were greater because they had grown beans and corn instead of export crops. (We suspect they were not.)

We have seen that when a government intervenes directly in the economy, it may set up a vicious cycle. The intervention leads to problems; the response is more intervention, and this leads to more problems. By 1981, the Ministry of External Commerce had set up enterprises for the export of coffee, sugar, cotton, beef, and tobacco; all growers were required to sell to these enterprises (Deere and Marchetti 1981:59). At the same time, domestic trade in basic foodstuffs became nationalized (Kaimowitz and Thome 1980:2). Prices of all export goods and basic foods were now government-controlled.

Not having price signals, the government was unaware of the growing demand for sugar in 1980; it therefore sold too much to Coca-Cola and did not have enough left over for domestic consumption (Collins 1982:131). Shortages appeared in other foodstuffs as well, and long lines began to form at stores, a common sight in countries where prices and production are centrally controlled. Naturally, hoarding followed. Here Sandinista supporters confuse cause and effect; they blame the hoarding for causing the shortages, not understanding that people hoard only when shortages are either upon them or imminent:

> Several other basic foodstuffs illustrate the same story: government programs to make food available at stable, affordable prices undercut by profiteering as well as by those holding food in "reserve," for fear of shortages (Collins 1982: 133).

In response to the growing shortages (and in keeping with the vicious cycle), the government decided to distribute credit (still at favorable interest rates) with greater care. Instead of as cash, credit would be granted in inputs such as fertilizer, seed, and tools (Collins 1982:113). There has not yet been time to study the effects of this decision in Nicaragua, but we have seen in other countries—Egypt (Chapter 6) and the Philippines (Chapter 2), for example—that the government knows neither the best fertilizers and seeds for local conditions all over the country nor the best ways to distribute them to peasants (by the teaspoonful or in hundred-weight bags). Through Adams et al. (1984), we have seen that cheap credit undermines rural development (Chapter 1). In the Philippines, Goodell (Chapter 2) found that peasants who received credit in kind accepted it but (possibly because it was not what they wanted) would not pay it back. It is, of course, difficult to transpose experiences from one country into another, but they are the only insights we have.

The next response to shortages was rationing. Collins (1982:120) found that rationing was "feared" by many persons he had encountered. Because of this fear, he pointed out (p. 134), the government therefore decided to call it something else, and "guaranty cards" were issued. However, as Collins perceived (p. 119), rationing has two disadvantages: first, because it implies lower than market prices, it subsidizes the rich as well as the poor; second, since Nicaragua is populated by thousands of tiny retailers throughout a country with difficult communications, rationing is very difficult to enforce.

To solve these problems, and in keeping with the vicious cycle, the government decided to go into retailing itself. By 1982 ENABAS, the Nicaraguan Basic Foods Company, had spawned into 100 supermarkets and "people's stores" throughout the country. In addition, ENABAS made arrangements with some 800 small retailers to sell at controlled prices goods that it would provide them. In exchange for their cooperation, government would see to it that these retailers received special favors: credit and supplies, both of which were in short supply. Once again, government was using its sovereignty to juggle economic commodities in favor of those who would agree with its political/economic system. Collins (1982:122) tells how ENABAS expected to control the market indirectly:

> To help consumers, ENABAS would store up enough of the supply of basic foods so that whenever private merchants speculated on rumored shortages or hoarded, it could release enough onto the market at a low and stable price to undercut speculators, without resorting to policing.

We see two problems. First, to combat hoarding ENABAS is itself hoarding. Hoarding comes from shortages, not vice versa, and when hoarding is done (no matter by whom), the shortages become more severe. Thus ENABAS hoarding will likely lead to more hoarding, not less. Second, the plan implies administrators of great integrity, who would have the power to sell ENABAS supplies on the black market at great gain to themselves. Our experience is that integrity, when tested in situations such as this, usually is found wanting.

Still there were other problems, which Collins (1982:124) has perceived:

> . . . Private traders appeared in full force in the countryside offering up to 500 córdobas per hundredweight (of beans); ENABAS could hardly compete with its price set at only 220. (In some areas the Sandinista-led ATC expended precious political capital with the campesinos trying to persuade them that the "correct" thing to do—"for the sake of the revolution"—was to sell to ENABAS at prices well below what they could be getting. Much to its dismay, the government felt compelled to forcibly stop some campesinos from trying to take their beans across the border into Honduras, where bean prices were much higher.)

Already we find a government that calls itself "popular" taking actions against its people. The bean growers whose activities it is trying to control are not the wealthy plantation owners of Somoza days; they are small farmers trying to sell the bean crop that the government has urged them to produce. We have pointed out that a more effective distribution will come from increasing the income of small farmers (so they can buy their foods); the government, through ENABAS, appears to be decreasing that income instead. By offering low prices for beans—and by making it illegal for farmers to accept higher offers—they are also discouraging production. The increases in the bean crop were wiped out in 1980–81, when it fell to only two-thirds of 1977–78; in the same year, the corn crop showed no increase (Collins 1982:109). The Sandinistas have apparently decided to subsidize the urban poor (and rich as well) at the expense of the rural poor, thus discouraging agriculture, as governments all over the Third World have done. Lappé and Collins have admirably pointed this out in their other writings.

Like Collins, Austin et al. (1985:26–7) also perceived the problems with ENABAS, but they too considered them errors of inexperience, without seeming to be aware that in other countries these same problems were inherent in centralized control of agriculture, persisting over decades:

> Whereas private traders paid cash and sold consumer goods, ENABAS offered cheques; other difficulties included staff and transportation shortages and insufficient producer prices. In 1980 ENABAS tried to centralize grain procurement without first using a transportation and storage network adequate to the task, which led to friction with private traders and producers. Because of the use of political pressure to sell to ENABAS in the absence of sufficient economic incentives, the private procurement network was sharply disrupted and reduced non-state urban grain supplies.

In the next paragraph, the same authors report that "ENABAS began to change its operational approach," by intervening further in the market, with "over 250 intermediate collection centres to be run by 'honest' private merchants selected by UNAG." Thus they repeat the faith expressed by Collins in the integrity of private Nicaraguans when placed in situations of great temptation for corruption.

There are still other ways in which the government thought it knew what was best for its people and discovered otherwise. One was to decide, as general policy, to decrease the spread of earnings between the highest and lowest paid employees in the public sector. An admirable thought, but it caused technically trained managers to leave the state farms in favor of greater opportunities elsewhere (Collins 1982:76). Another was to move the sprawling Mercado Oriental (Eastern Market), since it thought that smaller, neighborhood markets would be more convenient for its people. Its people had a different idea, however, and they continued to buy in the sprawler. Finally, Collins writes, "in the marketplace and even in lunch counters, you will find people distinguishing between 'beans' and 'EN-ABAS beans,' and commonly paying more than twice as much for the non-government beans."

After interviewing a large number of peasants in Matagalpa, Lowenstein, a *Wall Street Journal* reporter, wrote (6/20/84) that "support for the government here remains strong—and, by most reckonings, it is even stronger in areas such as Managua, the capital. Yet there is widespread dissatisfaction with the Sandinistas." Among the points of dissatisfaction was the direct intervention of the state in farmers' decisionmaking:

> The growers must sell to the state, instead of exporting directly. The government gets dollars for their coffee, pays the growers in local currency and cheats them on the exchange rate. Pasqual, a small grower, can't get a loan from the state-owned bank because he won't join a co-op. The farm of Jaime, who was a medium-sized grower, was expropriated. Another grower would like to sell out but fears that if he asked permission, it will simply be seized. "Is this free enterprise?" he asks.

The Indians

Living on the Caribbean coast, the Miskito, Sumo, and Rama Indians for centuries had farmed their land communally, but they held it in individual plots, with the harvest belonging in each case to the plotholder (NYT, 9/5/82). In hindsight, the government might well have declared the Indians already "cooperators" in no need of land reform. Instead, it decided to include them. Cooperatives would be formed, with the harvest shared according to need. The Indians so insisted on their traditional customs that the government yielded during the second year.

By then, however, it had intervened in other ways. Wishing to incorporate the Indians into their country, the Sandinistas provided health clinics with doctors, nurses, and assistants, opened schools, and began teaching literacy in Spanish (although this was dropped later when the Indians complained that it was not their language). While all these have appeared to outside supporters to be an advance, it is not clear that the Indians looked upon them as such. After interviewing a number of them, Bonner reported (NYT, 9/5/82):

> But many of the students, especially the adults, complain that there is too much political content to the instruction, according to a teacher. . . . And even Sandinist supporters criticize the government for not being sensitive to the Indians' culture.

This opposition led the government to assume that the Indians were their opponents. Already frightened by potential military intervention from the Contras (guerilla exiles), whom they suspected the Indians would join, the Sandinistas forcibly relocated thousands into settlement villages behind barbed wire.

In a pastoral letter of February 18, 1982, Catholic bishops of Nicaragua "verified reports of relocation of Indian communities without prior notice, the forced marches of women, children, and the elderly to relocation camps, the wholesale destruction of Indian communities, property and livestock, and the murder of Indians in the process" (Sussman of Freedom House, New York, letter to editor, NYT, 3/18/82).

Other reports of atrocities trickled in. J. B. A. Kessler, an advisor to the Moravian Church in Costa Rica and a regular visitor for eight years to the Miskitos, reported (WSJ, 12/16/83) that three armed Sandinista soldiers had invaded a church service to arrest two Miskito Indians. When the congregation asked them to wait until the service was over, the soldiers tried to arrest the Indians by force. A gun went off; some parishioners were killed, whereupon young men of the church killed the soldiers with their bare hands. To escape arrest, these young men fled to the jungle. Promised amnesty, they returned. But the government broke its promise and detained some of the returnees. (A high official of the Sandinista government told one of the authors of this book that the incident was correctly reported.)

When the Nicaraguan minister of Justice was asked by the United Nations Human Rights Commission to explain the forced relocation of approximately 14,500 Miskito Indians and the arrest and execution of some (along with other infringements of human rights), he admitted that Indians had been detained on a farm where they were told to "practice your religion, retain your customs, and sing your beautiful songs" (Nossiter in NYT, 3/31/83).

On June 7, 1984, the Inter-American Commission on Human Rights, an agency of the Organization of American States, reported the following (NYT, 6/8/84):

> Hundreds of Miskito Indians have been arbitrarily detained without formalities, under vague accusations of counter-revolutionary activities,

[and many] were placed in isolation for long periods, and in some cases, the commission verified they were tortured and illegally punished . . . . [The commission] has sufficient information to state that the Nicaraguan government illegally killed a considerable number of Miskitos as a reprisal [for the deaths of government soldiers in skirmishes with the Indians].

To us, the military threat of the Contras is not the question here. The real question is: Why were the Indians deemed a threat in the first place? We would argue it was a result of the active intervention of the Sandinistas in their land practices and other affairs. Had the government respected the traditional aloofness of the Indians and not tried to remold them after their own image, we can see no reason why the Indians would have wanted to become involved in any manner in a civil war in which they would have everything to lose and nothing to gain.

The Economic Crisis

For all its mathematical wizardry, economics does not yet have a way to "prove" the causes of the economic crisis in Nicaragua. On May 1, 1985, President Reagan declared trade sanctions against Nicaragua; these and the war of the Contras have surely taken a devastating toll. Although conditions have worsened greatly since the embargo, nevertheless the negative direction had been set much earlier.

The growth rate in per capita gross national product—positive in 1981 and 1983, negative in 1982—has also been negative in 1984 and 1985 (IDB 1986:252). The New York Times reported (3/8/82) that although gross national product grew by 8.1 percent in 1981, it was "still far below pre-revolution levels." The growth rate in agricultural output tapered off (to 0.3 percent in 1983 and then became negative (-0.2 percent and -3.3, respectively) in 1984 and 1985 (IDB 1986:252). Inflation averaged 30 percent (IMF:IFS) from 1979 to 1984 (latest information available), and the long-term foreign debt grew from the $1.6 billion inherited from Somoza (NYT, 3/8/82) to approximately $3 billion at the end of 1982 (increase taken from balance of payments; see Table 17.1). The New York Times reported (3/8/82) a "growing mood of disenchantment among the urban poor, who complain of wages falling behind prices and occasional shortages of basic goods." (The shortages have become more severe since that time.)

Even Sandinista supporters admit that state farms are running losses and are a drain on the treasury. Collins (1982:65) shows that "in 1980, the state farms got over 25% of the total agricultural credit, yet produced only 14% of the value of agricultural production. In terms of loan repayment, an officer of the national finance corporation told me that the state is 'our worst client.' He reports (p. 63) that when a U.S. visitor asked the director of a coffee farm how profits were divided, the reply was: "Well, we haven't had any yet to divide." Deere and Marchetti (1982:80) show:

344

The issue facing the agrarian reform at the moment though is whether the state farms will be generating any social surplus at all. Preliminary indications seemed to show that the costs of state enterprises were running far above expected, possibly pointing to an overall drop in productivity in this sector compared to the private sector.

Collins suggests that if the exports of state farms were valued at the black market exchange rate (or the "parallel" or "tourist" market), the farms would turn a profit. Since the government is the winner from exchange losses inflicted on state farms, all he has shown is that the government's finances have been sweetened by palming off a part of its deficits on the state farms. Overall, the outstanding debt of the government was 1,966.5 million córdobas in 1974: 4,320.0 million in 1978; and 36,327.5 million in 1983 (IMFGFSY 1985:621).

As early as September 1981, Frazier of The Wall Street Journal (9/15/81) was reporting "an economic crisis so severe that Nicaragua doesn't have enough dollars to import the machinery and raw materials it needs to keep its largely agrarian society functioning." So the government declared a national emergency. "It cut the national budget 5% . . ., slashed subsidies for food, transportation, and other items 10%, froze the government payroll, and imposed a 30% to 100% luxury import levy. It also threatened jail terms for acts of economic sabotage, said to include strikes, raising prices without permission and publishing false economic news."

By 1983, the reports of crisis were more numerous and more serious. Kinzer (in NYT Magazine, 8/28/83) stated:

> The disillusionment now setting in among ordinary Nicaraguans has more to do with chronic shortages, ration cards and long lines at stores.
> In the town of Jinotega, . . . I spent an afternoon in a small general store. Half the shelves were empty . . . there was no oil to be had. There was also no chicken, no soap, no rice, no eggs. I had noticed eggs in the market in Matagalpa, half an hour away by car, and I asked the store-keeper why she did not send someone there to buy eggs, so she could resell them in Jinotega.
> . . . "In Matagalpa," she said, "I would have to pay the official price for eggs, and when I got them to my store, I would not be able to charge a single penny extra. I couldn't make back what I would have to spend for gasoline. . . . If I charged a higher price, they would send a mob against me and paint, 'House of Thieves' on my wall. . . ."

On October 16, 1988, Stephen Kinzer reported in The New York Times:

> A survey of 2,892 children taken several weeks ago by the Ministry of Health showed that two-thirds were suffering from malnutrition.
> "We are seeing many cases of robbery of food, especially meat and grain, in quantities that are only enough to feed one person or a few people," said Ramón Rojas, a criminal court judge in Managua. "Without

a doubt, the country's economic crisis is a major factor in the increase in crime."

It is impossible even to guess the extent to which the economic crisis is caused by the war or by government policies. Surely both are at work. In Table 1, we find that agricultural output per capita dropped seriously at the time of the Sandinista victory (1979–1980), increased slightly from 1980 to 1983, but has been declining ever since.

These declines in production were translated into decreases in exports and a high level of imports compared with the pre-1979 years. The trade balance, positive before 1979, turned sharply negative (Table 2). With the help of a rescheduling agreement in 1981, generally considered to be favorable to Nicaragua, and exceptional financing from abroad (probably the Soviet Union), Nicaragua has been able to stave off bankruptcy and even increase its reserves from 1983 to 1985. But the overall deficit worsened in 1986. In 1987 reserves declined by $152.8 million (IDB 1988:464).

In a study of coffee producers in Nicaragua that bears out our general theme, Colburn (1984) found that although coffee production had not diminished significantly, nevertheless costs had been so increased that producer income had seriously declined:

> ... real income for coffee producers has fallen precipitously. In 1978–1979 a large profit was realized in coffee production, in part because

Table 17.1

NICARAGUA: AVERAGE PERCENTAGE CHANGES IN VALUE ADDED BY AGRICULTURE, TOTAL AND PER CAPITA, 1960–70, 1970–80, 1980–83, AND YEARLY 1984–87

Period	Total	Per Capita
1960–70	9.06	5.30
1970–78	3.89	0.31
1978–79	−15.30	−17.73
1979–80	−10.09	−12.50
1980–83	6.33	3.56
1983–84	−5.28	−7.49
1984–85	−4.79	−9.96
1985–86	−6.94	−11.85
1986–87	2.05	−1.41

SOURCE: Calculated from IDB, *Economic and Social Progress in Latin America,* 1982 report, Appendix Tables 1 and 9, pp. 346 and 354, respectively, and 1988 report, Appendix Tables A-1 and B-7, pp. 534 and 544, respectively.

Table 17.2
NICARAGUA: BALANCE OF PAYMENTS, 1978–86 (MILLIONS OF DOLLARS)

	1978	1979	1980	1981	1982	1983	1984	1985	1986
Exports	646.0	615.9	450.4	508.2	406.0	428.8	385.7	301.5	247.2
Imports (−)	−553.3	−388.9	−802.9	−922.4	−723.5	−778.1	−799.6	−800.2	−726.5
Trade balance	92.7	227.0	−352.5	−414.2	−317.5	−349.3	−413.9	−498.7	−479.3
Services and incomes earned	85.9	67.3	63.6	73.4	49.5	48.7	49.7	51.2	47.6
Services and incomes paid (−)	−213.0	−205.7	−246.4	−321.1	−297.4	−338.5	−364.8	−395.8	−375.9
Unrequited transfers	9.5	91.6	123.9	70.3	51.5	79.3	89.7	83.9	114.6
Balance on current account	−24.9	180.2	−411.4	−591.6	−513.9	−559.8	−639.3	−759.4	−693.0
Long-term capital	79.9	122.5	62.6	283.3	253.4	24.8	146.9	425.0	254.8
Short-term capital (exc. res.)	−173.1	−266.9	−19.9	24.0	31.3	22.6	106.6	−288.6	21.1
Net errors and omissions	−10.5	−38.5	−74.7	15.8	10.8	−87.3	10.3	137.8	−219.0
Counterparts*	1.6	37.8	4.7	1.0	1.3	0.9	0.7	−0.1	0.0
Total of above items**	−127.0	35.1	−438.7	−267.5	−217.1	−598.8	−374.8	−485.3	−636.1
Exceptional financing	55.1	0.0	241.9	235.4	177.7	742.5	679.6	496.2	515.5
Change in reserves***	−71.9	35.1	−196.8	−32.1	−39.4	143.7	304.8	10.9	−120.6

SOURCE: IMF:IFS (1988:539).

NOTE: Minus sign means debit, no sign credit, except for change in reserves, where minus sign means decrease, no sign means increase.

*Counterparts to gold monetization, SDR allocations, and valuation changes.

**May be roughly thought of as balance of payments surplus or deficit (−).

***Changes in reserves, less changes in liabilities construed as deductions from reserves.

of a high international price that year. In 1981-82, Nicaraguan coffee producers made little, if any, profit. . . . This drop in nominal income was exacerbated by the declining value of the córdoba.

Translating into dollars in order to include the impact of the declining córdoba, Colburn (1984:509) found that semimodern producers were earning $63.86 per quintal in 1978-79, which fell to $2.75 in 1981-82. Some of the decline, however, was due to a fall in the international price. Had that price remained the same, semimodern producers would have earned $7.35 per quintal in 1981-82. He did not have comparative figures for traditional and modern producers in 1978-79, but he showed that in 1981-82 these would have earned $13.78 and $10.83 per quintal respectively, had there been no change in international prices. In addition to the declining córdoba, most of the decline, Colburn argued, was due to government procurement requirements at prices fixed by the government, sharp increases in wages mandated by the government, and inefficiencies in distribution (such as when the government purchasing officers are located far from the coffee-growing areas). The return would have been so low as to cause the farmer to abandon his field and search for other employment, except that coffee trees are a fixed investment (sunk costs had already been paid); land would be confiscated if abandoned; and alternative employment possibilities were scarce.

Curiously, Austin et al. tell quite a different story from substantially similar data. In Table 3, we compare the information on coffee output from the two sources. Since hundredweight (used by Austin et al.) is similar to thousands of quintals (although the English measurement system is not quite clear on this), and since the figures are quite close for a number of years, we take them as equivalent and a rough check on each other. The only substantial difference is for year 1981-82.

Yet this difference in data may be crucial. At the least, it shows the unfortunate result of generalizing on trends in agriculture from a single year or even two years. Colburn, quite properly in our view, sees not much change in coffee output from the mid-seventies to 1981-82. Austin et al. (1985:24), on the other hand, report that "coffee production in 1982-83 was 25% higher than in 1977-78, a record high, and yields were 7% greater. However, adverse weather in 1983-84 caused a 32% drop in output." We submit that this interpretation is misleading, for it implies a consistent increase in output from Sandinista time on, except for 1983-84. Furthermore, while Austin et al. tell of an increase in yield, Colburn (1984:512) reports decreasing yields from 1978-79 on, as follows (in thousand quintals per hectare, the same source as in Table 3):

1978-79	10.48
1979-80	8.47
1980-81	9.73
1981-82	8.98

Table 17.3
COFFEE OUTPUT BY TWO SOURCES OF INFORMATION

Year	From Colburn (000 quintals)	From Austin et al. (cwt milled)
1972–73	762.5	na
1973–74	797.7	na
1974–75	890.7	na
1975–76	1,068.2	na
1976–77	1,205.6	na
1977–78	1,196.0	1,251
1978–79	1,415.0	1,263
1979–80	1,224.0	1,228
1980–81	1,284.9	1,285
1981–82	1,150.0	1,328
1982–83	na	1,568
1983–84	na	1,070

SOURCE: Column 1 from Austin et al. (1985:25), originally from CIERA based on INEC and MIDINRA, Statistics, 1984; column 2 from Colburn (1984:513), originally from UPANIC, "Estudios Económicos," 1982, verified with Banco Central de Nicaragua.

Finally, Austin et al. present their data in physical quantities and not in aggregate value or value added. In a major table that we do not reproduce here (their Table 1, p. 25), they showed increases in seven crops (sesame, bananas, tobacco, maize, rice, sorghum, and beans), virtually the same output for one crop (sugar), and declines in two (cotton and coffee), from 1977–78 and 1983–84. For livestock over the same period, they showed increases in three products (pork, poultry, and eggs) and decreases in two (beef and milk). Using international prices and Food and Agriculture Organization production data on the same products, we found that in 1983, the declining items constituted 46.15% of the value of the products that Austin et al. specified, and the increasing items only 14.85% (Table 4).

We would therefore fault Austin et al. on four grounds. First, they reported increases in coffee output based on an insufficient number of years. Second, they did not, as Colburn did, report that the incomes of coffee growers declined substantially. Third, since Colburn's article was published first, Austin et al. should have mentioned Colburn's data on yields and explained the discrepancy between their information and his. Fourth, they argued, *on the basis of numbers of products,* that agricultural output had been increasing and not—as would have been

Table 17.4

OUTPUT OF SELECTED CROPS AND LIVESTOCK AT
INTERNATIONAL PRICES, 1983 (THOUSANDS OF METRIC TONS;
PRICES IN DOLLARS PER METRIC TON)

Commodity	Quantity	Price	Value ($)	Percentage
Commodities that Austin et al. showed as increasing:				
Sesame	6	na	na	
Bananas	158	429	67,782	
Tobacco	3	3,792	11,376	
Maize	227	136	30,872	
Rice	162	172	23,564	
Sorghum	89	129	11,481	
Beans (dry)	47	394	18,518	
Pork	14	1,065	14,910	
Poultry	8	644	5,152	
Eggs	32	887	28,704	
Total			212,359	14.85
Commodities that Austin et al. showed as decreasing:				
Cotton	80	1,854	148,320	
Coffee	67	2,822	189,074	
Beef	53	1,149	60,897	
Milk	124	2,112	261,888	
Total			660,179	46.15
Commodity that Austin et al. showed as virtually unchanged:				
Sugar	3,000	186	558,000	39.01
Overall Total			1,430,538	100.00

SOURCE: FAO, vol. 37 (1983).
NOTE: Quantities for maize and cotton are listed as unofficial estimates.
For international prices, we selected for each commodity the price we
considered most appropriate; generally prices in the United States. International prices are used to avoid distortions due to overvaluation of the
córdoba.

proper—on the basis of total value or value added. Although agricultural
output did increase in 1983, overall it is significantly less than it was in the

late seventies, and on a per capita basis it has been declining since 1983 (Table 1).

These points, plus the general tenor of Austin et al.'s article—one of dismissing deficiencies in the government program as "temporary," without assessing their potential impacts on peasants and indeed without appearing aware of similar deficiencies in programs of other governments—would cause us to label their approach as one of "selective perception" of information designed to place the Nicaraguan government in a good light. Colburn (1984:501), on the other hand, was clearly aware of similar policies in other countries and their results:

> Comparative research on the newly independent states of tropical Africa suggests several provocative propositions about what might be expected in Nicaragua, where the new regime is increasing its power considerably in order to achieve more equitable development. Because of their historical development, the tropical states of Africa have more extensive state participation in the economy than is common in Latin America. This state participation is often introduced in the guise of establishing "African Socialism." Rhetoric notwithstanding, however, the African regimes have tended to pursue policies that are adverse both to the interests of most farmers and, ultimately, to the welfare of the entire polity. [Colburn goes on to explain how Nicaraguan policies on coffee have been similar.]

It has become customary in some circles to blame the Nicaraguan crisis on the military intervention of the United States. Surely this intervention has contributed, and it is also to be condemned as immoral. However, the crisis had already begun before the United States pressure, and it follows the same general pattern we have seen in other countries (such as Tanzania) where United States pressure has been absent. For these reasons, we believe the government and its supporters would do well to look beyond the United States in order to grasp the reasons for their economic failure.

The idea that economic deterioration results from national policies is reinforced by an international study completed in 1989, on which *The New York Times* reported as follows (Uhlig 1989:1):

> The confidential study, prepared by an international team of experts at the request of President Ortega Saavedra's Sandinista Government, uses formerly secret data to provide the most comprehensive view of the Nicaraguan economy since the revolution in 1979. It presents a picture of a devastated nation where consumption has been cut by almost 70% and where per capita output has fallen even below that of such wrenchingly poor countries as Haiti.
>
> The report's authors assert that recovery will be achieved only through a sweeping reversal of long-held Sandinista priorities, including a halt to land redistribution, a broad new emphasis on private production, and severe cutbacks in government spending for military forces and educational and medical projects.

Conclusion

How, on balance, do we see the Sandinistas? We find them a fervent group of high-meaning individuals, primarily intellectuals but with considerable support from workers and farmers, dedicated to restructuring their country in ways that will help the poor. They have improved medical care, have decreased infant mortality spectacularly, and have increased national literacy. They are supremely confident of their own abilities. Their confidence is so great that when their efforts start to fail, they see no wrong in themselves. The blame must lie elsewhere, as with uncooperative peasants, hoarders and speculators, and above all, with the harassing government of the United States. With this perspective, their response to adversity is to do harder what they have already been doing; to assume more power for themselves, thus perpetuating a vicious cycle.

These Sandinistas have taken on a task of herculean proportions: they have gone far beyond extinguishing the Somozas; they are trying to convert a highly complex, intricate economy, one with a criss-cross network of linkages among money, credit, prices, production, wages, taxes, government revenues, interest rates, exchange rates, and other economic variables—a network they do not understand—into a corporate marionette whose strings they will pull. They are trying to erase local cultures and local institutions of buying, selling, and lending that have been tested over time and to substitute their own, which are experimental. And they want to do this all at once.

We see them as highly naive, in believing that they can perform such a task. We also find them paternalistic, believing that when peasants and workers do not agree with their plans, then the peasants and workers have not grasped "progressive" thinking. The lower classes need to be "educated" into sacrificing for the revolution. Furthermore, we believe the Sandinistas do the peasants great injustice in demeaning their wisdom. We believe the Sandinistas are sincere and (at the top level) noncorrupt. But we suspect that local officials to whom they have given power (capacity to trade in the black market) are probably corrupt, and we do not know how long officials at the top will remain pure. The purity of powerful people is sorely tried when their tenure encounters pressures—either from the outside (as from the United States) or from within (as from a failing economy).

Addendum

After this entire book had been typeset, on March 2, 1990, the Chamorro government-elect announced its plan for land reform. Mark Uhlig of *The New York Times* (3/3/90) reported:

> [The government will] move immediately to return or make compensation for most land confiscated . . . and will sell many of the large state enterprises. . . . [It will] attempt to recover thousands of buildings,

farms, vehicles and other property now in the hands of members of the Sandinista National Liberation Front. . . . [It] does not intend to give back the land that belonged to Mr. Somoza and his associates, because it considers those confiscations justified. . . . In the case of unoccupied farmland, . . . the old owners will be able to apply for new titles. In cases where the land has already been given to small farmers . . . the original owners will be compensated with transferable coupons redeemable at special auctions of Government land. . . . [The new government promises] to give the small farmers who have already settled on the land a permanent title of ownership, rather than the titles provided by the Sandinistas, who generally give lifetime privileges to use, but not to own, the land.

These are the outlines of the land reform that we would have proposed in the first place. Let us hope that it will be put into effect, so that at least the Nicaraguan peasant will become "unbetrayed."

References

Adams, Dale W.; Graham, Douglas H.; and Von Pischke, J. D., 1984. *Undermining Rural Development with Cheap Credit*, Boulder, Colo., Westview Press.

Austin, James; Fox, Jonathan; and Kruger, Walter, 1985. "The Role of the Revolutionary State in the Nicaraguan Food System," *World Development*, vol. 13, no. 1.

Avery, Dennis T., 1985. "Central America, Agriculture, Technology, and Unrest," *U.S. Department of State Bulletin*, January.

Colburn, Forrest D., 1984. "Class, State, and Revolution in Rural Nicaragua: The Case of Los Cafeteleros," *The Journal of Developing Areas*, vol. 18, July.

Collins, Joseph, 1982. *What Difference Could a Revolution Make? Food and Farming in the New Nicaragua*, with Frances Moore Lappé, San Francisco, Institute for Food and Development Policy.

Deere, Carmen Diana, 1982. "Agrarian Reform in Central America and U.S. Policy: El Salvador and Nicaragua," paper presented at the Latin American Studies Association meetings, March 3–6, xerox.

Deere, Carmen Diana, and Marchetti, Peter, 1981. "The Worker-Peasant Alliance in the First Year of the Nicaraguan Agrarian Reform," *Latin American Perspectives*, issue 29, spring.

Dorner, Peter, ed., 1977. *Cooperative and Commune: Group Farming in the Economic Development of Agriculture*, Madison, University of Wisconsin Press.

FAO (Food and Agriculture Organization), 1983. *Yearbook*, volume 37, Rome.

IDB (Inter-American Development Bank). *Economic and Social Progress in Latin America*, annual.

IMF:IFS (International Monetary Fund). *International Financial Statistics*, monthly.

IMFGFSY (International Monetary Fund). *Government Finance Statistics Yearbook*.

Kaimowitz, David, and Thome, Joseph R., 1980. "Nicaragua's Agrarian Reform: the First Year (1979–80)," Madison, University of Wisconsin, Land Tenure Center, paper no. 122.

Lappé, Frances Moore, and Collins, Joseph, 1979. *Food First: Beyond the Myth of Scarcity*, New York, Ballantine Books.

Thome, Joseph R., n.d. "The Nicaraguan Agrarian Reform Process: 1979–82," Xerox, Madison, University of Wisconsin, Land Tenure Center.

Uhlig, Mark A., 1989. "Nicaraguan Study Reports Economy in Drastic Decline," *The New York Times,* June 26.

18. Eleven Short Stories

We now turn to eleven cases of land reform that illustrate our major thesis, but that, for reasons stated in Chapter 1, we decided not to write up in complete case studies.

1. Cooperatives in Turkey

In Western socioeconomic thought, cooperatives are widely associated with worker-initiative and worker-control. A truly democratic cooperative, formed by voluntary association, doubtless serves the interest of its members, but a "cooperative" imposed by the state, with rules being set by the state and membership compulsory, may be quite the contrary.

Consider, for example, Lemel's (1977:10) observations on a land reform cooperative in Turkey:

> . . . production costs are so inflated that virtually no income accrues to the farmer from merely cultivating his land. The co-op usually shows no profit to be distributed after the harvest. . . . Since the complaint of little or no income was repeated in each of the two reform villages I visited, a lot of money is being absorbed somewhere.
>
> The depth of disillusionment felt by co-op members was expressed when a woman thrust her head into the room in which I was seated with a group of men and blurted out, in Arabic, "Just look at the shape we're in. The government saddles us with expenses and we have no money left."
>
> . . . The prescription for a good reform which I elicited turned out to be: "Just give us the land and leave us alone."

2. Zambia: Humanism and Land without Value

Rent is not an evil, and there is no possibility of a rentless society. In land reform for equity, the task is to spread the enjoyment of rents as widely as possible, and especially to include the peasantry. In land reform for efficiency, we seek a system of rents that minimally distorts markets for factors of production and for final products. In Zambia, the interventions of a well-intentioned government fervently seeking equity have created rent-rewarding situations whose market distortions have sacrificed not only efficiency but probably equity as well.

The underlying ideology of the Zambian government is called humanism: that all economic transactions shall occur with human values paramount. In keeping with this principle, in 1975 all land held in fee simple was vested forever in the president, to hold on behalf of the people. Ownership was converted into 100-year leases, on terms set by the state. All assignments, subleases, mortgages, and any other charges required consent of the president (Bruce and Dorner 1982:17). Since land belongs to "all the people," its transfer from one to another shall be at price of zero; only land improvements shall be compensated.

The concept of land belonging to "all the people" requires clarification. Not "all the people" will occupy a given piece of land; "all the people" cannot jointly decide how a piece of land will be used; nor will the fruit of any one piece of land be divided evenly among "all the people." Even "the state" cannot do any of these things in bureaucratic collectivity, for all decisions made by the state "corporately" are really made by specific officials. If the land is profitable, then whoever—state official or private individual—makes the decisions, manages the land, and/or enjoys the fruit may be a rent-earner. Real humanism, to our mind, would require that the rents be apportioned as widely as possible, not that they be concentrated in the president or in his advisors. Bruce and Dorner (1981:22) point out:

> Zambia's guiding philosophy of Humanism seeks a more equitable society. What seems to be happening, however, is that in order to offset undue current benefits to some groups (or to provide special advantages, incentives and benefits to specific other groups) a complex system of subsidies of various kinds is introduced. Certain subsidies are necessary in any society. However, they also have a tendency to grow more costly over time, to develop a life of their own, to be offset with additional subsidies rather than eliminated when no longer called for, and to result in an ever-growing bureaucracy to enforce them.

The land reform in Zambia, therefore, is but part of a wider sociopolitical system ridden with inefficiencies that burden both rich and poor. From 1966 to 1981, Zambia's food production fell by an average of 0.2% per year per capita (NYT, 12/1/84). In 1984, the government issued a report, apparently leaked to *The New York Times*, which wrote about it as follows (12/1/84):

> In a report of unusual candor—and therefore not made public beyond the group of Zambia's creditors—the Government earlier this year offered a severe self-criticism. The two-volume document amounted, in effect, to a repudiation of a largely state-controlled agriculture, which eliminated incentives to the producer, fixed producer and subsidized consumer prices and replaced a free market with favored companies that enjoyed, according to the World Bank, "monopoly trading rights."
>
> . . . In recent years, major steps have been taken to improve food production. Producer prices have been raised and taxes lowered, prices decontrolled and agricultural spending increased. This has raised acreage under cultivation. . . .

[But] in the nearly unanimous view of African and western agriculture and aid experts working here, the country has run into severe constraints imposed by an ill-trained, unmotivated and inefficient Government bureaucracy badly prepared to perform the tasks that their monopoly position limits to them.

The story of Zambia illustrates the third of the three hazards previously mentioned: that a benevolent, paternalistic government, unaware of the end results of a given action, often in good will, makes requirements that bear the opposite of intended results.

3. Sri Lanka: Reform of Tea Plantations

In a study of the 1975 reform of tea plantations in Sri Lanka, Fernando (1978) raises provocative questions concerning the benefits of the reform to workers. While admitting that the study is done too early for definitive assertions, he nevertheless points to harbingers of ways in which the agricultural surplus may be skimmed off by the state.

Early among these was a jurisdictional question. Although a State Planning Corporation (SPC) already existed, the government created a new board, known as the Janawasama (People's State Development Board) to manage approximately 56% of expropriated estates, the SPC controlling the rest. The reason lay not in efficiency or dispersion of power, but in a certain minister's wish that the reformed land in his home area be under the jurisdiction of his ministry (Fernando 1978:16).

Furthermore, only a small fraction of expropriated tea lands was subdivided, by far the greater share being incorporated into state plantations. While this decision may have seemed sound, because the yield on plantations has historically been about twice that on small farms, nevertheless, as Fernando points out, there is no technological reason why this should be so. Kenya, for example, has already demonstrated the efficiency of small tea holdings.

While it is too early to make judgments, the situation is ripe for political inefficiencies. The state, as a monopsonist of labor, can extort value from the tea picker. There are certain indications that it may be doing so.

First, as Fernando (1978:23) points out:

> . . . The quality of management has decreased with the undue interference from members of the National State Assembly. In some cases, political favoritism determined the appointment of managers rather than qualifications and experience. There is the additional factor of a centralized management and bureaucracy in both the SPC and the Janawasama which could hinder the smooth functioning of the estates. In the case of tea cultivation and processing, "quick decisions" play an extremely important role. The Central Bank has already indicated that the SPC tends to curtail the decision-making power of those estate managers working under its jurisdiction.

Second, the government has simply replaced the plantation owners, with no improvement in the conditions of the workers (Fernando 1978:27):

> Allocation to individuals has been insignificant, especially in the case of tea lands. As a result of the reform, the state has become the largest landowner in the country, but that has brought no tangible change in the situation of the landless. The upcountry landless (assumed to have lost their land because of plantation expansion during the colonial period) have received no land from this program on any significant scale.

Ethnic discrimination may well play a greater role in government ownership than it did in private plantations. Many of the workers are Tamils from southern India, who do not carry the same political rights as Sri Lankan citizens (mostly Sinhalese). For example, foreigners are not allowed to receive land under the reform laws. While this distinction probably made little difference to the earlier owners, it is of considerable import to the nationalistic state.

Third, labor unions have raised complaints about the treatment of plantation workers (Thondaman 1975:121, cited by Fernando 1978:28):

> Workers have been forced out of employment for no bigger crime than trade union activity. Trade union rights have been denied and the new managements have refused to negotiate with unions to settle disputes.

4. Venezuela: Marginalization of Land Reform Beneficiaries

Instead of creating a vigorous, domestic agriculture, as had been intended, Venezuela's land reform has impoverished and marginalized its small-farmer beneficiaries. In addition, Venezuelan agricultural output has increased slowly and is less able now to feed the population than it was over twenty years ago. The main findings of Cox (1978) in a doctoral study at the University of Wisconsin's Land Tenure Center are comparable.

Although the reform had been intended to expropriate the latifundia of the north central plains, in fact it consisted mainly in the distribution of state lands, many of them unoccupied and of questionable value. But Cox found the major problems to lie in the system of agricultural credit, controlled prices, and government restrictions on the types of farming that reform beneficiaries might do. Below are some prominent examples.

First: Until 1969, reform beneficiaries were required to borrow only from the state-owned Banco Agrícola y Pecuario (BAP). But the great demand for loans exceeded BAP's capacity to manage them. Often loans were made without any examination of the beneficiary's credit record or purpose of borrowing, and sometimes no record was kept. Therefore, many loans were not repaid. Since delinquency is a "subsidy," borrowing farmers could compete unfairly with nonborrowing ones, and the privilege to borrow became a corruption-potent plum. BAP was close to bankruptcy by the mid-sixties (Cox 1978: 28). A new agency, Banco de Desarrollo Agropecuario, was founded in 1967, to service medium and large farmers. As a result, "medium farmers demanded more credit, were granted more, were paid more, and they repaid more than campesinos" (Cox 1978:29).

Second: Using credit as leverage, BAP steered small farmers into crop production rather than livestock, contrary to the national trend and contrary to an outlet they might have found more rewarding.

Third: Presumably to help small farmers, the government fixed minimum producer prices for nineteen crops and four animal products (Cox 1978:39). These would be paid by a government agency, the Corporación de Mercadeo Agrícola, to which crops would be delivered. However, some land reform beneficiaries, having received favorable credit, would nevertheless sell to private intermediaries and report to the authorities that their crops had been ruined. This would excuse them from debt repayment. With a de facto subsidy, these farmers were in a better competitive position than others who did not do the same. These other farmers, unable to receive credit from official sources and being excluded by law from the regular banking system, would sell their crops to intermediaries in exchange for illegal credit. Because they were competing with the "subsidized" farmers, who could afford to sell at lower prices, they were forced to sell at less than the minimum prices set by government. Thus these prices turned out instead to be maximum prices.

Fourth: To please its urban constituencies, the government also set price ceilings on certain farm products, which decreased the incomes of growers.

Fifth: Agrarian reform personnel "persuaded" farmers to place their lands into collective empresas campesinas, by offering credit. These would then be developed into vertically integrated companies, which would combine mechanization, supply of inputs, storage, and transportation with food production. We do not have financial information on these companies, but the fact that farmers were bribed into them with credit, and the fact of their vertical integration, which excluded competitive (cheaper) sources of credit, storage, and transportation, would indicate that farmers' incomes were sacrificed, probably to the benefit of the government officials.

It was therefore not the land reform, but the extra baggage that the government imposed on top of it, that deteriorated the welfare of the peasantry.

5. Paraguay: Authoritarian Government—Beneficial Reform?

Our pluralistic, balance-of-power argument is challenged by land reforms of authoritarian governments which appear to be beneficial to the poor, for example, those of South Korea and Taiwan. In the chapters on those countries, however, we argued that benefits the peasants have gained from their governments responded to and were limited by the amount of peasant political leverage. In Paraguay the case is different: an absolutist, apparently corrupt government, often called the "last of the Latin American fiefdoms," which severely restricts freedom of expression and movement, has instituted a liberal land reform advantageous to peasants who seem to lack political power completely. Much fertile land in Paraguay—stretching from Asunción east to the Rio Paraná—has been expropriated from latifundists and has been divided among peasants in private property.

The agrarian reform law of 1960 (law no. 662/60) authorized the expropriation of nonproductive private landholdings in excess of 10,000 hectares, and the Institute of Rural Welfare (IRW) was created in 1963 to foster settlements in the east, carved out of these expropriations. In an interview with one of the authors (Powelson) in Asunción, Manuel Frutos, who heads the IRW, declared that the reform was based on Christian, humanist principles. Frutos (1982:289) also writes that from 1960 to 1981, the IRW created 313,682 new properties, with 9,352,426 hectares. Whereas 91% of rural land was held by squatters in 1936, with 4% by owners and 5% by leaseholders, in 1981, 71% was held by owners, 11% by leaseholders, and only 17% by squatters (Frutos, p. 287). The International Monetary Fund wrote enthusiastically of the Paraguayan reform as follows (*IMF Survey*, 1/21/80:18):

> Since the early 1960s the Government's land colonization policy has been effective in bringing many thousands of families, mainly from small landholdings around Asunción, to develop new agricultural areas. . . . Compared with Paraguay's population growth rate of 2.6 percent annually between 1962 and 1972, the eastern region grew by 5.2 percent a year during this period, mostly because of growth in rural areas. . . . Agricultural output grew by an average 8 percent annually between 1973 and 1978. Much of the benefit of the increased activity went to small farmers, who account for the production of 60 percent of the cotton and 30 percent of the soybeans.

Admirers of the reform declare that it has been so powerful that: (1) there are virtually no slums (the scourge of other Latin American capitals) in Asunción; (2) Paraguayan peasants who have migrated to Argentina and other countries have been returning to claim land; and (3) agricultural production has increased spectacularly, with exports shifting from traditional timber to more promising soybeans and cotton.

Current research on Paraguay's land reform, being undertaken by Ben Marcus of the University of Texas, tells a somewhat different story. In a letter to Powelson (August 1984), Marcus wrote that

> . . . A substantial and rapidly growing percentage of Paraguay's agricultural market is controlled by large, mechanized enterprises against which the peasant cannot compete. Moreover, over half the growth in the

land area devoted to farms and ranches since 1956 has occurred in operations of 1,000 hectares and greater. The growth in Paraguay's agricultural production probably results more from the modernization of its agricultural sector and the expansion of these large, modern enterprises into formerly unexploited lands than from the participation of the peasant in the land distribution program.

Marcus believes that the Frutos data include the half of the country that is mostly unexploited. The 1981 Census of Agriculture and Cattle, he points out, found that, of all farm and ranch operators, 15% rented, 30% squatted, and 55% had title. Of this last group, 60% held definitive titles and 40% provisional. Therefore, the tenure of almost half the farmers and ranchers was still precarious.

Thus the land reform, which the International Monetary Fund found so liberal, may not explain at all Paraguay's increased agricultural output. But why were the officials willing to undertake a reform at all?

A most obvious observation might be that they found a common interest with peasants. Just as peasants are concerned with their livelihood, so also the officials are concerned for agricultural exports. Aware that incentives work, they instituted a liberal reform. But more questions are raised than answered by this observation. Why are Paraguayan officials willing to share the rents with peasants when apparently they do not have to? Are they different, in this respect, from officials in other authoritarian societies?

The answer, we believe, lies in cheap land. Even in its most fertile areas (the southeast as opposed to the Chaco in the north and west), Paraguay is land-abundant. According to Marcus, most distributions were from state lands. Even the expropriations did not bring great losses to the former owners, who were still left with 10,000 hectares each. The political élite therefore had much to gain at little cost.

Furthermore, during the seventies, with the influx of funds for hydroelectrical projects (Iguazú, Itaipú, and the beginnings of Yaciretá), plus their multiplier effects, the economy was sufficiently heady—and the "take" of the small number of officials sufficiently great—that they did not concern themselves with skimming off the cream from the small farmer. Agricultural exports were buoyed by the larger farms. The marginal utility of money was so low, and peasant contribution to agricultural exports so slim, that depriving peasants of their rent was not worth the political inconvenience.

During the eighties, the situation became more ominous. Yaciretá was slowed because of the world recession and scarcity of funds from abroad. Parguayan officials, holding the bonanza mentality of the seventies, hoped for oil discoveries to replace capital inflows, but oil remained a long shot. In the mid-eighties they became hard-pressed for funds, and they began the process—so familiar in other parts—of skimming agriculture.

361

The skimming was not done through the land reform laws, for other procedures were more convenient. Whereas the Paraguayan currency (the guaraní) had been freely traded for twenty years, in 1982 the government announced a new exchange control system, with a devaluation of approximately 25%. From then on until 1984, the guaraní was officially settled at 126 to the dollar for certain public sector payments and at seven rates ranging from 126 to 230 per dollar for others (IMF 1984:383); the free-floating exchange system was abolished; and the parallel market value deteriorated, with inflation, to approximately 450 guaranís to the dollar, before stabilizing in the neighborhood of 330.

The government now extracts the surplus from the farmers in the following way. Export brokers, to whom farmers are accustomed to selling their crops, are required to exchange dollars at the official exchange rate on the basis of presumed price (*aforo*) per unit in dollars. If the foreign price for soybeans or cotton falls below the *aforo*, brokers, to stay in business, must buy dollars at the parallel market rate in order to provide them to the government at the official rate. They recoup their losses by paying the farmers less for the crop. Although we were unable to obtain data on prices paid by brokers to farmers, we understand they declined significantly in this process.

The general principle is that an authoritarian, paternalistic government may indeed favor peasants if the cost to do so is not great, if times are prosperous, and if the payoff to it is high. So long as peasants have no leverage upon the government, however, the situation will rapidly change when the state comes under pressure. At that time, government policy will turn against the peasant, for his weakness and his relative prosperity make him reasonable prey for the recoupment of government losses.

6. Sub-Saharan Africa: Universal versus Local-Particular Tenure

Land reform tends to impose a universal tenure system upon a whole country, similar to those in MDCs. In many LDCs, however, the land tenure system has differed from locality to locality. How did these differences arise? For sound, technological reasons, or for historical quirks? Does tearing them down, in favor of national uniformity, destroy local culture and local agriculture? In many cases, we believe, it does just that.

The tribal tenure system in the Anloga area of the Volta region in Ghana, which specializes in shallot farming, exemplifies a logical evolution by consensus between the king of the Anlo and clans and lineages. Nukunya (1974) shows how new technology led to precise boundaries and formal methods of sale and mortgage instead of alienation through subterfuge: gifts (with token payments) because sales were not traditional. Benneh (1971) describes how the tribal land system has adapted to the needs of "a very intense farming system which involves irrigation, manuring, and rotation of crops in the narrow drainage ditches which run almost parallel to the coastline." The problem has been to make land heretofore subject to clan and lineage restrictions available to those particular farmers most apt to be efficient in shallot production. In conclusion, Benneh argues that "the high productivity which the system ensures has been achieved through the efforts of individual farmers who are illiterates. The system gives lie to the assertion, often made by experts of economic development in the Tropics, that the main obstacle to improvement . . . is the illiterate peasant farmer who responds negatively to innovations."

In modern, mobile societies a universal system of land tenure may be optimal, but too rapid a jump from particular to universal gives rise to opportunities for state officials to seize powerful positions away from tribes, destroying efficiencies such as those forged by the Anlo. Land reform must take place over time, responding to new condition after new condition.

This would be particularly so in a nomadic society. Haraldson (1974 approx.), who has studied at least thirty-eight nomadic tribes in various parts of the world, writes of them as follows:

> In many places, people have not occupied these inhospitable areas voluntarily, but intertribal fighting has forced them to seek refuge where no one else claimed the territory. Successively, they adapted themselves to survive in a strange environment as gatherers-hunters or pastoralists with domesticated animals, defending their territories against neighbours and intruders.

In Africa, there are degrees of nomadism. Some tribes move regularly, their livestock following the seasonal grazing; others are partially nomadic and partially settled; still other tribes are largely settled but do have a migratory pattern. As we saw in the case of Somalia, such tribes may make the most efficient use of marginal lands. To substitute a modern, "universal" tenure in these cases would not only invade cultures that have evolved over generations but would result in less efficient food systems.

Largely because of local differentiation in tribal patterns, Subsaharan Africa has not been prone to land reforms of the Latin American, Middle Eastern, or East Asian types. Instead, agricultural development, sponsored by central governments, impinges on local political and tenurial structures. Governments—and foreign advisors—are prone to believe that maximal production of foodstuffs depends only on a given technology (mostly developed locally) combined with well-defined institutions of marketing, credit, and supply. What is often omitted is that the "well-defined" institutions may be quite unacceptable to the people expected to participate in them. In a paper on land tenure issues in Africa, Riddell et al. (1978) point to a number of African states attempting to "formulate land policies which would give the state clearer rights in relation to the landholding kinship groups." They describe dangers inherent in a number of development projects whose implementation may conflict with traditional rights.

Bohannon (1963:101–115) goes further, indicating concepts of tenure quite at variance with the Western terrestrial map, which depends on a *geographical* grid. The Tiv (in Nigeria) posses a *genealogical* map; they "see geography in the same image as they see social organization." Territories, which are associated with lineages, are located spatially with reference to other lineages. The "map" of the Plateau Tonga of Zambia is "a series of points, each representing a rain shrine. . . . Rain-shrine neighborhoods were the basic territorial grouping, and they changed constantly as allegiances shifted with the creation of new shrines." The Kikuyu (in Kenya), on the other hand, possessed "a notion of territorial boundaries" which (among the three tribes mentioned) comes closest to the Western variant.

In studies of Botswana, scholars from the Land Tenure Center (University of Wisconsin) describe the misfortunes occurring when a central government establishes a uniform pattern of agricultural development without taking account of local cultures (Manzardo 1982; Rude et al. 1982; Brown et al. 1982). The authority of village headmen and village councils is already in decline, due to population growth and scattering of people into more distant areas. Instead of permitting this trend to work itself out, with revised or new agencies developed by villagers, the government has imposed a set of Village Development Committees, village extension teams, and village extension agents, in a uniform pattern throughout the country. These institutions have tended to undermine traditional authority further. Manzardo (1982: vi) reports that "lack of experience, lack of adequate training, and lack of extension support make it difficult for some Village Development Committees to be effective." Likewise, "village extension agents . . . are not effective as agents of change. Large territories and lack of transportation reduce effectiveness." It is too early to judge the effectiveness or ineffectiveness of this system.

Let us suggest the following historical sequence. In a tribal, land-abundant society, tenure depends on the technology of products that differ according to locality as to how they are grown and distributed. Thus each tenure system is location-specific, blending with socio-cultural forces. Often these include tribal hierarchies, caste differences, and gross inequalities in income and power. Such a tenure system is likely not to be "efficient" in a modern sense. However, with land abundance, the concept of efficiency is not paramount and may even be irrelevant.

As population grows, as economic development occurs in its neighborhood, and as land becomes scarce, the inefficiencies of feudal, hierarchical systems become revealed and a matter of concern. Likewise, population pressing on land may reduce the effectiveness of nomadic systems, and tribes may be rescued only by improved technology in agriculture, which will require tenure changes. It is then that radical land reform (as opposed to evolutionary change) becomes tempting. In this volume, we have argued in favor of evolutionary reform nevertheless, in which tenants themselves—neither the feudal owners of the past nor the government officials—bargain for new structures. We also argue that technological efficiency is maximized in this manner, as apparently it was in the shallot farming of the Anlo, rather than by the attempt to achieve a sudden, universal tenure system, imposed by government officials who may (1) know little of local circumstances, and (2) be potential gainers themselves from the new system.

7. Honduras

> Repeated studies in Honduras make it clear that the forest, in much of the present pine area, is the most advantageous permanent use of land. These studies show that if the remaining pine forests were to be used primarily for lumber and wood, if there were greater efficiency in logging and sawmilling, and if burning were curbed sufficiently to permit natural regeneration, Honduras could produce wood indefinitely at present or greater levels (Wheeler et al. 1982:22).

When all trees were nationalized in 1974 and placed under the new Honduran Forestry Development Corporation (COHDEFOR), and when COHDEFOR acquired substantial interest in wood processing and became the country's sole exporter of timber products to boot, the way was presumably opened for integrated exploitation that would maximize the country's principal resource. But in 1983, a U.S. presidential mission diplomatically reported that "COHDEFOR, in its nine years of existence, has accomplished much in transferring forest product industries and trade from the private sector to the public sector, but very little in better forest management" (Wheeler et al. 1982:24).

In fact, Honduras was rapidly becoming deforested. COHDEFOR had been awarded the exclusive right to sell stumpage (cutting rights) on both public and private timber. In principle, it was required to pay a stumpage fee to the landowner—the timber, not the land, had been nationalized—but it set this fee at only about one-quarter of its imputed free-market value. More often than not, the fee was not paid because property ownership was in dispute, or ownership records were not clear. Therefore, COHDEFOR treated the timber, in effect, as if it were free:

> COHDEFOR is both the supply source for timber and the only exporter of lumber. It sells stumpage cheap and likewise buys lumber cheap. It seems to maximize its receipts from assembly, reprocessing, storing, and exporting lumber, using its monopoly to extract margins of 50 to 100 percent. The domestic market, in which private industry is permitted to sell directly, is small. Most production, therefore, goes to COHDEFOR (Wheeler et al. 1982:27).

365

Because it holds a monopoly on timber, COHDEFOR has the power to make or break enterprises in any aspect of lumbering. Its price policies (low stumpage costs, high sales prices) have hurt both private and public sawmills. The former have largely gone out of business (hence the small private sector), while the public ones have subsisted through subsidies.

The greatest tragedy is the forest. With low stumpage value, the forest is treated as a free good. Peasants, ever needful of fuel and space for grazing and migratory agriculture, invade the forest, burn it, and cut it down. Because the logger pays only for the timber he takes, he has the incentive to remove only the best, leaving even slightly defective trees behind. Burning impedes natural regeneration, and there is no planting program. As a result, the forest is rapidly depleted.

To an outside technical observer, the problem is managerial: there is no reason why a government monopoly should not operate efficiently. Indeed, *in its own long-term interests,* COHDEFOR should increase stumpage costs and charge opportunity costs for the use of the forest, to promote regeneration. If the forests are depleted through continued mismanagement, COHDEFOR itself cannot survive.

There is, however, one point that sage management advice cannot overcome. Political appointees are ephemeral. Their best interests may lie in squeezing both the forests and COHDEFOR as much as possible during their terms of office, which may shortly be ended legally or violently. Although not strictly land reform, Honduran forests fit into a pattern: short-term functionaries, operating in their own best interest and from their own monopolies, and seeing advantages in exports to gain hard currencies, will degrade both peasants and resources, as well as the future possibilities of their countries.

8. Chile: Land Reform by Grace

Agriculture in Chile has been stagnating for half a century or more; it even declined by 5% per capita from 1948 to 1963 (Barraclough 1973:141). Why? First, high industrial tariffs had made farm equipment costly, thus discouraging modernization. Second, sharecropping was widespread. Sharecroppers have no incentive to invest in improvements, for the land is not theirs; owners do not invest because a large part of the return would go to the croppers. Third, as in the rest of Latin America, the hacienda has been viewed as an inefficient political and social system, which Barraclough (1973:28) describes as follows:

> The large landowners do not need to produce in order to survive . . . for the *hacendado* to maintain his social and economic power it is necessary that he maintain the peasants (*campesinos*) in a situation where they have low incomes, insecure tenancy, and few alternative sources of employment. He has a constant motive to limit rather than to raise his labor requirements.

For both efficiency and equity, Chile has long been ripe for land reform. Although there had been earlier reforms, a real transformation began with the law of 1967, under President Eduardo Frei. All farms greater than 80 "standard hectares" were subject to expropriation. (A standard hectare equals the amount of land capable of producing the equivalent of one hectare in the most fertile, irrigated areas.) These were to be placed in cooperatives for five years, after which the peasants would decide whether to continue cooperating or to divide the land into private farms. Before the five years were over, the Popular Unity government of Salvador Allende, which favored state farms, had been elected. Taking advantage of a provision in the law for an unspecified number of state farms (intended for research), Popular Unity turned every expropriated farm into a state farm.

In 1971, David Baytelman, the director of the Agrarian Reform Corporation, invited one of the authors (Powelson) to visit a state farm, and while driving there, he expressed the high hopes that the reform would overcome the inefficiencies of the past. The following is excerpted from notes taken of his conversation:

> Fifty years ago the land was producing seventy quintals of wheat per hectare, and now is is producing only five. In 1936, there were 250,000 cattle in Chile, and now there are only a few thousand more. You could fit all of California into Chile and have room for New Zealand left over. The California part of Chile could produce as much fruit as California, and the New Zealand part as much cattle. We have 20 million hectares of natural pasture, even more than New Zealand, but they have eight million cows to our quarter million. Whereas there are now 70,000 hectares planted in fruit trees, another 500,000 would be possible. Where there are now 100,000 hectares in vineyards, another 500,000 would be possible.

But all this did not come to pass. Before the military brought Popular Unity to an end in 1973, agricultural output had declined significantly. In that year it was only about 75% of what it had been, per capita, in the three years immediately preceding Popular Unity. Former owners had removed what equipment they could before the accelerated nationalization. During the Allende years, little investment was made, and already existing equipment was allowed to deteriorate.

Causes lay both in farm management and in the general management of the economy. Among the former, three reasons predominated. First, small farms (less than 80 standard hectares) were invaded by dissidents who split off from Popular Unity, declaring it was not radical enough. Allende objected publicly but did nothing. Neither the owners nor invaders would plant or invest, for their tenure was insecure. Since these farms occupied some two-thirds of Chile's land, the impact was not insignificant. Second, the government kept farm prices low, in the interests of urban workers. It tried to offset these prices by subsidies to state farms, but it could not keep

367

up with inflation. Low returns discouraged output, whether on private or on state farms; they did not provide the funds for seed or fertilizer, let alone tractors. Third, the question of *afuerinos* (persons who had previously worked on the *fundos* – the Chilean term for haciendas – but were not directly attached to them) remained unsolved. On many farms, peasants directly attached (former *fundo* peons) refused to let *afuerinos* work, for fear their membership rights would be diluted.

But improper general management of the economy also worsened agriculture. Workers seized factories and demanded higher wages and low-priced commissaries. Popular Unity's policy was to nationalize factories that had been seized (thus encouraging further seizures); to employ more workers than the factories needed; to pay wages much higher than labor productivity; and to subsidize the commissaries. Profits turned into losses, which the government subsidized, but workers' real incomes increased. To do all this, the government increased the money supply at an average annual rate of 182% (1970–73). Prices went up at an average annual rate of 205% during the same period. Businesses, whether private or nationalized, could not control costs, and with the exchange rate overvalued, exports plummeted and imports skyrocketed. The balance of payments, which had been in modest surplus at the end of the sixties, went into serious deficit. The $400 million of foreign reserves that the government had inherited melted away (Rosenstein-Rodan 1974:9). Needed imports could not be bought, for want of foreign exchange. Stores emptied, people hoarded against uncertainty, and farms could not afford the inputs they needed.

For many, the Allende years are a highly emotional matter. The intervention of the United States, the dedication of Popular Unity to the welfare of the poor, and the brutal dictatorship that followed the overthrow all have made objective assessment difficult. But in a book in which we call both socialist and nonsocialist governments to task for mismanagement, we must not exempt Allende's Chile. The subsidy of the poor could not have been continued without increased production – impossible because of no investment – so the poor in the end were the victims. Mismanagement does not justify foreign intervention; it does not excuse a torturing dictatorship; it is not an argument against land reform. But the accountability of the government is a point that supporters of land-reform-by-grace have not adequately addressed.

The overthrow of Popular Unity did not repeal the reform. The smaller farms, those whose illegal occupation Allende himself had decried, were returned to their former owners: 22.9% of total expropriations. The remaining 77.1% were scheduled to be turned into private farms in the names of the settlers (Stanfield 1976:2). The fact that the Allende government had not distributed a single title to a single farmer made it all the easier for a successor government to undo the reform. Stories of political favoritism abound, as choices had to be made on who would and who would not own a farm. We have no information to corroborate these stories nor any reason to believe they are not true. Many farm workers, now declared surplus, were laid off from their places on state-farms-turned-private.

Agricultural output immediately began to increase; per capita, the index for 1980–83 averaged 25% higher than in 1973, the year of the overthrow. It began to stagnate against in the mid-eighties, possibly because of authoritarian policies of the dictatorial military government.

9. Cuba: Experimenting with the Welfare of the People*

The Cuban Revolution has consisted of a series of experiments extending over a quarter of a century: in pure communism, in Chinese communism, and in the eighties, in Soviet planning. Each time the model has changed, the problem has remained the same: that an economy without incentives for production, without penalties for freeloading, and without prices that reflect scarcity of resources could not produce enough goods for its people. Despite sharp ups and downs, agricultural output—both total and per capita—declined during the sixties and experienced erratic growth during the seventies. This failure has led to nutritional deficiencies. Mesa Lago (1981:159), probably the most rigorous and specialized of Cuban observers among current scholars, reports:

> Rationed articles are often sold out before the turn of a customer thus provoking the long lines in front of state shops. According to various official estimates, rationing assured a minimum of 2,100 to 2,846 calories per day in 1977–78, but Dudley Seers reported that rationing in 1962—when quotas were higher—allowed only 1,307 calories for those older than seven and 2,155 calories for those younger than seven. . . . Those who have enough income supplement their diet by often eating in cafeterias and restaurants.

Nevertheless, Mesa Lago concludes that "although the national average per capita caloric intake has probably declined since 1962, rationing has been instrumental in making food distribution more egalitarian. As a consequence, low-income groups and rural areas probably have increased their caloric intake while urban middle-income groups have experienced a decline." Although caloric needs vary widely among persons, and caloric intake is not a sufficient guide to nutrition, nevertheless as averages, the quantities mentioned here appear on the precarious side. Furthermore, compared with the ideal conditions for agriculture in Cuba (flat, fertile land, abundant rainfall) and the experiences of other LDCs, Cuba's performance in feeding its people during the period of the Revolution would appear to be considerably less than might have been expected. Why?

*We are indebted to Carmelo Mesa-Lago for reviewing this section and offering his comments.

Cuban land reform was initially directed against foreign imperialism. The sugar and tobacco plantations and cattle ranches, largely owned by foreigners, were the first to be seized, in 1959. Smaller properties were not immediately reformed. Private farms still exist nominally, although they are now managed as part of the state system.

One reason for the slowness in agriculture has been the constant experimentation on basic structures. The authorities have tried to lead toward pure communism (no money, free food; they did not achieve this); they debated (and had difficulty deciding) between Soviet and Chinese models (with differing stress on urban versus rural investment; on equality of distribution versus wage incentives). When the reform began, the expropriated properties were divided into sugar cooperatives, other cooperatives, and state farms. In 1961, all ordinary cooperatives were transformed into state farms, and private farmers were required to join the Association of Small Farmers, which over time received more and more direction from the state. In 1963, all farms above 67 hectares were expropriated; thus the middle-sized farmer was eliminated. Compulsory procurement quotas (*acopio*) were instituted (Mesa Lago 1981:15). By 1968, all private farms were effectively under state management. Quite apart from which structure is "better" than others, the very capriciousness led to uncertainty, along with decapitalization and decline in worker productivity. Writing about the late sixties, Mesa Lago (1981:25) reported:

> Labor productivity also fell due to the negligence of work quotas, its disconnection with wage scales, the suppression of production bonuses, and the gigantic labor mobilization that disregarded costs. . . . Contrary to expectations the old "economic man" was not transformed and economic chaos ensued.

Rural-urban migration was stopped in 1964, but the retention of surplus labor on the farm could only decrease its productivity. Control was enforced through a state monopoly over employment, with a compulsory identification card for all job-seekers, Ministry of Labor authorization required for all transfers, and ration cards dependent on residence (Mesa Lago 1981: 128).

The failures of the sixties led to reassessment in the seventies, and a return to the Soviet economic model. Increasingly, private farms have been turned into collectives, and prices for compulsory quotas were increased. Wages were brought into line with worker productivity, and the creation of jobs depended on productivity, not need for employment. As a result, total agricultural output has increased, from 1971 to 1982, by an average of 3.9% in total per year and 2.8% per capita (FAO 1983:77). Three points should be kept in mind, however.

First, the increases have hardly compensated for the earlier stagnation. They may be nothing more than a "catching up," which might not continue. Second, increased productivity has led to some unemployment. An economy geared to absorbing unproductive labor on its farms cannot suddenly find jobs with the command that farms become "efficient." Third, the farmer on the field has no greater power to manage his affairs than before. Incentives in his favor may be just the "day's decision" by bureaucrats, subject to change as soon as a new ideology comes into vogue.

In addition, the few remaining private farms account for a disproportionate share of the increase in yield. From 1962 to 1968, the sugar yield on private farms averaged only 97% of that on state farms (which had been the high-productive plantations). Thereafter, yields on both increased, but those of the private farms increased more. In 1969 to 1973, private yields were 11% greater than those on state farms, and in 1974 to 1977 they were 17% greater (calculated from data in Mesa Lago 1981:138). Furthermore, Mesa Lago finds that tobacco productivity also increased more on private than on state farms. "Although private farms in Cuba do not operate fully under the market system," he reports, "they are the closest to that system that can be found in the nation. He goes on (p. 139):

> This performance is particularly important in view of the limitation imposed on private lands by the state, including the prohibition to sell the land except to the state, restrictions and penalties to sell their surplus in the market, obligation to sell a significant percentage of their crops to the state, social pressure to become integrated into cooperatives or into the state sector, and dependency on the state to get credit, seed, fertilizer, and tools.

In keeping with a current trend among socialist countries, the Cuban government permitted "free peasant markets" beginning in 1980; farmers were allowed to sell specified portions of their harvest at market-determined prices. In 1982 these were subject to a 20% profits tax, and in May 1986 they were peremptorily abolished, with the following statement by Fidel Castro (NYT, 5/20/86):

> The struggle against all kinds of exploitation and parasites is a struggle without truce, because such a deviation could damage the revolutionary cycle of the people. The free market became an obstacle to the development of the cooperative movement and was useful only for a group of intermediaries to get rich individually.

10. China: A Roller Coaster with More Downs than Ups

China has been on a roller coaster: during periods of "direct planning," when production was controlled by quantity quotas (1958–1960; 1965–1977), output has fallen. But when "indirect planning" has been in vogue—price incentives, procurement contracts, credit manipulation, and taxes—(1949–1958; 1961–1965; after 1977), production has increased. On balance, over thirty years, agricultural output is up, but state controls have so limited productivity increases, these increases have been so unevenly distributed, and the state has skimmed so much away that many peasants are worse off, nutritionally, than they were before the 1949 revolution. These are the observations of Lardy (1983:18ff., 44).

The Chinese land reform began even before the communist victory of 1949, when Mao's forces confiscated land and executed landlords in occupied territories. It was not that Chinese farms were large. Buck (1937:197), who studied 16,786 farms in twenty-two provinces as of 1929–33, found an average size of 5.36 acres in the wheat region and 3.09 acres in the rice region, with a standard error of .118 for the Yangtze wheat-rice region. Perkins (1969) also reports small size with low deviation. Furthermore, there was very little tenancy in the north. In the south, probably less than half the land was tenanted, with rents about 40% to 50% of the crop. The small sizes and low rate of tenancy would not seem to make China an appropriate candidate for land reform, least of all justify the execution of so many landlords.

When the reform did occur, tenants were converted into owners. In the early fifties, private farms were "encouraged" to join mutual-aid teams, then collective farms, which accounted for over 60% of the total by 1955 (MacFarquhar 1974:15). In 1958, over 90% of Chinese farms were combined into communes, which were divided into villages, and these in turn into production brigades and work teams. Each level owned its own machinery, equipment, and other assets. Each had different responsibilities for production and the division of income. Toward the end of the seventies, the communes were again being dismantled; farmers were again being permitted individual properties (but not the right to buy and sell land) and free markets of certain crops within certain areas; and farming decisions were more and more decentralized.

In addition to the major finding cited above, Lardy (1983) makes the following observations about the land reform and Chinese agriculture.*

First (pp. 1ff.): Although Chinese production shifted relatively from agriculture to industry, the distribution of population has changed little since the Revolution. China is still an agrarian country. Strict control over rural-urban migration and the registration of labor were the instruments for keeping people on the farm. Implied in this is surplus labor, with attendant inefficiencies.

Second (pp. 30ff.): The terms of trade for agriculture have been subject to central control. Depending on which planning ideology dominated politically (Mao favored direct planning, but he was not always in charge), the terms of trade would improve or deteriorate.

Third (pp. 32ff.): Private grain marketing was sometimes permitted

*We are indebted to Nicholas Lardy for reviewing the draft of this section, and for assuring us that our résumé is a fair representation of his findings.

(e.g., 1956–57; after 1978), sometimes not, and sometimes permitted in part and under specified conditions.

Fourth (pp. 36ff.): Communes have been required to deliver grain quotas to the state. Since 1953, grain transfers from one province to another have been controlled by the state.

Fifth (pp. 48ff.): Chinese planners appear unaware of the increases in productivity available through specialization and trade according to comparative advantage. During certain periods, they have insisted on self-sufficiency by regions, which has decreased agricultural output and the welfare of the peasantry. For example, grasslands were especially adapted to animal husbandry, their traditional use. During periods when self-sufficiency was demanded, peasants on grasslands were required to grow grain, which yielded much less income than livestock.

Sixth (p. 51): Peasants were required to sell grain to the state at one price, but to feed themselves, they had to buy it back at a much higher price.

Seventh (pp. 82ff.): Bureaucrats unfamiliar with agronomy would demand irrational, inefficient cropping patterns, such as triple-cropping of grain. Unit yield became the goal rather than maximum yield proportionate to cost. During the Great Leap Forward, communes were required to produce steel in backyard furnaces, inefficient not only because of size but because coal had to be transported to so many different places. In the meantime, trains were hauling coal instead of food, farmers were called away from harvests to tend the furnaces, food rotted in the fields, and peasants' home cooking pots were confiscated to compel them to eat in communal mess halls. Both MacFarquhar (1974:197) and Lardy (1983:152) found evidence in original Chinese documents of widespread starvation and death during the Great Leap Forward.

Eighth (pp. 94ff.): While private marketing was restricted, at the same time the state monopoly—with insufficient storage space, transportation, and budget—was often not able to market all the products peasants would offer.

Ninth (pp. 123ff.): The government profited greatly by being the sole buyer of raw cotton and sole seller of cotton goods, controlling prices in its favor.

Tenth (pp. 138ff.): Traditional sources of credit (landlords and rural loan associations) were eliminated, so that investment depended on government budgetary expenditures, reinvestment of collective income, and bank loans. The government control over these sources (or local party cadre control over income of collectives) enabled the state to follow an investment policy that favored industry over agriculture during most of the period. As a result, Chinese agriculture has been seriously undercapitalized.

Eleventh (pp. 145ff.): Since 1978, with a new administration, state credit has been directed more toward agriculture, farm taxes have been reduced, and terms of trade have moved again in favor of farmers.

Twelfth (p. 149): Foodgrain output per capita, which had increased from 285 kg. in 1952 to 302 in 1957, declined to approximately 205 in 1960 and did not regain its 1957 level until the early seventies. With increased farm output following the more liberal price policies after 1977, it rose to 342 in 1979 and remained at 326 in 1980 and 1981. However, inequality of consumption, both as between urban and rural areas and within rural areas, increased from the mid-fifties to the late seventies (p. 157), which has led Lardy (p. 159) to comment: "China is probably the only country to combine, over twenty years, a doubling of real per capita national income . . . and constant or even declining average food consumption." In his final summary (pp. 186–7), Lardy observes:

> The county-level data . . . suggest that absolute deprivation was widespread. . . . Programs . . . had not eliminated chronic malnutrition and had left wide variations in the level of life expectancy. . . . Government policy contributed to the immiseration of a significant portion of the peasantry. Policies that encouraged or even compelled the pursuit of self-sufficiency in foodgrains squeezed out the gains from specialized production based on local comparative advantage. . . . Population and migration policy has also exacerbated rural poverty. . . . Tax and procurement policy, at least until 1979, exacerbated rural poverty.

In these ways, the Chinese land reform and attendant policies have substituted state credit, state procurement and marketing, and state planning for institutions already developed in villages; have squeezed the peasant in favor of the state; and have reduced the efficiency of agriculture and decreased the country's ability to feed itself, just as other land reforms have done in many parts of the Third World.

In 1979, the government of China began to dismantle the communes by dividing the land into "private parcels," which peasants may use but not sell. Although the farmers are required to sell a certain crop quota to the government, they are allowed to sell the remainder where and when they will, at whatever prices they wish. The result has been a surge in small vendors seen both along rural roads and on city pavements.

Agricultural output surged, increasing per capita by a 4.52% annual average during the first half of the 1980s (Table 19.1). Grain production rose 34% from 1978 to 1984, or a compound average of 5% per year. Thereafter, however, it tapered off, and in 1988 it was no higher than in 1984.

Why? First, while the government allowed other prices to rise, it controlled the price of rice. In their new-found freedom, farmers shifted from rice to other crops. Second, investment in agriculture lagged. Without the security of owning their own plots, private farmers were reluctant to invest, and the government's investment dropped off because of its own fiscal problems.

By 1988, price controls had been reintroduced, and government officials were talking of a return to collectivization. Why? In part because of inflation, officially in the neighborhood of 9% per year, but privately suspected to be many times that amount. While this inflation is caused by deficit-ridden publicly owned industries and corruption at local levels, all of which are fed by the creation of money, the opinion is nevertheless widespread that it is somehow related to the liberalization of farm production and prices.

The government of China stands on the threshold of taking away the freedom that it gave, by its grace, to the farmers. The massacre of Tiananmen Square in 1989 shows that it possesses that power to do so.

11. The Philippines under Aquino

Kenneth B. Powelson*

Chapter 2 by Goodell was written before the election and coup of 1986. I too am a field worker in Philippine villages, and I have a later report. Although Santa Rina is not among these villages and no direct comparison is possible, the following comments do constitute a set of peasant impressions in one local area—plus events reported in the Philippine press—during the first year of the Corazón Aquino government.

First: The Masagana 99 Progam Goodell mentions is now ended, and all agree it was a failure. Militant farmers' organizations have demanded that outstanding debts be written off. Even before the end of the Marcos regime, farmers had become free to borrow where they liked, and informal mechanisms were being reconstituted in the countryside. Farmers still complain about lack of credit because large banks—both private and government—tend to absorb the national credit supply. These large banks are accessible only to larger farmers; only local resources are available for local needs.

Second: The land reform applied to rice and corn lands only, exempting a large portion of the country's land area and leaving many of the poorest tenants (i.e., in sugar) unaffected.

Third: Even in the areas affected by land reform, landlords converted their lands to exempted crops immediately after the proclamation. Others subdivided them among relatives until each piece was under the seven-hectare limit. They managed to date transactions before the land reform. Even Ministry of Agrarian Reform officials might be bribed to declare the land exempt. Political and family connections were likely avenues for unlawful exceptions.

*Kenneth B. Powelson worked with the International Institute of Rural Reconstruction in the Philippines, 1984–1987, assisting farmers in Cavite Province to cope with the land reform. The information in this section is a combination of his personal experience and his understanding of how the land reform law and bureaucracy operated.

Fourth: Landlords en masse declared their tenants' rights "under protest." This action, for which there is no penalty, not only gave them hope of exempting their lands after court action but also would tie up the process for some time in litigation.

A small community where I have been working for two years is an example. The land is going to be sold to a developer, but the tenants do not want to sell their rights under the land reform law. In other communities that I know, tenants in similar circumstances have been harassed, duped, or manipulated into forfeiting these rights. If the tenants lose their case, a whole community will be forced off the land and committed to a life in the streets or as landless agricultural workers. Not only are officials of the Ministry of Agrarian Reform unresponsive, but the landlord is protesting tenant rights without any legal basis to do so. The tenants do not have the funds to fight the court case. Thus it is unrealistic to suppose that they will ever own the land according to the provisions of the law. At best, we hope, the courts will recognize the rights of tenants to remain on the land for the time being, under current arrangements.

Fifth: The pricing formula established under Presidential Decree No. 27 has been widely violated. This decree provided that the value of affected land should be determined as the average yield of the three crop years before October 22, 1972, times the government support price of the rice at the time, multiplied by two and one-half. This formula would result in a land value of approximately 68% of current market price. But even that value was only suggestive; landlords were not required to accept it.

Barangay (i.e., village) Committees on Land Production, created by the Ministry of Agrarian Reform, were charged to prepare production data. But values based on their data were not given force of law. After months of money-wasting trips through the bureaucracy, many tenants were told by the Ministry of Agrarian Reform to go back and negotiate directly with their landlords. But without government and legal support, they were negotiating from weakness. In most cases, the negotiations led to agreements based on the full market price of land. Those tenants who accepted this value found that amortization payments—originally intended to equal rentals over fifteen years—were beyond their reach. Unable to make payments, they forfeited their rights.

Sixth: Even the conversion of share tenancy to leasehold has not been widespread. Under share tenancy, the landlord provides half of the equipment and materials used in farming, in exchange for half of the crop. As leaseholders, tenants would have to shoulder all costs themselves. In one village where I worked, both tenants and landlords preferred shareholding to leaseholding. The landlord requested tenants to sign documents stating that they had been offered leaseholds, to prove that he had abided by the law. They did so, with verbal reassurance that shareholding terms would remain informally intact.

Seventh: Sugar and coconut sales have been monopolized by Marcos

376

"cronies" through their control of the marketing boards. They have also controlled the major banks financing their operations. Planters were awarded a sugar quota—a guaranteed market at guaranteed prices. During the sugar boom throughout 1984 and into the first quarter of 1985, when prices reached an index of 405 (1980 = 100), the island of Negros was virtually a one-crop economy. Because of their assured market, planters had little incentive to increase efficiency. As the world market price of sugar plummeted to three U.S. cents per picul (compared with the 11 cents it cost to produce) and the U.S. quota was reduced to 21% of total production, many planters went bankrupt. Because of substantial losses and political manipulation within the marketing board, payments for the 1985 crop were made only to politically favored producers. Mills closed, and thousands of workers were left unemployed, some facing starvation.

What has been done since President Aquino has come to power? Promising steps include the breakup of the sugar and coconut monopolies, although the privatization of government-owned assets has been delayed amid reports that some of these companies are being managed by friends and political allies of the new government. Landlords are still politically powerful in the provinces and dominate the new legislature.

President Aquino herself lacks the political organization necessary to implement a reform independent of local political powers. Aquino had the opportunity to declare a land reform before the legislature first met, while she still possessed Mr. Marcos' decree-making powers. Her land reform decree declared the entire country subject to land reform, but left the critical elements of retention limits, compensation, and priorities to the new legislature.

Within this context, the legislature has passed a land reform law that guarantees full market compensation to landlords. Tenants will be required to pay for the land in installments over a thirty-year period. In these circumstances, the government is likely to gain, having paid for the land in government bonds while receiving payment in cash and produce. Tenants, faced with paying the full market value for the land, will not gain. The landlords, to the extent that the land reform can be implemented over their almost certain resistance, will very likely lose from the reform, if only because the value of the government bonds will depreciate.

Furthermore, there are indications that the government will continue to exercise a similar degree of bureaucratic control over the farming system as President Marcos did in his time (Chapter 2). The land reform bill states that "a basic qualification of a beneficiary shall be his willingness, aptitude, and ability to cultivate and make the land as productive as possible. The Department of Agrarian Reform shall adopt a system of monitoring the record or performance of each beneficiary, so that any beneficiary guilty of negligence or misuse of the land or any support extended to him shall forfeit his right to continue as such beneficiary." Likewise, the extensive provision of services anticipated by the government program makes the centralized system of bureaucratic farm administration likely. Village-level organizations are constituted to coordinate the delivery of government services and credit to farmers. To the extent that continued participation in the agrarian reform program is made contingent on the acceptance of certain combinations of government assistance, then these organizations can be used to the government's advantage—to the detriment of peasants.

The crucial question is how able the government will be to implement its reform while the political power of landlords in the countryside is still intact. Many Filipinos are openly pessimistic. They say that any prospect of reform using the same administrative machinery is likely to fail for the same reason that the Marcos reform failed—through unreasonable delays in administrative procedure, as landlords block the reform at every step of the way. While the current bill allows the government to take preemptive action in the face of delay, one wonders whether the new administrative machinery will be any more capable and efficient than the last and any less susceptible to landlords' influence in the face of their degree of local control.

In the sugar lands of Negros, the problem is more acute. The economy is in disorder, and the political situation is polarized. The decline of the sugar industry and the elimination of monopolies have reduced the economic clout of the *hacienderos,* to the extent that they are no longer the power brokers they once were. But they are threatening to take the law into their own hands by defending their lands with armed force if need be. The ability of the government to move decisively to expropriate their holdings will be a decisive test of its power to resolve the crisis.

Meanwhile, the New People's Army, gaining support from unemployed sugar workers, has declared that any government land reform is bound to be palliative. The Army will be satisfied only with the free distribution of land to the workers. Again, the ability of the government to effect a land reform will be key to defusing the crisis. Sugar workers who own their own sugar cooperatives are not likely to support either the government or the underground in attempts to further the reform.

The problem is compounded by the decline of the sugar industry. In Peru, not only was the government able to move decisively with the army to confiscate the sugar haciendas, but it was able to turn over the management of highly profitable enterprises to the workers' federations. In the Philippines, there is doubt whether a viable economy based on sugar production can be rebuilt. New crops are needed. Landlords with capital are unwilling to invest in long-term alternatives without the security of knowing that they will be the ones to harvest their crop. They doubt that they would be able to finance nonagricultural enterprises on the cash payment that the government would provide them. While sugar workers may be able to manage sugar cooperatives under favorable economic conditions, they are not farmers, and would not be able to move easily into other kinds of crops. Furthermore, the transformation of the economy requires investment in infrastructure, which is currently lacking.

Creating a framework for a healthy economy in a situation where power brokers on all sides are vying for control will not be easy. Until a political settlement is reached, the prospects for any recovery are slim.

The following interchange was passed on to me by a rural worker who prefers to remain anonymous:

> Wishing to eject a tenant, a landlord took his case to court.
> Judge (to tenant): Who owns the land?
> Tenant: The landlord.
> Judge: Then get off the land.
> Tenant: But sir, I have the right to remain on the land, according to Presidential Decree no. 27.
> Judge: This you should learn: the law in Manila is one thing, the law here is another.

References

Barraclough, Solon, 1973. *Agrarian Structure in Latin America*, Lexington, Mass., Lexington Books.

Benneh, G., 1971. "Land Tenure and Sabala Farming Systems in the Anlo Area of Ghana," *Institute of African Studies Research Review*, Vol. 7, no. 2, reprinted in LTC reprint no. 120, Madison, University of Wisconsin, Land Tenure Center.

Bohannon, Paul, 1963. "'Land,' 'Tenure,' and Land-Tenure," in Daniel Biebuyck, ed., *African Agrarian Systems*, Oxford, Oxford University Press, reprinted in LTC reprint no. 105, Madison, University of Wisconsin, Land Tenure Center.

Brown, Chris, et al., 1982. "A Study of Local Institutions in Kgatleng District, Botswana," Madison, University of Wisconsin, Land Tenure Center.

Bruce, John W., and Dorner, Peter P., 1982. *Agricultural Land Tenure in Zambia: Perspectives, Problems, and Opportunities*, Madison, University of Wisconsin, Land Tenure Center, Xerox.

Buck, John Lossing, 1937. *Land Utilization in China*, Nanking University Press, reprinted by Paragon Books, 1968.

Cox, Paul, 1978. *Venezuela's Agrarian Reform at Mid-1977*, Madison, University of Wisconsin, Land Tenure Center.

FAO (United Nations Food and Agriculture Organization), 1983. *Production Yearbook*, vol. 37, Rome.

Fernando, Nimal, 1978. *Land Reform in Plantation Agriculture: An Analysis of the Case of Sri Lanka, with Special Reference to the Plantations*, Madison, University of Wisconsin, Land Tenure Center, research paper no. 72, May.

Frutos, Juan Manuel, 1982. *Con el Hombre y la Tierra hacia el Bienestar Rural*, Asunción, Cuadernos Republicanos.

Haraldson, Sixten, n.d. (1974 approx.) *Nomads of the World: A Series of Slides*, Göteborg, Sweden.

IMF (International Monetary Fund), 1984. *Exchange Arrangements and Exchange Restrictions, Annual Report*, Washington, D.C.

Kanel, Don, 1978. "Land Tenure Issues in African Development," unpublished, Madison, University of Wisconsin, Land Tenure Center.

379

Lardy, Nicholas, 1983. *Agriculture in China's Modern Economic Development*, New York, Cambridge University Press.

Lemel, Harold, 1977. "Examination of the 1973 Turkish Land and Agrarian Reform and Its Implication: Observations in the Pilot Province of Urfa, 1977," *Land Tenure Center Newsletter*, no. 58, October–December.

MacFarquhar, Roderick, 1974. *The Origins of the Cultural Revolution, 1956–57*, New York, Columbia University Press.

Manzardo, Andrew, 1982. "Planning for Local Institutions of Development in the CFDAs (Communal First Development Areas) of Botswana," Madison, University of Wisconsin, Land Tenure Center.

Mesa Lago, Carmelo, 1981. *The Economy of Socialist Cuba: A Two-Decade Appraisal*, Albuquerque, University of New Mexico Press.

Nukunya, G. K., 1974. *Land Tenure and Agricultural Development in the Anloga Area of the Volta Region*, Staff Paper, University of Ghana, Legon, Accra, reprinted in LTD reprint no. 120, Madison, University of Wisconsin, Land Tenure Center.

Perkins, Dwight, 1969. *Agricultural Development in China, 1368–1968*, Chicago, Aldine Press.

Riddell, James C.; Parsons, Kenneth H.; and Kanel, Don, 1978. "Land Tenure Issues in African Development," unpublished, Madison, University of Wisconsin, Land Tenure Center.

Rosenstein-Rodan, Paul N., 1974. "Why Allende Failed," *Challenge*, May/June.

Rude, Andrew, et al., 1982. "Report on Local Institutions in Five Villages in the Southern District Communal First Development Area," Madison, University of Wisconsin, Land Tenure Center.

Stanfield, David, 1976. "The Chilean Agrarian Reform," *Land Tenure Center Newsletter*, no. 52, April–June.

Thondaman, S., 1975. "Towards a New Order," *Asian Labor*, vol. 23:121.

Wheeler, Richard O., et al., 1982. *Report of the U.S. Presidential Agricultural Mission to Honduras*, Xerox.

19. Conclusion: Who Advocates the Peasant?

Who advocates the peasant? Do Marxist revolutionary governments? Do the governments of "capitalist"* countries? Do the governments of the more developed world? Does the government of the Soviet Union, or China? Do private agencies like Oxfam and the American Friends Service Committee?

To Marxists, the class struggle is staged between "oppressors" (owners of capital) and "oppressed" (possessors only of their labor). While we agree on some Marxist points, on others we find the dichotomy too simple. Often the attributes of "classes" belong not only to powerful groups in "capitalist" societies, but to those in "socialist" as well. For example, the distinction between classes is often arbitrary. But the greatest error of modern Marxists is to assume that the improprieties so astutely uncovered in "capitalist" societies are either eliminated or greatly alleviated in "socialist" societies (Jones et al. 1982:xi, xvi).

Where Marxists find a single phenomenon—the extraction of "surplus value"—we discover two. First, we agree that the extraction is real. Although we do not define "surplus value" as the Marxists do (excess above a "labor value"), we do consider that peasants are exploited whenever powerful groups limit their choices, so that they receive less than the marginal product of their labor. Exploitation takes two forms: (1) limiting peasants' wages or profits (through price or wage controls), and (2) restricting their freedom to buy or sell. The powerful exploiters (monopolies) may be either private or state. The second is the quality that Marxists do not recognize: the inefficiency of state rather than peasant decisionmaking. State decisions, as this book has shown, tend to reduce the "surplus" in agriculture (however it is defined), simply because bureaucrats are not farmers. The losers may be peasants, the state, or consumers.

Another too-easy distinction of Marxists is that the principal decisionmakers in "capitalist" societies are motivated by "profit" while those in "socialist" societies are motivated by "service to the masses." One author's (Powelson) experience as economic advisor to government in "capitalist" countries is that many civil servants are just as loftily motivated in favor of

---

*We use quotation marks for commonplace terms that are unsatisfactorily defined. But we do not wish either to digress or to confound ourselves by trying to define them.

the peasant as are those in "socialist" societies. They are also just as sure that they know better than the peasant how to improve his welfare. On the other hand, our reading of events in "socialist" as well as "capitalist" societies—and this is a main thrust of the present book—is that governments, to keep themselves in power, divert profit (surplus) from peasants to themselves. In "socialist" states, for example, peasants are often asked to "sacrifice for the revolution" (Nicaragua, Chapter 17). Thus neither concern for the peasantry nor profit-seeking belongs exclusively to one mode of government rather than another.

We can agree with some elements of Marxist rhetoric, however, but we find them poorly applied in Marxist states. Foremost would be "power to the masses!" Had we coined this phrase, it would mean freedom for the peasants to structure their own societies—to select private farming, cooperative farming, or state farming as they wished. In Marxist states, this term generally connotes state decisions presumably *on behalf of* the peasants. But peasants have never selected state farms of their own volition; they submit only under coercion. Rarely have they selected even total cooperatives—complete farming in common—the exceptions being religious communities such as the Hutterites in America and the Israeli kibbutz (Dorner 1975). Often, however, peasants have voluntarily formed cooperatives for specific purposes, such as buying and selling, and these are the ones we favor, totally managed by peasants.

Is it enough to grant that peasants would *prefer* to make their own decisions? Would their decisions promote the welfare of others: industrial workers, consumers, professionals, retired people, and so on? We argue yes, in the long run, which leads to the question of efficiency.

As a preliminary indicator of efficiency, we show (Table 1) agricultural growth rates for several of the countries studied in this book, plus a few others, divided into more-developed economies, less-developed market economies, and less-developed controlled economies. These distinctions are not exact. Not only might "more developed" and "less developed" be qualified, but—with greater hazard—control is always relative; there is no way objectively to compare controls of different types. But we have argued in Chapters 7 and 18 that Bolivia and Paraguay should be deemed "less controlled" than others, and we add the Ivory Coast to boot. Since it is not easy to find LDCs with few controls, our list is short.

This table is indicative only. Not only do we not have a large enough sample for statistical analysis, but each country's data are affected by many other variables than degree of control. Nor is the overall index always a good measure of efficiency. Some countries, Indonesia, for example (Chapter 15), have inordinately weighted their exports, disproportionately pushing up their indexes. But domestic food supplies and peasant welfare may deteriorate. While we have pointed out that declines in African agriculture do not correlate with the drought (Chapter 4),

Table 19.1

AVERAGE ANNUAL RATES OF AGRICULTURAL GROWTH PER
CAPITA, 1960S, 1970S, AND FIRST HALF OF 1980S, FOR
SELECTED COUNTRIES

Country	Sixties	Seventies	Eighties (1st half)	Overall
More developed				
Canada	0.36	1.40	1.67	1.04
France	1.77	1.34	1.28	1.50
Germany, West	2.98	1.19	2.52	2.17
Germany, East	1.23	1.19	1.77	1.32
Italy	1.23	1.50	−0.05	1.08
Spain	1.66	1.37	0.94	1.40
United Kingdom	1.59	1.82	2.17	1.80
United States	0.73	1.91	−0.30	1.00
U.S.S.R.	2.65	−0.31	1.23	1.18
Less developed, market				
Bolivia	1.71	−0.20	−1.77	0.25
Ivory Coast	2.46	1.36	−1.19	1.29
Paraguay	−0.47	1.26	0.58	0.43
South Korea	1.26	1.88	0.62	1.38
Less developed, controlled				
Algeria	−2.41	−1.29	0.40	−1.40
Botswana	−0.06	−5.05	−4.51	−2.95
China	0.36	1.40	4.52	1.61
Egypt	0.19	−0.98	−0.07	−0.33
El Salvador	−0.40	−1.38	−4.74	−1.66
India	−0.11	0.43	2.06	0.54
Indonesia	0.28	2.30	3.13	1.66
Iran	0.64	−0.12	−0.32	0.14
Mexico	−0.16	−0.14	−0.71	−0.26
Nicaragua	1.87	−2.88	−5.42	−1.49
Peru	−0.83	−2.39	−0.45	−1.38
Philippines	−0.29	1.97	−1.19	0.43
Somalia	−0.12	−4.73	−2.04	−2.35
Tanzania	2.31	−1.80	−1.89	−0.17
Turkey	0.32	0.95	−0.14	0.48

Table 19.1 (Continued)

Country	Sixties	Seventies	Eighties (1st half)	Overall
Venezuela	0.96	−0.15	−1.47	0.03
Zambia	−0.54	−1.88	−0.87	−1.14

SOURCE: Calculated from United Nations, Food and Agriculture Organization Yearbooks, 1972, 1983, and 1986.

NOTE: "Sixties" means the 1961/63 average index until the 1971/73 average index (10 years). "Seventies" means same for 1971/73 to 1981/83 (10 years). Data for the sixties are calculated from FAO indexes with 1961–65 = 100; they are spliced onto data for the seventies, from FAO indexes with 1974–76 = 100 (1971 and 1972 being the splicing years). Figures for the first half of the eighties are from FAO 1986, from 1979/81 to 1984/86. The "overall" is the weighted average of the first three columns.

nevertheless the drought did take its toll, for example in the dramatic Somali decline during the seventies. The substantial increases in Indonesian and Philippine output in the seventies, compared with mediocre performance in the sixties, were in large part generated by "miracle rice" of the Green Revolution. Paraguay's increase during the seventies, compared with a desultory performance in the sixties, was caused in part by capital inflows associated with dams on the Rio Paraná. Bolivia's decreased output in the seventies is exacerbated by political instability during that decade. In some countries, official indexes may be underweighted because black market sales are not detected.

The U.S.S.R. showed impressive growth in the sixties, only to slow down and stop in the seventies. That the government attributes the slowdown to its control is manifest in its liberalization policy. The significant output growth of China in the seventies—which continued on into the eighties—is also widely attributed to liberalization (Chapter 18). We have argued (Chapter 12) that South Korea's growth in the seventies stems from price subsidies. This might suggest that bias against the peasantry is not, after all, inevitable from an authoritarian government. (Taiwan is another example; Chapter 13.) By adopting liberal policies, an authoritarian government can stimulate agricultural growth and peasant welfare—witness not only South Korea and Taiwan, but also the People's Republic of China. The big question is whether the liberalism of these countries reflects the long-term leverage of peasants or the current whim of rulers. This is not easily answered for any of them, yet it may spell the difference between continued or aborted promotion of peasant welfare.

Despite these qualifications, the *overall* picture is one of exuberance in the market economies (including those of more-developed countries) and desultory performance in the controlled economies (including the U.S.S.R. in the seventies). The positive performance of market economies is brought out by Wade Sinclair in an article entitled, "The World Isn't Dying for American Farm Products Anymore" (*Washington Post Weekly*, 1/13/86). While Sinclair does not point this out, the great advances he cites in Third World farming took place either in countries where land reform has been deemed "unsuccessful" (e.g., India and Bangladesh) or where its restrictions have been relaxed (e.g., China). Most of the negative signs in Table 1, by contrast, are in the "controlled" group.

Let us examine these negatives more closely, by dividing the "controlled" LDC economies into three groups: (1) those with primary products (sugar, coffee, etc.) that are more for export than for domestic consumption; (2) those producing mainly for domestic consumption; and (3) those with primary export products that are also widely consumed at home.

Peru, Egypt, Tanzania, Indonesia, and Mexico illustrate the first group. In each of these countries, *the state has co-opted the export crop far more than it has domestic crops. It has also diverted scarce capital and scarce credit away from domestic crops to export.* In Chapter 14, we found that Peruvian sugar is much more controlled than crops on the sierra. In Egypt (Chapter 6), the government has grabbed cotton more than it has other crops. In Tanzania (Chapter 4), regulations affect especially sisal, cashew nuts, coffee, tea, pyrethrum, and tobacco; in Indonesia (Chapter 15) sugar; in Mexico (Chapter 3) sugar, cotton, and henequin. Apparently, we now come closer to the arguments of *Food First* (Lappé and Collins 1979) than we appeared to do in Chapter 17 (Nicaragua). *Food First* advocates do err by ignoring comparative advantage—Lardy (1983) demonstrated this for China (our Chapter 18)—but they are right to the extent that governments have, *in non-market ways*, advantaged exports over domestic production.

Turning to the second group, we find a new explanation for liberalism in Bolivia. In Chapter 7, we argued that the Bolivian government was too disorganized to control the peasant effectively, though it much wanted to. *But Bolivia does not have a primary export crop*—its principal agricultural products are for domestic consumption—so it is perhaps not worth the trouble for the government to control the peasantry. However, the revolution of 1953 did nationalize tin, the principal export! On the other hand, we hear rumors that coca, a clandestine export crop, has been monopolized by the military government. The drug traffic in Paraguay has also been a government monopoly, it is said. Since these rumors are not easily investigated, we leave the matter there, except to comment that if they are true, they fit easily within our hypotheses.

Countries with diversified crops cut across our first and second groups; they may or may not also possess a principal export. Only with difficulty does a government control a diversified farmer. In Egypt (Chapter 6), the government found it easier to intervene with small farmers (who could grow only one crop) than with large farmers (who could diversify). Although wheat is the dominant crop in Iran (Chapter 5) and Pakistan (Chapter 11), many other crops, grown for the local market, were difficult to control. Since all countries produce diversified crops for domestic markets, the relationship between concentration and control would be a useful one for study. We only speculate on it here, but we recommend it to others for future research.

South Korea (Chapter 12) and Taiwan (Chapter 13) represent the third group. Here, rice is a major crop for both domestic consumption and export. Both countries were rice baskets for Japan; indeed, control over agriculture was initiated in both places by the Japanese, and the postwar governments merely adopted Japanese-formed institutions.

Two generalizations come from this. First, the governments of these countries exerted their control more easily than did those of others in our case studies. They simply stepped into an existing situation. Similar examples would be African governments (not covered in this book) that inherited marketing boards from the British (Bauer 1954; Bates 1981, 1983). Second, however, the peasants of both South Korea and Taiwan appear to have greater leverage on their governments—in the sense of acquiring greater concessions—than have peasants under other authoritarian governments. Both governments, for example, have been less willing to turn the terms of trade against farmers than have other authoritarian governments studied in this book.

There may, of course, be many reasons. Both governments have been liberal in their total economies (in ways beyond the scope of this book); this liberalism may simply have been extended to agriculture. (Authoritarianism has been mainly political.) In addition, however, peasants producing both for export and for domestic consumption may gain more leverage upon their bureaucrats than peasants who may be "divided and ruled" in other countries.

We hesitate on these conjectures, for they require more investigation. Nor must we be deceived by the economic successes of Taiwan and South Korea, for they possess many of the same attributes of other LDCs: monocrop agriculture for export; earlier domination by a colonial power that used them to its advantage; present government assuming the instruments of that colonial power. We are not so sanguine as some about the ability of these NICs (newly industrializing countries) to thrive in the long term just because they are liberal *at the moment*. We believe that significant changes in politics are essential for the economic exuberance to perdure.

* * *

We now return to the question that began this chapter: who *really* advocates the peasant? The governments of more-developed countries, such as the United States? The U.S. government has promoted land reforms in Japan, Taiwan, South Korea, Bolivia, Chile, and El Salvador. The British government helped buy out British landlords in Kenya, Zambia, and Zimbabwe, so land might be distributed to African owners. President de Gaulle undercut the settlers in Algeria, to quicken independence and land reform. All these reforms confiscated value from former landowners (many of them constituents of the initiating government) and contributed to substantial changes in power structures.

Marxist rhetoric holds that the United States advocates land reform only because reform is inevitable. By managing the reform itself, the United States can minimize its consequences. U.S.-sponsored reforms, according to this rhetoric, divide lands into private ownership rather than into collective or state farms; their purpose is to prolong a dying capitalism.

This rhetoric is not entirely correct. Both the Chilean land reform under President Frei and the Salvadoran reform under the junta (and later under President Duarte) included collective farms. Chilean farmers were to vote after five years on whether they wished to continue as collectives. In El Salvador, collectives would be indefinite on the large farms; private property would predominate only on the smaller ones. Forced cooperatives were also integral to the Taiwanese and South Korean reforms.

Our own perception of U.S. policy is therefore different from the Marxist one. In Latin America, the "backyard" of the United States, U.S. government goals are twofold: to prevent international communism and to keep the country "quiet" (subdue guerrilla warfare). If land reform is convenient to those goals, the United States will promote it; if not, it will not. Consistent with this hypothesis, the United States will promote only land reforms that do not lead to communist-style state farms. While we do not defend these hypotheses here, we submit them as reasonable interpretations of recent history.

Neither the U.S. nor the Soviet government advocates peasant control over farming decisions, except perhaps rhetorically. The central government has encroached upon peasant prerogatives in many countries in which U.S. influence has been great—the Philippines, Egypt, Iran before the shah's overthrow, South Korea, Taiwan, Peru, and El Salvador—but the U.S. government did not lift a finger in opposition. Governments where Soviet influence has been great have also encroached—Algeria and Ethiopia, for example—but of course Soviet ideology already favors central control. Nor does the World Bank advocate peasant decisionmaking. With its imposition of policy from abroad (especially its "structural adjustment loans"), the World Bank presents itself as a super-policymaker, reinforcing the control over peasants by central governments (provided, of course, these governments follow the policies of the bank and the International Monetary Fund).

By contrast, we argue that true advocates of the peasantry promote the peasant's control over his own farming structures and freedom in his own decisions. Thus we conclude that no foreign government or international lending agency qualifies as advocate, any more than do the national governments we have studied.

What of the outside private agency? In Peru (Chapter 14), a group of Cornell anthropologists intervened to modify a culture. (Intervention by anthropologists, as opposed to aloof observation, is at best controversial; the Vicos experiment has been much criticized on this point.) They performed a land reform "by grace," which truly enhanced the capacity of peasants to form their own structures and make their own decisions. But the experiment was out of context with the overall Peruvian reality; it succumbed when central institutions were imposed throughout the country without regard to local variants.

In its projects in Mali (AFSC 1982) and Somalia (in both of which Gunn, author of Chapter 8, participated) and among the Hmong in Cambodia, the American Friends Service Committee (AFSC) has quietly helped peasants acquire needed skills while it has carefully not intervened in their policies. It has therefore become one of the few advocates of the peasant that we know (Powelson 1984:109). But even the AFSC succumbed to an ideology when it implied—as did Oxfam also—that peasants in El Salvador (Chapter 16) favor one side's land reform over the other's (Berryman 1983). In fact, neither of these sides is interested in allowing the peasants a deciding voice.

To strengthen his leverage without interfering with his decisions is perhaps the only way that outsiders can successfully advocate the peasant. But this appears to require a religious devotion not widely found. We conclude pessimistically that, with perhaps a few exceptions, peasants must be their own advocates. In future writing, we hope to show that they have indeed been their most effective advocates in the past, in dismantling feudalism in Western Europe and Japan, and we see no reason why history should be changed in the twentieth century.

Those who would become external advocates of peasants would therefore do well to understand, strengthen, and respect their cultures. Instead of supplanting those cultures, instead of destroying their methods of coping through outside "assistance," instead of incorporating peasants into "integrated economic plans," instead of imposing modern institutions created in capital cities or abroad, external advocates might help peasants integrate their own cultures into modern society.

References

AFSC (American Friends Service Committee), 1982. *Tin Aïcha, Nomad Village*, Philadelphia.

Bates, Robert H., 1983. *Essays on the Political Economy of Rural Africa*, Cambridge, Cambridge University Press.

Bates, Robert H., 1981. *Markets and States in Tropical Africa: The Political Basis of Agricultural Policies*, Berkeley, University of California Press.

Bauer, Peter T., 1954. "The Operation and Consequencs of the State Export Monopolies of West Africa," *Journal of the Royal Statistical Society;* reprinted in Bauer, *Dissent on Development,* Cambridge, Mass., 1972.

Berryman, Philip, 1983. *What's Wrong in Central America, and What to Do about It,* Philadelphia, American Friends Service Committee.

Dorner, Peter, ed., 1975. *Cooperative and Commune: Group Farming in the Economic Development of Agriculture,* Madison, University of Wisconsin Press.

Jones, Steve; Joshi, P. C.; and Murmis, Miguel, 1982. *Rural Poverty and Agrarian Reform,* New Delhi, Allied Publishers, on behalf of Enda, Dakar, Senegal.

Lappé, Frances M., and Collins, Joseph, 1979. *Food First: Beyond the Myth of Scarcity,* New York, Ballantine Books.

Lardy, Nicholas, 1983. *Agriculture in China's Modern Economic Development,* New York, Cambridge University Press.

Powelson, John P., 1984. "International Public and Private Agencies," in John D. Montgomery, ed., *International Dimensions of Land Reform,* Boulder, Colo., Westview Press.

Index

Lechín, Juan, 132, 133
Lenin, V. I., 10
Less-developed countries (LDCs), xiii-xiv, 7; efficiency of land reform, 382, 383–84tbl, 384–86; food first policy, 336
Lewis, Paul, 180
Liga Nacional Campesina (LNC) (Mexico), 37
Local-partner tenure systems, 362–65
López-Portillo, José, 55

Macapagal (Philippine politician), 15
McKinsey & Company, 71
Magaña, Alvaro Alfredo, 311, 312
Magsaysay, Ramón, 15
Mahir, Ali, 108
Mali, 3, 388
Mao Zedong, 10, 372
Marcos, Ferdinand, 15, 16
Marcus, Ben, 360-61
Marei, Sayyid, 111, 112, 113, 115
Marketing systems: Algeria, 177–79; Bolivia, 130, 135, 137–39, 141; dualistic systems, 130; Nicaragua, 338–42; nomadic pastoralism, 153–54, 159; Pakistan, 221, 223, 225; peasant systems, 11, 130; Peru, 278–80; Somalia, 158–59; Ujamaa villages, 75–76
Marxism. See Communism
Masagana 99 program (Philippines): advantages, supposed, 21; banking services, impact on, 22; black market, 29; corrupt practices, 28–29; credit system, 17–19, 24; distribution system for chemicals, 20-21, 24–25; expenses charged to peasants, 27–28; failures of, 23–24; fertilizer policy, 18, 19, 20-21, 23, 24–25; government control as goal of, 33; innovation stifled by, 30, 31–32; peasants' attitude toward, 28, 33; pesticide policy, 18, 19, 21–22, 24–25; post-harvest facilities, 23, 27; practical results, 24–29, 32–33; private sector, comparison with, 21–22; private sector credit and, 29–33; purchases of products, 21, 26–27; quality control, 27; retail sector, impact on, 22–23; self-perpetuating nature, 26; termination of, 33, 375; theory behind, 16–17
May, Clifford, 1, 2
Mendoza, Juan, 137, 138–39

Menon, Achutha, 191
Mexican Food System (SAM), 55–56
Mexican land reform, 9 (see also Ejidos); in Atencingo, 50-52; black market, 48; corrupt practices, 45; cotton production, 46, 47tbl, 48, 50; counterreform movement, 36; credit system, 39–40, 41tbl, 42, 48, 56; efficiency of, 383tbl, 385; export crops, focus on, 52–53; gradual approach, 35–36; irrigation policy, 42–46, 43tbl, 44tbl; in La Laguna, 46, 47tbl, 48–50; Mexican Food System (SAM), 55–56; in Morelos 52–53; output, impact on, 5, 56–59, 57tbl, 58tbl; peasant conflict with state bank, 48–50; peasant-government relationship, 36–39; peasant leagues, 37–39; sugar production, 50-51, 52–53; in Yaqui Valley, 53
Middlemen. See Private sector credit
Ministry of Water Resources (SRH) (Mexico), 44–45, 52
Miskito Indians, 342–44
More-developed countries (MDCs), xiv, 7, 383tbl
Morelos, Mexico, 52–53
Mozambique, 1
Muhammed Ali Pasha, 107
Muthoka, Matheka, 2–3
Mwanza African Traders' Cooperative Society, 63
Myrdal, Gunnar, 6

Nasser, Gamal Abdel, 114
National Agrarian Federation (CNA) (Peru), 280
National Agricultural Cooperation Federation (NACF) (Korea), 240-43, 241tbl, 242tbl, 244, 245
National Agricultural Credit Bank (NACB) (Mexico), 39
National Fertilizer Corporation (NFC) (Pakistan), 228
National Food Plan (PAN) (Nicaragua), 338–39
National Grains Authority (NGA) (Philippines), 21, 23, 26–27
National Revolutionary Movement (MNR) (Bolivia), 132, 133, 136, 137, 141
National Rural Credit Bank (Mexico), 40, 42
Nawag experiment (Egypt), 112–13
New People's Army (Philippines), 378

Shah of Iran, 85, 86–87, 88, 91
Shallot production, 362–63
Sharecropping: Chile, 366; Indonesia, 295–96
Sheep raising, 169–70 (see also Nomadic pastoralism)
Shortages and hoarding, 339–40
Siles Zuazo, Hernán, 132
Sinclair, Wade, 385
Socialism. See Communism
Socialism and Rural Development (Nyerere), 67
Socialist villages (see also Ujamaa villages): Algeria, 172–74
Society of Social Interest (Peru), 274, 275, 286–87
Solidarity union, 10
Somalian land reform, 145, 388; agricultural growth rates, 383tbl; alternatives to, proposed, 162; communal ownership, 146, 152–53; drought and, 149; external agencies, influence of, 146; fertilizer policy, 156; failure of, 150, 160-62; goals of, 146, 147; "helplessness of peasants" attitude, 161; large-scale projects, 157–58; livestock industry and, 155–57, 160, 161; marketing, credit, and import/export institutions, 158–59; nomadic pastoralism and, 147, 153–55, 158; output, impact on, 157–58; overuse of land resulting from, 157; pesticide policy, 156; private ownership, focus on, 147–49; rationale for, 146–47; settled agriculture, inappropriateness of, 156–57; settlement programs, 149–50; smallholders, impact on, 158; social organization, impact on, 159–60; state farms, 157–58; state ownership, implementation of, 149–50; traditional survival strategies and, 151–52
Somoza family, 323, 324, 337
South Korea. See Korean land reform
Soviet Union, 9, 10; agricultural growth rates, 383tbl, 384, 385; support for land reform programs, 387
Spain, 383tbl
Sri Lankan land reform, 357–58
State Egyptian Cotton Organization (SECO), 115
State farms: Chile, 367; Cuba, 370; Nicaragua, 324, 326–28, 344–35; Somalia, 157–58; Sri Lanka, 357–58; Tanzania, 68; Ujamaa villages, 68

Sub-Saharan Africa, 362–65
Subsidies: Chile, 367–68; Egypt, 121; Nicaragua, 330, 331–32; Pakistan, 212, 217, 223, 224tbl, 225; Peru, 279, 281; unfair competition through, 7; Venezuela, 358–59; Zambia, 356
Sugar production (see also Indonesian sugar production): Cuba, 371; Mexico, 50-51, 52–53; Pakistan, 225–27; Peru, 281–83, 284tbl, 285; Philippines, 376–77, 378; small-scale production, 338

Taiwan Provincial Farm Bureau, 260
Taiwanese land reform, 6; compulsory rice sales to government, 260, 261–62tbl, 263tbl, 264–65, 266; efficiency of, 386; expropriation of land, 255, 256tbl, 257; farmers' associations, 260, 263–64, 266–67; fertilizer barter program, 260, 264–65, 266; government acquisition of surpluses, 264, 266; incomes, 257, 258tbl; in-kind payments to landlords, 257; Japanese occupation and, 253, 260; liberalization of, 384; motivations for, 254; output, impact on, 264; pre-reform landholding patterns, 253, 254tbl; public land, sale of, 255, 256tbl; redistribution of land, 259, 259tbl; redistribution of wealth, 257, 265; rent-reduction program, 254–55, 256tbl; rice production, 253–54, 260, 261–62tbl, 263tbl, 264; success of, 253; taxes, hidden, 257, 263tbl, 264–65, 266, 266tbl
Tanganyika Africa National Union (TANU), 62, 64, 65, 68, 71
Tanzanian land reform, 6, 10 (see also Ujamaa villages); black market, 76; centralized government, establishment of, 62; cooperatives, compulsory, 65–66, 67tbl; cooperatives, voluntary, 63–65, 67tbl; efficiency of, 383tbl, 385; failure of Nyerere's policies, 61, 81–82; independence and, 61–62; parastatal companies, 78–80; private farming, moves toward, 80-81; terms of trade, 77, 78tbl, 81; traditional methods of land management and, 62–63
Tapioca production, 186
Tea production, 357–58

400

About the Authors

John P. Powelson is a professor of economics at the University of Colorado at Boulder. He is the author of *The Story of Land* and the coauthor (with William Loehr) of *The Economics of Development and Distribution* and *Threat to Development: Pitfalls of the NIEO*.

Richard Stock is an assistant professor of economics at the University of Dayton. He is actively working on local development issues in Dayton.

Cato Institute

Founded in 1977, the Cato Institute is a public policy research foundation dedicated to broadening the parameters of policy debate to allow consideration of more options that are consistent with the traditional American principles of limited government, individual liberty, and peace. Toward that goal, the Institute strives to achieve a greater involvement of the intelligent, concerned lay public in questions of policy and the proper role of government.

The Institute is named for *Cato's Letters*, pamphlets that were widely read in the American Colonies in the early 18th century and played a major role in laying the philosophical foundation for the revolution that followed. Since that revolution, civil and economic liberties have been eroded as the number and complexity of social problems have grown.

To counter this trend the Cato Institute undertakes an extensive publications program dealing with the complete spectrum of policy issues. Books, monographs, and shorter studies are commissioned to examine the federal budget, Social Security, regulation, NATO, international trade, and a myriad of other issues. Major policy conferences are held throughout the year, from which papers are published thrice yearly in the *Cato Journal*.

In order to maintain an independent posture, the Cato Institute accepts no government funding. Contributions are received from foundations, corporations, and individuals, and other revenue is generated from the sale of publications. The Institute is a nonprofit, tax-exempt, educational foundation under Section 501(c)3 of the Internal Revenue Code.

CATO INSTITUTE
224 Second St., S.E.
Washington, D.C. 20003